David English is the Associate Editor of the London *Daily Express* and also a British television commentator on current affairs. He was a correspondent in the United States for six years, two of which he spent as a White House reporter. He covered the 1960 and 1964 Presidential campaigns. In his last two years in the United States he was chief of the *Express*'s seven-man New York Bureau, and during that time visited all fifty states in the Union. In 1965 he returned to London as Foreign Editor and was promoted to Associate Editor in 1968. During the campaign he was in charge of a team of twelve *Express* writers who were assigned to the election. The team was composed of experts on American affairs, and included reporters who had first covered American politics in President Roosevelt's time, as well as younger writers who had never visited the United States before. Mr. English commuted across the Atlantic to direct the team, but as the campaign developed he moved his wife and three children to New York "so that I could see them for the odd weekend without having to fly six thousand miles every time." Age 37, he lives (in non-election years) in London, and describes himself as a "totally committed America-phile."

DIVIDED THEY STAND

DAVID ENGLISH
and the Staff of the
London *Daily Express*

PRENTICE-HALL, INC., Englewood Cliffs, N.J.

DIVIDED THEY STAND
By David English and the Staff of the London *Daily Express*

SBN 13-21620-0-8

Library of Congress Catalog Card Number: 69-19113

Printed in the United States of America

T

Prentice-Hall International, Inc., London
Prentice-Hall of Australia, Pty. Ltd., Sydney
Prentice-Hall of Canada, Ltd., Toronto
Prentice-Hall of India Private Ltd., New Delhi
Prentice-Hall of Japan, Inc., Tokyo

For Derek Marks—
Who said it was a good idea

The *Daily Express* reporting team assigned to
the 1968 Presidential campaign:

Richard Kilian
Ross Mark
Rene MacColl
John Ellison
Jeremy Hornsby
Ian Brodie
Ivor Davis

PREFACE

AT THE BEGINNING OF 1968 I FLEW TO NEW YORK FOR A CONFERENCE
of the *Daily Express* American bureau chiefs to plan our coverage
of the Presidential election.

What sort of campaign would it be? How many men would we
need? What were the major issues that should be analyzed and
explained to British readers? It was a long conference and, when I
left that night to catch a familiar New York Central train to
Scarsdale where I was to dine with some old friends and neighbors,
I was profoundly depressed.

America's problems went very deep and it was everyone's opinion
that the tensions of the election would bring them to a dangerous
crisis point.

Henry Lowrie, the Bureau Chief in New York, celebrating his
twenty-third year in the United States, had gloomily predicted that
everything was breaking down. "I've never known this country in
such a state," he said. "And I think that 1968 is going to be the worst
year that any of us has seen here."

In that, he was right. It was a terrible year. But it was also a very special year and one I would not have missed.

Some time later, talking to Daniel P. Moynihan, who now heads the White House Urban Affairs Office, I had mentioned the apprehension one felt at the beginning of '68.

"Europeans are always looking at America and expecting it to come apart," he said.

"But if you look closely enough you will find that the system is built to withstand stress . . . even the stress we're going to get in 1968 . . . and you will no longer be surprised when America doesn't fall apart."

We decided that we would look closely. And in 1968 the *Daily Express* gave the most detailed coverage an American election has ever received in its pages.

In this it was matched by British and European television, who between them devoted hundreds of hours to live coverage.

The reason was absolutely clear. The problems facing the United States were not isolated to that side of the Atlantic. They were the same kind of problems which sooner or later must beset every modern industrial country. Many of them are already here in Britain to some degree or another. This is why public interest in the American scene was so intense.

So Britain had much to learn in observing America during the year but when making this point to Americans I found that it was matched by a counterpoint. "We have some things to learn from you," said Eugene McCarthy one night. "You're looking at this marathon election and you must see clearly the things we avoid looking at. You must see its faults."

From that came the idea of this book. It would be an account of the campaign as seen by friendly foreigners . . . entirely written from a British perspective, emphasizing the things which struck us as important, or bizarre, impressive, or astonishing.

Any definitive account of a U.S. election must come from the work of more than one person. It is impossible to cover all the candidates, travel all the miles or visit all the places involved in the vast campaign that America endures every four years. As the writer I was fortunate in the fact that I worked with old colleagues, all British and all experienced at the same kind of reporting.

My thanks are due to the team which was always in the field with the candidates and always ready to assist me when I would descend, usually at an inconvenient moment.

In particular, I should like to mention Richard Kilian's long trek with the Nixon campaign, which produced some deeply revealing interview material and a superb account of the Nixons on election day. I should like to thank Ross Mark for his limitless knowledge of Washington affairs; Rene MacColl for his wisdom and insight gleaned from covering seven Presidential elections; Jeremy Hornsby for his moving story of the Seidensticker family; John Ellison for his McCarthy coverage; Ian Brodie for his work on Robert Kennedy and civil rights, and Ivor Davis for his reports from California.

When I express opinions as "the visitor" they are my personal opinions but very frequently they reflect a combined viewpoint as well. We spent many heated but rewarding hours discussing the events of the year.

Thanks are due to many others. To Henry Lowrie for his total recall of American personalities and events in the post-war period; to Ivor Key for his work on Ronald Reagan; to John Grant for his assistance on the labor front; to Susan Kingston for handling the most complicated travel arrangements imaginable and never failing; to James Nicoll for his help with the vote tabulation; to Robin Esser, the *Express* Features Editor, and Stewart Steven, the Foreign Editor, for their assistance in editing the final manuscript and to Harold Keeble and Eric Raybould for their constant encouragement, particularly in the darker moments.

The greatest encouragement of all came from my wife, who traveled many thousands of miles with me and whose affection for America is exceeded only by her understanding of its people.

Finally, a sincere thank you from us all to two super girls who did some of the hardest work of all—our researchers Ina Sherman and Sharon Schlein. Without them we would not have made it.

David English
Fleet Street
London
December 1968

CONTENTS

CONTENTS

.1.

THE DISUNITED STATES

THE VISITING BRITON'S FIRST REACTION TO THE UNITED STATES
is invariably a mixture of envy at what the country has and exhilaration at being there to taste it. Mild anti-Americanism is
endemic to the British. There is nothing vicious in it; it is gentle
and ironic. It forces the Briton to recognize his own nation's
shortcomings while chuckling at the tiny pomposities with which
Americans choose to embellish their virtues, virtues that, he admits, make them more succesful than anyone else in the search for
prosperity.

But, at the beginning of 1968, the visitor experienced neither
exhilaration nor envy on his arrival—only a bewildered anxiety.
Something had gone wrong with America. Deep divisions, always
visible but not always of prime urgency, had by some imperative
chosen simultaneously to demand attention: the black against the
white, the rich against the poor, the established against the in-
novating, the war makers against the peace lovers. The result was

1

a confusion of priorities and a paralysis of will, bringing the decade to an end in total contrast to its beginning.

For, at the beginning of the 1960s it seemed, both in Britain and within the United States, that the promise and potential of America would be fulfilled in a decade of political and sociological renaissance. There was no hint of the neurosis to come. When British visitors—writers, businessmen, artists, tourists—went to America in those days, the vibrance and the thrust of American confidence were immediately infectious. How backward and dull and middle-aged everything seemed at home compared with the sense of adventure and purpose in America. How slow it seemed compared to the urgency of facing up to all kinds of problems with new solutions.

It was American optimism most of all that filled the visitor with wonder. There was a sense of possibility in the early 1960s that seemed to infect everyone with the conviction that America would forge a new world—made in the U.S.A.—that would be exported to all mankind.

Most Englishmen, most Europeans in fact, believe that John F. Kennedy was the man responsible for this feeling. It was as if his unique personality served as a catalyst for the energy and the hopes of American people, fusing them together to release a new sense of purpose. The problems were there when he took over. The civil-rights issue was about to explode. Southeast Asia was on the brink of war. The economy was not right.

But the attitude toward all these problems was one of confidence. They could be solved. There *were* answers; America had the talent to find them, and they would not be the old, hackneyed ones but new and imaginative—even revolutionary—conceptions.

Coming from England, then sunk in Tory lethargy and contentment, the American attitude was overpoweringly refreshing. It was no accident that it was at that time that the "brain drain" from Britain to the United States first appeared as a serious problem to the British government.

Today it is possible to argue that President Kennedy only "managed" problems and that had he lived he would have displayed no greater skill than the next politician at unraveling the tremendous complexities of our age.

Now in the year that the United States began its third and last Presidential campaign of the 1960s—the 46th in American history —nothing quite balanced. The immediate problems of America

2

were poverty and hunger, and across the country they were there for the naked eye to see many times a day. Yet they were subordinated to the furore over the Vietnam war.

There had never been a war like it. Fought on the American global frontier against Communism, the battle raged through the eastern days while the western hemisphere slept. The names of the battlefields were unpronounceable . . . sharp, barking syllables in an ancient Oriental tongue latinized by a Portuguese priest centuries ago. The enemy was unseen and unknown, the ally unpredictable and ungrateful.

This war was brought home to America in a way that no other war has been brought to the home front short of invasion. The scenes of battle came flashing daily onto the great color-television screens that dominate American drawing rooms. There, numbed by repetition, the American public sated itself with vicarious action brought by satellite from the front lines. The nightly ritual, like some never-ending serial, had the paradoxical effect of making the war more unreal and less understood with every 24-hour performance.

In any case, as everyone said, it was not a real war. It was not a declared war. It was not even a war with very clear goals. Daily the casualties mounted, draft calls increased, and the army of General William Westmoreland grew larger. But it was not an official war.

There was no wartime spirit in America. Nor were there any signs of a committed nation sending its sons to die in an unknown country for a cause known to be right. There was no rationing. There were no shortages. Least of all was there any sense of national unity, except in one area. In 1968 Americans of all races and classes were united in one emotion, an emotion totally foreign to the American thinking, at least to white American thinking. Americans were almost without exception gripped by frustration, a frustration so powerful that many people feared that the nation was heading for a nervous breakdown.

The hawks were frustrated by restrictions that prevented the mightiest nation in the world from eliminating North Vietnam overnight. The doves were frustrated by the stupidity that went on pouring endless men into a military machine that was unable to impose a solution. Negroes were frustrated because they were recognized as true Americans only when they fought in the war but denied that recognition when they came back as heroes. The diplomats were frustrated by their failure to produce any alternative solution. The politicians were frustrated by their inability to shake the public from the frustration that gripped it. The economists were frustrated by their failure to control inflation and the ever-increasing pressure on the dollar.

The sense of frustration was so overpowering that it was almost physical. It expressed itself in many different ways. The visitor traveled to Westchester early in January for a dinner party with some old and valued friends. He was anxious to discuss this mood of helplessness that seemed to be gripping America. But, before the log fire while the drinks were being poured and the preliminary chatter about children and acquaintances was being got out of the way, he perceived a curious by-product of the frustration around him. It was an aversion to talking about the war. Perhaps it was a fear that breaking the self-imposed censorship would ruin the evening and perhaps put an end to friendships now precariously balanced between "doves and hawks."

So the conversation was about the latest aids to easy living. A new shaving cream had been developed; it was aerosol-packed, and heated itself when placed on the cheek. Marvelous. Everyone had color televisions now; portables cost only $250 in the discount stores. Incredible. Wall Street was fantastic. Everyone was richer. Salaries went up. So indeed were costs. But the well-being of white-collar suburbia was intact, growing more transistorized and seemingly untouched.

"But what about the war?" the visitor asked. The question was answered by a resigned shrug from the host and a swift "We're not going to talk about that" from the hostess. She quickly moved the conversation into a discussion on the cinematic potential of John Osborne's latest play *Inadmissible Evidence*. Would it translate to the screen? From there it was inevitable that one should be asked whether or not the character of the solicitor, Maitland, was meant to be symbolic of "Britain in decline."

And so the visitor found himself talking about his own country when he really wanted to talk about the United States. Afterward he realized that unspoken despair about the war had been present throughout the whole evening, even though it had not been mentioned. It was as if by talking trivia the ultimate, insoluble argument over Vietnam could be placed in a mental deep freeze. Which, of course, it could not.

When later one of the people at that gathering was asked why no one had talked about Vietnam, he replied: "Well, we're all confused about it. We talked about the war in the past for so long —without getting anywhere except into some damned unpleasant arguments—that there's nothing else to say. I guess there's some kind of unspoken moratorium on the subject. We analyzed and dissected the whole situation, and we've exhausted the subject."

For a visitor it was profoundly depressing. American purpose and optimism, once so intoxicating to an Englishman, had gone. They had been replaced with what? For the middle classes, a feeling of affluence gone stale. For the poor, an aggressive bitterness. And for everyone, a strange, undermining anxiety.

By comparison, Britain, with all its problems, seemed a happier and more carefree nation—and much more youthful. Perhaps the British were sitting back and waiting to let the Americans come up with answers to most of the problems that ailed the world. More likely the scale of difficulties in Britain suddenly seemed dwarfed by the immensity of the problems facing the United States.

A nation of 200 million people in a bountiful land felt the volcanic discontent of 30 million among them who were not receiving their share of the bounty. It was a major irony that, while it spent millions of dollars to store surplus farm produce, America still countenanced the hunger of millions of its citizens.

The Citizens Board of Inquiry into Hunger and Malnutrition in the United States issued in May 1968 a one hundred-page report in which it stated that 10,764,000 Americans were suffering from hunger. Another 20 million, 75 per cent of them under seventeen, were less than adequately nourished. Yet, after months of wrangling over the administration's request for $25 million emergency food bill, Congress appropriated $10 million, less than $1 a year for the really hungry American.

This unevenness in the slicing of the American cake was high lighted by *Fortune's* survey of the richest Americans: two men with personal fortunes of more than $1 billion, six others with more than $500 million, and 153 with net worth of more than $100 million. Richard Strout, writing as "T.R.B." in *The New Republic*, commented, "Millionaires who pay no taxes and poor people who go hungry—this disparity is the most dangerous social fact in America today."

The question was how long would millions of Americans be content to starve passively? Already in preceding years big-city riots had become as much part of the American way of life in the blazing summer months as the barbecue and the beach party. And the menace of the underprivileged brought fear to the doorstep of every urban middle-class home in the country.

Fear is contagious. In 1960 one rarely walked in New York City's Central Park or along certain stretches of the West Side or in the back streets of Harlem if one was white. But in 1968 many white Americans were afraid to walk up and down their own streets. A poll taken in the cities showed that 48 per cent of urban dwellers were frightened to leave their homes after dark and did not do so unless it was absolutely essential.

Much of New York's East Side, it seemed, was barren and soulless, with the population nervously entrenched behind locked doors. Eight years ago these same streets throbbed with life at night—a tremendous contrast to London, where everything stopped at 11:00 P.M. But now, with its new night life, London streets are crowded and New York streets abandoned. The difference is that, in London, people are not afraid to walk their own streets.

In New York and Washington this summer the conditioned fear one's friends felt swiftly infected the visitor. In the early hours of a New York morning, after several vain attempts to call a cab, a host urged him to stay the night, sleeping on a couch, rather than to walk the few blocks from 51st Street to 56th.

It was ridiculous. So the visitor walked through the empty streets. Two or three times, as other wanderers appeared, he felt himself tensing, ready for an attack. He could sense the tension in the others too, and each would pass warily on guard, prepared for sudden violent aggression. When he arrived at his hotel the visitor relaxed, pondering on the extraordinary situation that had forced him to walk through one of the most affluent and delightful areas of Manhattan with almost as much apprehension as he had felt in the back streets of Saigon. But such was the atmosphere of fear and despair.

It became mandatory for one's friends to produce new weapons and confess with self-conscious aggressiveness that they were going to "protect themselves." Against what? Against "them" they said, and they meant the Negroes.

Many of these people were those who, a few years ago, were supporting the civil-rights movement. Now some of them carried guns. Much of this fear came not so much from the riots—which had hardly touched their islands of affluence but had instead been confined to the ghettos, which few of these people had ever seen —but from the pronouncements of the new Negro leaders.

White liberals took the threats of the Negro militants far more literally than did many Negroes themselves. One afternoon the visitor spent several hours talking to a colored Vietnam-war veteran who had lost both legs. Sergeant Jack Jones of Philadelphia was working as a radio technician and could walk with stiff pride on his new artificial limbs.

"Rap Brown?" he laughed. "I'm 36 years old, and I've seen the world. Hell, I know that I don't get the squarest of deals, because I'm colored, but you don't think I'm going to take the yelling of a 23-year-old boy seriously, do you man? I mean, who would?"

How many Negroes shared his view was difficult to assess. The younger ones, living in a world of rising expectations beyond their reach, were less inclined to do so. The raging appeals of black nationalism found their target among them. But the white population found it hard to differentiate between rhetoric and reality.

This difficulty seems always to have been a characteristic source of American instability. One remembers reading how, in the great Depression, millions of middle-class Americans believed that they were threatened by an impending Communist revolution. That the mass of the unemployed was still as devoted to the capitalist system as was the Wall Street establishment went largely unperceived. Today too one finds many middle-class Americans terrified of black uprisings reminiscent of the "slave rebellions." The rantings of the extreme Negro leadership have intensified this fear. The aspirations and longings of the Negro masses to exist as ordinary Americans were largerly being ignored.

In any case, the one thing the visitor, coming from a welfare state, could see was that the social engineering of the United States was totally outdated where it existed at all. Both white and black knew it without knowing how best to change it. But then American reaction against welfare statism was still strong.

Though American adults were divided, an even more bewildering development was the revolt of the nation's youth. All the surging liberal enthusiasm that John Kennedy had released in young Americans had turned sour. In its place was a futile nihilism. As individuals or in groups, more and more young Americans were choosing to reject those precepts of American life that their parents held dearest. The depths of their hostility to the adult world were something never seen before.

In San Francisco the visitor sat with some young students and asked them what they wanted from life. "I want love, man," said one. The visitor brusquely rejected the comment and asked whether or not the young could talk in anything except platitudes. So the conversation turned serious, and the student explained himself this way:

> I don't know really what I want, except to say that I know what I don't want to be. I don't want to be like my parents and all their friends, because their lives are so pointless. . . . The trouble is that I'm afraid I will grow up to be like them. We all will I suppose unless we can change society. That's why we're so hostile. We're not really hostile; we're just trying to fight our way out of the trap we're being dragged into.

That the youth revolt was so inarticulate made it even difficult for adults to understand. But adult America was frantically worried about the division between itself and the young. The most amazing thing about young America's hostility to the adult world was its implacability. When young Americans did not choose to attack with demonstrations and riots, they did something even more frightening. They disengaged themselves. They did so by surrendering in ever-increasing numbers to escapist drugs. And they did so by living in total contrast to the affluence around them.

The visitor was astounded to find in New York—and other American cities—numbers of perfectly fit and able young men and women begging. The shocking thing was that they had none of the physical appearance of beggars—they were tall, strong, products of well-nourished childhoods. They seemed perfect specimens to go out and fulfill the American dream. Then one realized that by begging they are demonstrating their total rejection of that dream, that this action of self-abasement is their way of showing contempt for the prospects offered by the American way of life.

So the confusion and futility began to infect every sector: the decaying cities with their characterless business centers, deserted at night as the whites fled to the suburbs; the financial world, fighting a losing battle with inflation and the gold drain; government, responding more slowly as crises came faster and leaders accepted that their control over events was beginning to break down.

At the beginning of 1968 the visitor thus saw that America was deep into a new age: The Age of Anxiety.

Conceivably some Americans would challenge this conclusion. Yet all could not be well with a people whose television industry in the first quarter of 1968 took its advertising revenue in this order: Anacin headache tablets $4,618,500; Alka-Seltzer stomach remedy $3,993,400; Salem menthol filter cigarettes $3,552,700; Winston filter cigarettes $3,321,600; American Telephone and Telegraph $3,295,200; Bayer Aspirin, $3,110,500; Bufferin headache tablets $2,929,500; Listerine antiseptic $2,401,000.

And it was not just the obvious problems—the new issues like the Vietnam war, the growth of drug taking, Negro militance—that were causing this anxiety. It was something more: a helplessness in the face of a great sweep of technological events that seemed to be crushing man's individuality and deciding his destiny against any wishes of his own.

The visitor saw this reaction in his own changing attitude. All the things that had in the past signified America's progressive lead over the rest of the world took on a new dimension. The motor highways—the great cement arteries that span the nation—came to seem despoilers of the countryside. People drove along them like automatons, the pleasure of a drive in the open air gone forever. And the very air itself was poisoned by the fumes of multiplying technological complexes. The toxic output was so high that some scientists began to worry that carbon dioxide was increasing too fast for nature to handle.

So the industrial poison spread into the waters of once lovely rivers and magnificent lakes, turning them into sewers. Effluence is a by-product of affluence. And still the industrial machine ground on, unstoppable. One hundred thousand tons of sulfur dioxide belched forth every day from America's industrial chimneys; daily a quarter-million tons of carbon monoxide were emitted from 90 million cars. (The technocrats forecast that by the year 2000 there would be almost 200 million cars.) And people began to wonder, "Where will it all stop?" Those who thought a little more deeply asked, "Are we going to be capable of stopping it?"

Americans at the beginning of 1968 thus began to be aware that there was something to fear, though the shape of the threat was unclear. But the experience of fear itself was traumatic because it was contrary to all that they had been brought up to believe. Progress and the future had always been considered ends in themselves. In 1968 America wondered.

There was no room for smugness on the part of the visitor be-

9

cause, whether the world likes it or not, the United States sets the pattern of existence for the West—and for much of the East as well. The problems of America are the problems that all of us have to face. And this deep, unspoken fear of the technological imperative that sweeps man along in its path has its parallel on the other side of the Atlantic.

The British writer, C. P. Snow, has a theory that the difficulty of solving problems multiplies geometrically in relation to the size of a nation. That is if Britain, with 54 million people, has the same problems per head of population as does Sweden, with 8 million people, Britain needs, not seven but thirty times the money and effort to solve them. The United States with a population 25 times that of Sweden probably needs 200 times the effort. "And," says Snow "the ratio works in reverse."

This then is why the world looked more closely at America in 1968 than perhaps ever before. For, if the United States could handle its problems, then the smaller countries could surely solve theirs. If the United States failed, however, the future was uncertain for everyone. The visitor hoped, for himself and his fellow countrymen, that 1968 would be a year in which the United States would break out of its frustrations and find its way back to a path of decision and enlightenment.

His hope lay in the unique American conception of democracy, which gives the people a chance every four years to find a leader to match the times. The task before the American people at the beginning of the 1968 election campaign was formidable in the extreme; it was a testing time as never before. The year would show how the American system and the American people would stand up to that test.

PRESIDENT IMPERFECT

THE PRESIDENT OF THE UNITED STATES IS FREQUENTLY DESCRIBED AS "the most powerful man in the world." Many people believe that he is. The one man who would argue from strength against the description is Lyndon B. Johnson.

Toward the end of 1967 there was something of a minor political furore in Britain when the opposition press reported that Prime Minister Harold Wilson had indicated his wish to break away from the traditional system of cabinet rule in Britain and to introduce a government along American lines. This course, warned the newspapers, was dangerous. Mr. Wilson was attempting to do what no other British Prime Minister had ever dreamed of. He was trying to invest himself with Presidential *power*.

Whatever specter that comment may have raised in Britain, in Washington it produced only ironic laughter. Presidential power? At that time the President's lieutenants were being given almost third-degree treatment by a Senate committee, his war policy was under attack from leading members of his own party, and a vitally necessary tax increase to stabilize the economy was frozen at the whim of an Arkansas congressmen, the 59-year-old Wilbur Mills, who, as Chairman of the influential House Ways and Means Committee, refused to pass the increase unless the President agreed to cut Federal spending. Finally, Democratic Senator Eugene McCarthy of Minnesota was going around the country saying that President Johnson should not serve another term.

So, at the time when Harold Wilson was yearning for Presidential power, the President must equally have ached for the rigid party discipline that is the basis of the Prime Minister's authority. Mr. Wilson's power was limited by the tradition that all major policy decisions in Britain are made jointly by the cabinet. Of course, the Prime Minister appoints that cabinet and, as Harold Macmillan showed in his "night of the long knives," he can unappoint it just as quickly. But at all times he must maintain a majority in the cabinet, and that cabinet must always reflect the sentiment of the party as a whole. That is how the Prime Minister is prevented from getting ahead of his position.

There is no written constitution in Britain; the checks and balances are customary rather than ordained, and therefore the British system is more flexible. In 1967 the American Civil Liberties Union made a comparative study of individual freedom in Britain and America. Its conclusion was that, although the American has more guarantees of freedom than does the Briton, the latter has more freedom in fact. The difference is that the United States—as Americans will proudly tell you—has a government of laws. In Britain there is a government of men, understood as such.

In Washington in 1968 the visitor was bound to ask, as so many Americans were asking, were the laws outdated? Were the checks and balances, so precisely written into the system in order to make it run smoothly, beginning to paralyze it?

It was the prime purpose of the Founding Fathers to deny the occupant of the Presidency dictatorial powers. With their experience of colonial government—they were virtually the first self-governing colonies in the British Empire—they sought to combine the two offices of head of state and head of government in one person with constitutional checks, vested in Congress and the Supreme Court, on his prerogatives.

In the leisurely, reflective pace of eighteenth-century life, the American system worked. There was time for reasoned debate, time to adjust and regulate Presidential power. And the men in Congress were among the finest in the land. But now we are in the technological age, an age in which decisions are taken at computer speed and then, in many cases, have to be ratified by machinery that moves at the pace of a covered wagon.

In Washington it seemed that the outdated precepts were in early 1968 beginning to produce a Constitutional crisis in the United States. It is true that men of quality still go to Washington (although today there are more of them in the executive branch than in the legislative branch). One of the most impressive aspects of American life is that powerful businessmen who earn huge salaries will abandon them to serve their country, shouldering huge responsibilities for the maximum Cabinet pay of only $35,000 a year.

It is also true that at the lower levels of government service there are young men of enormous talent, products of an excellent educational system. The financial rewards that they can secure in government service will always be less than commerce can offer. But they choose government, and they choose it because it can offer, if nothing else, the facilities for research and the kind of equipment that not even the biggest corporation in the land can match.

They are able to plan and project for the future. They can recommend decisions based on the ultimate in immediate research. But to obtain action—to have requests for decisions recognized, let alone implemented—they must convince the Congress of their necessity. And the U.S. Congress is a traditionally conservative body. Its seniority system places the real power in the hands of the oldest and often most reactionary legislators: the committee chairmen who hold hearings and who hammer out legislation. These men are, in the eighteenth-century tradition, suspicious of and hostile to the ever-increasing pressures of the government machine. Congress has shown clearly that it is not going to be rushed into anything, particularly by the new science of cybernetics or the ever-proliferating bright new scientific civil servants.

The frustration among clever government workers in Washington, therefore, goes very deep.

Charles Warden came to Washington at the age of 35 as Special Assistant on the President's Council of Economic Advisers.

His views on the role that Congress plays in his special sphere of activities—strengthening the dollar at a crucial period when the pound sterling, the first line of defense, had crumbled—were bitter. He told the visitor:

> It is incorrect to imagine that Congress is thoughtful, wise, understanding, or even conservative. It is also incorrect to imagine that Congress is thoughtful, wise, understanding and liberal, for Congress is neither conservative nor liberal by bias but instead is blind, ignorant, and dumb. Its senses are somehow cut off, not linked to any reflective brain.
>
> Every Congressman knows that he has to go back to his electorate every two years. He is acutely aware that his political life is at stake. This enforces a sort of political myopia on everything he does. The Congressman is conscious only that he must stay in the public eye and stay there in a favorable way. His political survival requires that he surrounds himself with news and drama, sometimes when there is no news or drama.
>
> In the debate on taxes last year we had the spectacle of Senator William Proxmire making headlines with statements that were completely out of character, with statements that were out of role with a graduate of the Harvard School of Business Administration. But Senator Proxmire saw that he could not make any political headway by joining the Administration, so he became an arch critic, and to hell with the nation's fiscal policy.

Yet Warden, who has been in Washington for two years, wants to stay on, despite lucrative commercial and academic offers. He has a Ph.D. degree from Harvard University, served in the armed forces, and worked as a senior economist with the Ford Foundation for eighteen months before Gardner Ackley, chairman of the Council of Economic Advisers, invited him to join the White House money team.

"During budget times, from November to February each year, it means working fifty to eighty hours per week and seven days per week," he says. "Either my wife or my stomach would give out with much more of it."

Warden feels that Congress particularly frustrated the best interests of the country in delaying the 10 per cent tax-surcharge bill, which the nation's best economists almost unanimously urged, to help cool off inflation. "Congress does not have by any means

14

the system of analysis on which to base sound judgments on the budget," he says.

So plans got lost, discarded, or thwarted in the body of Congress. America, once the fastest-moving nation in the world, was like a champion sprinter trying to do the hundred-yard dash with a ball and chain around his ankle. It could move very fast for three yards; then it had to stop and pull the ball forward. And so in a peculiar way it not only slowed down in 1968; in some ways it actually stood still as well.

The irony of the situation is that few Presidents in this century have understood the workings of Congress better than did Lyndon Johnson. The visitor was struck by his similarity to Harold Wilson in this respect. Wilson is the supreme parliamentarian of his generation. Johnson was the superb congressional fixer of the 1950s. In many ways the problems that the two men faced were similar, although Britain's were small in comparison to America's.

"We need a Winston Churchill," said a Tory critic once, bemoaning Britain's problems, "and all we've got is a mini L.B.J." Cruel but not altogether untrue.

Both men rose (and thus suffered in the comparison) because tragedy smote outstanding leaders. No one needs reminding that President Johnson reached the White House only because an assassin's bullet felled his predecessor. It is sometimes forgotten, however, that Harold Wilson became leader of the Labour Party only because first Aneurin Bevan and then Hugh Gaitskell died at the height of their powers.

Neither man emerged from the classical centers of political power and influence. Both took pride in the fact that their origins were humble. Wilson was always keen to draw a favorable comparison between his Yorkshireman and Johnson's Texan. Both men believed passionately in the politics of pragmatism, both sought their power from the center, and both sought consensus. Both understood politics better than they understood principles, and both understood principles better than they understood people.

Both enjoyed the trappings of power and patronage. Both were jealous of their images, sensitive to criticism, and suspicious of conspiracies against them when none existed. Both enjoyed love-hate relationships with the press. Both had an almost messianic sense of their own importance. They were capable of great generosity and also of petty spite. Neither easily forgot a slight.

But, above all, at the beginning of 1968, both suffered the same fearful political handicap. Neither of them was believed by his people.

Lyndon Johnson, in a moment of anguish, asked one day, "Why should Ho Chi Minh believe me when the newspapers and the broadcasters in my own country won't accept my word?"

A political joke then current in Washington went, "Frankly I won't believe anything is true until L.B.J. denies it."

Somewhere in mid-Atlantic the word spinners, always anxious to soften the hard truths of Anglo-Saxon, came up with the necessary euphemism. There emerged, on each side of the ocean, a "credibility gap."

The gaps arose not solely from disbelief of individual statements made by Wilson and Johnson but rather from growing suspicion of their motives.

Throughout the history of political thought, it has been argued that dictatorship would be the ideal form of government if only one had a foolproof system for choosing the perfect and benevolent dictator. As there is no such system, the idea has been rejected by democratic theorists.

But Wilson and Johnson appeared to be joining Charles de Gaulle in the belief that the leader must know best and, consequently, that, because *he* knew his motives to be good, any method of achieving them was legitimate. This path leads to the death of democracy. Wilson was prompted to take the first faltering steps along that path because of his belief that he alone knew how to raise the siege of Britain's economy. Johnson, on the other hand, believed that he alone could handle Vietnam. His first step was taken after the Gulf of Tonkin incident. It was prompted by his special knowledge of Congress.

In the summer of 1964 a number of American warships were reported to have been attacked on the high seas by North Vietnamese torpedo boats. Skeptics are still unconvinced that a serious attack was made; some even doubt that any incident took place at all. But at the time the reports raised American blood pressure to the level of apoplexy.

Johnson used this mood to rush the Gulf of Tonkin Resolution through Congress. It was just the excuse he needed. The American President does not have the legal right to declare war. He can order American troops into action only to defend the nation. The Constitution reserves to Congress the right to declare war. What the Tonkin Resolution did was to give the President carte blanche in Vietnam, allowing him full powers to prosecute the war in any manner that he saw fit.

The Vietnam situation was fast-moving and ever-changing. To the man in charge, especially one who believed that he has some sort of divine ordinance in the matter, it was essential to have powers to move fast in order to contain any sudden threat. But, in assuming such powers, Johnson made what was later revealed as his greatest mistake in the way that it affected him and his Presidency. The Vietnam war had already grown on an ever-swelling stream of American involvement. But now, the President handed on a plate to his critics—in and out of Congress—the charge that it had become not America's war but Johnson's war.

Insistence on the Resolution was an act of political self-destruction that clouded not only Johnson's reputation in relation to the war but also his many excellent achievements, particularly in civil rights, of which he could rightly be proud.

Soon the sleight of hand used to secure those powers began to produce a backlash in Congress. Its members became gradually more hostile. The suspicion began to grow that perhaps the President had too much power, and an attempt was made to repeal the Gulf of Tonkin Resolution.

At a hearing before the Senate Foreign Relations Committee on August 16, 1967, legislators reexamined the President's powers. It is worth repeating what a Constitutional specialist and college professor, Ruhl Bartlett, had to tell the committee about the Founding Fathers' apprehensions regarding the Presidential office that they were creating:

> They were deeply impressed with the power of the British Crown to declare war and were fearful of establishing an executive authority that might develop monarchical tendencies. They feared that the desire for achievement, or fame, or prestige or the exhilaration derived from the exercise of power, or belief in its superior wisdom regarding the national interest might lead the executive away from the necessary restraints of Constitutional government.

This then was the office for which at least eight men would compete during the 1968 election year, an office of supreme responsibility, enormous complexity, and unquestionable frustration. It is an office that Americans endow with almost worshipful respect.

Yet in one of the profoundest paradoxes of their society, Americans very rarely yield to the President the respect that they shower on his office. Once a man walks through the tall, iron gate of the mansion at 1600 Pennsylvania Avenue, he becomes the target for the most extraordinary verbal abuse. The last four Presidents of the United States had been lambasted with disgraceful epithets and cruel innuendos. They were called feeble-minded, fools, crooks, dilettantes, adulterers, traitors, liars, megalomaniacs, playboys. Perhaps the dichotomy is the direct result of the Founding Fathers' determination to give the President power but not to trust him entirely.

Congress, which exemplifies this determination and uses its powers to advise and consent when it thinks fit, does not, however. stint on things material. An economist has estimated that a private citizen would have to acquire an annual income of between $90 and $100 million to live in the style of a President.

To support him in the discharge of his towering work load, the President has a "magic carpet" service of assistants, transport, and communications.

Under law he has assigned to him six administrative assistants; a legal adviser; a special adviser who is sometimes now known as "Assistant President"; three principal secretaries for appointments, press, and correspondence; three military aides; a personal physician; and a detail of Secret Service agents who guard him from the day of his election until he quits office. His personal staff numbers 255, and he has immediate access to thousands of government and private experts in any field in which he requires special guidance.

Eight telephone switchboards, each with 500 duplicate extensions, manned around the clock can link the President to most of the world at any time. More than three hundred people operate this complex communications network. Their job is to see that the President is the most "in touch" man in the world. And he is. In a boat on the Potomac, in his car in the Texas hill country, in a jet high over India, President Johnson can pick up a telephone and talk to anyone at a moment's notice.

The financial rewards of the Presidency are impressive. Mr. Johnson's salary was $100,000 a year. In addition, he received $50,000 in taxable allowances and another $40,000 for travel and entertainment. His accommodation in the White House, with its lovely rolling lawns, was free. (The mansion has been valued at $60,000,000. Its annual upkeep, also paid from the public purse, was $735,000 a year in 1968.)

The 36th President of the United States inherited this position of power in the aftermath of John Fitzgerald Kennedy's assassination in Dallas, November 22, 1963. Lyndon Johnson was 55 at the time, an ambitious man who had long wanted to be President in his own right, not as a substitute.

He took his sudden elevation in stride. And, in a moment of national trauma, he preserved the continuity of the office and calmed the nation. In those early Johnson days, with the image of Kennedy's death still sharply etched in every memory, the new President really moved his country forward. It may be forgotten now, but, far from slowing the Kennedy administration's impetus, Johnson actually speeded it up. The deadlock between the President and Congress was broken, and much of the Kennedy legislation, so long held up, was passed with extraordinary speed. Suddenly Congress was acting in a way that it had not acted since Franklin D. Roosevelt had taken office. In short succession, the Tax Reduction Act (based on the—to some—heretical economic theory of Federal spending to stimulate the economy even at the expense of a balanced budget) and a dramatic new civil-rights bill were passed. They were great victories and, though some believed that the President succeeded in getting them passed only because of the catastrophic events in Dallas, that was only half the story.

The fact is that President Johnson used these events—and his unquestioned brilliance in dealing with Congress, together with nationally televised and broadcast speeches that appealed directly to the American people—to get his way and secure legislation for the betterment of the American nation.

It seemed at that time that the fundamental strength of American purpose in the 1960s was not to be weakened by the death of President Kennedy. Indeed, many people started to say that Johnson would do more to implement Kennedy's ideals and conceptions than Kennedy could ever have done himself.

But the chemistry of national leadership is extremely subtle. And from the beginning there were clues that things might not go so well. The biggest clue was in the personality and character of the substitute President.

On Christmas Day 1963 the new President talked to corre-

19

spondents invited to his Texas ranch. Those were the days before the "credibility gap," and the President and the White House press corps were still enjoying what was to be a very short honeymoon. On that Christmas morning the President, dressed in "suntan" levis and hand-tooled Texas boots, took the correspondents on a tour of his home. It was a totally American thing to do and absolutely engaging to a British member of the press corps.

His pride in his home was blatant but winning, an unaffected enthusiasm. The love of all things Texan was so innocent, so completely without guile, that it was quite infectious. He displayed an ornate black Mexican saddle and Indian artifacts gathered by his grandfather. Pointing through a window to a field spread with a veil of green, he said, "That's some fine winter oats for our Hereford herd." Scottish brass kettles gleamed beside paintings of western scenes. The books on the shelves showed a catholic taste, ranging from Robert Browning's letters to Isabella Blagden, Balzac, Gautier, and gastronomical guides to Europe.

The tour continued into the front garden. There the uninhibited President of the United States had his audience admire the heated swimming pool, the green lighting for the trees, and the piped-in music system. He pressed a button and stood reverently as "Hark! The Herald Angels Sing" boomed in full stereophonic sound across the ranch.

Then—quite suddenly—there occurred an incident so jarring, so out of keeping with the occasion, that the British correspondent asked himself whether or not he had imagined it. Americans quickly assured him that he had not.

In the middle of the conversation the President's older daughter, Lynda Bird, joined her father. He slipped his arm round her waist and gave her an affectionate squeeze. She was wearing a Christmas-red dress with a flying panel in the front of the skirt. The President, his eye taking in the lines of the dress, suddenly broke off his anecdote and put his hand under the panel, patted his daughter's stomach, and said to his audience, "It's just the style of this dress —no matter what you men are thinking."

It was the kind of remark that an eighteenth-century British country squire would have made to guffaws of amusement. It was the kind of remark that may still have some currency in twentieth-century Texas. But among the international pressmen standing there that Christmas Day it caused embarrassment for the girl and themselves. The only person who seemed unembarrassed was Lyndon Johnson himself.

This sort of gratuitous crudity was to impede the President's capacity to communicate with the people around him and, through them, with the nation and the world. His lack of style came to be compared often with the dead President's distinctive sophistication; his earthy humor and habits contrasted with the Kennedy "grace" and "charisma." The comparisons were inevitably unfavorable.

It was a tragedy of his Presidency that this largely irrelevant matter of style obscured and hindered what might have been a remarkable custodianship of America's highest office.

Style did not much matter in the 1964 campaign. The Republicans nominated Barry Goldwater, a man who believed that the future lay in the past. Johnson, anxious to prove to the world and to himself his right to be President as the people's choice, campaigned with fervor and drive and produced a record-breaking result. He received 60 percent of the popular vote, carried 44 states, and returned to Washington with a heavily balanced Democratic Congress. In the Senate Democrats held 68 out of 100 seats and in the House of Representatives 295 out of 435.

Governing in his own right, Johnson moved ahead. Despite his Texas background, his record on civil rights and social welfare was a good one. He had a program for dealing with many of the problems that he foresaw for the second half of the decade. Under his prodding the 89th Congress set about converting that program into law. First Medicare—a national health scheme for those over 65—was introduced, then more civil-rights legislation; Federal aid to education, antipoverty legislation, and establishment of the Department of Housing and Urban Development (whose first Secretary, Robert Weaver, became the first Negro in the Cabinet) were accomplished.

During the campaign President Johnson had started talking about the "Great Society," and now it seemed that he had the power and the influence really to shape that society. Some of his detractors scorned the phrase. One observer said at the time, "the title the President has suggested for his era in American history is typically Texan—at once grandiose, vague, noble, and corny."

It seemed an unfair comment. Most people in Washington at that time perceived the President's sincerity. His words rang true when he said:

We are in the midst of the greatest upsurge of economic well-being in the history of any nation.

Our flourishing progress has been marked by price stability unequaled in the world. Our balance-of-payments deficit has declined, and the soundness of our dollar is unquestioned. I pledge to keep it that way. I urge business and labor to co-operate to that end.

We worked for two centuries to climb this peak of prosperity. But we are only at the beginning of the road to the great society. Ahead now is a summit where freedom from the wants of the body can help fulfill the needs of the spirit.

We do not intend to live—in the midst of abundance—isolated from neighbors and nature, confined by blighted cities and bleak suburbs, stunted by poverty of learning and an emptiness of leisure.

The Great Society asks not only how much but how good, not only how to create wealth but how to use it; not only how fast we are going but where we are headed.

Fine words, but, tragically, the lofty ambitions that they expressed remained only a politician's promise—all because of the Vietnam war.

Empowered by Congress to take whatever action he thought fit on Vietnam the President's first act of foreign policy after his election was to Americanize the war. Ironically this move was the very thing that he had warned against while campaigning. He had won his huge majority because the American people were afraid of what Barry Goldwater might do in Vietnam if he gained power. Yet American planes began to bomb North Vietnam on February 28, 1965. By the middle of the year a huge American army was building up in the South.

At that time, President Johnson believed that the American people could have both guns and butter. Surely the great American economy could support a tiny colonial war without losing pace for a second. But Vietnam was to become the most expensive war of its size in history. By 1968 it was costing the United States $82 million a day to prosecute, and everyone at home was feeling the pinch, particularly the poor. The Great Society had become an empty catchphrase.

The President's popularity declined with the lengthening of the war. It is said in Europe and repeated in the United States that the Americans are a dynamic people who like to "get things done" and that they do not have staying power for a long course of action—

22

only for quick results. This, of course, is, like so many other conceptions of America, a myth—as the briefest glance at American history will show.

But Americans in 1967 were saying it about themselves in relation to the war. The frustration was beginning to show, and they were looking for an excuse to get out. The President, who had committed himself and his country to the Vietnam brushfire, was naturally surprised at the apparently uncrushable strength of North Vietnam and the Vietcong. But he was bewildered by the attitude of a huge segment of the American people, who rejected the war and began to campaign actively against it.

In 1967 the President discussed this problem with the visitor: "Duties fall to nations as they do to individuals," he said. As he conceived it, it was America's historical duty to be in Vietnam. "Two thirds of the world's population are in Asia, and this is where the immediate future of mankind is going to be resolved. . . . America must be there."

He spoke with what seemed historical farsightedness. It was not merely a question of holding the line or even of the domino theory, he said. The facts were that, if Asia were to fall under the domination of Chinese Communism, the gap between the "haves" and the "have-nots" would grow wider. Peking's brand of Communism could not produce the drive or the technology necessary to raise the living standards of Asian peoples to a Western level. Only a massive effort of Western technology—a huge investment of men, money, and machinery—could lift the Asian peoples into the twentieth century, he said. It would be an unrelenting struggle, but it was absolutely necessary for peace. If the gap became wider it had to end in a terrible conflict between East and West.

The Vietnam war had to be fought, he added, to show that America was committed to Asia and intended to play a part in its development.

But what of the antiwar feeling in the United States? the visitor asked. Did that not indicate that the American people were not behind the grand design for Asia?

The President answered quietly. He thought that opposition to the war was exaggerated: "Nobody likes war. I do not enjoy a duty which causes me to send American boys to be killed in that faraway land." But he added that, regrettable though the war was, he believed that the American people understood the issues and would not flinch from their duty.

23

The movement against the war makes headlines because it is composed of beatniks and so-called "intellectuals" and newspaper columnists. But the real American, though he hates war, is not prepared to let his country down. Of that I am sure. If you get out among the ordinary people you will find it to be the case. And you know each month tens of thousands of those Vietnam troops are coming home. They understand the realities, they talk to family and friends, and that's something you have to count. It means a lot more than the shouting of the protesters.

The President spoke simply and with conviction. He had not successfully communicated to the American people the grand strategy involved, however, and by 1967 it was too late.

Toward the end of that year the President began to face up to this fact. The polls showed more and more of the American people turning against him. At first, he put his unpopularity down to the columnists. The people, he believed, were still for him. In the great silent center of America he would get his response.

But slowly it became apparent that opposition to himself and the war was not a peripheral thing. It cut right across the nation at almost every level. It was producing personalities and movements that threatened not only President Johnson's chances for a second term but also the whole traditional structure of American politics. It was clear that the 1968 elections would take place amid crisis and turmoil.

.3.

The Undeclared War

By the beginning of 1968 American casualties in the Vietnam war had passed the 150,000 mark. Of this number 20,000 had been killed since the United States first became involved in 1961. So rapidly was the death rate climbing that it was probable that more than 20,000 men would die in the election year alone.

Casualty figures, like all statistics, are impersonal. They cannot convey that most of the men who die are young and uncomplaining. They do not reveal that wounds in this far distant war are more hideous and appalling than military surgeons have had to face before. Nor do they reflect the home-front casualties, the parents, wives, or girls for whom the only cushion for the shock of a loved one's death is the personal delivery of a telegram by an officer of the United States armed forces.

A casualty ceases to be a statistic only when we know him. The visitor thought that he could find out better what the war meant to America—and what it was doing to the country—if, instead of

25

analyzing 20,000 deaths (the Pentagon had them all neatly tabulated), he were to look closely at just one.

James Seidensticker was born on August 4, 1947. His mother, Patricia, chose the Rockaway Beach Hospital on Long Island for her confinement because the doctor who had delivered her first son, Howard, a year before was still there. Howard Seidensticker, Sr., was a tall, reserved, but friendly and just sort of man. He was a second-generation American; his grandparents had come from Germany. During World War II he had served as a marine and had fought in some of the bloodiest battles against the Japanese in the South Pacific.

During one leave he had married a tall girl with a mass of red hair, Patricia Willnauer. Her grandmother had come from County Mayo in Ireland, which probably accounts for the hair. Patricia was a placid sort of girl, with an equable temperament, and her fine cheekbones revealed character.

Unlike her husband, Patricia's brother James had not fought in World War II. He suffered from a congenital heart condition that made him ineligible for war service. This disability affected him badly. On New York's grubby buses and the big, uncomfortable railway coaches that ran from Pennsylvania Station under the East River and out to Long Island, people would stare questioningly and accusingly at this young man, apparently fit and well but *not* in uniform. James Willnauer and his family never forgot those stares.

Patricia was extremely fond of her brother, and she named her second son after him.

The main preoccupation of the Seidenstickers, as of most Americans, was to improve their standard of living. When Howard Seidensticker, Sr., came out of the marines, they moved into a tiny frame house with only two bedrooms in Elmont, Long Island. Nine months after the birth of James, they followed the ever-spreading pattern of suburbia out to Wantagh on the south shore. There they moved into a bigger Cape Cod house, a style of building similar to a British bungalow but with dormer windows set into the roof to ventilate the attic rooms.

The young Seidenstickers were happy in their new home. Wantagh was a further step toward realizing the aspirations that they shared with millions of Americans. It was definitely middle-class. And, like so many American suburbs, it cloaked itself in the respectability of things English as if to lend an aura of tradition to its new roads and shiny mass-produced houses. Its street signs read, "Chelsea Road," "Kent Road," "Derby Road," and so on. The Seidenstickers lived on Cambridge Road, and they loved the name.

Wantagh was typical of America in its lack of variety. It did, however, manage to stamp its own breed, to whom patriotism and the approval of all things American seemed desirable in themselves.

As movies, television serials, modern literature, have created a world-wide impression of American suburbs as the epitome of sybaritic decadence and corruption, this may come as a shock. Perhaps there is a stratum of suburban society in which the boredom of affluence leads to insecurity, casual sexual liaison, and disturbed children as a matter of course—but it is fairly hard to find.

In places like Wantagh, where the upper working class fuses with the lower middle class—if one can use such British classifications—there is a resourceful strength. This is the solid bourgeois background of America, more aggressive than its British equivalent, less smug than the French. Here are respect for the community, a powerful sense of family life; above all, religion, still strong, exerts its subtle influence through the generations. The "real" America is often described as the farmlands of the Midwest. But that was fifty years ago. The "real" America of today is the suburb.

Suburban life may not be the ideal life, but it was what millions aspired to, and the fact that the suburbs are for the most part territory forbidden to the Negro population shows only how much Negroes are excluded from the real America.

So James Seidensticker, a white, Roman Catholic child, a third-generation American, was born into this suburban existence, and it molded him. When he was five he attended the Beech Street School kindergarten in Wantagh, and his mother gave birth to a third son, Richard. She was probably relieved to be that much more certain of a male heir—because there were already fears for young James. He was found to be suffering the same heart condition this his uncle had, and Patricia Seidensticker was told by doctors that her second son was unlikely to see his teens. His year at the kindergarten passed safely, however, and he moved on to the primary grades in the Beech Street School. This part of his education was free, paid for by local rates and taxes.

Before classes started each day James, like all American school-children, would stand before the "stars and stripes," or a picture of it, place his hand on his heart, and recite the national Pledge of Allegiance: "I pledge allegiance to the flag of the United States of America and to the Republic for which it stands, one nation under God, indivisible, with liberty and justice for all." Then the children would sing "America"—"My country 'tis of thee, sweet land of liberty, of thee I sing"—to the tune of the British national anthem.

In the holidays and evenings after school, James' playmates in the flat, dusty, scrub-filled dunes of the shoreline, were the Buckley girls. The Buckleys were the Seidenstickers' best friends. At times the two families seemed almost one. Tom and Mary Buckley lived in the house opposite and had three daughters, Mary Jo, Monica, and Faith.

Like the Seidenstickers, the Buckleys were strict Roman Catholics. At mass every Sunday young James sat next to Monica Buckley. She was a year older, but, from his third birthday, they were inseparable.

In 1955 when James, nicknamed Jim, was nearly eight, the Seidenstickers moved again. Wantagh was becoming built up, and with still another new baby, daughter Audrey Jude, they needed more room.

They chose Brentwood, in Suffolk County, Long Island, 42 miles out the dreary, single track that carries the Long Island Railroad trains from Pennsylvania Station in Manhattan to Ronkonkoma, the Indian name for "bottomless river."

Shortly afterward the Buckleys moved out to join them. Taxes had gone up in Wantagh, and, like the Seidenstickers, the Buckleys wanted to move to where there was still open country. Besides, when the Seidenstickers had moved, it had been almost like splitting the family. The district was perhaps a shade lower in class than Wantagh but the white clapboard house on Bruce Lane, near St. Joseph's Academy for Young Ladies, was bigger and better— and there was more country.

Vines covered the big trellis outside the kitchen door, providing a cool place to sit during the hot summers when flies swarmed beyond the wire-mesh doors. Beneath the front windows crouched a row of young cypress and yew trees, and in spring brash yellow forsythia splashed its way up the walls almost to the eaves.

By English standards Brentwood was more a garden suburb than a village. Oldish Colonial-style clapboard houses were dotted pink, gray, and yellow among the tall pines that blanketed the area. The suburb's center, such as it was, consisted of shops and services clustered around the station, which was only a wooden shack beside the dirty brown ribbon of the railway. The trains seemed to tower over the station, and it was a steep climb into their long, sparsely-furnished, and uncomfortable carriages. Most people used automobiles.

In Brentwood Jim attended St. Anne's School next to St. Anne's Church. He did well there. His grades were always in the A-B category, though his best subject was mathematics. Participation in organized games like baseball and football was out because of his faulty heart, but that did not stop him from being popular. He and a boy called Nicholas Fritz were the best-liked kids in their class.

When he was thirteen he left St. Anne's and went to Brentwood High School. Already his father, who marked off the children's height in pencil on the inside doorframe, had noted that he was going to be a very tall boy. He was talkative and outgoing and early showed a love for dancing—but he was also serious and sensitive. When he was but nine, he and Monica Buckley had been playing in the yard when Monica broke her arm. At the hospital he had cried for hours at the thought of his friend's pain.

At the time that he entered high school he was thinking of becoming a priest. The notion faded, but he stayed extremely close to the church among the pines. He also became a very patriotic boy. When he was sixteen, he attended a baseball match, and, when some people near him failed to stand during "The Star-Spangled Banner," he cajoled them into rising.

Jim's penciled height on the doorpost was past the six-foot mark when, at seventeen, he entered Suffolk Community College. He planned to stay there two years and then to take a mathematics degree at New York University, which would be a further two-year course.

It was 1964; in the same year his Uncle James underwent open-heart surgery and died. He was buried in Pinelawn Cemetery up the railroad track past the Negro-populated old Indian settlement of Wyandanch.

The horrors of another war on the other side of the world were beginning to matter to the American public, whose sons were already killing and being killed. But, as long as he stayed on his full-time higher-educational course, Jim Seidensticker knew that he would not be called to the colors. So the war in Vietnam did

29

not concern him, he was happy at college, and he spent all his spare time with Monica Buckley.

Their days together were long and lazy. Sometimes they joined in the "beer and franks" beach parties that were the teen-age mode on the island; sometimes they just sat at home doing jigsaw puzzles, which they loved, or played cards with the younger children or watched television westerns, which she enjoyed.

He liked to play records and read poetry; his favorite poem was "The First Fig" by Edna St. Vincent Millay. The Seidenstickers' living room was a cozy place to curl up in. The chairs were deep, chintzy, and comfortable, and a big old wooden rocker loomed over the television set. On the shelves were all sorts of ornaments, mementoes of holidays, and china statues of old American infantrymen. On the wall hung four needlework pictures of "olde" American towns that Monica had embroidered.

It was a fine year while Jim was at college. Monica, who worked in a local store, had bought an old 1957 DeSoto car for $200 and later she gave it to Jim; then he gave it back to her, and after a while it caught fire, and they "junked" it. But the car was fun while it lasted.

Financial problems were pressing on the Seidenstickers. The community college was free, except for a small charge for books and so on, but living was costly. To live decently Mrs. Seidensticker felt that they had to be a two-job family. Her husband, who drove a cement-mixer truck, averaged about $7,000 a year, despite layoffs. Mrs. Seidensticker took a job driving a school bus, which brought in about $100 a week. But the outlays were huge. The monthly mortgage payment was $125, gas for cooking and heating $50, water $10. And there were about $600 a year to pay in local taxes.

The two years at New York University were going to cost more than the Seidenstickers could afford. So in June 1966 after a year of attending college full time Jim went to work for a company that made audiovisual educational aids. He planned to continue his education in night school.

Three weeks after informing the authorities that he had left college, Jim Seidensticker received the letter notifying him that he was to be drafted into the army.

The draft boards and their workings were one of the most controversial subjects in 1968 America. Each board dealt with a local area, and each month it was told by the Defense Department how many men it would be required to produce. All boys were eligible from the age of eighteen upward, though some were exempted —for instance, those who enlisted in the Coast Guard or National Guard—and some, like those attending college full time or volunteering for the Peace Corps, were deferred.

Jim did not mind being called up. He had frequently criticized the draft dodgers, and he never questioned an American's duty to serve his country when called. His mother worried about his heart. It was a miracle that he had lived so long. When the time came she would have to decide whether or not to tell the authorities.

On the doorframe Jim's height had reached six feet five.

The hot summer passed easily enough. Every Sunday Jim went to visit his Aunt Louise, the widow of his dead Uncle James; when he did not find her at home, he knew where to find her in the cemetery. He had acquired an old Chevrolet and a Weimaraner, a short-haired gray sporting dog called Baron.

One evening the following November, Baron, who was tied up in the yard, tried to jump the fence and was hanged on his collar. For a long time Jim was inconsolable. Then he acquired a budgerigar. Mrs. Buckley's mother was almost blind, and Jim often went over to "baby sit" with her. She gave him the bird; he called it Cosmo and kept it in a cage in the kitchen over the brass bell that his mother used to call the family to supper.

Around the turn of the year he went for his army medical exam. His elder brother Howard, whom everyone called Buzz, had already passed the higher standards for the military police. But what about Jim's heart? He had taken his decision. He would say nothing. Perhaps the thought of his uncle's unhappiness influenced him. Perhaps it was just patriotism, perhaps just pride. Whatever it was, it swayed his mother too, and she kept silent. Jim passed not only the ordinary medical exam but also, made the higher grade needed to join his brother in the M.P.s.

On February 7, 1967, Jim Seidensticker entered the army. He was sent to Fort Jackson, South Carolina, for eight weeks of basic training. After five days it was found that he had a cyst at the base of his spine. It was infected and dangerous, and he was told that eventually he would need an operation. But he wanted to stay with the same batch of recruits, so they kept him going by swabbing out the sore and packing it. Letters to his mother told her how painful it was when he had to stand guard at night, but the fear of appearing to be a "dodger" prevented him from requesting relief. He stuck it out until the cyst healed.

31

Then he went to Fort Gordon, Georgia, for special training as a military policeman. He was in transit on Ash Wednesday, and he wrote home that he felt a terrible sinner because he had missed mass and no cross of ashes had been placed on his forehead by a priest. This religious ritual is so important and so widespread among America's Catholics that on Ash Wednesday even New York policemen can be seen with black smudges on their foreheads.

Jim Seidensticker finished the training as a military policeman with distinction and was posted to the 293rd M.P. Company at Ford Ord, California. On August 1 his mother received an extraordinary letter. He told her that, although he was still not 21 and did intend to continue with his studies after the army, he would like to get engaged to Monica Buckley.

Patricia Seidensticker was flabbergasted but delighted. She had always thought of them as brother and sister. She phoned Mary Buckley, "What do you know, Jim's written saying he wants to get engaged."

"Who to?"

"Who to! Why to your Monica!"

The two ladies went immediately to inform Monica of Jim's intention. It was the first that she had heard of it, and she reserved her decision. But, when Jim phoned as usual the next Sunday, she was waiting to accept the proposal that his mother insisted he make. Now Jim had a fiancée.

Thanksgiving in 1967 was on November 23. This American holiday dates back to the time of the Pilgrims, who celebrated their foothold in the New World with feasting and prayer. Traditionally the fare consists of the native staples that saved them after their European crops had failed: turkey, cranberry sauce, and sweet potatoes.

The Buckleys sat in the warm kitchen of the Seidensticker home. All around the soft wood-paneled walls were glowing copper utensils and rows of spice and herb bottles—oregano, spiced curry, raisins, mint. Pinned up over the massive eighteen-cubic-foot refrigerator and deep freeze—necessary to most Americans because of their once-a-week shopping habits—was a painted wooden plaque depicting the American flag with the Pledge of Allegiance.

During Thanksgiving Dinner in this cozy setting Jim called from California to say that he was coming home for a month's leave on December 1. After that he would be going to Vietnam.

One of the first things he did when he came home was to buy

Monica her engagement ring. A diamond it had to be. He did not know much about engagement rings, so he enlisted his mother's help. Jim dipped into his savings and took out a loan on an insurance policy that he had started when he was seventeen, and he and his mother went off to neighboring Patchogue, where they bought a fine, single-stone ring for $340. Monica was very proud of it.

The day before Jim's leave was up there was a farewell party. All the Buckleys were there, of course, and any other friends who cared to drop in. Mrs. Seidensticker's hospitable table was laden. There were fresh ham (Jim's favorite), cold cuts, salted butter and rye bread, celery and olives, pretzels, potato chips, and melba rounds (small circles of toast) to be thrust into sour-cream-and-onion mix or one of Mrs. Seidensticker's other "dips." They drank beer, root beer (a dark nonalcoholic beverage that tastes rather as Friars Balsam smells and is made, as its name implies, from roots and herbs), sarsparilla, highballs, coke, Pepsi, and, best of all, French champagne, which they had bought especially for the occasion. One bottle they left in the refrigerator for a welcome-home toast when Jim should return from the war.

As the evening passed, forty or fifty friends and neighbors dropped by. There were no special invitations. Everyone knew big, gangling Jim and liked him, and the Seidenstickers were friendly people who did not stand on formality. And so people kept coming into the open house with its feeling of warmth and affection. They were still coming at 2:00 in the morning. Mrs. Seidensticker made the family's favorite punch, which she mixed from white wine, frozen strawberries, and ginger ale.

Many people were taking photographs for their albums, and the Christmas tree was bright with colored lights and glass balls, gingerbread houses and tin soldiers. They played records, and they played charades. They did card tricks, and they did brain teasers and quizzes, which were a favorite family pastime.

For the Seidenstickers it was an evening without parallel. Yet that kind of evening was repeated a thousand times across America as young boys, scarcely yet men, said their farewells before traveling halfway around the world to take part in a war that had not even been declared.

James Seidensticker was not regretful at going. Like his family, he believed that the Americans were right to be in Vietnam, that they were doing a necessary job in containing Communism. In

33

fact, he was very proud to be going. His patriotism was not based on politics—the Seidenstickers were split, the father voting Republican, the mother Democratic; it was deep and inborn.

The next day they all piled into the family car, a Mercury Comet, and drove to Kennedy Airport. There James joined John Smith, another M.P. and a friend of his from a couple of towns away, and they said their farewells. Jim and John, after many colored photographs had inevitably been taken of them for the family album, boarded the United Airlines flight to California.

During the picture-taking Jim's father commented that Jim had filled out his normally slim six feet five inches; he weighed 215 pounds, his heaviest ever.

Jim expected to wait for a few days in Oakland, California, before taking the plane to war. In the event it was only 36 hours before he boarded the commercial flight to Vietnam. Once there, he counted himself lucky. He wrote home immediately that he was fortunate not to be attached to the infantry; he had been posted to Tansonnhut Air Force Base as a guard at General Westmoreland's headquarters. He was in the 716th M.P. Battalion.

Back in Brentwood Mrs. Seidensticker tidied up after the party. For Jim's leave they had decorated the house with many American flags and models of military trucks, jeeps, and so on. Over Christmas they had taken them all down, but at Jim's insistence she had left a tiny flag in each of the two end copper mugs that lined a shelf in the kitchen. She thought of him as she dusted them each day.

And every day she received a letter from Jim, as did Monica. In every possible spare moment, it seemed, he wrote home. It occurred to his mother sometimes that there was a sense of foreboding in the way he wrote, but she tried to put it out of her mind.

Jim had been in Vietnam about three weeks when he wrote that he and his comrades were looking forward to celebrating their first Lunar New Year holiday. "The Vietnamese call it Tet," he wrote.

The Vietcong launched a massive offensive right in the heart of Saigon early on the morning of January 31. The defending forces reacted with chaotic desperation. Jim's group of military policemen leaped into a truck and raced to the assistance of an American unit under heavy attack in the city. After racketing through the streets of the Cholon area they turned into an alley to join their comrades. At the other end of the alley the beleaguered Americans recognized a trap. They fired warning shots over the truck. The M.P.s, thinking it was the Vietcong firing, drove straight down the alley. Halfway down, they were hit by grenades, claymore mines, and a hail of small-arms fire.

At 3:15 A.M. on January 31, in the first hour of the Tet offensive, all seventeen M.P.s in the truck died. One of them was John Smith. Another was James Seidensticker.

Back in Brentwood, Long Island, they heard the news of the offensive, and they knew that it was in the area where Jim was stationed. Patricia Seidensticker tried to listen to all the friends who said that everything would probably be all right, but in her heart she knew otherwise. Her fear increased so that she found it difficult to sleep. Two days passed. Then on February 2 she stayed home from work to look after her youngest daughter, Geraldine, who was sick. She was tidying the front room when she saw two shadows pass the window; she knew what they meant, and, in a way, it was a relief.

She opened the door and saw the military man, Colonel Alves, and Father Armshaw, the priest from St. Anne's. She slammed the door on them. They waited, and she thought better of it, opened the door, and said, "It's my son Jim." It was 9:00 in the morning and sunny, when the embarrassed Colonel recited the formal notice of death as he was obliged to do. Father Armshaw, who had known all the Buckleys and Seidenstickers since they had moved to Brentwood, did not know what to say. He tried: "You must come in and sit down." But Patricia Seidensticker did not hear him.

That day the army telephoned the news to Howard, Jim's brother, who was stationed in southern Germany; he obtained permission to fly home.

In Vietnam the machine began the highly personalized V.I.P. treatment that the Army gives its dead. Jim Seidensticker's body was taken to a "killed in action" clearing station, where army morticians, who worked ten hours at a time without a break, took care of it, cleaning the wounds and composing the youthful features. Then they sealed it in a plastic shroud and put it into a gleaming steel coffin, the standard issue Military Sealor Casket. They draped a new flag over the casket and put it in a plane along with dozens of others, each with its own flag. The army flew the caskets back across the ocean, pausing only briefly for refueling. The caskets were unloaded in Dover, Delaware, before the creases

35

in the flags were fully shaken out. And there, where Old Glory still covered new dead, Howard Seidensticker in full-dress uniform waited to take his brother home.

There were orders that the casket not be opened because it was hermetically sealed. Howard sat beside it in the guard's van all the way to New York City.

At Pennsylvania Station, at 1:00 in the morning, Howard and the casket were met by Michael J. Grant, Brentwood's funeral director, and they drove back quietly along the dusty road to the accompaniment of occasional barking of dogs. It was very cold. They went to Mr. Grant's big, impressive, Colonial-style funeral parlor, its pillars picked out by street lamps under the pines, and they put the casket in big wood-paneled room with wall-to-wall green carpeting and deep, comfortable chairs. Then they lit votive candles, which would burn until they took the casket to bury it.

The next day on local radio station WBIC the news was broadcast, and all the flags in Brentwood were flown at half-mast. At 2 Bruce Lane the letters began to flow in. There was one from Chief of Staff General Harold K. Johnson: ". . . you may rest assured that all of us will continue to do our utmost to bring eventual victory so that your son's sacrifice will not have been . . ."

There was a letter from another Johnson, the President: "Calling on young Americans to suffer great pains and even loss of life in Vietnam is the most agonizing and painful responsibility of my office . . ."

A letter from Jim's company captain in Vietnam gave details:

> James was a member of an alert platoon responding to hostile activity in the Saigon/Cholon area when ambushed. He was hit with small arms fire and shrapnel from an explosive charge. Death was immediate and he did not suffer from his wounds.
>
> The events as described above were confirmed by other members of the alert force and you can rest assured that everything possible was done to try and save James's life.

From the Brigadier General commanding Jim's M.P. Brigade: "On behalf of the members of the 18th Military Police Brigade, I extend our sincere condolence on the untimely death of your son James. James was respected by his associates and performed his assigned duties in a dedicated and efficient manner."

All these letters said much the same thing, that Mrs. Seidensticker's boy had died a hero and had given his life for his country and all those other things, but Mrs. Seidensticker knew that they sent the same letters to the mothers of all the other dead sons. Only the name was different.

They buried Jim Seidensticker on Friday, February 16, 1968. He was not yet 21. The service was held in the cool interior of St. Anne's, with its rounded wooden ceiling and three aisles and fourteen rows of pews, which could hold perhaps 300 people.

To the Seidenstickers' astonishment the church overflowed, and sixty people could not get in. Father Armshaw conducted the service as Jim's casket lay in the light of the yellow and crimson stained glass reflected by the pale-green walls with their brightly painted stations of the cross. Then everyone went out into the cold air across from the school, where Jim and his friend Nicholas Fritz, who was killed a little later, had studied and played.

The cortege, which included forty cars and a five-car police escort, followed the expressway to Pinelawn and St. Charles, the Catholic cemetery alongside it. The main part of the funeral was paid for by the government. There was a standard rate of $250 for these purposes; transport, the casket, embalming, and the flag were provided.

But there was allowance for only one car, and the Seidenstickers had to hire four extra at $37 each. There was an escort of seven soldiers in full dress, and they fired a 21-gun salute, three shots each; then a bugler played taps.

St. Charles Cemetery was huge and green, and low cypresses scattered among the uniform rows of little headstones laid out in blocks like a city. There are notices saying that one cannot put plastic flowers or jars on the graves, and listing visiting hours. To Howard, still escorting his brother, it seemed a particularly cold and windswept day.

The mass of flowers and wreaths were placed on the grave in block eighteen. The only wreath that they did not put on the grave was one in the form of the flag of the Union, for patriotic Americans know that Old Glory must never be allowed to touch the ground.

After the service the flag from the casket was given to Mrs. Seidensticker, who gave it to Mr. Seidensticker, who gave it to Monica. In the car on the way back Monica returned it to Jim's mother, who kept it on the television set in the parlor until she could make a proper case for it.

That night everyone sat around a long time in the kitchen, where the two little flags still rested in the copper mugs and Jim's budgerigar Cosmo still chirped in his cage. The bottle of champagne waited in the refrigerator. They talked about the war and that year's election, and somebody said, "You know, if Jim had lived until August he would have become old enough to vote for the next President."

Each morning before dawn in the White House situation room —which looks like the foreign desk of a large news agency—a senior civil servant prepares a series of reports that have come in through the night and seals them in a thick envelope. Another official takes them through the deserted building to the Presidential elevator, which goes up to the mansion's living quarters. There he is checked by the all-night Secret Service guard and hands the envelope to the night usher. It is taken instantly to an aide who is on duty outside the President's bedroom door throughout the night.

When the President wakes—usually before 7:00 A.M.—the aide puts the envelope on a bedside table. Almost immediately a waiter brings in tea and toast, and Mr. Johnson begins to read situation reports from around the world. Invariably the first one deals with the Vietnam war.

The President would probably have been informed of the death of James Seidensticker the same day that Colonel Alves was breaking the news to James' mother in Brentwood. In the Presidential report, however, James was only another digit in the total figure of American troops killed in the previous 48 hours.

As the Tet offensive raged that early February, casualties were extremely high. Three hundred sixty-seven Americans were killed the first week of February. The initial success of the Communist offensive staggered the American people. It appeared that the administration's Vietnam policy had been a total failure. All the high promises, all the confident forecasts from the White House, all the implacable predictions from General Westmoreland's headquarters in Saigon appeared to have been quite empty in view of shattering success of the enemy's attack.

.4.

New Course on Campus

In February 1968 the United States entered its seventh year of military involvement in Vietnam. By May 1961 there had been 685 American military advisers assisting the Diem regime in the South. President Kennedy increased this figure by one hundred special-forces commandos, who went into the field.

By the end of 1962 there were 10,000 American troops in Vietnam. This figure expanded to 16,500 in 1963. As the internecine political struggle in South Vietnam weakened the viability of the government in Saigon, the United States continued to increase its forces to prevent total victory for the Communists. By 1965 the draft intake had been doubled, and 125,000 Americans were involved in the war. The escalation continued. In the next year the American forces tripled to nearly 400,000, and the end of 1967 the troop commitment had reached 475,000, higher than at any one time during the Korean war.

With each successive increase, the American people were promised results. They were told that the enemy was demoralized, that the South Vietnamese government was securing the countryside, that all American troops would start coming home by Christmas 1965. But all the Pentagon prophecies proved wrong.

Christmas 1967 was the thirteenth Christmas that the American nation had been at war in 26 years. But never before had a war been fought with less enthusiasm.

American opposition to the war in Vietnam was slow to crystallize. For the first few years the American people did not feel the strain. Regular army men fought the war, casualties were few, no economic pressure was imposed, and few moral questions were raised. But, as the war dragged on, as more and more young men were sent east, and as success seemed further away than ever, the protests began. They naturally started among the professional Left, with pacifist support. Then they spread. And their most fertile ground was the young people who were being called upon to do the fighting.

It was difficult to say just how much the protest was motivated by selfishness—a refusal to be involved and perhaps killed in an unpopular war—and how much by pacifist idealism. But many students declared that they would go to jail rather than fight—and some did.

In 1967 1,300 young Americans were indicted for violating the Selective Service Act, and 748 were convicted, in effect choosing jail rather than military service. Many more simply left their homes and "got lost" in the big cities. Others decided to leave the country, emigrating to Canada or Europe. By the end of 1967 the authorities had a list of 15,310 draft "delinquents," an extremely high number in a country where people are brought up believing that patriotism is a major virtue.

The Justice Department formed a special unit to prosecute the dodgers more vigorously. But nevertheless, as the war escalated, so did the number of Americans putting into practice the antiwar cry, "Hell, no, we won't go!"

Under this kind of pressure the draft boards themselves began to show indecision. The rate of conscientious objection to the war increased enormously, to almost double what it had been in World War II. From 1947 to 1967 22,000 young men had won exemption on grounds of conscientious objection.

The main resistance to the draft came from middle-class groups. They had the education, the ability to organize, and the political awareness to channel belief into practical action. Antidraft organizations began to spring up in all the major cities. They offered all kinds of assistance to young Americans who wanted to avoid service—legal advice on how to obtain deferment; literary and theological advice for conscientious objectors, who had to write their reasons for not wishing to fight; and, finally, "underground" advice on how to enter Canada or change identity.

Apart from this "practical work" the antidraft committees started a political guerilla war. They staged demonstrations. They picketed the draft boards and staged "sit-ins," attempting to paralyze the boards' work. They publicly burned draft cards, and they tried to stir American youth into a mass refusal to serve in the war.

The irony was that most middle-class young men could avoid the draft by legal means. Nearly 2 million Americans turn eighteen and become subject to call-up each year. But the total number needed by the forces was well under 1 million, so there were plenty of deferments to be granted. All university students were automatically deferred, as were postgraduate students. And, as many Americans study until the age of thirty and the maximum age for the draft is 26, staying in school was one sure way of evading service. (In February 1968, as the result of pressure from the National Security Council, postgraduate deferments were virtually abolished.)

Lieutenant General Lewis B. Hershey, the 74-year-old Director of Selective Service, ordered the draft boards to hit back. Those students who had already been deferred yet persisted in the antiwar campaign suddenly found their deferments canceled. The battle moved to the courts, and several such cancellations were reversed. But, as the fight became more bitter, the hard-line draft boards continued to withdraw deferments granted to what they called "troublemakers."

A personal view of why students were against the draft, revealing the mixture of idealism and anger at the disruption of their private lives, was given by Roger Rapoport, a University of Michigan senior and editor of the *Michigan Daily:*

> Four years ago, the University of Michigan commencement speaker was Lyndon B. Johnson. He told graduating students "Your imagination, your initiative, and your indignation will determine whether we build a . . . Great Society." If the President came back to Michigan for my graduation . . . he would be met by a wave of indignant students.
> Why are the students so angry? Let me offer a personal

41

explanation. Ideally, I was counting on going to work in some form of journalism. After 17 years of education I felt interested in taking a job that would let me use what I've learned in school. But threat of the draft has changed all that. I'm not opposed to defending my country. I would have fought in World War II and would be willing to fight now in a similar "national emergency" if one developed. But I am not willing to fight in Vietnam.

For one thing Congress has never declared war there, has never explained who we were fighting or why. I seriously doubt the wisdom of going 10,000 miles to fight on behalf of a country led by a military clique where a "democratic" election means the runner-up gets put in jail. As a future journalist, I'm not enthusiastic about defending a country that censors its press and expels an American correspondent for pointing out that the South Vietnamese Army does not fight very well. Moreover, I don't see any point in fighting for the freedom of a country (South Vietnam) that punitively drafts students who are involved in anti-war protests.

The deepening civil unrest over the war seemed at the beginning of 1968 without question the major issue of the coming campaign. But, as the year continued, it became clear that it was not. It was more a trigger, exploding a series of parallel issues and bringing to the surface the deeper, more complex problems in American society.

One of the more extraordinary of these problems was the generation gap in the United States. The overwhelming impression that hit a young Briton coming to the United States was that he had landed in a petrified, middle-aged society. He was astonished because it was the last thing he expected.

But the image of a dynamic, fast-moving economy; of a hard, aggressive business community; and of the most advanced technology in the world was blurred by reality. After London New York—at least socially—seemed middle-aged and much of the rest of America even more old fashioned.

First, there were women's clothes. Hemlines were where they had been in London four years before. Some of the younger girls wore modest miniskirts, but the microskirt was a bizarre rarity, whereas the British had happily come to accept it as a natural way of life.

Men's clothes seemed strangely dated and conformist too, although many stores and clothing manufacturers sought to tempt their male customers to join the fashion revolution. Another extraordinary thing to the visitor was the compulsive urge among American disk jockeys to play over and over again the old musical standards of the 1940s and 1950s. Of course, one found "beat" stations on any American radio dial, but this fact only underlined the polarization in radio entertainment. There were stations for the young and stations for the middle-aged, and in many cities the stations for the middle-aged were more popular than the others.

America has its "pop" groups, and some of them were great, but they were not granted the same national stature that their equivalents received in Britain. The American daily press virtually ignored the existence of pop groups as professional entertainers. In Britain, where the top-twenty disk charts were printed in the newspapers, weekly features on the record scene were accepted reading. To a large extent young and old bought the same records and shared the same tastes. In America this was not so. The middle-aged continued to prop up their idols from the past; the same singers kept singing the same songs ten years later, and a specialized industry was developed for the young.

In entertainment this industry seemed to extend well beyond the pop-record business. The great stars of American television were the same old faces of the previous decade. Indeed the whole of American television seemed gripped by some strange computerized production system, in which the dial was set at the instruction "update but do not change."

Even the surprise hit of 1968, Rowan and Martin's "Laugh-In," was based on the British television formula that produced "That Was the Week That Was" and "B.B.C. 3." The two stars were both in their forties.

The relentlessly middle-aged look of the American television screen was exemplified by the national newscasters Chet Huntley and David Brinkley, 57 and 48 years old respectively, and Walter Cronkite, who was 52. The field reporters all seemed to be in their late thirties or middle forties. In Britain the star newscasters were in their thirties (I.T.N.'s Andrew Gardner, 36, and Leonard Parkin, 38, and B.B.C.'s Michael Aspel, 35) and the reporters younger still.

The comparative merits of these men could not be fairly assessed because of different national techniques, but the point is that the British used younger men throughout the whole television scene. The biggest impact made on British television in the last four years was that of David Frost, and Frost was still only 29 years old.

The same difference could be noted in the newspaper industry, whose executives in Britain always seemed to be younger than their American equivalents. Of course, it can be argued that these differences existed in relatively fringe areas of society, mostly communications, the arts, and fashion. But it is these highly visual industries that condition society to accept more fundamental change.

The British establishment reacted instinctively and traditionally to the youth revolution by seeking to absorb the revolutionaries into its ranks. It did so by giving them opportunities that they had not had before, and by amending the law to give young people more rights and more power.

Apart from the youthful breakthrough in the fields of communications and design, there was an increased willingness to give young men their heads in commerce and industry. More important, the educational authorities voluntarily handed over to the students a great deal of control in university administration. British students sat on all main committees and had their say in every sphere of college life, except the appointment of staff and admission of students.

And, as far as the students' private lives were concerned, the authorities did not interfere. If British students wished to sleep together on or off the campus, that was their affair and, apart from informing them about and, in some cases, seeing that they were supplied with, the latest contraceptive aids, the authorities left them to it.

British students reacted to the case of Linda Le Clair at Barnard College with disbelief. The twenty-year-old Miss Le Clair, from New Hampshire, had moved into a West Side apartment with her boyfriend while studying at Barnard College, Manhattan. She was brought before the school authorities, who charged her with violating residence regulations. She was found technically guilty, and it was recommended that she be denied the privilege of using the campus snack bar and cafeteria. She then left school of her own accord. It was beyond the belief of British students that this kind of thing resulted in punishment.

Similarly, British policemen and officials thought it a joke when they heard stories that their American counterparts in some cities could be dismissed for having mistresses instead of wives.

The American author, William Burroughs, a determined anti-establishment figure, told American students in 1968: "I have just come back from Britain where it is *terrible*. There's no sign of protest against authority there. The young are passive . . . they're not doing anything." Burroughs was wrong. The young in Britain *were* making their changes in a traditionally conservative society —and making money at it.

In America such was not the case. The United States gave its young greater educational opportunities than did any country in the world; 45 percent of all high school graduates went to college in 1967. But, once there, they were expected to conform to American university rules, which in many cases were almost Victorian.

It must be said that the majority of young Americans were prepared to accept the rules as laid down by adult society. James Seidensticker and boys like him, who grew up in the middle-income suburbs, did not rebel. They went off to fight without questioning their duty.

But students were emerging as a political force around the world: in Latin America, in Europe, even behind the Iron Curtain. America could be no exception, and the Vietnam war speeded up this political involvement, introducing an entirely new and significant element into American university life. Student political groups dedicated to change, notably the Students for a Democratic Society, began to proliferate.

The leaders of these groups were usually children of wealthy parents, who had grown up not in towns like Brentwood but in the really exclusive suburbs and "villages" that surround most large American cities. They were the products of homes that had given them every luxury. Many were Jewish. All were intelligent and highly educated. Several surveys have suggested that only about 2.6 per cent of American students were dedicated political activists and extremists, whereas another 5 to 10 per cent showed interest and went to rallies. They tended, however, to be in the top 10 per cent, the brightest pupils, and they were capable of arousing many of the remainder to action.

The movement started in 1964 at the University of California, Berkeley, where the modern form of American student protest through civil disobedience was born. By 1968 Berkeley was still a hotbed of discontent but had gone far beyond the orderly sit-ins of the "free speech" movement. The campus buildings of the Naval Reserve Officers' School were twice dynamited in the wake of antiwar meetings, and violent campus demonstrations were commonplace.

This type of demonstration now spread across America. In the first six months of 1968, the National Student Association reported, there had been 221 such protests. Many had ended in battles with the police. The theory of civil disobedience had been promoted by the more militant agitators to a more extreme "social revolution." This policy was put to the test at New York's Columbia University early in 1968.

Columbia—with 20,000 students—was, according to the extremists, superbly situated for the type of confrontation they needed. It was in one of the less busy areas of Manhattan, straddling the low rocky hills known as Morningside Heights in the northwest section of the island. Its halls and libraries were spacious and elegant, in contrast to most of the houses of the area, which were run down and overcrowded. Its visibility as a prosperous establishment was thus enhanced by its proximity to a bursting ghetto community. The pressures that these uneasy neighbors exerted on each other were key factors in the campus disruption of April and early May 1968.

The Negro living in Morningside Heights, which is also called "West Harlem," had little reason to regard the university as a benificent institution. Although it already covered a lot of land, it was always expanding. Families had been evicted and homes pulled down to make way for new college halls.

The need to do something for the nonstudent population of the area dawned upon the trustees of Columbia nine years ago. Plans were prepared for a gymnasium and swimming pool, which the community could share with the students. Yet, ironically, this gesture eventually became the catalyst of disorder.

Close examination of the plans revealed that the community's section of the gym was to be in the basement, taking up only 11 per cent of the total area and with a swimming pool much smaller than that for students. Worst of all, however, to reach the basement, the local residents would have to enter by a back door, whereas the students would use the front. This arrangement was viewed as a grotesque humiliation. The trustees had left themselves open to emotional charges of discrimination against blacks. The gym was no longer regarded as a gift from Columbia to a grateful community. Instead, it became an example of Columbia's condescension, an expression of corporate arrogance.

When in February 1968 bulldozers began clearing the site, local Negroes and some students promptly sat down in the path of the machines. Twenty-six of the pickets were arrested. By reacting with swift force, the authorities drew the attention of many others on the campus to the controversy. The mass of New Yorkers also heard of the arrests but could not understand why the blacks should complain when someone was trying to do them a favor. The journey to catastrophe had begun.

The campaign against the gymnasium was led by the Columbia chapter of the Students for a Democratic Society. A radical revolutionary group, against "racism, oppression and imperialism," S.D.S.'s avowed aim was to destroy American society. S.D.S. members worshiped the late Che Guevara overlooking his trinity of failure (as a doctor he did not practice, as Cuba's Minister of Economics he was ignorant of the economy, and as a guerilla leader he was caught in the simplest of ambushes).

The S.D.S. used the gym issue and Columbia's link with the Institute for Defense Analysis, a research arm of the government dealing with weapons and war techniques, to whip up student unrest to the point of rebellion. It brought this confrontation to a head finally by occupying four of the halls on the campus.

By then the events at Columbia had become a national issue, seeming to illustrate once more the continuing fragmentation of the American way of life. There was no room for compromise. The leader of each side perfectly represented, in his own implacable way, the forces he commanded.

At the head of the university there was its 64-year-old president, Grayson Kirk, a man with the kind of *Who's Who* biography that made one wonder how he ever found time to do anything. He held an enormous number of trusteeships and directorships. He was even a member of the sedate Athenaeum Club in London! For his services to education and for helping with secretarial work at the founding of the United Nations Organization, he was one of the few Americans to have been made a Knight Commander of the British Empire, which meant that, had he been a British citizen, he could have called himself Sir Grayson Kirk.

He had been President of Columbia for fifteen years, and during that time there was no doubt that the university was a tough landlord. Some of the families evicted to make way for Columbia's

47

expansion had their mail, water, and heat services cut off in a most arbitrary manner. At the time of the campus rebellion Kirk was a director of Socony-Mobil, IBM, two investment firms, the Consolidated Edison Power Company, and a savings bank. This list gave weight to the S.D.S. complaint that university trustees were more concerned with the profits of America's military-industrial complex than with the problems of students or hardships in Harlem.

The head of the Columbia chapter of S.D.S. was twenty-year-old Mark Rudd. During all his young adulthood there had been war in Vietnam. Like so many of his white contemporaries, Rudd came from a secure upper-middle-class background, with two cars in the garage of a comfortable home in Maplewood, New Jersey.

His parents had worked hard to heal the scars of the Depression. They were determined that the upbringing of Mark and his older brother would be happier than their own had been and free from anxieties about money. When Jacob and Bertha Rudd, the children of emigrants from Lithuania and Poland, were married in 1933 they had, as she recalls, "only about three dollars to our name." Without a job, Jacob went into the army, coming out as a lieutenant colonel in 1947. Then came fourteen years as a civilian supervisor for the Defense Department until he started his own real-estate business. In a revealing comment, he told *The New York Times*:

> I was a member of the depressed generation and my greatest concern has always been making a living. Mark doesn't have to worry about that so much and we're glad he has time to spend on activities like politics. He's never cared about material things anyway. He'd just as soon sleep in the woods as anywhere.

Mark grew up a typical all-American boy, a ham radio enthusiast, an active Boy Scout, always near the top of his class in school. He became politically active in his second year at Columbia and swiftly became president of the local S.D.S. chapter. The depth of his political passion is shown in an open letter that he wrote to Grayson Kirk: "If we win, we will take control of your world, your corporation, your university and attempt to mould a world in which we and other people can live as human beings. Your power is directly threatened since we will have to destroy that power before we take over."

48

There was never any hope of a reasonable agreement between these two opponents. Six days after the occupation began, one thousand New York policemen moved in and, with brutal efficiency, cleared the campus. One hundred six people, among them many curious bystanders, needed medical treatment after it was over, fourteen of them policemen.

Three weeks later, at the beginning of May, S.D.S. members occupied another building and were once more removed by the police after a violent battle. It was a Pyrrhic victory for Kirk and the authorities, however. S.D.S. was the real winner on two counts. The Columbia trustees agreed to consult with Harlem representatives before doing any more about the gym, and the university also agreed to break its "institutional" ties with I.D.A.

On August 24 Grayson Kirk resigned as Columbia's president. He would have been obliged to retire in October anyhow, but, of course, his departure was regarded as the establishment's price for having allowed the disorders to get so badly out of hand.

The best postmortem on the Columbia events came from the independent commission appointed by the faculty and headed by Archibald Cox, former Solicitor-General of the United States and a key member of President Kennedy's brain trust. Its 50,000-word report denounced the police brutality, strongly indicted the university administration, and criticized the students for using "disruptive tactics." But it stressed that student behavior was "in no way commensurate with the brutality and did not excuse or even mitigate the blame resting upon the police." Describing the second clash, the report did not mince words: "Hell broke loose. Whether the students had a fair chance to return to their rooms is a matter of dispute. Some police first warned the students; others chased and clubbed them indiscriminately." Of the underlying causes of the student disturbances Cox said, "The hurricane of social unrest struck Columbia at a time when the university was deficient in the cement that binds an institution into a unit."

The report attacked the authoritarian manner of the administration and the aloofness of the faculty. It also criticized the ambiguous official attitude on what kind of demonstrations were acceptable on campus. As for the neighboring community, Cox commented unfavorably on Columbia's indifference to the poor, the "manner in which Columbia has pushed her physical expansion," and the university's harassment of tenants in order to evict them. The report said, "Columbia cannot flourish in upper Man-

49

hattan until it establishes a new and sounder relationship with its present neighbors."

Most important of all, the report rejected the theory that the troubles were primarily the result of a plot by a revolutionary group. Whatever the feeling at the beginning of the affair, it said, there was no question that when it was over the grievances toward Columbia were felt by the majority of all students.

The Columbia example inspired aggressive demonstrations at other colleges across the country. At Boston University 125 Negroes held the administration building for a day until the president agreed to recruit more black students. At Colgate University 500 students sat in the main offices for five days until officials agreed to scrap a system of selecting candidates for fraternity houses that excluded blacks. The South became involved when 1,500 students at Duke University in North Carolina held a sit-in until the trustees raised wages for the college canteen staff from $1.15 to $1.45 an hour. Even at Princeton, despite its staid reputation, 500 students marched in support of reducing the trustees' powers.

Students left their universities and accepted call-up, many with burning resentment. They took with them their experience of anti-authoritarian revolt from the campus and adapted it to the parade ground. And so was born a growing antiwar movement within the ranks of the U.S. Army itself. The movement, a loose association of G.I.s in Vietnam and in the huge military installations in the States, was helped and funded by peace groups, including Vietnam veterans who had been demobilized. Five "peace coffeehouses" were opened, each one in a garrison town, to attract the custom of disaffected soldiers.

One of the busiest was in dreary Columbia, South Carolina, where the vast camp of Fort Jackson handled 23,000 new recruits in basic training at a time. The atmosphere in the coffeehouse was deliberately relaxed and friendly to provide an oasis of contrast to the grimness of the first weeks in barracks.

No one could miss the antiwar atmosphere. A wall poster showing a soldier on patrol said, "Fly Far Eastern Airways . . . this vacation visit beautiful Vietnam." Protest songs by Bob Dylan and Joan Baez came from the jukebox. Copies of several underground newspapers were on every table. They reported on G.I. grievances from around the world, thus promoting a sense of cohesion among doves and encouraging them to further individual acts of defiance against the military system. A popular button worn by the young soldiers of the movement bore the letters "FTA"—a sardonic dig at the promises of "fun, travel, and adventure" in army recruiting posters. Another badge simply said, "Bring *me* back alive."

One evening the visitor sat with three soldiers in this coffeehouse and listened to them talk about their frustrations.

Drill Sergeant Bob Cookinham, 21, had been wounded three times during his year in the Vietnam front lines. He said:

> There's no way I can justify what the United States is doing there. I was drafted very much against my will, and now I just want to let people know my opposition to the war. Over there I wasn't fighting for my country because I cannot rationalize our actions. But in battle I knew I had my own skin to save. The only thing you learn in Vietnam is to look after good old number one.

Cookinham's comrades-in-arms had all known that he was antiwar, but he did not ram it down their throats. He explained, "In the line that's a quick way to get a bullet in the back from a lifer"— G.I. slang for an N.C.O. who has signed on for twenty years. This risk did not seem to discourage a former history student, Private Joe Cole, aged 24, from Atlanta. A quiet but intense man, he expected to go to Vietnam shortly and wanted to use the chance to spread peace pamphlets. "It will be very meaningful for me to continue to agitate against the war once I get over there," he said. His activity meant that he might face a charge of subversion or even sedition. He shrugged: "Yes it could be three to five years' hard labor. But I am only carrying on the protest I started on the outside. I have been carrying a placard in marches for years."

Another private, Steve Kline, 21, told of the day that he had staged his own war protest, a pray-in on his knees outside the camp chapel. An enraged military policeman yelled, "Stop prayin' and start moving." When Kline refused, he was dragged off to the guardroom, his hands still clasped together.

The dedicated activists were only a tiny minority of all the men called up, but, like the Columbia leaders, they tended to be the brightest recruits, potential officer material and able to influence others.

To senior military minds, such a coffeehouse so close to the camp must have seemed a nest of snipers that could not be cleaned out. N.C.O.s told recruits, quite wrongly, that the place was off limits.

Troops who went there were later interrogated by intelligence officers and the F.B.I. For all the harassment, however, the place attracted at least 150 soldiers every Saturday night.

There was no doubt that protest among young people against academic authoritarianism and against the war was growing into a potent force. Amorphous, in some ways inarticulate and confused, it nevertheless encompassed a large percentage of the brightest young people in the United States. The extreme element—anarchist, Marxist, or Trotskyist—hoped to weld the protest movement into a revolutionary force.

One of the factors contributing to belief that it could do so was that no establishment figure seemed remotely to understand what youth was feeling. This gap between the generations only increased the frustration and cynicism of young America. The Kennedy image still lingered on in the person of Senator Robert Kennedy. But, although he made sounds of disquiet about the war, he refused to launch an all-out attack on President Johnson.

So who was there? To answer that question one now has to begin an account of the election campaign proper. The date was October 26, 1967, the place the University of California at Berkeley, and the speaker Minnesota Senator Eugene McCarthy.

He was talking about the war:

> As I see it, we have reached the point now—I think we reached it, really, a year ago—in which you can no longer morally justify what we are doing in Vietnam, certainly not the escalation of the war. You cannot make a legal case for it; and certainly it appears also that you cannot even make a military case for our involvement there. And, if one wanted to add a fourth judgment, not even a political case. Because as we have moved along month after month, those nations which had perhaps given us honest support—or at least lip support—began to draw away. And this is a serious loss for the United States. We were founded, really, in the appeal of the Declaration of Independence, when we said that what we were doing we wanted to have approved by the decent opinion of mankind. So today, some one hundred and eighty years later, I think we still have an obligation to be concerned and to seek to conform, in some degree, to what the decent opinion of mankind is with reference to our involvement in Vietnam.
>
> My special concern over the last few weeks has been with what, of course, has been in evidence for a long time—a kind

of continuing expansion and escalation of the war. It is rather curious, I think, that more and more, as the war has become more involved and difficult to explain, that the Pentagon has begun to use Latin words. This is not necessarily bad, but George Orwell, writing . . . about the Russians and the Hungarian Revolt and some of their activities, pointed out that it was very convenient to use a Latin word to more or less obscure things which were very unpleasant. He described then what was called "pacification." He said all this means is that you machine-gun the villages; you drive the people out into the roads; you burn houses; and this you call "pacification." It has almost direct application, at least in use, as we apply it today. He gave some other examples—"rectification of boundaries"—but he did not list the word which is most popular today in the lexicon of our administration—"escalation." "Escalation," a Latin word, which is presented to us almost as though it freed anyone who is involved in decision making from personal responsibility, as though this was something which was happening to you, and you could at no point cut it off. It was always too early or too late. It is a kind of continuum. There is no point at which the escalator stops. You might say, "Well, we might have done that then, but we have passed that point," and, "We might do it in the future but not now." This is always the wrong time to suspend bombing or to use the "enclave" concept of General Gavin or whatever the particular proposition might be.

There had been other speeches against the war in and out of Congress. Doves like liberal Democratic Senator Wayne Morse of Oregon had opposed it consistently. So now did Republican Senator Thruston Morton of Kentucky. So did South Dakota's Democratic Senator George McGovern.

But it was something in the way that McCarthy expressed his views rather than the views themselves that made his speech different. There was nothing in his personality to suggest that he could spark the affection and devotion of the young. Middle-aged, middle western, and academic, McCarthy was uncompromisingly adult in his words and actions. He was a relatively obscure political figure who had never tried to be "with it."

A more unlikely folk hero it was difficult to imagine. Yet that is what he became. McCarthy did not know it when he sat down after his Berkeley speech, but from that moment the mysterious political forces that combine to make vintage election years were already

53

beginning to gravitate toward him. He was engulfed and propelled into a series of events that future historians may well regard as a turning point in American politics. For Eugene McCarthy gave meaning to a phrase that was being used yet not widely understood. He was the spearhead of "the New Politics."

.5.

The McCarthy Challenge

THE ORIGINS OF THE VARIOUS EFFORTS THAT FINALLY CULMINATED IN the emergence of Eugene McCarthy are obscure. But one can place the beginning at about the time a particular joke button hit the market early in the summer of 1967. The button, produced by an audacious manufacturer with a keen sense of the commercial market, was emblazoned with the motto "Dump Johnson." It caused a mild scandal—and large sales—when it appeared. It sprouted on the lapels of students around the nation—and behind the lapels of a lot of adults who should perhaps have had a greater sense of propriety.

Campaign buttons are an American political tradition that has infiltrated every social stratum. In the late 1960s they spread beyond politics and became a national pastime. In recent years some of the humor on buttons had become increasingly offensive. At the beginning of 1967 a very sick lapel button indeed began to compete with "Dump Johnson." It said, "Where are you Lee Harvey Oswald, now that we really need you."

This kind of sickness and viciousness was to become a feature of the 1968 election. But by the fall of 1967 the Oswald button had made its brief impact and had finally been shamefacedly junked. The "Dump Johnson" button, however, continued to sell. It appeared on so many lapels that many people, young people above all, began to believe that the "Dump Johnson" movement was for real. Suddenly everyone began to ask, "Who is the man behind this campaign?" The answer at that moment in fact was no one. There was no campaign, no organization—just a top-selling button.

But the button was giving ideas to a few isolated groups of people who prided themselves on being ahead of the political cartwheel, in this case liberals and some moderate student leaders who had been of the opinion for some months that the time had come to do just what the button suggested.

At last, selling heavily on the open market was the first proof that their sentiments might, after all, find a ready echo in the hearts of sufficient voters even to sway an election, or at very least to give a political campaign enough momentum to teach the administration a salutary lesson—and perhaps even to help achieve the overriding goal of all such liberals: to end the war in Vietnam.

The man who was most instrumental in transforming the sentiment on the button into a movement that would have a profound impact upon American politics was Allard Lowenstein. Lowenstein, 38, was a lawyer and teacher who earned a steady but not excessive income teaching Constitutional law at City College in New York. He had, in addition, a moderate private income from a chain of ten New York restaurants owned by his family, four of which were grouped in a company of which he was a director.

He lived on the unfashionable West Side in an apartment with his wife Jennifer, baby son Frank (born, in fact, at a most difficult moment in the negotiations leading up to the declaration of McCarthy's candidacy), and a turquoise trim-line telephone that was habitually engaged and through which Mr. Lowenstein spun his web of influence around the nation, regardless of the hour or day.

He habitually went tieless in a crumpled shirt and a mackintosh golfing jacket. Admirers urged him to dress better, in order better to play his political role, but Lowenstein was deaf to all such appeals. (Ironically, the only dark suit he had, which he had taken to New Hampshire to wear on primary night, was stolen from his hotel room, leaving him looking penurious as ever.)

The other extraordinary fact of Lowenstein's makeup was his

social conscience, which never let him alone. He was constantly and deeply concerned by a whole variety of issues and had been called a "liberal gadfly." The judgment may have been less than just. Certainly driven by conscience, Lowenstein began during his student days at the University of North Carolina to interest himself in civil rights. By 1950 he was head of the National Student Association, the ubiquitous forum of American student opinion.

He went on to become a director of Martin Luther King's Southern Christian Leadership Conference and in 1963 moved to Mississippi, where the civil-rights movement was blossoming. He brought in other students, put the first glimmerings of a political movement among Mississippi Negroes on a sound footing, and was instrumental in strengthening their realization that the vote, properly used, was a powerful weapon. Injustice, racism, suppressed minorities—such were the issues that preoccupied Lowenstein in those days.

By the summer of 1967 he was a force to be reckoned with in rebellious liberal circles. He had just organized the well-publicized series of "end the war" letters to President Johnson from Peace Corps workers, students, and businessmen. The year before he had narrowly missed being nominated on a "Democratic Reform" ticket to contest the seat of Republican Leonard Farbstein in a New York City congressional-primary election. Lowenstein had advanced beyond mere dreaming. He had become a skilled professional.

By 1967 his main preoccupation was not simply opposition to the war itself but also the notion that protest against it was "getting hooked on a narrow radical-pacifist base," as he put it.

He believed—and the buttons were there to prove it—that the war protest went far deeper into American society, right into the very entrails of the Democratic Party itself. And—long and convinced Democrat that he was—he decided that the time had come to channel the mounting anger of the young, of Peace Corpsmen, of businessmen, and of the man in the street into a new, clear, viable movement inside the Democratic Party itself, in order to change the whole course of policy in November 1968.

The "Dump Johnson" slogan was exactly the mood Lowenstein had been seeking, though he never used the phrase. "I considered it far too discourteous. Stop Johnson was as far as I ever went," he said. Lowenstein was looking ahead to the possibility of overturning President Johnson in the party convention the following summer and replacing him with his own candidate—a candidate ready not only to end there and then the Vietnam war but also to respond to the new liberalism sweeping the young.

Nowhere else in the world could one single individual with little money, no big political pull, and few powerful friends ever conceive of selecting a man—through the normal democratic process —to be the nation's leader. The mere idea would have been enough to get him committed in most countries. But America is America. It is a country built for the Lowensteins of this world. To him the idea was perfectly feasible, and he set out to put it into motion.

He mounted his first offensive that August at the National Student Association's annual conference at the University of Maryland. It was natural enough that he, as a distinguished ex-president, should be there. He launched into a brilliant speech about the Vietnam issue, the failings of the administration, the need for change; he urged students themselves to consider what action could be taken to bring these issues home to the American people. It is your future, he told them; protect it. The speech transcended all else on the agenda and became the key theme of the conference.

The next day Lowenstein agreed to address a meeting of student leaders, the presidents of college unions and the editors of student papers. But first he had to dash back to New York overnight in answer to an urgent message that his son was about to be born. He stayed in New York just long enough to see the birth through and hurried back to Maryland.

The meeting was packed. Lowenstein agreed that the objective —indeed the necessity—must be to find a candidate. A candidate, he promised them, would be forthcoming. Meanwhile, a principle had to be firmly established, a principle declaring that if the nation were to be redeemed the administration had to be changed. For, until the principle was seen publicly to exist, until the demand for a change was everywhere apparent, there would be little chance of persuading a man of stature to pose his candidacy.

Then Lowenstein had to produce. He decided to tour the nation, seeking out the key men in the Democratic Party organization whom he knew or suspected were as concerned as he was about the manner in which the country and the Vietnam war were drifting into deeper and deeper disaster.

He had never lacked friends at the grass-roots level of the Democratic Party organization (his wife had reacted with some dismay when he handed her a list of one thousand political names to be invited to their wedding). It was to these people that Lowenstein—financing himself and with no organization or official support—now addressed himself. His first call was to the San Francisco home of businessman Gerald Hill.

Hill headed an organization called the California Democratic Council, a respectable and influential group of well-to-do people who were working to inject a new spirit of radicalism into the party from the inside. After a series of meetings and speeches organized by Hill, Lowenstein obtained the consent of the C.D.C. to put forward for the California primary election the next summer—the single most important of the primaries, controlling 174 delegates to the Democratic convention—a slate of delegates pledged to support a "peace candidate."

It was a neat formula, for if successful it would virtually tie up a substantial block of California votes for Lowenstein's as yet unfound candidate. Hill agreed to help carry the Lowenstein movement forward to a national level. The C.D.C. pledged $1,000 in California, and Lowenstein matched it with $1,000 in New York to set up an organization pledged to carry the word to the Democratic Parties of the fifty states.

The "organization," when it emerged, turned out to be Curtis Gans, a graduate-student friend of Lowenstein's from university days and a former wire-service reporter. From his Washington home—while he and Lowenstein worried about how to pay the phone bills and the air fares—Gans toured the nation seeking groups of people who would respond to the Lowenstein challenge. After him came Lowenstein himself—to speak, to cajole, to enthuse; "to stick in the hypodermic needle and activate them" was how he put it.

He went to Iowa, Wisconsin, Ohio, Indiana, Minnesota, and so on. He spoke to crowded public meetings, to small party gatherings, to overflow campus audiences. Everywhere he went he left behind him the framework of a new organization—dedicated to changing the existing order of things—and the seeds of a new thinking.

In California he linked up with Robert Vaughn; the "Man from U.N.C.L.E." actor had started another splinter group, the Dissenting Democrats, who were taking full-page advertisements in the Los Angeles Times calling for support from all who believed that Johnson should go. Vaughn had gathered nearly 10,000 names.

Lowenstein did a deal with the Dissenting Democrats and brought the Vaughn organization into his own group—now becoming known as the Concerned Democrats. The intergroup deal was that Vaughn's organization should spread its ad campaign to the major newspapers of the nation, calling for names of people who would join the Dump Johnson campaign. Lowenstein's Concerned Democrats organization would move in in the wake of the ads and organize the sprouting groups. Ten thousand names a state was the aim.

Hill joined Lowenstein as cochairman of the Concerned Democrats. Donald Peterson, Democratic chairman of Wisconsin's 10th district and an important early defector to the C.D. movement, was another cochairman. By the end of October an embryonic organization of still-unknown power was in existence. But what was desperately needed if it was not to drift apart through lack of momentum was a candidate.

Lowenstein, the aspiring kingmaker, was totally persuaded from the response that the prince he now had to produce from the political hat would be assured of sufficient support to carry him to the convention and an open challenge to Johnson. Very few shared his view. Pollsters and pundits alike declared Lowenstein's band hopelessly wide of the mark. "They believed I was either a stalking horse for Bobby Kennedy—or just a plain nut," said Lowenstein.

The first name that sprang to every mind was, of course, that of the young Senator from New York. He would, indeed, have made the Lowenstein bandwagon an ideal leader. His views on Vietnam were sufficiently radical. His age, his heritage, his experience at the side of his brother all contributed to the necessary public appeal. Kennedy was on close terms with Lowenstein, whom he admired and consulted.

He was understandably the first man whom Lowenstein approached with his grandiose plan to overthrow the regime. The first meeting took place in August 1967 on an airliner carrying Kennedy to California, where he was expected at a dinner for his friend Jesse Unruh, Speaker of the State Assembly and the most powerful California Democrat (he subsequently pledged himself to lead a Kennedy delegation to the convention).

Lowenstein recalled: "I told him we were going to defeat Lyndon B. Johnson for the party nomination in 1968. He just laughed. I told him that with him we could do it very much

60

more easily but that we were going to do it and we would do it with him or without him."

It was the beginning of a long and often emotional series of meetings between Lowenstein and Kennedy. Lowenstein said much later that at no stage did Kennedy ever mislead him. "I knew that his instinct was to run. But he had no concept of politics. He did not and would not believe the support was there. I had no illusions at that time that he would ever risk it." After eight meetings Lowenstein knew that he had to find another candidate. He wrote Kennedy off.

The next man on his list was General James M. Gavin, hero of World War II and a reputed Democrat, who had served as Ambassador to France under John Kennedy. Gavin was known to be opposed to the Vietnam commitment. Militarily he retained considerable influence; General Westmoreland was a close friend and had been his chief of staff when he commanded the 82nd Airborne Division in World War II. Nationally he would have the stature to end the war.

Politically he was the sort of man who could (like General Dwight D. Eisenhower before him) be sold to the nation as a father figure with the prestige and status to change the course of American politics. Already Hill and Lowenstein had sent him a telegram from San Francisco urging that he interest himself in their campaign. Then Lowenstein flew to his office in Boston to put a firm proposition before the General.

Gavin listened sympathetically. Then he announced that he was not really their man. He was, he said, a Republican. He had come to believe that the only way to defeat the Johnson commitment to Vietnam was by working toward the emergence of a Republican Party peace candidate. Lowenstein commented, "I thought he was wrong, and I tried to persuade him so, but his mind was made up."

The third man on Lowenstein's short list was Senator George McGovern, a liberal from South Dakota and an outspoken dove. But there was a serious problem with McGovern. He was up for reelection in South Dakota in 1968, and peace talk was not calculated to impress his local constituents, whatever success it might have had elsewhere.

McGovern, in the estimation of the liberal Democrats, was not a man whose future services in the Senate should be jeopardized if it was possible to find an alternative candidate. Lowenstein indicated that his organization would prefer a man less fettered by his own domestic political considerations.

Eugene McCarthy had interested Lowenstein for some time, but he wondered whether or not the Minnesota Senator had the appeal and the sustained determination for a long campaign. Then two things happened that made the choice of McCarthy inevitable: first, his courageous antiwar speech at Berkeley, which students all over America were discussing, and, second, the entry into the field of Republican George Wilcken Romney.

Romney was an exceptional man. Brought up in the Mormon faith, he had entered politics after making his name as a brilliant president of American Motors. As Governor of Michigan he had hovered on the brink of Presidential aspirations all through the decade. But was his appeal broad enough to make him a national figure? Would Americans vote for a nondrinking, nonsmoking, moralizer of unflagging energy? In 1966 it seemed that they might. In that year the Mormon Romney won a landslide victory and began his third term as Michigan's Governor. Overnight he shot to the top of the national preference polls—beating President Johnson by 54 to 46 per cent.

From these intoxicating heights, Romney believed that he had only to fight to win. But, as soon as he began campaigning, his popularity began to decline.

In September, when Lowenstein was meeting with his students, Romney made sensational headlines when he explained on a Michigan television program why he had changed position on the Vietnam war. True he had supported it. True he had gone to Vietnam and had publicly endorsed the American position. Certainly he had been optimistic about results. But he had changed his mind. He had come to realize that he had been "brainwashed" by the generals and diplomats in Saigon.

It was an honest statement and one that could well apply to many others who had run the public-relations gauntlet in Saigon's P.R. Alley. But the choice of the word was disastrous. Potential American Presidents are not supposed to be the sort of men who can be "brainwashed," and overnight Romney's popularity began to decline.

Meanwhile Lowenstein was having a series of meetings with McCarthy in Washington. He outlined his organization, explained the chances, and pleaded for a decision. While McCarthy was considering, Romney, fighting desperately to stop the disintegration of his campaign after the "brainwashing" disaster, adopted the principle of when in doubt press on. On November 21, 1967, he became the first man officially to announce his candidacy for the Presidency.

Now there was no time to lose. McCarthy told Lowenstein that he would run, and nine days later he announced publicly that he would seek the Democratic nomination. He thus challenged the leader of his own party and spelled out quite clearly that the issue would be the Vietnam war.

One of the few decorations on the deep-blue walls of Eugene McCarthy's quiet office in the Washington Senate was a white medallion in bas-relief of the head of Sir Thomas More, the English martyr who died denying Henry VIII's right to declare himself spiritual head of the Church of England. McCarthy's bookshelves were packed with the works of More and commentaries upon them, together with such tomes as the *Summa Theologica* of Thomas Aquinas and St. Augustine's *Confessions*.

McCarthy had a profound affection for "our blessed Thomas More," as he calls him, and More had an equally profound influence on McCarthy's thinking. No doubt nothing could be more flattering to the Senator than to suggest that in his attitude toward the administration that autumn of 1967 and in the stand he was preparing to take there were parallels with the story of the English martyr. But nevertheless it is so. The similarities won him the epithet "Gene McCarthy—the Man for This Season."

McCarthy was no firebrand revolutionary but a man who stood firm behind the sanctity of traditional law. The events of 1967 and his conviction that they represented a total failure of the nation's leaders to recognize or rise to their responsibilities were forcing him to speak out. "There comes a time when an honorable man simply has to raise the flag," he said.

The flag that he was ready to pin to the mast called for total reassessment of the Vietnam war and the commitment of the United States in Southeast Asia. McCarthy delighted in turning to More's *Utopia* (a book that had been compulsory reading for his sociology students at the College of St. Thomas in St. Paul, Minnesota) to find a parallel for Vietnam. More wrote of his imaginary perfect state, which had blundered into an unfortunate overseas war:

Once upon a time they had gone to war to win for their

63

king another kingdom to which he claimed to be the rightful heir by virtue of an old tie by marriage. After they had secured it, they saw they would have no less trouble in keeping it than they had suffered in obtaining it. The seeds of rebellion from within or of invasion from without were always springing up in the people thus acquired.

They realised they would have to fight constantly for them or against them and to keep an army in continual readiness. In the meantime they were being plundered, their money was being taken out of the country, they were shedding their blood for the little glory of someone else, peace was no more secure than before, their morals at home were being corrupted by war, the lust for robbery was becoming second nature, criminal recklessness was emboldened by killings in war, and the laws were being held in contempt—all because the king, being distracted with the charge of two kingdoms, could not properly attend to either.

At length seeing that in no other way would there be any end to all of this mischief, they took counsel together and most courteously offered their king his choice of retaining whichever of the two kingdoms he preferred. He could not keep both because there were too many of them to be ruled by half a king, just as no-one would care to engage even a muleteer whom he had to share with someone else. The worthy king was obliged to be content with his own realm and to turn over the new one to one of his friends, who was driven out soon afterwards.

"That's it flat out, isn't it?" McCarthy said of this passage. "There you have the description of a war that so distracts a society that it fails to respond to its problems at home." And he added: "I have always looked upon More as the first modern man, the first *political* man. He was forced to make a kind of individual and personal choice at a time when there was great upheaval, significant and political changes not really very different from those we face today." To consider McCarthy as a saint would be absurd; he is a tough and realistic political in-fighter. Yet there were many in the fall of 1967 who believed that he was heading for political martyrdom.

McCarthy was born in March 1916 in the Minnesota farming hamlet of Watkins (population 744). His father was a livestock breeder of Irish descent; his mother came from a family of German immigrants. In 1968 his father at 92 was still supervising the family farm, and McCarthy himself had a lively knowledge of the land and farming affairs. He received his secondary and college education at St. John's University in Collegeville, finishing in two years less than the prescribed eight and collected A-level passes in everything but trigonometry.

His games, which he played well, were ice hockey and baseball. Six feet two inches tall, well built, and tough, he excelled in both and almost reached professional standard in baseball. But the influence most at work in his life was the intellectual liberalism of the Benedictines at St. John's, where he later returned as a novice to study for the priesthood. After a year he left to marry Abigail Quigley, a good-looking and decisive girl whom he had met while teaching in North Dakota.

McCarthy's return to secular life and a job teaching sociology at the College of St. Thomas came at a time of unrest and upheaval in Minnesota politics. Hubert Humphrey, later Vice-President of the United States, was leading a campaign to weed out strong Communist influences that had infiltrated the Democratic and Farmer-Labor parties in the state. McCarthy joined the fight. By 1948 a new party had been formed under a coalition arranged by Humphrey's liberal forces, and McCarthy successfully stood for the first of five successive terms in Congress.

In 1959, after a relentless battle at the polls that few backed him to win, McCarthy upset an incumbent Republican to gain entry to the Senate. As a committee member he was involved in some of the major issues of the day—taxation, agriculture, and the congressional supervision of C.I.A. activities—but gained the scantest reputation as a lawmaker and introduced no major bills. With his relaxed and casual manner and ready quips, he was often accused of laziness, a charge that he refuted strongly. He reminded critics that since 1960 he had written four books and averaged 125 major speeches a year outside the Senate. "Do they expect me to go to the Senate and do push-ups?"

In 1960 the name Eugene McCarthy first became a national byword for a reason as strange as his campaign against Johnson appeared in the fall of 1967. At the Democratic convention that year he led an astonishing and quite hopeless attempt to gain the party nomination for Adlai Stevenson, the liberal intellectual whom he so admired. His nomination speech for Stevenson was the greatest of that convention and no doubt of Gene McCarthy's career. His daughter Mary later said: "He often wishes now he had never made it. Every time he speaks, people expect him to reach those heights again, and he just cannot do it."

McCarthy's preoccupation with Vietnam did not really begin until January 1966. Then, as a member of the Senate Foreign Relations Committee, he joined with fourteen other Senators to urge the President to continue the bombing pause on Hanoi. The appeal fell on deaf ears; four days later Johnson broke the 37-day hold-off. McCarthy from then on devoted himself to needling, to questioning, criticizing, and challenging the administration's conduct of the war.

By August 1967, when Undersecretary of State Nicholas Katzenbach declared that in modern times it is the President and not Congress who has the right to wage, if not technically to declare, war, McCarthy was afire. He stumped out of the hearing, saying to E. W. Kenworthy of *The New York Times:* "This is the wildest testimony I ever heard. There is no limit to what he says the President can do. There is only one thing to do—take it to the country."

The next McCarthy explosion came in mid-October, when Secretary of State Dean Rusk in a "yellow peril" press conference linked Vietnam with the fight against Communist China. Replying in a bitter speech from the Senate floor, McCarthy called the American endeavor in Vietnam "a costly exercise in futility," accused the administration of trying to secure "an anti-Communist bastion in South Vietnam," and upbraided Rusk for his specious references to the "yellow peril."

Then along came Lowenstein, who decided that McCarthy was his man. There were other influences at work on the Senator. He had already discussed the issues—but less explicitly his own candidacy—with his family. He had four children: Ellen, twenty, then attending Georgetown University's School of Foreign Service; Mary, an eighteen-year-old sophomore at Radcliffe College, who took a leave of absence to help in her father's campaign; Michael, sixteen, a high-school student and the silent one in the family; and Margaret, twelve, attending Catholic Stone Ridge School in Maryland, where some of the Kennedy children were her classmates.

Mary, the most politically active of the four, was deeply involved in the whole issue that was so troubling her father's conscience. She was equally deeply concerned in the student movements springing up in the wake of the Lowenstein campaign and in the general spirit of defiant protest that had burgeoned on the campuses that year.

Mary brought home student friends who talked with the Senator in the Washington house that he had recently rented from his old friend, columnist Walter Lippmann. McCarthy was thus tuned into the ideas and preoccupations of youth. "He was always a great guy to have around; you could talk to him easily, and he always understood," said one of Mary's friends, who knew the family well.

The Senator was also lecturing regularly at colleges throughout the nation, and there too he heard the objections and the reservations not only of students but also of many faculty members, with whom he had so much in common. "He realized that what youth was seeking was leadership, not freedom to drift," said Mary, who openly counseled her father to run. "I told him a political life was meaningless unless you were ready to stand up for your ideals." The political realities were also pushing McCarthy toward a run on his own. His future was bleak. Joining Robert Kennedy, even had Bobby shown any enthusiasm for such an alliance could hardly have led McCarthy to the Vice-Presidential nomination, for both men were Roman Catholics, and no party would have risked such a ticket.

There were friends in the Senate who were persuaded that McCarthy had tired of the routine of Congress, that he was bored with the ritual and irritated by the futility of it all. His moral rage at Johnson was certainly at its height. He felt that, if ever his time was to come, it had to be then.

The night before he announced his candidacy on November 30 he telephoned Mary at Radcliffe and told her of his decision. His wife, Abigail, had been against it, but he had won her over. He told Mary—she wrote his words down immediately afterward—"It is a question of whether there is any purpose in politics beyond yourself."

Lowenstein, meanwhile, knowing that he at last had the candidate so essential if his cause was to be kept afire, was already working on a different problem. He had to postpone the Conference of Concerned Democrats, which was to have taken place during Thanksgiving week at the Blackstone Hotel in Chicago, so that McCarthy could open his campaign before the people on whom he would depend for support and organization.

67

Desperate switches were made in the booking arrangements, and telegrams were sent to all delegation leaders, urging them to confirm that they could fall in with the date change. The telegrams, without explanation, were signed "McCarthy," Lowenstein's way of signaling the importance of what was to follow.

The announcement, when it came in Washington on a snowy morning, was not overinspiring. On the first poll taken, 58 per cent of those questioned did not know who the candidate was. The phone rang all day in McCarthy's office, but by evening no single Senator had pledged his support, and only one of the 247 Democrats in the House of Representatives—Don Edwards of California—had publicly come out for the peace cause. It was to stay like that for many weeks.

When the 500 leaders of the Concerned Democrats and 10,000 others met to see McCarthy open his campaign in Chicago on December 2, Lowenstein was jubilant. He was introducing the troops to their general, the general to his cause. He openly regarded McCarthy as a full-fledged candidate who could, with the help of the organization already assembled, go as far as the party convention and, with any luck, into the final run for the White House.

McCarthy certainly did not see any such prospect. For the Senator, it was a chance of putting before the public the issues that he had been trying—with insignificant success—to raise on the Senate floor; it was a protest to which he was morally committed.

For most of the delegates the aim was twofold: to do something concrete about Vietnam and to do it by raising such a public hullabaloo around the polls that Washington could no longer ignore it. It was really immaterial *who* led them, but a figurehead they had to have. McCarthy happened to be the man who came to hand. "He may as well have been an asterisk as long as he had a name," said one.

In view of the excitement and heady enthusiasm in the air, it was an unfortunate day. Ten thousand people packed the ballroom of the Hilton Hotel, where McCarthy was to make his announcement, and another 2,000 thronged outside. The band played "Happy Days Are Here Again," then "Hello Dolly" until a frantically waving aide cut them short in midbar. ("Hello Lyndon" was the L.B.J. theme song, a smash hit at the White House.)

Lowenstein made a long speech, John the Baptist announcing the Messiah. "We are not trying to beat somebody with nobody.

We are trying to beat nobody with somebody," he cried among cheers.

When at last Eugene McCarthy stood up—a gray man, with gray eyes, gray hair, gray suit—some of the ardor began to cool. After he had spoken for twenty minutes, some listeners were dozing. He spoke of the Dreyfus case in France and compared the burning issue of Vietnam to the Punic Wars in Rome.

"Yes, but we're fighting Ho, not Hannibal," muttered one disconsolate delegate.

Asked afterward why he had failed to switch them on, he replied, "But at this stage of the campaign what would you have me galvanize them to do?"

He angered Lowenstein and the organizers by refusing to speak again for the 2,000 people outside. Lowenstein said much later: "I saw him as a candidate. He saw himself as a moral protester for a cause. That was where the early troubles lay."

And troubles there were. A team closed in around McCarthy —more a loyal band of supporters than any sort of political organization. From the Concerned Democrats organization Curtis Gans, Harold Ickes, Jr., and Mrs. Sarah Kovner moved in. Ex-C.B.S. newsman Blair Clark took over as campaign manager; he was later joined by Richard Goodwin, former White House speech writer for Presidents Kennedy and Johnson and adviser to Jacqueline Kennedy on the publication of William Manchester's *The Death of a President*. Former Associated Press newsman Sy Hersh came in as press secretary. And, as organizer of the Students for McCarthy movement there was Sam Brown, a young student who persuaded his wealthy father he should quit Harvard's Divinity School and devote himself to the cause.

Little of the enthusiasm of the Concerned Democrats appeared to rub off on the candidate in those vital early days. According to the accounts of Lowenstein and his friends there was constant friction as McCarthy insisted on "just pacing myself."

Lowenstein replied angrily that, if the pacing went on much longer, the movement would lose all the momentum it had gained. "We owed so much to that guy—it was just so great that he had the courage and the moral determination to offer himself to us. It is a debt we shall always remember. But then, this . . . ," said Lowenstein later.

The Senator was a man who disliked early rising, so a series of 6:00 A.M. factory-gate appearances was canceled. "I'm not really a morning person," he said. On another occasion he mused among the handshakes, "This is sort of a strange ritual." And "Oh those factories!" he lamented, in an exchange with Bobby Kennedy.

He was at first reluctant to allow his wife and daughter Mary to join him, though they were later to campaign actively. While Mrs. McCarthy visited women's clubs and gatherings, Mary spoke at schools and colleges. Once a reporter who found her talking to a group of nuns asked, "But do nuns have the vote?" "They do," replied Mary. "They also pray, which is more important at this stage."

By mid-January, the opinion polls rated McCarthy nowhere. Most of the press, when it bothered to report him at all, considered him a joke. Enthusiasm among the organizers of the Concerned Democrats was sagging as their candidate's campaign meandered on in a series of well-phrased speeches and urbane asides that did little to turn on the uncomprehending voters.

But the Senator's scholarly analysis of Vietnam, his condemnation of the administrative methods and the style of Lyndon Johnson, his claim that there had been an "alienation" of youth that he was seeking to overcome ("A lot of politicians lingered on a good deal too long after the last war; then with the discovery of penicillin the process was accentuated. But your turn must not be long delayed. I want to bridge the generation gap.") slowly increased his prestige on campuses across the nation.

Around the person of the "gray rebel," as one columnist tagged him, was gathering one of the most curious phenomena in America's political history. For in New Hampshire "the children's crusade"—or "the kids," as everyone called them—was forming ranks.

.6.

NEW HAMPSHIRE: THE CHILDREN'S CRUSADE

NEW HAMPSHIRE IS BY REPUTATION A DOUR STATE, WHOSE PEOPLE —proud of the reserve inherited from their British ancestors—are regarded by Americans as the least expressive and the least responsive in the Union. Richard Nixon remembers his own first visit to the state as a candidate in 1960, immediately upon his return from Warsaw, where, as Vice-President, he had been mobbed and showered with flowers by the enthusiastic citizens. "When I complained to my campaign manager that, in contrast, nobody here seemed to want to say more than a curt 'good morning,' I was told that a 'good morning' in New Hampshire was worth a garland of flowers any day in Warsaw," he recalls.

It is in this state—the Granite State, as it is known, as much for the character of its population as for its geology—that the American election campaign officially begins, with the first of the primaries. As a factor in the campaign New Hampshire's importance is more psychological than political. The first primary has an exciting freshness about it, a first-night atmosphere in which anything can happen. The candidates are eager, the audience anticipatory, the political correspondents full of enthusiasm. The fact that this state has fewer than 1 million people and can muster only four electoral votes hardly seems to matter.

The primary-election system is regarded in Europe as a superb example of the American democratic process. Britain in particular has become fascinated with it. The Conservative Party is experimenting in some areas with a British version of the primary to secure the "best" candidates for parliamentary election.

Fourteen states and the District of Columbia conducted direct primaries in the campaign. The rules varied from state to state, but, in general, the system gave the voters some say in deciding the best man to run for President. It worked this way: In each primary state voters registered as Democrats or Republicans (usually), and on Primary Day each stated his preferences for candidates within his own party.

In some states the voters were asked to vote directly for Presidential candidates. In many states, including New Hampshire, voters could "write in" names that were not officially on the ballot. In others they voted for groups of delegates committed to one or another of the candidates.

The primary gives the public the chance to state its choice in most cases, but not in all. That choice is implemented by the states' delegates going to the convention committed to vote, on the first ballot at least, for the candidate with the biggest support in their state.

The two parties thus did not confront each other in the primaries. Instead, they indulged in internecine warfare, Republican against Republican, Democrat against Democrat, and this struggle went on for seven months until—in theory—each party had eliminated the weak and only the best man was left. Then the real fight against the opposition's best man began, and it was to be a duel of champions.

The whole system is comparable to those Roman mass gladiatorial contests in which dozens of fighters eliminated each other in different amphitheaters until only two were left to decide the championship before the Emperor.

The difference was that in this modern gladiatorial contest, instead of being killed, the losers were only politically wounded, and, after the conventions, they were expected to fall in behind the respective victors and give him all their support until Election Day. The system did not always work that way and certainly did not do so in 1968.

From on-the-spot observation of the primaries, it was clear that they were not quite as flawless as they seemed from the other side of the Atlantic. They prolonged the campaign and depleted the energies of the candidates. In 1968 they cost vast sums of money, and they did not necessarily bring out all the important issues. What is more, because fewer than one third of the states held primaries at all they could not be conclusive.

It was apparent that a candidate could secure the nomination without winning a single primary election and that the only way for the system to work effectively would have been as a national institution, replacing both the individual primary elections and the national-convention nominating system.

Nevertheless, the visitor approached the New Hampshire primary with all the anticipation and excitement of a racing journalist up early on Epsom Downs in the weeks before the Derby. The primary offered an opportunity to see the contestants exercising in an all-out gallop; it would reveal their strengths and their weaknesses and help to set the betting odds; and, most of all, it would bring a merciful end to the candidacies of the nonstarters, thinning the field and leaving only the strongest to fight it out.

One thing is always certain about New Hampshire at primary time: It is bitterly cold. It is possible to see why the early settlers named this colony after Hampshire. The pine trees and the greenness evoke that lovely southern English county. But England's Hampshire is gentler than its namesake, particularly in winter.

The cold of a New England winter explained something of the character of the New Englander. Traditionally he was said to be resourceful but stubborn, taciturn but with a sense of humor, shrewd but honest. In New Hampshire these Yankee characteristics were highly prized, and an immigrant from, say, Chicago would adopt them like a chameleon. Within a few months he would not only look as if his ancestors had arrived on the *Mayflower;* he almost certainly *claimed* that they did as well.

But, although all New Hampshire people liked to think of themselves as fitting a single image, campaign managers divided the state into two: To the north there was a rural population of

73

farmers and landowners, well-to-do businessmen, and retired professional people. Their attitudes had always been strongly conservative and, according to opinion polls, they were markedly hawkish on Vietnam. To the south were the industrial towns. Like its counterpart in the Old World, Manchester—the largest population center—was a brash and bustling mill town, where the beauty of the rolling hills and endless pine and spruce forests gave way to a main street with little to commend it but the local discount stores and supermarket complexes. In Manchester was a block of hard-working, comfortably-off voters more concerned with overtime pay than with Vietnam. In 1968 traditional union allegiances made them an apparently easy target for campaigners who were urging that President Johnson's name be written in on Democratic ballots. Their attitudes were further influenced by the *Manchester Union Leader,* which had the reputation of one of the most violently conservative organs in the United States.

Such was the bleak territory McCarthy had to face, and naturally there were many friends and supporters who advised him to ignore it, among them his wife and campaign manager Blair Clark.

One of the most compelling arguments was the makeup of the voting lists. Of the state's 345,000 voters, 148,000 had registered as Republicans and only 89,000 as Democrats. The rest were independent, for an interesting reason. On Primary Day a New Hampshire voter must take either a Democratic blue ballot card or a Republican red one. An independent who chooses either card in the voting booth is automatically listed as a voter for that party and can vote no other ticket in future primaries, unless he gives a clear ninety days' notice (before the primary date) of his decision to change. The result is that New Hampshire primaries are customarily marked by small turnouts because of numerous abstentions by independent voters who habitually prefer not to vote in primaries.

In addition the New Hampshire voter is a notoriously fickle creature. In 1964, by a fluke never satisfactorily explained, the Republican majority went to Henry Cabot Lodge—at the time Ambassador in Saigon 12,000 miles away—on a write-in vote that defied all the prognostications of the day and resulted from a last-minute campaign mounted by his supporters and strongly backed by his son.

If only McCarthy were prepared to wait for the second primary election on the 1968 list, in Wisconsin on April 2, he would have a far more satisfactory track for a trial gallop—or so the argument ran. Wisconsin adjoins McCarthy's home state of Minnesota. There he would find people—and a political climate—he knew very well. Why be tempted to the snowbound political wastes of New England?

Afterward, McCarthy claimed that it was "just my sense of politics" that had pushed him into overriding his advisers. His reasoning was that, if one was mounting an idealistic political campaign aimed at allowing the public to protest at the polls, then it was better to take the hard road and expose oneself to the greatest risks and the toughest opposition from the outset. In the first days of January, therefore, McCarthy entered himself for the New Hampshire primary.

George Romney came into New Hampshire with all the fervor of a preacher who has found a new tribe of unbelievers to convert. He believed that his own sincerity would go down well with the New Englanders. He was like them himself, he told friends—religious, self-disciplined, a worker rather than a playboy, a man of integrity and character—and if there was one thing New Englanders understood and respected it was character.

So at 5:00 A.M. on January 12, the first official day of the New Hampshire primary-election campaign, Romney was up and ready and in high spirits. He had gathered an impressive press caravan one hundred strong (a collection of mingled courtiers and hecklers that assembles round every hopeful candidate at the beginning of the election year and stays with him until he drops out or wins), and he had, he believed, a good organization.

But the pressmen who had been assigned to Romney did not look particularly happy about their luck as they gathered in the conference room of the Sheraton-Wayfarer Motor Inn in Manchester at 5:30 A.M. The mood was quiet and sullen. Romney, the most alert person there, was first-naming around the room, refusing proffered coffee (he never drinks it on Mormon principle) and smacking his hands in anticipation of at last making contact with some actual voters who would shortly have the power to mark his name on a ballotpaper.

Once the stand-up breakfast was over, Romney led the party through the motel lobby and paused at the low double doors. His police escort informed him that the thermometer was showing seven degrees below zero. The candidate did not care. He was euphoric as he plunged into the biting cold. "Come on, come on!" he yelled.

The actual first moments of the campaign were a shambles. Romney's entourage drove fifteen miles across country to Nashua, where he was to "pump the flesh" outside an electronics plant. Everyone wanted to see whose hand he would shake first. But the only hand the accompanying press saw was that of a policeman. In a traffic tangle outside the factory gate, Romney was allowed through while the rest of the convoy was held up.

Romney first stood right outside the factory entrance, on a narrow sidewalk, but the police and television crews prevailed on him to move into the more open area of the car park across the road. It was agreed that he should stand at the entrance, trapping every unsuspecting worker who arrived and obliging him to run a gauntlet of pressmen and cameras, culminating in the Romney glad hand. The latter consisted of a firm handshake with the right hand while the left hand grasped the target's right elbow, a firm "look me in the eyes" smile, and the words—mechanical after the first few minutes—"We've got to get America back on the track —back to fundamentals. I appreciate your support." It was hardly a detailed program, but it was about as much as anyone was prepared to stand around and hear in that cold.

Most of the workers appeared bemused or indifferent to the experience. One woman said, "I agree entirely," and a few people smiled briefly before hurrying into the warm building. After a few minutes, however, Romney was sufficiently encouraged to say, "The people of New Hampshire are even more friendly than I expected." The cry was taken up during the day by his aides.

After two hours at the factory gate, Romney took off on a precisely calculated tour of southern New Hampshire, an area of small mill towns, the one part of the state where the Democrats have a numerical edge. His style was that of a salesman closing a deal. The lack of embarrassment with strangers that he had first learned as a Mormon missionary in Britain in the 1920s was very apparent. He bustled up to one elderly woman shopper on the main street of Manchester and said in his usual breezy manner, "Hi, I'm George Romney."

"No you're not," she retorted. "If you say you're George Romney, you're lying."

"Madam," George Romney retorted, "I never lie."

At 10:40, together with his wife Lenore and a clutch of followers, he filed into the office of Robert Stark, Secretary of State for New Hampshire, and presented his petition. Stark gave him an immediate letter of reply, saving, as someone remarked, the postage on two letters.

By dinner time the press had followed Romney in and out of countless stores, restaurants, supermarkets, and houses. His technique never varied. It was going to be an old-fashioned, "meet the people" campaign, based on the belief that a hand shaken is a vote won and that personal magnetism is what really counts.

After dinner—hamburgers in a drug store—the press bus headed for Exeter Academy, a boarding school for boys between the ages of fourteen and eighteen based on the British public-school system. The idea was that Romney should demonstrate how he could communicate with youth. It turned out to be an embarrassing evening. The students—candidates for the establishment of the future—showed a cool, instinctive scorn for Mr. Romney. Within a few minutes of his starting to speak they were yawning at his jokes and laughing cynically at his serious points.

Mrs. Romney, a woman whose air of permanent Midwestern innocence makes her seem a perennial debutante, was the only person in the room following the speech with the right facial expressions. When Romney attacked rising crime in the streets, declaring that America had a rape every minute, she looked suitably shocked. But only seconds later she looked ready to die: The student body had risen en masse to give a rousing cheer at this record.

The embarrassment grew. "Let's call a spade a spade and have the chips fall where they may," declared Romney, and the youthful audience cried "Hear, hear!" in delight at his clichés. The applause and laughter had sophisticated and ironic cruelty about them. Romney looked bewildered, and his aides were disconcerted.

But at the next stop—an inaugural ball for the newly elected Mayor of Bedford—there was warmth and affection for the candidate. He shook everyone's hand. "Congratulations," he said. "With people like you we can get this country moving again."

At midnight, eighteen hectic hours after the predawn start, the first day's campaigning was over. "Is it going to be like this all the time." asked a German reporter, who was covering a primary for the first time.

"No, worse," replied an A.B.C. cameraman.

77

"My dear fellow, that's impossible," put in a British reporter. "The buses will be leaving the motel at 7:30 A.M.," called out a Romney aide. "Please be in the press room at 7:15." The campaign was under way.

Richard Milhous Nixon was almost as familiar to the average Briton as he was to Americans. His enigmatic quality had always fascinated writers, and through the years Nixon had been given more television and newspaper coverage in Britain than any other American politician, including the Kennedys. To the British, Nixon's very personality encapsulated those American qualities that exacerbate the hate side of the love-hate relationship between the two countries. A willingness to subordinate everything to ambition, a gutter fighter's deadliness when cornered, a lack of style, a questionable integrity were all regarded as epitomizing the dark and doubtful side of the American character.

Yet there had always been a reluctant admiration for Richard Nixon among the British. His toughness was respected, his courage recognized, and his resilience appreciated. Losers who will not lie down have always had the affection of the British people. And so, in and out of the spotlight, they followed his career through their newspapers, and it was with a feeling of certainty that they anticipated his return to the ring in another comeback attempt as 1968 approached.

On the other hand, many Americans seemed surprised, if not actually shocked, at the re-emergence of Richard Nixon as a serious, and then the leading, Presidential contender. The difference, it was said, was that Americans do not like losers, particularly three-time losers. This aphorism was to be repeated many times in the campaign by Richard Nixon's opponents.

Understandably, many Americans took comfort from repeating it, for Richard Nixon's recent record was not impressive. In the United States, a loser's image was considered fatal—except by Richard Nixon.

His narrow defeat by John F. Kennedy in 1960 should have finished him. The failure of his comeback in the battle for the governorship of California in 1962 ought to have been the end. His whining bad temper at his defeat was highlighted by his attack on the press: His comment, "You won't have Nixon to kick around any more because, gentlemen, this is my last press conference," suggested that even he thought so.

Once again Nixon resurrected himself in a half-hearted last-minute drive for the Republican nomination in 1964. Once again he lost. But each time he lost he learned. He learned how to lose with better grace. And in 1964 he lost not only gracefully but also sportingly, and, as a loyal party man, he campaigned long and hard for Barry Goldwater.

During the course of that disastrous Goldwater campaign, Nixon dug deep into the grass roots. The gallons of lukewarm coffee and the hundreds of half-eaten chicken dinners were worth it. He rubbed shoulders with local party chairmen and officials as one of them. Contacts were made and friendships renewed. It was the beginning of yet another comeback.

Senator Goldwater won only six states, and his claim to be party leader was obviously worthless. Who was to fill the vacuum? Richard Nixon. Within a week after the election, he declared, "Those who divided the party this year cannot unite it." It was a beautifully calculated strike, scuttling all the other contenders with one devastating blow. Not only did it finish Goldwater, but it also damaged both Romney and New York Governor Nelson Rockefeller, who had refused to campaign for the national ticket. Just to be certain, Nixon singled out Rockefeller as the "principal" divider.

Three weeks later Nixon and Goldwater met with former President Eisenhower at the Waldorf Towers Hotel in New York. Nixon was able to dictate terms. Goldwater's party chairman, Dean Burch, had to go, he said. Goldwater left the meeting knowing that he was no longer party leader. "Richard Nixon," he said "now has the biggest hand on the wheel."

A month later Burch was out, and Ray Bliss, a long-standing friend of Nixon, was in. And, when the congressional elections of 1966 got under way, Nixon was ready. In 165 congressional districts in 35 states, Nixon campaigned in support of the local man. The theme of his speeches was an all-out attack on President Johnson himself.

The elections were sensationally successful for the Republicans. The party gained three Senate seats, eight governorships, and 47 congressional seats. And with those wins came promissory notes, notes that could be cashed at the Republican convention in Miami Beach in 1968.

On February 1, 1968, Richard Milhous Nixon once again announced his candidacy for the Republican Presidential nomination.

The way the announcement came was intriguing. It hinted at a new, cooler Nixon approach to politics, one closer to his own character. "I am an introvert," he had always said, and that is what he was, a natural loner who was also capable of donning various masks as the occasion required.

On this occasion no mask was necessary. Reporters were called to Nixon's apartment at 531 Fifth Avenue and handed a copy of a letter addressed to the voters of New Hampshire. In it he announced his intention of running. His six years in Congress and eight as Vice-President, plus eight ensuing ones as a private citizen, had, the letter said, given him the experience and the perspective "necessary to provide the new leadership" that the nation required.

> During 14 years in Washington, I learned the awesome nature of the great decisions a President faces. During the past eight years I have had a chance to reflect on the lessons of public office, to measure the nation's tasks and its problems from a fresh perspective. I have sought to apply those lessons to the needs of the present, and to the entire sweep of this final third of the 20th century.
>
> And I believe I have found some answers.

In New Hampshire Governor George Romney was still determinedly shaking hands, despite a bruising experience in Concord, where an angry citizen, finding his hand seized in a firm Mormon grasp, had yelled before the television cameras, "Take your hands off me, or I'll sue you!"

Mr. Nixon's letter made it clear that he would use different tactics: "You can't handshake yourself out of the kind of problems we've got today. You've got to think them through and that takes a lifetime of getting ready." The Nixons, it was announced on Fifth Avenue, would leave the next morning to start their campaign in the Granite State.

Governor Romney's campaign began to move beyond farce into straight tragedy. Everywhere he went he was tormented by his brainwashing comment. His standard reply to questions about it was, "Well, I think my statement on that has been misrepresented enough without my getting into it tonight."

Often he received an equally standard gibe, "How would you know the real facts even if you heard them?"

This painful exercise in self-flagellation was to come to an end just 29 days after Nixon entered the race.

On Sunday, February 25, William Johnson, Romney's campaign manager in New Hampshire, was asked to fly to Washington to discuss the crisis with Leonard Hall, the national campaign chairman.

The two men met next morning. Foremost in their minds was a poll of voters taken a few days before by Market Opinion Research. It showed that Richard Nixon would win with 70 percent of the Republican votes and that Romney could hope for little more than 10 percent. There was no point in doubting the accuracy of the polling organization; it was a Detroit company and belonged to George Romney himself.

Similarly unfavorable results had come in from all the other states where Romney hoped to campaign. The poll had to be shown to Romney, who was on his way to Boston. More important, he had to be told what to do. More was involved than just his being made to look foolish. There was an important commitment that could not be ignored. That week America's 25 Republican governors were meeting in Washington. They expected Romney to tell them how he was doing in his campaign, as he had promised them at a previous meeting in White Sulphur Springs, Virginia.

Johnson and Hall worked out Romney's options. He could renege on his promise. He could deliberately lie, say that he was doing well, and chance a last-minute revival. Or he could tell the truth and, having told it, get out. Both men believed that the last choice was the only one. It would give the governors plenty of time to consider the men they wanted to support.

The poll was sent to Romney and a meeting arranged at his Boston hotel, the Ramada Inn, on Tuesday night. Apart from Johnson and Hall, Travis Cross, the Governor's able press secretary; Jonathan Moore, his foreign-policy adviser; and Richard Van Dusen, another close aide, also attended. Johnson outlined the position. He spoke for nearly an hour. All the time Romney sat looking at the ground, listening without expression. From time to time some of the others joined in, but there was no escaping the reality.

Just after 10:00 Romney said good night to his staff. "I'm going to sleep on it," he said. "You'd better prepare the draft statement of withdrawal in any case."

The five men sat there, sad but relieved. They knew that Romney would accept the decision. They were his men and grieved that his effort had proved meaningless so early in the campaign, but such was the camaraderie and openness around Romney that they knew they could talk honestly to him and receive only respect in return.

At 7:30 the next morning the five gathered in Romney's suite. Eggs and toast had been ordered, and before they sat down Romney told them: "I've thought it out, and I'm withdrawing." He looked at the prepared statement, made a few alterations, and, with a beaming smile, attacked his breakfast.

Everyone around the table relaxed. Jokes were exchanged. Laughter filled the room. Instead of a wake the breakfast became a celebration. They had extricated themselves from an appalling situation by facing things honestly and communicating in time. It was a great relief.

There was only one thing left to do. A list of supporters to be told in advance of the formal announcement had to be prepared. With breakfast things cleared away, the party began to compose it, the first name being that of Lenore Romney, who was already campaigning for her husband in Wisconsin.

And so, on February 28 at 5:00 P.M. at the Washington Hilton Hotel, George Romney delivered the first shock of the campaign. He withdrew.

At once the third man, Governor Rockefeller of New York, came into the headlines. Nelson Rockefeller was an American aristocrat. A multimillionaire, an art lover, a brilliant administrator, he had chosen in middle age to enter politics. In Britain this choice was an aristocratic right, though it was being increasingly challenged. In America aristocrats have to change their style a little before the necessary public acceptance comes their way, which is why Nelson Rockefeller was such an intriguing man.

Overlaying his sophistication and breeding was a veneer of forced beer-hall camaraderie. He nudges, winks, and calls everybody "Fella"—like a coach in one of those Hollywood movies about college football. It seemed totally artificial and rather absurd, but it could not really have been so, because Nelson Rockefeller had three times been elected Governor of New York State and had proved that politics was his natural environment.

To the people he was "Rocky"; to him they were *his* people. He seemed to have a sixth sense about how to talk to them and deal with them; whether or not he would have had the same effect without the friendly neighborhood politician's routine is really immaterial. His appeal went far beyond traditional Republican voters.

82

His techniques and his liberalism had always enabled him to cut deeply into Democratic strength. Yet these same successful qualities had put him in a curious and paradoxical position in American political life.

Because his methods and ideals often conflicted with the traditional thinking of the Republican Party, he had alienated himself from the party machine. In 1968 Nelson Rockefeller had far more enemies inside the party than outside.

In Britain one is taught that both great American parties are loose federations, each encompassing a range of political thought from ultraliberalism to fundamental conservatism. This extreme simplification cannot possibly prepare a visitor for the Byzantine complexities of the American political scene.

The parties *are* great alliances among different power groups. The Democratic Party, combining labor with groups of intellectuals and academics, balancing hard-line southern segregationists with the Negro block vote all under the same banner, is the most extraordinary popular front that democracy has ever produced. Somehow since the 1930s the Democrats, through sheer political genius and organization, had succeeded not only in holding these fratricidal groups together but also in making them work in relative harmony.

The Republicans, on the other hand, a smaller, less professional party, had been in disarray for 36 years. Their only taste of power had come with Dwight Eisenhower, the professional father figure whom they had elevated to national leadership from outside the party.

The Republican Party was less pragmatic than the Democrats and more principled, so—although it is the younger of the two parties, having been founded in 1854—it is much more linked to the old America. Republicans embody the Puritan ethic in their philosophy and seem to be the party of the white Anglo-Saxon Protestants, known as "Wasps."

This heritage can result in two different kinds of thinking. It can produce an individual who, thanks to his own work and dedication, can make his own destiny in this world—and should be left alone to do so; it can also produce a sense of duty, an almost Victorian zeal for the organization of good works to improve mankind.

The Republican Party was a curious alliance between small and medium-sized businessmen from the hinterlands and America's

83

giant corporations. For a long time the corporations provided not only the money to sustain the party but also much of its intellectual leadership. Certain executives—secure in their positions of power in finance and industry—had for years arrogantly assumed that they had a right to lead the party. And they suffered from a classic weakness of elite groups: They lost touch with the rank and file.

This particular elite pushed the Republican Party toward definite, perhaps paternalistic, liberalism, which increasingly angered Republicans in America's West and Midwest. Because Nelson Rockefeller was the epitome of the Republican liberal, he became an object of hatred for those right-wing Republicans who abhorred the idea of state interference in the life of the individual. They were "conservative," and they believed in the old American virtues, in leaving a man alone to make his way or to fall by the wayside, depending on his drive and initiative.

Rockefeller's methods of public financing for projects that had been traditionally the playground of big private money were contrary to every precept of their Republicanism. His refusal to fight the New York State elections on Republican Party lines instead of basic civic issues further riled other Republican leaders.

In 1960 the Republican Party had chosen Richard Nixon, a middle-of-the-roader, as its Presidential candidate and had seen him narrowly defeated. Many Republicans from the Midwest and Southwest blamed Rockefeller for this defeat, for they knew that, in a secret agreement with Nixon, he had virtually dictated the party platform.

For the next few years, the conservatives worked until they were able contemptuously to overthrow the eastern leadership in a political coup d'etat, which resulted in the disastrous Barry Goldwater campaign against Lyndon Johnson in 1964. Rockefeller had attempted to rally the moderates and the liberals against the right wing and had emerged catastrophically.

At the party convention he was booed and jeered from the platform. Publicly he faced charges of trying to divide and break the party. His private life, after the divorce that ended his first marriage and his remarriage, became the subject of a scandalous national witch hunt, and across the country the Rockefellers were criticized largely because of Happy Rockefeller's decision to relinquish custody of the children of her first marriage in order to start a new family with the Governor. When the hue and cry died away, the commentators concluded that the name Rockefeller would never again figure on the lists of Presidential nominees.

It was a conclusion shared by the Governor. He told friends that he would fight one more election for another term as New York's Governor. Against the odds, he won. Afterward, holidaying at brother Laurance's Puerto Rico house, he told his immediate circle that he was happy to see the end of national politics. To another intimate, flying with him aboard his private plane *Wayfarer* last September, he said, when quizzed about his plans for 1968: "You do not understand what these campaigns take out of me physically, nervously, and psychologically. I never want to do it again."

And, as the inevitable questions began at the beginning of 1968, kept saying "no." He was at last living a settled domestic life. Happy came up with him each week to Albany, the state capital, bringing their three-year-old son Nelson, Jr., with her. Together father and son would play in his office behind the door marked "Executive Chamber" and around the huge desk in the great red-carpeted state cabinet room, upon which little Nelson loved to clamber so that he could stand up and be taller than his father.

Rockefeller adores his small son. In 1968 he was preoccupied with the problems of New York, for which he had grandiose plans. He was content. To enter the lists would mean an end to it all. In any case, as he told friends, it was not a question of whether or not he could win the Presidency—he believed that he could; indeed the polls consistently showed his popularity. (In 1960, after narrowly defeating Richard Nixon, John F. Kennedy said that he would have lost had the Republican Party run Rockefeller.) It was a question of whether or not the Republican Party would let him win. Knowing the depth of the feeling against him within the party, he felt pretty certain that it would not.

So Rocky sat back and left the field to Romney. Many of his opponents saw this move as a political ploy, but those who talked to Rockefeller at the end of 1967 came away convinced that it was no trick. Rockefeller had lost his appetite for the Presidency.

But all that had to change. When Romney took his decision to pull out, he told the men with him, "Nelson is the only man in the party who can stop Nixon now." It was important, he said, that the governors be encouraged to rally to Rockefeller. But Rockefeller had to be forewarned; Romney told Hall that absolute priority must be given to informing Rockefeller in advance of the withdrawal.

On the morning of the announcement, Rockefeller was airborne en route to his New York office after his customary two-day spell in Albany. That afternoon at 3:00 P.M. he was due to leave with Happy for Washington and the Republican governors' conference. It was not until midday that he heard the news. Unable to reach the Governor personally, Hall had phoned George Hinman, the political adviser who masterminded Rocky's electoral machine.

Hinman was waiting in the office to break the news to Rockefeller. But neither man was able to make contact with Romney in Washington. "I'll talk to him when I get there," said Rockefeller and left with Happy and his staff from La Guardia Airport.

In the air, press secretary Leslie Slote put on headphones in the pilot's cabin to listen in on Romney's news conference. He recorded the details for the Governor, for whose arrival all Washington was waiting. At the airport Rockefeller bounded for a phone booth. Before he faced the press and his fellow governors, he wanted to talk directly to Romney at his hotel. The first phone booth had only a credit-card phone. He leaped to the next one, then found that he had no dime. He disappeared to find change. Slote found a coin and was about to put it in the box when the Governor returned, similarly armed. "Here take this," he urged Slote.

"Aw, Governor, have this one on me," said Slote and put him through to Romney, who begged him to announce his own candidacy.

Rockefeller went to his Washington home on Foxhall Road for a conference with his brother, Governor Winthrop Rockefeller of Arkansas, and Governor Spiro Agnew of Maryland. Heavy pressure was put on him to declare himself ready to accept a draft at the Republican convention. His team believed that at least 16, maybe more, of the 25 Republican governors would support Rockefeller, but the problem was would they be ready at such an early stage to rush in and show their support? Neither Rockefeller nor Hinman believed that they would. The tactic of "wait and see" was adopted.

The reasons were quickly evident. Nixon, heavily engaged in primary electioneering, was already urging that, if Rockefeller was going to run, he should start battling on democracy's home ground, in front of the people. The intention was plain; late on the scene, Rocky would have his nose bloodied in a way already too painfully familiar to him.

Rockefeller paused. He had no wish to engage his wife in a second round of that sort of electioneering; there were voters in New Hampshire who still vividly recalled scenes in 1964 when Happy, pregnant with young Nelson, was left standing because no one would offer a chair to a divorced woman. But some sort of gesture was desperately needed if advantage was to be taken of the moment.

When at last Rocky and Happy arrived at the Washington Hilton conference at 8:00 P.M., they were mobbed—"as if Rockefeller had not only announced but won," wrote one reporter.

"Wonderful, terriffic," said Rocky. "We want to win. The party needs unity. I'm exactly where I was before. I'm not making any move." Then came that involuntary wink. "You are winking at me Governor," said a newsman. "I'm not winking at anybody," said Rocky.

Later he said: "I was accused of dividing the party once. I do not want that ever thrown in my face again." The remark showed a touch of the old resentment, but it was not the last word. Finally came the statement that everyone had been awaiting.

> The party must decide who it feels can best represent it and who it thinks can best command the confidence of the American people and best serve the country. The Republican Party has two objectives. It wants to remain united. It wants to nominate someone who can get enough independent and Democratic votes to get elected. I am not going to create dissension . . . by contending for the nomination, but I am ready and willing to serve the American people if called.

The Rockefeller charter was struck. Ahead, if he were to have the slightest chance of success, lay a long and painstaking task. As it was too late to get on the ballot in the primaries, he had to persuade the delegates from the fifty states, one by one, group by group, to support a "draft Rockefeller" movement at the Miami convention in August. All the skill, influence and money the Rockefeller machine could command would be required to do it.

This way to the Presidency had never in recent years succeeded. Already a poll of the loyalties among delegates expected at Miami showed that Nixon commanded 621 out of 1,333, just 46 short of the total number needed to secure the nomination in August. Rockefeller's showing: 434 delegates. Could Rockefeller stop Nixon? It was the question being asked everywhere across the country, except in the quietly carpeted suites of offices where the Rockefeller machine purred imperturbably on. There it was hardly ever mentioned. The Rockefeller forces were still not campaigning anywhere, nor was there any intention of starting. The Governor was not a candidate. But across the country a spontaneous campaign for Rocky, a yardstick for his nomination chances, was under way.

He would see how the write-ins went in New Hampshire. But the vote there would make little difference to him. To Nixon, on the other hand, it meant a great deal. He would have preferred to trounce Romney at the polls and so secure a massive victory. But that was of little importance. What was important was that the new low-key, good-humored Dick Nixon had been on show for a month—and everyone was agreeably surprised. Indeed Nixon was meeting with something he had encountered seldom before: affection.

His was not a showy campaign like Romney's, nor was it an original one like McCarthy's. It was solid and professional. It did not make too many headlines, but at that stage Nixon did not want headlines. In any case, the headlines in New Hampshire belonged to McCarthy.

The men who began the McCarthy drive in New Hampshire were David Hoeh, thirty-year-old associate director of public affairs at Dartmouth College, who had toyed with state politics before; and Gerry Studds, also thirty, a history teacher at St. Paul's School in Concord.

Both men were young, enthusiastic, energetic—eager for change. Both were impatient of the conservatism that permeated the Democratic machine in the state; both saw in McCarthy a chance of protesting at least against the authority of men like Governor John King and State Senator Tom McIntyre, both strong Johnson loyalists.

The only headquarters that the limited McCarthy budget could afford was a disused and decaying storefront on Pleasant Street Extension, off Main Street in the state capital, Concord. The former tenants had left for a more advantageous site. By mid-January Hoeh and Studds had taken over. Across the drab gray-painted brick front, they stretched the red, white, and blue banner reading "McCarthy for President." In the next few days the first of the student staff arrived to begin from scratch the sort of political organization that could cost wealthier candidates millions of dollars to achieve. First came Sam Brown, later organizer of the McCarthy student working force. With him came the first volunteers.

Just back from the Peace Corps in India was John Barbieri, 23. He arrived by bus with $20 and call-up papers instructing him to report for induction February 27. With the help of the organization, Barbieri had his call-up postponed until March 20, after the primary; he set about organizing a mass mailing campaign to 100,000 homes across the state.

From the physics laboratory at Cornell University came 25-year-old Joel Feigenbaum. He used the analytical techniques of the lab to organize the door-to-door canvassing campaign. Typical of the first girls to join was graduate student Dianne Dumonoski. Dianne had traveled in Europe, taught Negro children in the South, and demonstrated with the peace marchers at the Pentagon.

"I was looking around for something else to do. We had heard vaguely about McCarthy; then I was told there was a Students for McCarthy representative on the campus. I called to see him out of curiosity—and he asked me if I could leave for Concord in an hour." Dianne went, with a sleeping bag and one suitcase. She spent the next six weeks sharing a home with a Concord family on the "help McCarthy" list. Her office task was to organize and assign the student volunteers who were expected to pour into the state to join the "children's crusade."

The first jobs were thankless enough. The early volunteers—they numbered about fifty—set out in the snow to find every town and village hall in the state. In ill-lit filing rooms they copied out by hand the lists of Democratic and independent voters. The results began to trickle back into the Pleasant Street headquarters—half a dozen names here, a score there, hundreds from the town wards. Helpers in Pleasant Street laboriously typed out the growing lists.

The candidate's early showings were rated poor by the kindest critics. His speeches lacked bite, his electioneering lacked style, and the opinion polls were giving him a maximum of 12 percent of the Democratic vote: symptoms of a cause lost before it ever really saw the light of day.

But, little by little, the McCarthyites were compiling a complete

89

dossier on the identity and whereabouts of every Democratic and independent voter in New Hampshire. The results were logged in colored crayon on huge wall sheets. Each county, each town, each village, and each ward was charted with details of registered Democrats and independents and beside them an analysis of the area's 1964 voting returns.

Copying and adding machines and even a calculator were moved in. A group of Yale students "borrowed" the university's electronic brain and programmed it to discover from past voting records which areas were likely to be most open to the McCarthy challenge.

The machinery was in place for one of the most astonishing grass-roots operations in the history of American politics. The aim of the McCarthy crusaders was quite simply to visit in person every household with a potential McCarthy voter and to explain to its members on their doorstep just what McCarthyism meant and why it was essential to consider it as an alternative policy in 1968.

There was good reason for this direct appeal. One month before polling day few voters in New Hampshire knew who McCarthy was (an alarming number thought that he was some sort of reincarnation of the late Senator Joseph McCarthy, the notorious anti-Communist witch hunter of the 1950s), and even fewer had any idea of what his policies really were.

To achieve such a goal required a labor force unmatched even in the most expensive political circuses. But from New England universities like Yale and Harvard, from colleges like Radcliffe and Smith, from Washington, D.C., from Columbia University in New York, from midwestern campuses like Michigan and Ohio State, the volunteers began to pour in, as Sam Brown's Students for McCarthy organizers went to work. They came by Greyhound bus or hitchhiked across the states.

Anyone who could lay hands on an automobile was urged to bring it too. Some came in old jalopies; others borrowed the family cars—with or without permission. To the open and growing alarm of McCarthy's professional entourage—"We were none of us quite sure just where it was going to stop or how it might rebound on us in the form of offended voters," said campaign manager Blair Clark later—the student army in New Hampshire grew to more than 2,000 strong ten days before the balloting. Some were weekend workers only; others cut classes or simply dropped out of school to join the McCarthy cause. Their ages ran from 17 to 25 and up—about half were old enough to vote themselves. Brown remarked, "They are all arriving sober—an unprecedented phenomenon in students."

McCarthy calculated on election eve that the average I.Q. rating of his volunteer army was 162, "and that is about fifty higher than the average at the White House."

Most of the students who rallied to Pleasant Street Extension had already been activists in the series of peace marches and youth demonstrations that marked 1967. Many had been among the 10,000 demonstrating before the Pentagon. Others had led the protest marches through New York City. Some had involved themselves actively in the civil-rights issue, teaching in Negro schools or working in the ghettos.

But now they were involved in something quite different. They were engaged in the processes of democratic government, taking part in activities that only six months earlier they would have spurned. Politics had seemed to the majority to offer no scope for effective protest, an activity to be left in the hands of the adults who had captured and corrupted it.

The candidate's daughter Mary summed up the changing attitude of her generation: "Demonstrations are one thing, but power lies in the vote. That is what the kids are realizing. That is why they are all here."

When Senator McCarthy finally comes to weigh his achievements in 1968, this one must count heavily among them. McCarthy called for—and worked toward—"the bridging of the generation gap." The evidence of New Hampshire suggested that he was doing just that—and significantly more. For not only young people were joining ranks behind him. A notable cross section of the academic community of America was also rallying to his cause.

To tens of thousands of university professors, teachers, and administrators across the nation, the mild-mannered McCarthy, with his quiet intellectual approach and his refusal to join in what he dismissed as "the razzmatazz" of politics, was a natural choice. In the America of 1968 these men and women no longer rated insignificantly in the power structure of the nation. Colleges were among the fastest growing institutions in the land. Education was America's biggest industry. The academics were for the most part profoundly disturbed at what was happening at home and in Vietnam. They were in a position to transmit that disquiet not only to the students but through them to millions of families. They were in a position to exercise enormous power and influence both directly through their writing and speeches and indirectly in their contributions to the thinking that shaped political campaigns, including McCarthy's.

On those frost-nipped days in New Hampshire the issues were beginning to emerge and to take shape. It was becoming evident that, as the showdown among the multitude of power units that make up American society approached, a new and significant force had to be reckoned with: the community of intellectuals who were no longer prepared to stand aloof from the political processes of America.

But, just as the thinking of the students, the shock troops of this revolution, had changed so now did their habits. The power they sought lay in the hands of the rural and urban middle-class voters of New Hampshire, people to whom the hippy image was repugnant. To alienate them would be suicidal.

Ann Hart, the five-foot, twenty-year-old daughter of Michigan Democratic Senator Philip Hart, was put in charge of the necessary transformation. As the kids poured into the Pleasant Street Extension, she would line them up for a critical inspection. Beards were banned for canvassing; brethren who sported them were politely but firmly told that jobs would be found for them indoors in the postal department unless they shaved them off. Miniskirts were frowned upon if they rose to more than two inches above the knee, and in the early days many hems were let down for McCarthy! Slogans were everywhere. "Be neat for Gene—and press your pants." "Be clean for Gene—and get your hair cut." Some young men even cold-shaved their beards on arrival in the first ecstasy of the new cause.

Ahead was only hard work. Ann Hart lost eighteen pounds in three weeks of New Hampshire duty. And conditions were far from comfortable. The boys slept in sleeping bags on the floors of church halls and gymnasiums hired or lent by churches and local authorities. Girls were put up in McCarthy supporters' homes. "Those who came for a love-in didn't stay very long," said Dianne Dumonoski.

For the visitor the exhilaration and enthusiasm were totally

92

infectious. Here were the vitality and idealism of America combined in these tremendous young people; they gave an entirely new dimension to politics. New Hampshire had never seen anything like it before, and neither had America or the world.

The line that the young canvassers were told to plug was that Eugene McCarthy was offering "an alternative" to President Johnson. The word "alternative" was indeed a key word in the whole McCarthy operation, much more so than the name of Vietnam itself. A poll after the voting showed that only 22 percent of the McCarthy support was a result of his stand on the war. The vote was basically an anti-Johnson vote and reflected growing irritation and resentment throughout the country at the Johnson regime and its apparent inability to deal with the issues that combined to harass and frustrate the American voter.

The Tet offensive in Vietnam had rocked every voter and reopened the credibility issue. The administration had long been claiming that the war was being won, yet in the week immediately before the New Hampshire vote America lost a record 542 soldiers killed in Vietnam—a fact that the young canvassers played on hard. ("But do you think the moral issues involved are really worth the lives of 542 American boys?") Then, astoundingly, just two days before the vote it was reported that General Westmoreland had requested another 200,000 troops for the war. To meet any such demand would have involved a massive call-up of reserves and an extension of the draft. Every parent of a young son had cause to worry.

Of course, for everyone prepared to listen there were two who did not want to hear. But the McCarthy brigade was compiling an even more detailed analysis of the vote potential. Each address visited was rated on a five-point scale—from number one ("favorable to McCarthy") and number two ("uncertain but possibly favorable to McCarthy") to number five ("unfavorable to McCarthy"). These returns were also being fed to the Pleasant Street Extension, where they were carefully analyzed.

All was going well, but there was a big problem: money. Already the campaign in New Hampshire had, by Hoeh's reckoning, cost about $160,000 for radio and television spots (the local stations were demanding cash before the transmission of any political propaganda). Hoeh said: "It's not a lot, but it's a heap more than we originally budgeted. I don't yet quite see who is going to pay

93

the telephone bill, the rent, or the electricity charges." At that stage too McCarthy had at last decided to go all out for victory and was buying more radio and television time.

His main backers were Howard Stein, the young president of the Dreyfus Fund (who installed a Wall Street ticker tape in his room at the Sheraton Wayfarer, where he cranked away at copying machines turning out McCarthy literature), who was said to have contributed $100,000; Arnold Hiatt, vice-president of the Green Shoe Manufacturing Co. of Boston; bearded Martin Peretz, a Harvard social scientist with independent means, who gave a fund-raising cocktail party for McCarthy in Boston; Lyndon Johnson's tailor, Harry Roth; and June Degnan, a California heiress whom McCarthy subsequently appointed his national finance director. Potentially more money was available—if McCarthy showed progress.

By the beginning of March—about ten days before the primary —the smell of victory was seeping into the McCarthy camp. The polls showed increasing support. The student movement was becoming national phenomenon, as more and more young people flocked to join; the last weekend 3,000 were turned away.

Some 60,000 doorbells had been rung, and the majority of the 89,000 registered Democrats had been reached in person, or at least by mail. Most striking of all was the wave of alarm that spread through the Johnson camp which was then organizing the write-in campaign for the President; its success had been so taken for granted that little work had been done. Then a panic policy, locally known as "the overkill campaign," set in. It rebounded sorely.

Governor King opened a radio and television onslaught, branding McCarthy as unpatriotic. King called him "a spokesman of surrender" and declared that any large vote for him "will be greeted with cheers in Hanoi."

"It may be greeted with cheers in Hanoi, but they'll be cheering in a lot of other towns right across America as well," replied the urbane Gene. Bobby Kennedy—and a lot of other previously unconcerned Democrats—chimed in to defend McCarthy's right to speak out.

Finally, on election eve, in an open smear campaign, the Johnsonites attacked McCarthy for allegedly demanding a free pardon for draft dodgers who had slipped abroad. A technician at the Manchester radio station—a McCarthyite—learned what was afoot, phoned McCarthy headquarters, and alerted the Senator hours before the tapes went on the air. McCarthy was able to reply with a dignified statement before the polls opened in the morning.

By then—his friends dated it from those last ten days of the New Hampshire campaign—a subtle but unmistakable change had occurred in McCarthy. His style had become more buoyant, his step springier, his smile broader, and his speeches more telling, as he took the measure of his audience. Students had insisted all along that McCarthy "grew on you." "We like the way he deals with these issues seriously, intelligently from an intellectual base and not on a sloganizing basis. The cheering is over. This is the sort of guy we need—a man who takes time out to read books," said one graduate helper from Harvard.

McCarthy had become keenly aware that he was no longer an asterisk at the head of an amorphous band of rebels but a man becoming an accepted leader in his own right. He even consented to appear in an ice-hockey match after supporters had distributed thousands of plastic windscreen scrapers showing McCarthy on skates above the slogan "McCarthy cuts the ice."

Everywhere he saw evidence of an imminent moderate triumph at the polls (he said later that he had believed through the last week that he would top 30 percent). Eugene McCarthy was no longer merely a protester. He was a full-fledged Presidential candidate.

"I believe I can make it to the convention and beyond," he said just after the primary, which gave him an impressive 42 percent of the Democratic vote. (A postvote survey by pollster Louis Harris revealed that McCarthy lost voters over 35 years of age to Johnson by 51 to 38 percent but carried the under-35 vote 49 to 44 percent. High-school-educated voters went against him 55 to 35 percent but college-educated voters were behind him 51 to 42 percent.) The high horse of principle that he had mounted with so many misgivings in November had become in New Hampshire a white charger, which his supporters believed capable of carrying him to the gates of the most important castle in the world.

95

.7.

Once Again the Round Table

The word on everyone's lips that night was "beautiful." As a late New England blizzard swirled outside, it passed from mouth to mouth among the young, motley, and excitable followers packing the halls, corridors, bars, and conference rooms of the handsome and expensive Sheraton Wayfarer Hotel.

It started with the candidate's daughter Mary. As McCarthy acknowledged the first round of youthful cheers, she slipped onto the platform, threw her arm round his neck, and whispered, "You are beautiful, Daddy, just beautiful." She had played a deep and not yet fully understood role in the drama that led up to that night. She had earned the right to offer first congratulations.

From there the word spread through the jostling, eager crowd, among the sophomores in their bright skirts and colored wool tights, among the graduate students with ties pulled away from open collars, among the hugging couples helping themselves to endless Coca-Cola in paper cartons from the soda machine: "It's beautiful, man. It's just the most beautiful night I've ever lived."

Plump and jolly Mary Lou Oates, the assistant press secretary, who had worked three days and three nights without sleep, sat in the bar beside her boyfriend, Bruce Page, over a bourbon on the rocks. She was sobbing and laughing with elation. "We no longer have a contender. We have a candidate," she said.

The reason for all this exuberance could be found by following the footbridge that led over the waterfall and old mill pond on the hotel grounds to the conference suite, now taken over by the telex network, the adding machines, the calculators, and the banks of telephones belonging to the combined television services.

There the results of the New Hampshire Presidential primary election were being received, sifted, and analyzed by the computers and flashed onto the big master scoreboard before the viewers of the nation. From there the figures were relayed across the bridge to the hotel's coffee-and-sandwich room, transformed into the election-night headquarters of Senator Eugene McCarthy. There, on a board made of pieces of colored paper clipped out all that day by the Senator's attendant army of student volunteers, the figures were revealed to the heaving mass of young supporters. Klieg lamps lit and overheated the scene. Movie and television cameras closed in upon it; the Huntley-Brinkley news report, the nation's top news-and-comment program, was being broadcast live from there that night.

But it was the figures that entranced the excited audience. Starting with the first trickle of results—from Portsmouth, the only town in New Hampshire with electronic counting machines, and from Laconia, a rural township in mid-state—it slowly became apparent that something much more significant than most had ever dared to hope for was happening in New Hampshire.

The first results showed Eugene McCarthy, the Vietnam peace crusader from Minnesota, receiving an astonishing 40 percent of the vote against the President of the United States, Lyndon B. Johnson. The kids cheered as pundits warned that, with only 12 percent of the votes in, it was far too early to draw conclusions. The percentages could still change radically.

But such change did not come. As the city results began to trickle in, particularly those from the textile towns of Manchester, where a virulent campaign had been conducted against the mild-mannered Senator—the percentage did begin to dip. But at 36 per-

97

cent they stuck fast. And, as the night wore on and the Coca-Cola machine was refilled, it climbed again. The computers spelled out their unchallengeable message: The Senator was assured of more than 40 percent of the total Democratic vote in New Hampshire.

It was then that he came onto the platform beneath the colored-paper scoreboard for the first time. The man who had been called a "joke" only one month before, the man without a political friend in America who would seriously back his quest, was fighting his way into the room before a phalanx of movie men, cameramen and a press corps more than 100 strong, all eager to pump his hand and gather the first victorious quotes. His aides, who had previously begged for publicity for their candidate, began to push and struggle to help their man through the narrow door garlanded with red and blue streamers. Eugene McCarthy was handling his first outward signs of political success well.

On the platform it seemed for a moment that the man whom many had chided for his pedantic speaking—he still liked to quote Sir Thomas More at length in his speeches—had been transformed. He gave what looked very like the V sign as the audience screamed, "Victory, victory!" and "We want Gene, we want Gene!"

He told them what they wanted to hear: "I have been helped by the most intelligent volunteers in the history of U.S. politics." He said that he had always believed that he could bridge the "generation gap" and that now he was proving it: "I think the returns are not only encouraging but what we deserved because of the sort of campaign we put on. We started out with confidence that if people would listen to the case we were making they would respond."

Respond they did. When the final results were verified next morning, McCarthy had won a total of 22,810—42 percent of the 54,333 Democratic votes cast. President Johnson's share was 48 percent, or 26,337 votes. More important on the bread-and-butter level of American politics was that McCarthy, even with his minority vote, had captured 20 of the 24 convention delegates from New Hampshire; they were pledged to vote for him on the first nominating ballot for the Democratic Presidential candidate.

This victory was achieved entirely through another gross blunder by the Johnson organization men. In New Hampshire there are, in effect, two elections: the "beauty contest" vote for the Presidential choice and another, practically more important, vote for delegates to the national convention. On the Democratic ballot the McCarthyites had entered in every district the same tightly controlled "slate" of 24 delegate names, the exact number to be elected. The Johnsonites, in contrast, had allowed each district to draw up its own slate. The result was that McCarthy's supporters voted solidly for the McCarthy "slate," whereas Johnson's greater support was split over a wide field. When the votes were counted, the McCarthy group had racked up the victory. Almost simultaneously it was announced that the McCarthy organization had won fifteen delegates at the Minnesota state convention.

As the students hitched lifts and boarded buses to leave the scene of victory and Eugene McCarthy planned his return to Washington, it was clear that whatever the future would bring, a very important change had already been wrought by the New Hampshire primary in the thinking, attitudes, and interests that are constantly at work inside the complex political machine of the United States. This accomplishment alone was probably more than Senator Eugene McCarthy had ever hoped for when he set out.

He had demonstrated that within the framework of the Democratic Party itself (and presumably on the national political scene as a whole) there existed a profound mistrust of the manner in which the Johnson administration was managing the nation's affairs. In spite of opinion polls that seemed to point consistently in the opposite direction, he had proved that there was a significant segment of the electorate that yearned for a quick and resolute end to the war in Vietnam. That he had done so in the Granite State of conservatism, of reserved but steely loyalties to federal principles, made the lesson yet more striking. That he had done so with a paid campaign staff of five in the teeth of national and local opposition from the Democratic Party's established leaders; on a pinch-penny budget; and with an organization comprising some 500 undergraduates and graduate students, reinforced on weekends by massive influxes of manpower from universities throughout the Northeast, made this primary unique in the political history of America.

Inevitably, the whole affair was dubbed "the children's crusade," and the candidate was not above calling himself Peter the Hermit, in reference to the mad monk who led that ill-fated medieval ex-

99

pedition to the Holy Land. But the modern crusade reminded Americans that, since the Johnson landslide of 1964, 12 million young Americans had been added to the voting registers; by 1972 another 13 million (only about half the McCarthy volunteers enjoyed the vote) would swell that total. Most of these young people, held ideas and principles foreign and even perhaps repugnant to the established order. They were no longer prepared to stay silent and inactive. In New Hampshire they tasted first blood: By reason and persuasion they had swayed many of their elders.

One young Harvard man said that victory night: "We were not prepared to tolerate their indifference to us much longer. Had they not listened to us this summer there would have been troubles. But now perhaps it is changing."

As the young staff members turned in, six to a room in one wing of the Sheraton Wayfarer, it was plain that the children's crusade was on the march.

Down at the Sheraton Carpenter Hotel in Manchester, where Johnson's campaign manager, Bernard Boutin, was staying, all was gloom as results poured in. Boutin delayed to the last moment phoning the results to Johnson aide Marvin Watson at the White House. Hopes that Johnson would carry the northern town of Berlin had proved unfounded. By 10:40 P.M. one of the two bars provided for the Johnson "victory" celebrations had closed; there were only 26 people left drinking in the Johnson camp.

Meanwhile McCarthy asked for poet Robert Lowell on the telephone. Lowell was the first to hear the victory news from McCarthy himself. Minutes after McCarthy had hung up, the phone rang, with a call from New York. It was 12:20 A.M., and the caller was Bobby Kennedy. There was a desultory conversation. Bobby congratulated McCarthy on his success. McCarthy said afterward, "Kennedy made a tired crack about 'all those mornings at the factory gates.'"

Pressman Sy Hersh commented, "When you've just had a political success no one wants to hear from Bobby Kennedy."

It was the first reminder to the McCarthy group that in New York, far from the scene of the action, others had been closely following the course of the New Hampshire campaign. But still no one forsaw the events of the next 24 hours. No one imagined that Kennedy was about to cut in on McCarthy.

Lowenstein had himself visited Bobby at Hickory Hill about

three weeks earlier. There had been what Lowenstein described as "a very emotional exchange of views; we were both swallowing very hard, and Bobby was very worked up." Kennedy said that he could see no way of running against Johnson; a declaration would look like the extension of a personal vendetta, and there seemed little chance of winning on the main issues: the conduct of the Vietnam war and of the internal affairs of the nation.

Kennedy added, as Lowenstein recalls, "Now your friend McCarthy has ruined everything because he cannot win in New Hampshire—the result can only be that he will make Johnson look even more powerful."

Lowenstein replied: "You do as you want. But those of us who have the honor of the country and the world at stake cannot sit this one out, and we are not doing so." Lowenstein repeated afterward that to his mind Kennedy's instinct was then—as it had always been—to run, but his assessment of the political power of the protesters was hopelessly at fault.

The people around Kennedy kept insisting that an incumbent President could not have the nomination snatched away from him. It had not happened in 84 years, since Chester A. Arthur had lost the nomination to James G. Blaine. Kennedy could not risk blotting his record for 1972 by splitting the party in 1968; that was the consensus among the "Irish Mafia" that still kept in touch through long-distance telephone calls and dinner-party meetings. But events were moving fast. First there had been the Tet offensive, which completely exploded the administration's propaganda on the Vietnam war. Then came the capture of the American "spy ship" *Pueblo* by the North Koreans and two days later a call-up of 14,787 air-force and navy reservists.

While the Tet offensive was still raging, Kennedy consulted his appointments diary. On Thursday, February 8, he was to speak at a book-and-author luncheon in Chicago, a good platform in the Midwest. He called in Adam Walinsky and speech writer Richard Goodwin (who later joined McCarthy) and, in the calm of his Senate office, outlined for them what he wanted to say about Vietnam and the illusions that had been destroyed by the Tet offensive.

Previous major policy speeches on the war had been committee jobs; nuances had been kicked around by the Kennedy "brain trust," subtleties had been honed, and always the result had failed to say what Kennedy really felt about the war. Instead it always reflected how far he thought he could go without splitting the party or inviting charges of treason from the President.

In the Chicago speech he abandoned that caution. Fighting from the opening paragraph, Kennedy said, "Our enemy, savagely striking at will across all of South Vietnam, has finally shattered the mask of official illusion with which we have concealed our true circumstances even from ourselves." He attacked the Johnson administration's claim that the Tet offensive had been a Communist failure because it had been unable to ignite a popular uprising against the Americans. Kennedy said, "How ironic it is that we should claim a victory because a people whom we have given twenty thousand lives, billions of dollars, and almost a decade to defend did not rise in arms against us."

The speech was well received by the members of the writing fraternity at the lunch. It was also praised in editorials across the country. And the next day, to his delight, Kennedy learned that more than one thousand congratulatory telegrams had been sent to his office in Washington. This warm response demonstrated how potent any end-the-war policy would be at the ballot box.

On Thursday, February 29, L.B.J.'s commission to examine the 1967 race riots in American cities issued its report. After eight months of hearings the commission, under the chairmanship of Illinois Governor Otto Kerner and aided by a strong panel of legislators and officials like New York Mayor John Lindsay, had come to a strong, though rather obvious, conclusion. America, the commission found, was in danger of becoming two societies: "one white, one black, separate but unequal." Massive infusions of funds were needed to give blacks more education, welfare, jobs, and housing, the commission declared.

The report produced headlines and comment everywhere, except publicly from the White House. L.B.J. alone among politicians, had nothing to say. Not until five days later did he pass any comment, and then he said only that he welcomed the report. By then the report was selling, as an instant paperback, at the rate of 100,-000 copies a day. It was a talking point everywhere. Yet President Johnson promised no action.

Coming on top of the disillusion of the Tet offensive, Johnson's silence on the Kerner report was the second big landmark that made Bobby want to run. By the first week of March the emptiness suffered by Kennedy and his aides after his decision not to run was disappearing. A new momentum was picking up. On Monday,

March 4, they received the results of a secret private poll taken in California. It showed that Kennedy could defeat the forces of Johnson and McCarthy in a three-way primary race in America's most populous state.

The findings were not enough to convince the bulk of the "Irish Mafia," but two members were swayed by them. They were Manhattan lawyer Fred Dutton, of whom Kennedy had said, "He has one of the best political brains in America," and Kenneth O'Donnell, a former White House aide to J.F.K., another lawyer who preferred working behind the political scenes to practicing law. The poll, the Tet offensive, and the riot report convinced them that Kennedy should run.

Another argument began to emerge: that if Kennedy did not run he would ruin his chances for 1972 rather than enhancing them by preserving the unity of the Democratic Party. With McCarthy a declared peace candidate, the argument ran, Kennedy could not stand on the sidelines preaching against the morality of the war but hanging back from action because the time was politically inconvenient. Dutton said later that he was personally worried about the 12 million or so Americans who would have the Presidential vote for the first time in 1968. Millions of them were among Kennedy's warmest supporters, the students and recent graduates to whom he made more sense than any other politician.

Dutton became convinced that to deny them the opportunity to vote for their hero in 1968, the year in which they wanted to end the war in Vietnam, would irreparably damage Kennedy. Those 12 million, possibly disenchanted with Kennedy forever, would pose a permanent problem. This bitterness would also influence the young people who would be eligible to vote for the first time in 1972 but who, though voteless in 1968, were still eager to turn out at campus meetings to give Kennedy the ecstatic welcomes that later became a feature of his campaign. To alienate these two blocs, these two generations of the young, would have been disastrous, Dutton argued.

But Dutton and O'Donnell were alone among the senior advisers. Theodore Sorensen, the scholarly author of so many of President Kennedy's best speeches, and a man who exulted in politics, was against the Senator's running. So were Teddy Kennedy and Steve Smith (husband of sister Jean), who had masterminded Bobby's brilliant senatorial campaign in New York State in 1964. Arthur Schlesinger, Jr., was against it, and so were Robert McNamara,

103

labor leader **Walter Reuther,** and William vanden Heuvel, another lawyer.

On Tuesday, March 5, despite this opposition, Kennedy asked Teddy and the staff to start making discreet inquiries among Democratic Party leaders across the nation. When, inevitably, this maneuver leaked out (in *Newsweek's* "Periscope"), Kennedy's office blandly explained that staff members were just trying to establish the primary procedures from state to state, so that they would know how to eliminate Kennedy's name from the lists should enthusiastic locals seek to put him on the ballot. This explanation was patently ridiculous. It was inconceivable that Kennedy, after plotting his brother's campaign for four years, did not know the primary laws like the back of his hand. But if he or his staff did not they could be looked up in any reference library in Washington.

In fact every state Democratic Party chairman across the country was being tested for his reaction to a possible Kennedy challenge to the President. Not surprisingly, this casual poll produced many "no"s, a turndown from almost every state in the Union. But one could not really expect party chairmen, well aware of the potential wrath of L.B.J., to cast aside all political discretion and say yes to an uncommitted and unannounced Kennedy.

Even worse for Kennedy, however, the dovish senators who were sounded out in Washington were equally reluctant to associate themselves with him. Idaho's Frank Church turned him down flat. Only one, Senator Joseph Clark of Pennsylvania, gave Kennedy a pledge of support. That was on March 5.

On Sunday, March 10, Robert Kennedy, aged 42, in peak physical condition, still tanned from his late-January skiing holiday, was on the brink of a tumultuous week in American politics.

Kennedy spent the weekend of March 9 at Hickory Hill, his farmhouse-style home across the Potomac River and twelve miles from the center of Washington, with his wife Ethel and all ten children. They did not know that it was to be the last normal family weekend of his life. With the Irish fatalism ever present beneath the Kennedy's New World vigor Bobby never forgot that life is at the mercy of events. The memory of Dallas and the awareness that it could be repeated were always in his mind. But, buried deep, they did not interfere with his enjoyment of his family.

On Tuesday he and Ethel sat up and watched the television reports from New Hampshire. The result surprised, even astonished,

104

him. He picked up the phone and made a call to congratulate McCarthy.

The next day was frantic with activity. It began at 6:00 A.M. with phone calls. They went on all morning. The whole Washington press corps was trying to corner Kennedy. At 11:45 he allowed newsmen to confront him in a corridor of the new Senate Office Building. Was he going to run for President? His precise answer: "I am reassessing the possibility of whether I will run against President Johnson."

Kennedy's timing was undoubtedly inept. McCarthy was not allowed to savor even twelve hours of glory before Kennedy stole the headlines. His announcement, coming when it did, seemed self-serving, and it triggered immediate resentment, particularly among McCarthy's young supporters.

On the same Wednesday morning Kennedy explained in a brief interview with *The New York Times* that he had previously refrained from becoming a candidate out of fear that he would split the party "in a very damaging way." He would have looked like "a spoiler," as if he were conducting a personal campaign against the President. But the McCarthy vote made it obvious that the party was already split. Kennedy said: "The primary demonstrated that there is a deep division in the party. It clearly indicates that a sizable group of Democrats are concerned about the direction the country is going."

At 5:00 P.M. Kennedy confirmed that his comment about "reassessing" had not been a slip of the tongue. His Senate office issued rather detailed reasons for such reassessment. As spelled out by his press secretary, Frank Mankiewicz, they were:

1. Profound concern over the Vietnam war, underlined by the Tet offensive and testimony given the previous week by Secretary of State Dean Rusk to the Senate Foreign Relations Committee, which showed no crack in the administration's official war policy. (Dragging in Rusk was rather gratuitous. Kennedy had known that there was no policy change without waiting for Rusk to tell him.)
2. Concern at L.B.J.'s silence on the Kerner report.
3. Concern that Richard Nixon, who as Republican contender was leading all opinion polls, would offer no suitable alternative to L.B.J's policies.
4. The extreme personal discomfort that he would feel at failing to take up the fight, in view of all the circumstances.

105

Meanwhile McCarthy arose at 9:00 A.M. and held a press conference at the Sheraton Wayfarer. He was at once asked—and pressed for an answer—whether or not he believed that Robert Kennedy would step into the race. "You'd better ask him about that" was the reply. He restated that he would not step down and denied for what seemed the thousandth time that he was a "stalking horse" for Kennedy.

At lunchtime he left for Washington, having heard the first news of Kennedy's reassessment statement before boarding. Unruffled, he lunched in the first-class cabin and read poetry. When he arrived in Washington, he noticed for the first time that one of his fellow passengers was Tom McIntyre, the Johnson loyalist behind the last "draft dodgers" smear campaign. "You've got no cause to be traveling first class today," Senator McCarthy quipped and jauntily stepped down the ramp.

On the tarmac an aide handed him a full copy of the Kennedy announcement. He drove to his Senate office, where he had no sooner arrived than he received a call from Kennedy asking if they could talk. McCarthy invited him to drop in. A few minutes later there was another call. Could they meet in Teddy Kennedy's office, neutral ground in a way? McCarthy agreed.

It was a cold encounter. Kennedy congratulated McCarthy once again. McCarthy thanked him. Silence ensued. Then Kennedy spoke: "You've read my statement?" McCarthy nodded. "Well I want to say in the light of events that I have no alternative but to reassess my position." He talked on about the split in the party and the need for change.

If either man had thought that there might be an opening for an alliance, he was disappointed. After fifteen minutes McCarthy left, and reporters noticed that his hands were shaking. He went straight home, still outwardly urbane to the tagalong press, but underneath he was seething.

He knew that Kennedy's mind was made up. It seemed an act of piracy backed up by the magic of the Kennedy legend, the Kennedy fortune, and the ruthless political strategy of the "Irish Mafia."

At 6:30 P.M. on that seemingly unending Wednesday Kennedy left the Senate Office Building for the C.B.S. Washington studio to appear on Walter Cronkite's 7:00 news show. The interview lasted eleven and a half minutes and was an emotional and affecting appearance. Kennedy told Cronkite: "We have to move in a different direction. I think that some of those in the administration are now cut off from some of these other possibilities . . . which would be in the interest of our people and the interest of world peace."

As Kennedy went on the air, the practicalities of organizing a White House campaign from scratch were being weighed by that old gang of President Kennedy's. It convened from 7:00 onward at 950 Fifth Avenue, in Steve Smith's apartment.

Edward Kennedy was there; so was Pierre Salinger, J.F.K.'s old press secretary and then a vice-president of Continental Airlines. Historian Schlesinger was there, and so was O'Donnell. Theodore Sorensen was there even as the White House was trying to trace him in connection with a policy matter.

Fred Dutton described the scene later:

> People drifted in and out all evening. Sometimes the group all talked together; other times they broken into smaller groups. A lot of conversation concentrated on whether Kennedy should run. Some people were still not convinced he should. Sorensen was against. Teddy was against, but would swing behind the family name if Bobby decided to go.

After Cronkite's show Kennedy drove to Washington National Airport and took the 8:00 shuttle to New York. He went straight to the caucus at Smith's apartment, staying until 1:00 A.M. He told the group that conflict with L.B.J. would be brutal, an uncompromising blood letting. By that evening Kennedy was also well aware that the charge of opportunism and of riding on McCarthy's success would be an added problem, at least for a while. He was disappointed that his old supporters, apart from O'Donnell and Dutton, were still not completely convinced that he should run. But each man gave him an assurance that night that, if he did decide to run, he could rely upon 100 percent support and help.

Kennedy flew back to Washington the next morning and went to his suite of offices in the Senate Office Building. He had six interconnecting rooms in that rather clinical place. The corridor and the front office—the one with "Please Walk In" on the door— were under seige from newsmen all day. There was an air of frenetic activity in the whole operation. Mankiewicz and Walinsky buzzed in and out of doors like flies—but with no time for more than a word with old friends and no time at all for strangers. The secretaries, mostly attractive and in their mid-twenties, spent hour after hour fielding phone calls from the press and from well-wishers and cranks.

By midafternoon more than 2,000 telegrams had arrived—no accurate count was ever made—and secretary Melody Miller was sorting them into "friendly" and "unfriendly" piles. There were never more than a handful of unfriendlies; all the rest welcomed Kennedy's reassessment announcement and urged him to run. One that now yielded a classic campaign slogan came from Evanston, Illinois; it said, "We want Camelot again." Other samples: "Go, Bobby, go"; "Let's get *him* out of the White House" (a clever play on L.B.J.'s egotism and his pet dog named Him); "A Kennedy in the White House would restore truth and prestige in the world, dignity and honor to the office, and the pride we lost November 22, 1963." Melody Miller was an old hand at broadcasting and handled herself like a professional in front of a microphone. As the radio and television men had no one else to interview that day, she became the star attraction for a while, giving breathlessly enthusiastic summaries of the flood of cables.

The St. Patrick's Day weekend was coming up, and all the girls wore badges saying either "Irish Power" or "Kiss me, I'm Irish." Everyone was delighted that the Senator was getting into the race, that suddenly they had been catapulted into the campaign that they had thought they would miss. As one of the girls said quietly, "It would have been awful to spend the summer dealing with complaints from New Yorkers while the real action was being played out elsewhere."

Kennedy hardly stirred from inside his office. Teddy came at 2 P.M. and left an hour later, making no significant statement to the newsmen on his departure. Sorensen spent most of the afternoon inside. At 6:00 Kennedy walked from his office across 400 yards of lawn to the Capitol to vote on a Senate amendment. He was in no mood for talking at all. His shoulders were hunched, his hands in his pockets, his eyes fixed on the ground—a man deep in thought and relishing the chance for some fresh air and the opportunity to be left alone for a few minutes.

At 6:30 Kennedy left the Senate Office Building for Hickory Hill. He would probably have given anything for a quiet evening at home in uninterrupted thought. But three weeks earlier invitations had gone out to the editors of thirty small newspapers from upstate New York, a vast part of his constituency that he, as a U.S. senator, was always at pains to ensure was not overshadowed by the problems of New York City. The guests were due at 7:30 and could not be put off. At the last moment Kennedy invited Jack Newfield, his latest biographer, an author of the "new left," and assistant editor of *The Village Voice*.

Newfield later described the scene to the visitor:

> We were seated at separate tables, and I was put with a bunch of Republicans. They were terrible, and I began a big argument with them. Kennedy was at a nearby table and caught my eye and winked.
>
> Kennedy spent a lot of the evening out of the room and on the telephone.
>
> You know, I don't think those editors had any idea at all of the drama that was being played all around them.

The editors left around 11:30, but Newfield stayed, chatting with Mankiewicz, Ethel Kennedy, and others for another hour and a half, as Kennedy himself drifted in and out of the conversation.

When Newfield left, Kennedy came out onto the steps with him and asked, "Do you think I'm making a mistake?"

Newfield says: "I knew then he had definitely decided. I told him I thought he should run."

Next morning, on Friday, March 15—the Ides of March—Kennedy shunned the Eastern Airlines shuttle which links Washington and New York every hour and traveled first class on American Airlines 8:30 A.M. flight. Like the shuttle, this flight was as familiar to Kennedy as buses are to most people. He used it for commuting between his constituency (New York state) and the capital, and had been known to make up to a a dozen of the $18 flights in a week. He preferred American where you were served coffee and had elbow room in which to work.

Newfield went with Kennedy and later quoted several significant comments:

> To break with the party that made my brother President isn't an easy thing for me to do. I keep thinking that I represent something more than just myself, but then people say I'm doing this just out of opportunism and ambition.
>
> I just feel more natural now that I'm going to do it, now that I can react naturally to events and issues again.
>
> My brother Ted still thinks I'm a little nutty for doing this, but he's an entirely different kind of person. You just have to march to the beat of your own drummer.

Later he told the visitor that, when he discussed the whole thing with his wife, the specter of Dallas had arisen once again. "There's no knowing where this could end," he had told her.

She had looked straight at him and replied, "You should go ahead—no matter where it ends."

Kennedy added, "Only the most emotional people are really for my doing it, like Ethel, my staff, and all my sisters. . . . It was a lonely, intuitive decision. I just felt I had to run at this time. It was something inside me telling me I had to go."

From La Guardia Airport Kennedy went to Steven Smith's for another staff meeting. This time Schlesinger, Dutton, and Smith were there. Kennedy confirmed his decision to run and asked them to start thinking about organizing what became known as the "instant campaign." He told Smith, "This is going to cost us a lot of money."

But the Kennedy millions were available, and funds were not the impossible hurdle that they would have been to a nonmillionaire candidate. Later Smith organized contributions, but at the beginning the campaign was bankrolled entirely from family resources.

At 11:30 in the morning Kennedy left for a round of long-standing engagements in his constituency and what became known as "the day of the hints."

British journalists, when they first come to the United States, are astonished at the power and presumption of the American press. Many of the scenes already described could not have appeared in Britain because the press would not have been allowed to intrude. The siege of Kennedy's office would have been impossible in most Western European countries, for private offices are simply off limits to pressmen.

In their total presence, the television cameramen and newsmen seem at first to exert pressure out of all proportion to their task, as if they were manipulating the whole scene. They are like puppet masters making the politicians dance to their schedules and deadlines.

But that is only an immediate impression. Detailed observation reveals that the politicians have swiftly balanced affairs by manipulating the media to further their own aims. And a perfect example occurred on Friday, March 15.

Kennedy intended to time his announcement to hit the massive Sunday papers with their 50 percent higher sales. He also wanted prime television time on a Sunday when Americans would be watching their sets in relaxed family settings, undistracted by other affairs. But it was necessary to provide a "build up" to achieve the right kind of drama for the actual announcement. Hence the day of the hints, on which the Kennedy organization, directed by Pierre Salinger, exploited the press and television to the full.

Hint number one came at 12:30 on Friday at the mock-Tudor home of Mrs. Anita Richmond in Garden City, a leafy suburb on Long Island. Although the visit was on his schedule he was late for lunch with more than a thousand people, and he decided to cut it, with apologies to Mrs. Richmond. Then an aide from the Long Island Democratic Party told him that 75 women had been waiting an hour and a half and that a lot of nice people would be offended if he did not show up. Kennedy ordered the car to turn round.

At Mrs. Richmond's he spoke briefly of how delighted he was to be in Long Island. Then one of the women asked, "How can I help you?"

He replied, "Well you can help me in this great effort I am about to make."

The women oohed and aahed. None of them was left in any doubt that Kennedy was going to run. But when was he going to announce? That question was answered by hint number two, when Kennedy arrived at the Garden City Hotel for lunch at 1:30. Mobbed by newsmen, he promised to answer all their questions the next day. His Washington office explained that he would take over the Senate caucus room for an announcement at 10:00 A.M. Washington was quick to note that it was the same room in which his brother Jack had declared his Presidential candidacy in 1960.

The lunch was the most unlikely function in that whole unlikely week. It was held by the Sky Island Club of Long Island, which once in a while invited some celebrity to one of its huge lunches, held in the Garden City Hotel ballroom, and then exposed him— as the fall-guy—to unbridled ragging.

Kennedy was an easy target, and the hearty jokesters who formed the backbone of the club had prepared sketches lampooning his hair, religion, children, and money. At the last minute they slipped in a sketch directly related to his election reassessment, in which he was depicted trying to make political deals with everybody in the race, including Nixon and George Wallace. Kennedy laughed at that bit, but he became plainly embarrassed when three lightly clad belly dancers from a local theater made overtly sexual undulations right under his nose. He deliberately became absorbed in his notes, though later he raised a laugh by asking if he could take the girls home for his sons.

The opening monologue was by comedian Joey Adams, a second-division copy of Bob Hope, and reflected the same sort of humor. (Sample: The new Archbishop of New York had not come because he did not want to kiss Bobby's ring again.) Club members whooped with laughter, and Kennedy took it all in good stag-party spirit.

Live microphones were scattered along the top table, and one picked up hint number three. Kennedy was talking quietly to Leonard Hall, and when local radio station WMCA played back the tape, it uncovered this exchange:

Kennedy: "Do you think I'm crazy?"

Hall: "The New Hampshire primary carried a big message. What will McCarthy do?"

Kennedy: "He is going to stay in. So it's going to make it tough, much tougher."

Hall: "Are you going the primary route?"

Kennedy: "Yeah."

Kennedy was twitted by newsmen as he left the lunch about what he had said to the housewives. "I can't remember what I told them," he said.

"Well I'll remind you," said an aggressive radio reporter, and he repeated the quote. "Now what do you say about it?" the reporter asked.

"I say what you just told me," said Kennedy, making everyone laugh. It was obvious that he was not going to answer any questions until the caucus room.

After lunch he drove about three miles to Westbury Manor, an elegant roadhouse, for a reception with local Democrats. In a light-hearted, off-the-cuff speech, delivered to a modestly well-to-do gathering of about 150, he gave hint number four: "These are important days in Washington. We're very busy down there, and I'll have an announcement to make about that tomorrow morning."

"Do it now," one of the audience yelled, and Kennedy just grinned back, while everyone else laughed and cheered.

The Kennedy caravan left around 4:20 for the 5:00 shuttle. Just after 6:00 P.M. Kennedy was back at Hickory Hill, carrying the evening papers with big Kennedy headlines.

He settled down to a long staff meeting with Sorensen, Schlesinger, Mankiewicz, Dutton, Walinsky, and Jeff Greenfield, 24 years old and a year out of Yale law school, another of his speech writers. This gathering was primarily concerned with drafting Kennedy's announcement speech. Al Lowenstein was invited to come later.

He was astonished at the phoned invitation. Kennedy came straight to the point saying, "Al baby, I've decided to take your advice and run."

Lowenstein mumbled something about the timing not being very happy. Afterward he said: "I felt Bobby could only hurt himself by this policy. I didn't think it was opportunism myself. Just Bobby suddenly letting his instinct take over to get into the fight."

He hurried to the Hickory Hill meeting. Sorensen had master-minded the announcement speech, making sure that it contained no direct attack on Lyndon Johnson. Lowenstein made sure that there was no attack on McCarthy. The result was an ambivalence toward the Minnesota Senator; the line was that both men were in the race and a decision was up to the voters.

Lowenstein warned that McCarthy would take the news badly and that anti-Johnson forces might be so badly split that their efforts would cancel each other out. It was essential he said that McCarthy be told in advance exactly what was to happen and how it was to be presented. Kennedy agreed. McCarthy must be told that night and who better to tell him than the candidate's brother Teddy?

Messages were sent to McCarthy, then campaigning in Wisconsin, to expect Teddy, who left the house that moment to fly to Chicago, where he took a small chartered plane to the rendezvous with McCarthy. McCarthy was not to alert the press and spoil the announcement.

So McCarthy quietly left his entourage at the Executive Inn at Sheboygan, on the shores of Lake Michigan, and motored sixty miles up the lake to Green Bay, where he was due next day. The explanation given to the abandoned press corps was that he had gone to join Mrs. McCarthy, who had been speaking in Green Bay and was staying there overnight.

Shortly after 1:00 A.M. a C.B.S. television team that had gone to Green Bay to cover a scheduled McCarthy appearance the next morning, in which he was to answer the Kennedy challenge, was astonished to see Edward Kennedy and two of McCarthy's aides—

Blair Clark and Dick Goodwin—mounting the freight lift to the sixth floor of the Northlands Hotel. McCarthy, thinking that Teddy might not arrive until the morning had gone to bed; awakened, he dressed hastily, leaving off his undershirt in his hurry, and received Teddy in the sitting room.

Later he said: "It was hardly worth the trip. It was kind of a goodwill mission—a courtesy call—and I appreciated very much the effort Ted Kennedy made in coming out. It was a long flight there and back to Washington simply to say what was going to be announced." Kennedy was carrying a black clip-up briefcase, and, as he was leaving the suite, McCarthy noticed that one of the two clips was open. "You'd better close that briefcase properly Senator, or people outside will think we've really been talking business," he said mildly as he showed his visitor out.

McCarthy, outwardly unflappable and witty as ever, was inwardly seething. The protest on which he had embarked had become a cause that could, he believed, carry him into the final battle for the White House. No one was going to cheat him of it now. Later McCarthy quipped bitterly, "I do not understand how the Irishman who says he is going to run against another Irishman the day before St. Patrick's Day can expect the relationship to be a peaceful one."

The battle pennants were up. Those caught in the middle were in despair. Lowenstein sat in Washington and said helplessly: "Who could have foreseen this? The only people who will benefit are the Republicans." In his depression he decided to pull out of McCarthy's campaign and concentrate on the sidelines. Those sidelines resulted in his running for Congress himself in the 5th Congressional District of New York, which he won by 4,000 votes. "I certainly do not wish to go to Bobby," he said.

Precisely at 10:00 the next day Robert F. Kennedy entered the Senate caucus room where his brother had announced his candidacy eight years before. He was wearing a lightweight suit of telegenic dark blue; Ethel trooped behind him with nine of the ten children (baby David was left at home). It was four years, three months, and twenty-three days since John Kennedy had been assassinated. During all that time, as L.B.J. was quoted as saying, Bobby had been a potential candidate. Now he would be a declared one.

Kennedy's style was crisp and purposeful. Old hands noted that

114

his hesitation, his "er-er"-ing had gone. He came to the point straight away with the same words that his brother had used: "I am announcing today my candidacy for the Presidency of the United States." Modulating the Sorensen prose nicely, Kennedy continued:

I do not run for the Presidency merely to oppose any man, but to propose new policies. I run because I am convinced that this country is on a perilous course and because I have such strong feelings about what must be done that I am obliged to do all I can. I run to seek new policies, to close the gaps between black and white, rich and poor, young and old in this country and around the world.

He talked of the disillusion over Vietnam and the ignoring of the Kerner report. Then he said, "No one who knows what I know about the extraordinary demands of the Presidency can be certain that any mortal can adequately fill it." He went on to cite his record in J.F.K.'s administration—his service on the National Security Council during the Cuban missile crisis, the Berlin crisis, the Laos conference, and the nuclear test-ban treaty. In what were to become familiar terms he spoke of the starvation of children in Mississippi and the depressed areas of Eastern Kentucky.

The most confused part of the announcement was his assurance that his campaign would not be in opposition to McCarthy's but "in harmony" with it. In California, he said, he hoped that his forces and McCarthy's would work together "in some form or another" in the primary. He would run on the same ballot as McCarthy in Oregon and Nebraska, but "In no state will my effort be directed against Senator McCarthy. Both of us are campaigning to give our forces and our party an opportunity of selecting the strongest possible standard bearer for the November election."

Finally he stressed that his decision reflected no personal animosity or disrespect toward L.B.J., who had served President Kennedy with the "utmost loyalty" and "was extremely kind to me and members of my family in the difficult months which followed the events of November 1963."

He concluded: "I do not lightly dismiss the dangers and difficulties of challenging an incumbent President. But these are not ordinary times, and this is not an ordinary election. At stake is not

115

simply the leadership of our party or even our country—it is our right to moral leadership on this planet."

The irrevocable decision, the first step toward the tragedy in the kitchen of Los Angeles' Ambassador Hotel—had been taken.

In Wisconsin McCarthy watched, still outwardly cool and inwardly enraged. He fingered his mouth as he listened. Then he went on "the box" himself to make a controlled and effective reply in which the bitterness peeped through:

> I am not prepared to deal with anybody so far as my candidacy is concerned. I committed myself to a group of young people and I thought a rather idealistic group of adults in American society. I said I would be their candidate, and I intend to run as I committed myself to run. . . . [to] people who were prepared to raise this challenge against the Johnson administration at a time when it seemed to me a lot of other politicians were afraid to come down into the playing field. They were willing to stay up in the mountains and light signal fires and bonfires and dance in the light of the moon. But none of them came down. They were not even coming in from outside—just throwing a message over the fence. It was a little lonely out there in New Hampshire.

Outside—and in the days that lay ahead—he needled Kennedy continually. That afternoon, sitting patiently for two hours in his campaign plane, which was grounded by a hydraulic leak in the undercarriage, he said: "I don't want Bobby Kennedy. I do not want his money nor his talent nor his organization. I just need running room; I don't want the track cluttered."

A series of cracks aimed at Kennedy were to follow. That same night McCarthy spoke at a fund-raising dinner in Indianapolis: "Today we have heard of the arrival of an alternative to the alternative. I think most Democrats will be concerned to try an alternative first." Blistering into the old days of John Foster Dulles' brinkmanship, on which McCarthy blamed many of the problems of the 1960s he said: "We are left with the legacy of his old love letters. The trouble is he'd written them to every girl in town." Later he gibed, "I have been urging for some time that the young should involve themselves more in politics. Unfortunately some people seem to be taking me too seriously."

Answering a questioner who asked if Bobby was not better qualified to be President, McCarthy poured scorn on Kennedy's government service and recalled that he had been advising his brother at the time of the disastrous Bay of Pigs expedition. "It is rather like saying we need a plumber for President because there are 54 bathrooms in the White House," he said.

McCarthy's cold and unrelenting attitude was echoed by his young campaigners. It was clear that the primary battles ahead would be bitter with no quarter given.

But the fact that the opposition was suddenly divided brought scant comfort to Lyndon Johnson in Washington. New Hampshire had shown what sort of challenge a virtually unknown senator could mount against the President. Now he faced an attack by the man who bore the most evocative name in the Democratic Party, a man with money and drive and organization. There was no longer just a revolt in the Party; there was outright civil war.

.8.

Abdication American Style

The president of the United States was openly being defied, and his politics was being challenged by not one but two charismatic members of his own party. In Washington there was only one question: How would Lyndon Baines Johnson react?

The President reacted in a way that no one anticipated. He withdrew completely from the campaign. His decision silenced his critics, staggered Washington, and reverberated around the world. What was so intriguing was that no one had considered such an eventuality—yet it was the move of a master politician.

It came at the end of a dramatic television speech in which he announced reduction of bombing over North Vietnam and an effort to scale down the war, in order to get peace talks started. He spoke for 35 minutes, and then, looking up at the camera, he said: "Finally, my fellow Americans, let me say this."

And, as on so many occasions in the past, President Lyndon Johnson invoked the memory of his predecessor John F. Kennedy.

It was a signal that Americans—and British reporters—knew only too well. The President was reaching his peroration.

Many listeners, satisfied that there would be a partial halt to the bombing, that peace was—if not around the corner—at least a faint possibility, switched off their televisions and went to bed, perhaps a little more confident than they had when they arose on that Sunday morning of March 31. And so they missed the most dramatic move of the President's entire political career.

Plainly and simply, at the close of his speech President Johnson renounced all ambition to stand once more for the most powerful elected office in the world:

> With American sons in the fields far away, with America's future under challenge right here at home, with our hopes and the world's hopes for peace in the balance every day, I do not believe that I should devote an hour or a day of my time to any personal partisan causes or to any duties other than the awesome duties of this office—the Presidency of your country.
> Accordingly, I shall not seek, and I will not accept, the nomination of my party for another term as your President.

Few secrets during President Johnson's occupancy of the White House had been better kept than this one. The Washington press corps, normally alert to events of such major significance had already filed its dispatches, based upon the advanced text of the President's speech, which included everything but the renunciation.

Yet all the signs were there and had been there for many months. Towards autumn 1967 President Johnson had perceived that his unpopularity was real. He was tired, and he was embittered. He began to weigh the alternatives before him as the election year approached. Then it became apparent that he could choose not to stand for a second term. As early as the previous autumn he had asked General Westmoreland what would be the effect of such a withdrawal on troop morale in Vietnam. George Christian, the President's press secretary, said later that in October 1967 he had actually gone so far as to make a preliminary draft of a withdrawal speech. Republican Senator Everett Dirksen remembered a drink with Mr. Johnson in his study at the White House at which the President had declared, "I'm not a candidate for anything."

Hubert Humphrey was advised to pack his bags and get on the road so that people would know who he was. All Johnson's closest

119

friends and confidants—Robert McNamara, Justice Abe Fortas, Governor John Connally of Texas, and Secretary of State Dean Rusk—knew the direction of his thinking. Few permitted themselves to believe it for more than 24 hours at a time.

Even Lady Bird Johnson, whose dearest wish it was that her husband retire for reasons of his health, did not know for sure whether or not the statement—so painstakingly prepared and dropped into the teleprompter by an army signalman only an hour before Johnson's scheduled appearance—would actually be delivered.

Once before the President had made a firm decision to renounce and then had hung back at the last moment. The distinguished columnist Drew Pearson described in *Look* the faintly bizarre circumstances surrounding this earlier incident. The President had informed his friends and aides that he would make his announcement at the close of his State of the Union message to the Congress on January 17. His original intention, said Pearson (who wrote his article after having gone to the White House for an invited chat with the President), had been to bow out rather more flamboyantly. The peroration to the ponderous State of the Union speech had been carefully worked over by the President himself, by Christian, by Special Assistant Horace Busby, and, of course, by Mrs. Johnson.

Quoting the President's explanation to Hubert Humphrey, Pearson reports:

> When I got to the right place in the message I reached into my pocket to get the excerpt and found it wasn't there. I had given it to Lady Bird before she went off to the beauty parlor. When I got back home I raised Cain with Lady Bird.
>
> "What the dickens did you do with that message?" I asked her. Then we went into the bedroom and found it by the telephone. I don't know how it got there. I guess I must have put it there myself.

The subconscious motivation that made the President "lose" the renunciation message before addressing Congress provides fascinating speculation. It certainly gave him a chance to change his mind. Perhaps he was waiting for an indication of a change in his fortunes, that the public would come round to supporting his policy. Or perhaps he was waiting for a final sign that it was time to go. If so, he got the message from New Hampshire.

The world believed, correctly or incorrectly, that the President himself—not the office but the man—was the greatest single barrier to a peaceful settlement of the Vietnam problem. When such a belief becomes widely enough held, it is transmuted into fact.

By coupling his resignation to a bombing pause the President was removing the peace talks from the arena of American domestic politics, and by this move he made it hard for the North Vietnamese to refuse to meet him.

But there was more to the move than that. In political matters President Johnson's intuition is often as sound as his vanity is grand. He was already doubting that he could win a second term. He more than anyone else—perhaps because he was the cause—sensed the unprecedented turmoil and the shocks to come in a campaign year.

The President had correctly judged that he could not secure peace while running for the Presidency. Yet only by securing peace could he win, and he knew that Hanoi would *never* hand him the one thing that would enable him to win another term. His proud Texas background made him perfectly able to gauge—with almost Oriental precision—the amount of "face" involved in the peace negotiations. The only way to get the peace talks started with any chance of success was to show the North Vietnamese his recognition that he had lost face and to renounce a second term.

"Face" has always been as important to President Johnson as to any Eastern Communist leader. He judged correctly that, although it might seem to the men in Hanoi and Peking that he was losing face by stepping down, the move would make the reverse impression in the West. He knew, too, that the way a Western politician loses face is to go down to a massive electoral defeat.

To campaign in the climate of 1968 would expose him more than ever to personal abuse, humiliation, and almost certain defeat, which he was not prepared to accept.

On the other hand, peace, if he could secure it, would have to be credited to his courageous act of self-sacrifice. That would be something for the history books. And President Johnson was intensely interested in his place in history. So he made his decision, and at 9:40 P.M. on the night of March 31 he took the plunge. The broadcast over, Lady Bird embraced him—she seemed both approving and relieved.

Around the world the news was received with absolute astonishment. The picture of a political leader setting himself up as sacrificial lamb for his fellow countrymen was sufficiently rare to silence even adepts in the fine art of the instant quotation. Of America's political leaders only Eugene McCarthy rose to the occasion: "I look upon this as a personally sad and difficult moment for a man who has given so many years to the service of his country."

The international press, save predictably for the Soviet news agency Tass, which accused Johnson of "maneuvering"—was strangely united in admiration and relief. Few questioned the President's sincerity; most applauded him warmly and wholeheartedly for facing up to the truth about himself and the world. Reading the British papers the following day, full as they were of panegyrics, Prime Minister Harold Wilson observed sourly, "I suppose that's one way of making sure one reads one's own obituaries."

Lyndon Johnson did not want to read his obituaries, but he was determined to be recorded by posterity as a statesman and not as just another politician. To that end, his decision to end the bombing had not been taken lightly but had been reached after the most detailed examination.

The story of this decision-making process illustrates the President's penchant for relying on the advice of men he trusts and working within the self-imposed confines of "consensus." Men close to L.B.J. insist that at no time in the conduct of the Vietnam war did he act on impulse, and the available evidence supports their statements.

By the beginning of March the President had rejected a plea from General Westmoreland for a major infusion of troops in Vietnam. Weighing heavily with Johnson at that stage was the opinion of former Secretary of Defense McNamara that the great American bombing fleet had failed. It was bolstered by the belief of former Undersecretary of State George Ball that the only hope for peace in Vietnam lay in political negotiation.

By the end of 1967 President Johnson had put together a small, elite band of men representing both Republican and Democratic, as well as military and civilian views; he relied on these men for strategic guidance on Vietnam. This cadre had no official title but was generally referred to in the White House as "the informal advisory group." By March 1968 President Johnson was using the group as a sounding board for advice he received from his top Cabinet and White House advisers.

The "informal advisory group" included General Omar N. Bradley, who had been theater commander in Western Europe during World War II and subsequently Army Chief of Staff; General Matthew B. Ridgway, former Commander of the 8th Army in Korea; General Maxwell D. Taylor, former Chairman of the Joint

Chiefs of Staff and close military adviser to President Kennedy; Dean Acheson, former Secretary of State to President Truman and respected consultant to all presidents since; McGeorge Bundy, former chief White House adviser to Presidents Kennedy and Johnson, now President of the Ford Foundation; C. Douglas Dillon, former Secretary of the Treasury to President Kennedy; Cyrus Vance, former Deputy Secretary of Defense (later appointed to the Paris peace-negotiating team); Arthur Dean, a New York lawyer who is a power in the Republican Party and had represented the United States at the Korean peace talks; and George Ball, former Undersecretary of State and close adviser to Presidents Kennedy and Johnson.

On the evening of March 18 these men met for dinner at the White House, with the intention of conducting a full-scale review of all aspects of the Vietnam war. They studied, with a brilliant array of administration officers, not only the status of the war but also its political and social effects at home.

President Johnson had summoned them for this vital meeting while still deliberating on his own future. Out of it came the bombing pause—and probably the arguments that made the President finally decide to renounce.

To brief the informal advisory group, the President had gathered at his dinner table what amounted to the inner corps of the National Security Council, the top policy-shaping group in the nation. Included were Secretary of State Dean Rusk; Secretary of Defense Clark Clifford; Ambassador-at-Large Averell Harriman; Undersecretary of State Nicholas Katzenbach; Assistant Secretary of State for Far Eastern Affairs William Bundy; General Earle Wheeler, Chairman of the Joints Chiefs of Staff; Richard Helms, Director of the Central Intelligence Agency; Professor Walt Rostow, Special White House Assistant for National Security Affairs; Deputy Secretary of Defense Paul Nitze; Deputy Assistant Secretary of State for Far Eastern Affairs Philip Habib; George Carver, the C.I.A.'s chief Vienam analyst; and Major General William DePuy, the Pentagon's top expert on counterinsurgency.

Remarks over the dinner table were of a general nature, coming mostly from Rusk, Clifford, and Rostow. But before dessert was served some sharp questions were being flung at the Administration men by the "group."

George Ball at last sensed support among his fellow advisory-group members for his view that a conference-table solution was now the only way out. The group began to bombard administration officials with arguments that the bombing campaign had failed in all its major objectives and that the United States was being plunged deeper and deeper into economic and social malaise by the Vietnamese conflict. The American presence in the world was being diminished as a result of the war. And the government had not really made a sufficient effort to get talks started. Why not? It was "nonsense" to say that such an initiative could not be taken without jeopardizing the military position.

President Johnson said nothing as the exchanges flashed around the dinner table. He sat, his face expressionless and only his eyes moving as the debate surged back and forth.

Over coffee General DePuy and Carver briefed the advisory group on the continued influx of Communist troops and the impending threats to major population centers, including Saigon, Danang, and Hué, as well as to the fighting zones.

The briefing that received the most attention came from Philip Habib. He dealt realistically with the impact of the Communist offensive during the Tet holiday. As he assessed the situation, there was little hope of producing stability in South Vietnam under the stresses of war in the foreseeable future.

On the morning of March 19 the advisory group reassembled in the White House to discuss the previous night's briefings. That afternoon they advised the President to take fresh peace initiatives and to relinquish the policy of escalation. Some say that President Johnson appeared surprised by this opinion, in view of the group's previous advice over several months. He subsequently sent for Habib and other experts and subjected them to a tough questioning session in the White House that lasted late into the night. Between the fateful conference on March 18 and his speech on March 31 President Johnson frequently conferred with Clark Clifford, not only on the military aspects of Vietnam but also on slippage in the situation at home. Others were brought into the discussions, which sometimes went on into the night. The President interviewed at least sixty people on the situation before he spoke on March 31. At all times he behaved like a poker player, his face grave and showing nothing of what was in his mind.

In Britain, where the news media have not yet penetrated officialdom to the same extent as in Washington, such meetings could have been discreetly handled, and the risk of exposure would have been mild. In Washington there was a very strong chance that some of the sixty would talk. Indeed, some of them did. That the meetings were going on was known. But so enigmatic was the President's behavior that not one reporter had any indication of what he planned, nor did any columnist add up the facts and make a deduction.

President Johnson has always been secretive and suspicious toward the press, which is why American newsmen make special efforts to pry into his plans in advance. But in this case, the greatest story of all, he deceived everyone.

On Saturday, March 30, he discussed the whole Vietnam situation with McNamara over lunch. That afternoon he went through the draft of the announcement (excluding the addendum on his withdrawal from the Presidential race) with McNamara, Clifford, General Wheeler, Bill Bundy, Walt Rostow, Christian, and speech writer Harry C. McPherson, Jr.

His firm decision called for the suspension of bombing over 90 percent of the populated areas of Vietnam. The die was irrevocably cast.

The repercussions in the United States came swiftly. In New York trading on Wall Street surged to a record high of 17,730,000 shares at skyrocketing prices, surpassing the previous record of transactions made on "Black Tuesday" 1929, when the market plunged, triggering the Great Depression.

Of course all this activity completely bewildered orthodox Marxists around the world, conditioned as they were to believe that American big business encourages the war for economic reasons. What they failed to understand is that business is the most sensitive barometer of a nation's health and that Wall Street had perceived that the destructive effects of the war were not only limited to Vietnam itself but could be felt in America as well. Once the war had been ended, America could get on with its unfinished domestic business, business that would be far more profitable to Wall Street and the American people than would an unpopular and unfruitful colonial war.

The Gallup Poll, the first to sample popular reaction scientifically, showed that 49 percent of the population now approved the way President Johnson had handled his office, a rise of 13 percent from the mid-March figure. It was the greatest single popularity increase recorded for a President since Harry Truman's 13 percent rise during a four-week period in 1947. The mid-April poll also showed that 64 percent of those surveyed approved of the President's decision to limit the bombing, against 26 percent who disapproved and 10 percent who were undecided.

Once President Johnson had lived by the polls. But, however flattering their results, they were not about to influence him at this stage. His mind was made up. The political reasons were clear, but the personal ones counted too. Like many people who are insensitive to other people's feelings, Lyndon Johnson is extremely sensitive where his own affairs are concerned.

All politicians must of necessity develop thick skins to protect them from the abuse that their profession draws. In a democracy, particularly in the United States, where the press is far less restricted by libel laws than it is in Britain, the politician can expect his private life to be mercilessly exposed.

Former British Foreign Secretary George Brown—a man of strong personality—has had more than his share of this kind of publicity. It was an American newspaper, *The New York Times*, that first reported London political gossip about Brown's exuberant behavior after a few drinks. Only then did the timid British press join in, but once it had—and had gotten away with it—it proceeded with a vengeance.

Brown has said: "Few directors of big corporations would last a week if this kind of publicity were played upon them. I don't mind reading in the paper that I had too much to drink. But what about my wife? What about my children? It's them I want to protect."

One difference between British and American politics is that in America the dirty work is more often in the open. Lyndon Johnson had long inured himself to the kind of attack that George Brown found difficulty in weathering. But during 1967 he became a victim of a new and significant form of attack. It was the kind of political abuse not heard since the eighteenth-century outpourings of Grub Street in Britain.

A number of controversial decisions by the U.S. Supreme Court had made it possible to publish material that previously would have been labeled obscene if not pornographic. The major impact of these decisions was to alter radically the structure of the best-selling book lists, which now contain novels that in a previous decade could only have been bought illegally.

But the Court decisions also unleashed a new and unpleasant development, which can be described only as the politics of pornography. Its outlet is the underground press, a number of newspapers

126

run by antiestablishment groups and aimed specifically at young readers.

The underground press takes advantage of the permissive society to assault the very freedoms that society grants it. It seeks to shock, using four-letter words to attack revered institutions. At their most intelligent, the underground newspapers are astringently refreshing. But all too often they are merely boring, badly written, and tediously immature—unless one happens to be a victim of their poison.

Lyndon Johnson through 1967 and 1968 was their major victim. If there was one thing on which the underground press seemed united, it was a combined attempt to smear the President as a man, a husband, and a human being. The technique was to present apocryphal stories of his personal life interwoven with the foulest type of sexual fantasy and told in the language of the gutter.

After Mr. Johnson announced that he would not seek renomination the observer spent some time in the White House discussing the underground press and its unspeakable campaign against the President with George Christian, the White House press secretary. He asked the obvious question: "Did the President know the kind of things that were being written about him?"

Every attempt was made to protect the family from seeing the publications, said Christian, but eventually the President did discover what was being written. "He treated it with the contempt it deserved," added Christian. "But there are some kinds of filth you can't wipe out of your mind. I could see what it was doing to him. No man can be the target of that kind of blind unrelenting hate and survive."

Christian added that he and Mrs. Johnson had counseled renunciation because of the effects of this pornographic attack on the President. Christian, in quoting the President's reaction, repeated the sentiments of George Brown: "The President felt that he could withstand this kind of filth. But he was worried about what it would do to Mrs. Johnson and the girls."

One wondered why America permitted such publications. It was all part of the strange indecision gripping the country, a failure to determine the difference between genuine freedom and license. President Johnson was one of the early targets but later in the campaign the backlash to this permissiveness was to have a powerful political effect, swinging the uncommitted center voter to the right.

But the President was under personal attack from more than just

127

the underground press. Senator Dirksen, a lifetime friend of the President, tells this story:

I was going through my mail before the President came on television. In the mail was a booklet entitled "In the Name of God, Mr. President, Stop This," and it was signed by 25,000 ministers, members of the cloth, who preach the word of God. How would you feel if you had done everything you know how to do to stop a war and then had this dumped on you?

Placards proclaiming "Murderer," "Assassin," "Baby Butcher," displayed wherever Mr. Johnson went, could not have been a pleasant background for an already inordinately sensitive man. As this kind of inflammatory attack increased daily the Secret Service became openly worried about the President's safety. "This sort of atmosphere is sick," said one Secret Service official. "And it's just the sort of thing to drive psychos to the point of doing something homocidal."

Security precautions were intensified to the point at which it was virtually impossible for the President to function as a politician. He had to travel in a car heavy with armor plating by secret routes at unannounced times. He had to cancel public meetings not only because he might be assassinated but also because he would certainly be publicly humiliated.

A senior Presidential aide said later: "The intensity of the attacks upon the President grew, and they became to be aimed at his very office. It could not long survive this. We don't mind dissent, but not dissent with a built-in plague.

For Lady Bird Johnson, a sturdy and devoted wife, there was a classic reason why her husband should step down. Lyndon Baines Johnson was a strong man, but his health was far from perfect, and the stresses of his job had, in the previous year, aggravated a chronic ailment—diverticulitis—that had bothered him for eight years.

He had had heart attacks in the past and his doctor had warned him to give up smoking and drinking. During his term as President, he had undergone surgery for removal of his gallbladder and for kidney-stone trouble. Mrs. Johnson did not hide her feelings. The President's health could be endangered by another campaign and an additional four years in office. She felt that he should not consider it.

128

All these factors led to his decision at the end of March.

But one reason was paramount. At that time President Johnson grasped it fully, and realized that it gave him little alternative but to renounce a second term: The country was divided, and only an enormous event could end that division.

President Johnson saw this truth more clearly than others perhaps because he had always wanted to be a leader acceptable to everyone in America. His ambition, his dream, had been to unify the American people. He had often said that he wanted to be "President of all the people."

The United States is not a homogeneous country like Britain. It is a complex mixture of ethnic groups and creeds. The true American is still being formed. It is each President's task to take the formation a stage further. President Johnson had hoped, with his plans for a Great Society, to shape this unifying process at a rate that historians would regard as remarkable.

But in March he finally accepted the great irony. All his plans, all his seeking for consensus, had achieved the opposite effect. He was the great divider.

At that time President Johnson believed that there was only one way to reunify the nation. It was a way that appealed to him. It would enable him to do things that normally he could not do. It would enable him to make his mark on history. It would enable him to win his way back into the hearts of the American people.

As he saw it, one man had to stand above politics. One man had to be the center of detachment, an embodiment of American continuity—a continuity that could not be disrupted by political warfare. Only one man, he believed, was capable of doing that job. That man was Lyndon Baines Johnson himself.

.9.

Can Black Ever Be Beautiful?

At 6:01 P.M. ON THURSDAY, APRIL 4, 1968, MARTIN LUTHER KING WAS shot dead by a sniper as he stood on the balcony of the Lorraine Motel in Memphis, Tennessee. To many outsiders this shooting was confirmation of their picture of barbarism in American politics. To white Americans it was a reminder of the violence in their society. To black Americans the event was merely another illustration of what the murders of Malcolm X and Medgar Evers and the wounding of James Meredith had already revealed: that any man who tries to speak for the American Negro inevitably risks finding himself at the wrong end of a rifle barrel.

In the immediate aftermath of King's death, Negro grief exploded into violence. In the weeks after the assassination, Negroes rioted in 125 cities, and 68,000 troops were required to contain them. Thirty-nine people died, all but five of them Negroes; 3,500 were injured, 20,000 arrested, $40 million worth of property destroyed and $10 million worth of goods stolen. The thick, black smoke from a dozen blazing ghettos made symbolic funeral pyres for King's policy of nonviolence.

Television satellites flashed pictures around the world, providing

130

instant testimony to black America's despair. In Moscow, London, and Rome people sat in the comfort and safety of their own living rooms and watched burnings in Baltimore, killing in Chicago, and total anarchy on the streets of Washington, D.C., the capital of the United States. The riots were on a scale unprecedented except for a country on the verge of revolution. The United States survived them, but the scars remained in the blackened, burnt-out ruins of urban districts that the Negroes had destroyed. Parts of Washington looked like London after the blitz. Indeed, Washington suffered most of all. Perhaps there was something symbolic in that. Of all the big cities in the United States, Washington was the first in which Negroes had become a majority of the population.*

In the chaos of the cities, grief easily turned to greed. In Washington the statistics spoke for themselves. Sixty-one clothing stores, 57 liquor stores, 53 groceries and supermarkets, 23 furniture stores, 19 drug stores, and 19 dry cleaners were looted and destroyed. Wherever one looked one saw Negroes grotesquely weighed down with goods. There was almost a festive spirit among the looters. For years Negroes had been taunted by commercials on television and newspaper adverts eulogizing the goods that characterize middle-class living in the consumer society. Most Negroes could not afford them. Now they were helping themselves and no one was stopping them. The Washington police, under strict orders not to provoke trouble, kept their guns in their holsters and watched as windows were smashed and mobs picked the stores clean. They arrested only Negroes who let themselves be isolated from the mob.

Not all the looters were underprivileged, as the observer saw for himself. On 14th Street he watched a carnival crowd scramble through the shattered windows of a shoe shop. As he stood there, a brand new Mustang motor car (which costs about $3,000) drew up at the curb, and a beautifully dressed Negro girl leaped out and began to fight her way into the shop. The broken glass tore her suit, and she came close to hamstringing herself, but within a few minutes she emerged triumphantly bearing two shoe boxes. Then she guarded the car while her husband fought his way through the mob and grabbed a pair of chelsea boots. Exultantly they climbed into their car under the eyes of the passive police and

* In mid-1968 the U.S. Census Bureau estimated that the population of the District of Columbia was 850,000 people, of whom fewer than 300,000 were white. The District school board stated that there were 151,147 children in the District schools, of whom 11,783 were white and 139,364 Negro.

131

drove away. Two blocks farther on, where the Negro crowds were thinner and the police out in force, the driver of the Mustang reverted to law-abiding citizen and stopped for a red light, whereupon he was promptly arrested by a policeman who had spotted the shoe boxes on the seat. The value of the loot could hardly have exceeded $30.

Negro attitudes toward white people in America are complex and not always honestly expressed. But Negroes will sometimes talk to Englishmen or Europeans more freely than to their fellow Americans. In the course of a year the observer met many American Negroes, all with different stories to tell. Yet diverse as the stories were, a common thread ran through them: Negro lives reflect the heritage of all that black America has suffered over the last 300 years. Perhaps the most hateful feature of that heritage was slavery which Negroes in America endured for two centuries. Even the surnames of most American Negroes came from white slave owners. In Britain people will boast that their ancestors were hanged as pirates or highwaymen, but there is nothing romantic about bearing the name of a man who held one's ancestors in bondage. This awareness adds outrage to the multitude of other racial pressures. (Some black militants have rejected Christian surnames entirely, preferring to be known by names of African or Muslim origin.)

After years of seeking to gain full acceptance as Americans through the usual channels of social change in America—and some of the achievements, like the 1954 Supreme Court decision overturning segregated education, were once hailed as monumental—the Negro mood was increasingly less patient. This impatience was most dramtically expressed in the riots that broke out during the 60s in city ghettos across the nation. President Johnson appointed a commission to investigate the disorders. When the commission's report was published early in 1968 (*Report of the National Advisory Commission on Civil Disorders,* commonly called the "Kerner report" after the Chairman, Illinois Governor Otto Kerner) its most astonishing finding was that America was in the process of becoming a divided nation—black against white. The Negro revolt included assaults on many of America's established social institutions. One institution that came under major attack were the police forces.

To city Negroes policemen often have appeared to be enemies. This point was brought out by the Kerner report as a prime factor in the 1967 riots. Even if a policeman was black, he still stood for authority, and authority was against the Negro—and likely to be brutal or abusive. In a special *Look* issue on the cities, Claude Brown wrote: "In Detroit, there are still stories, truthful or not, about the numerous rapes of Negro women who were arrested by white policemen during the rioting. One story has it that a soul sister, who was four or five months pregnant, was raped by a white policeman in the police station. What is of great significance is that the climate of Detroit makes such a tale credible and Negroes believe it."

At first sight American policemen are a pretty terrifying prospect to people brought up under the dignified law and order maintained by the British bobby. Their uniforms are scruffy, their mien insolent. They do not show the formal politeness of a British officer. They appear undisciplined and dangerously tough. Yet their side of the story is worth hearing too. "Sure I beat up some Negro hoodlums," one Cleveland cop said. "What do you think this whole thing is, the romper room? We are engaged in a war, and we are fighting for our lives much of the time. We don't get extra combat pay like the troops in Vietnam, you know." Police authorities in various American cities were making attempts to improve their community relations, but the policemen themselves often refused to cooperate. San Francisco had a widely praised program that seemed to have been effective in curbing riots, yet after five years its young founder, policeman Dante Andreotti, quit because white policemen refused to help to the extent of having simple forms filled out by the young Negro unemployed on their beats.

Sullen black faces, militant national leaders, and bitter contempt for those Negroes who have profited from the white power structure all awaken in a Briton memories of past colonial nightmares—but they occurred in remote African or Asian territories and not in his own homeland. It brought no pleasure to the visitor to see the great anticolonial power facing inside its own borders the same situation it had condemned around the world. That situation was ironic but tragic, for America could not take the final recourse of the colonial power and simply pull out. The problem had to be solved.

Aware of the almost incurable antipathy between Negroes and police, Chicago authorities fell back on a solution well known to such colonial experts as the British . . . they ceded many police functions to the Negroes themselves. These tribal police—for that is what they were—were formed from the urban gangs that had already split the ghetto into various principalities. First among

133

them were the Blackstone Rangers, whose national reputation arose from wide television exposure of various entertainment groups sponsored by them. They were about 1,000 strong and were led by 21-year-old Jeff Fort, a short, slim, arrogant youth.

Fort had immense power in the Chicago ghetto. He could mobilize his followers at a few minutes' notice, and their weapons included heavy machine guns. They also envisaged antitank guns as a defense against armored police trucks. (Indeed, one renegade Ranger testified in June that nearly $1 million of Federal aid to the Rangers had been spent on grenades and other weapons, though the accuracy of this charge has not been established.) Yet Jeff Fort said: "Our purpose is to organize to provide ourselves with security and houses and education and jobs, because no one else will do it for us. The way to stop the killing is that we will police our own areas ourselves."

According to Reverend Norman Theiss, one of the many ministers who acted as intermediaries between Chicago's ghetto children and the larger community: "The movement of these kids has done good for the churches because it has forced them to be relevant to life today. But the kids are the only force that can now keep order in the ghetto."

In 1968 a lot of important white men were trying hard to say and do things that would sound good to Negro ears. Most aspiring white politicians really had no other choice, and with the exception of George Wallace, they worked hard to win the Negro. But Robert Kennedy appeared to be the one white politician whom Negroes accepted. He was in Indianapolis on the night of King's death, and he went into the Negro district, a small figure hunched against the cold and blinking in the glare of a television spotlight operated by a Negro technician. "Those of you who are black," he said, "can be filled with bitterness, with hatred and a desire for revenge. We can move in that direction in this country, or we can make an effort, as Martin Luther King did, to understand and replace that violence with compassion and love."

He looked at his audience very slowly and added, "I can feel in my heart what many of you must be feeling." He paused again, and they knew what he was going to say, even though he had never said it in public before: "I had a member of my family killed, and he was killed by a white man." The Negroes listened to him, and they came out of the ghetto to vote for him. In California and Indiana Negroes showed what their bloc votes could do. They gave those primary elections to Kennedy.

Nevertheless, to many Negroes, any vote was a vote to put a white man in power. When, on October 7, 1967, Thurgood Marshall took his place as Associate Justice of the U.S. Supreme Court, many Negroes congratulated themselves on a great step forward, just as they had done when Robert Weaver became the first Negro member of the Cabinet. Indeed, Roy Wilkins, head of the National Association for the Advancement of Colored People, saw fit to say:

> Justice Thurgood Marshall towers above the cynicism. He dwarfs the smarties and their flippancies. He makes real the promise of America for the hundreds of millions over the globe who hope and pray and yearn. For here is the grandson of a slave, come from a people tricked and flayed by the maladministration of justice risen to the place where he and his fellow jurists have the last word on equal justice under law.

But Wilkins did not seem to represent younger Negroes' thinking. Many of them asked, "Isn't it about time we stopped talking about it, because why should it need special comment simply because Marshall is black?"

The end of 1967 had also brought the election of the first two Negro mayors of big cities—Carl Stokes in Cleveland, Ohio, and Richard Hatcher in Gary, Indiana. But, as a Negro in another city said: "God help Carl Stokes. Two months after he takes office Cleveland Negroes will be bitter and impatient because Carl hasn't solved their problems." Resentment among the Negro masses against the Negro middle class—"those better blacks"—had grown ferocious during the 1960s. To one European, the obvious affluence of Negro professional men in New York was quite startling. He saw Negroes better dressed than their British or European counterparts, driving bigger cars, and living in better homes, and he was tremendously impressed because it was contrary to what he had expected.

Too often the improving material position of American Negroes is ignored in the drama of persecution. By 1968 23 percent of American Negro families had annual incomes of more than $7,000, compared to 53 percent of white families. Negroes were advancing into white-collar business enclaves. In the first part of the decade there had been a 50 percent increase in Negro employment in professional and managerial jobs and a 48 percent increase in clerical jobs.

Nevertheless there was still a long way to go. The percentages were still out of balance. Eleven percent of the American people are Negro, yet in 1966 Negroes held only 5.9 percent of the country's professional and higher technical jobs and only 6.3 percent of the clerical jobs. The percentage of managers, officials, and proprietors who were Negroes was 2.8, less than a quarter of the representation one would expect on a proportional basis. On the other hand, Negroes constituted 25.3 percent of America's laborers and 21 percent of the service workers.

The one impressive figure was in education. In 1960 fewer than 4 percent of Negro males went to college. By 1966 the figure had increased to 7.4 percent, and by 1968 it was above 8 percent.

So progress was steady though slow. But, however impressed one was by the statistics, a visit to the slums of Harlem revealed a picture of genuine poverty and despair. The Negroes there had been left behind and were ripe for extremist exploitation. They knew that they did not have the same opportunities that white men had and that to achieve comparable success Negroes had to try very much harder.

And so the inevitable polarization between "them and us" continued to grow through the election year. It provided fertile ground for black extremists. "Sure you can be a white nigger if you want to" they said to the poor, "but you have to sell out your black heritage first and just ape the white man's ways. Do you want to do that?"

And now any Negro who adopted an assimilatory attitude toward the situation was called an "Uncle Tom." The time, it seemed, was already too late for reason. Old phrases and old aspirations were no longer any use. For decades integration had been the aspiration of American Negroes and white liberals interested in their plight. Most Negroes one met in those days wanted nothing more than to live as their white brothers did. They wanted good food, comfort, opportunity, money in the bank, education for their children, and no more hardships and defeats than the next man, whatever his color.

But, in the previous few years and particularly in 1967 a different attitude had emerged. One Negro in Detroit harangued a group of white journalists: "You think you are doing us a favor by wanting to integrate us. You think we should be allowed to participate fully in the kind of America you built. Man, that's not a favor. That's an insult. You really think *we* want to be like *you?*"

These activists were of quite a different breed from the integrationists. Its overtones were paranoid and racist. They wanted separation. To be absorbed into the white man's way of life would be

136

just as castrating as servitude, they argued. The alternative would be a Negro nation within a nation, characterized less by voluntary apartheid than by refusal to accept anything that did not come from the Negroes' own heritage. One of the foremost proponents of this view was Ron Karenga, a small, stout man who affected a shaven and polished head; clothes that seemed borrowed equally from Mao, Nehru, and Kenyatta; and speech that seemed composed of quotations unconnected with what anyone else might be saying.

Karenga was the head of US, a Negro organization with head-quarters in Los Angeles. Outside his office a sign urged "Just Try to Be Black." To a visitor inside his office he said: "Nationalism to us is a need and not a response. I'd feel it even without white oppression. We will not be absorbed. We will be active, not passive." In the US gospel, a small $1 book called *The Quotable Karenga*, he observes: "The purpose of a nationalist should be to build and make the black nation eternal. . . . The seven-fold path of the blackness is to Think Black, Talk Black, Act Black, Create Black, Buy Black, Vote Black and Live Black."

During 1968 the Black Panther Party for Self Defense in California, the all-Negro group of militants, emerged nationally on the American scene. The Panthers' influence on the election was minute although Eldridge Cleaver, who was called the Party's minister of information, ran in some states as the Peace and Freedom Party's Presidential candiate. (In California, Cleaver was not on the ballot because the Secretary of State ruled the 33-year-old Cleaver was two years too young to run for the White House.) But the Panthers ended up possibly the most striking and disquieting black organization.

They first gained prominence when their members, carrying loaded shotguns and rifles, pushed their way past a startled sergeant at arms in the California State Capitol building in Sacramento on May 2, 1967 and went onto the floor of the Assembly. They were protesting a bill, which was later passed, restricting the carrying of firearms. At that point the Panthers were regarded merely as a noisy group, not to be taken too seriously.

There are no reliable figures for the Panthers' strength in membership. They are strongest in California where there are probably two hundred active members buttressed by the hidden sympathies of a sizeable part of the Negro population. Panther groups have also sprung up in other cities—Seattle, Los Angeles and New York—but they too are believed to be small. The Panthers appeal most directly, perhaps, to young discontented Negroes who accept the Panther advocacy of combatting "the colonialist white establishment and white racist pig cops, the fascist cop and the white power structure."

It is strange that American Negroes should even contemplate, as many do, the creation of a separate national entity for themselves, for they are as American as the Latvians, Poles, Germans, Dutch, Russians, and Chinese who have also settled in the United States. These groups, for economic and emotional reasons, have clung to their ethnic identifications while quickly becoming Americanized. Yet the Negroes, many of whom have been in the country as long as the Englishmen who started the whole thing, talked of reversing one of the most enormous social tides in modern America: the homogenization of different peoples into one great nation. It made one realize how deep their alienation went.

There were, of course, still some Negroes who wanted to follow the "white way." Homer Waterman, president of the Booker T. Washington Negro businessmen's association in Detroit, said: "The point about the Negro is that he is first and foremost an American and so he has to win the American way. If a man tries hard enough he can make his way in business and get a good living for his wife and his family. I did it, and I believe anyone can do it."

A similar belief was expressed by veteran boxer Archie Moore, who decried the tendency of young Negroes to complain of their fate and circumstances. "We made it because we had a goal, and we were willing to work for it," he said. "Don't talk to me of your 'guaranteed national income.' Any fool knows that this is insanity. Do we bring those who worked to get ahead down to the level of those who never gave a damn? The world owes nobody—black or white—a living. God helps the man who helps himself!"

At the beginning of the Presidential campaign, there was a suspicion among politicians that the Negroes would stay away from the polls in droves unless they found a candidate like Kennedy, with whom they could positively identify.

In the McCarthy camp there was a long battle over whether or not to distribute a recording of part of one of Martin Luther King's speeches, in which he seemed virtually to be endorsing McCarthy. In the end it *was* issued, in the Negro ghetto of Watts in Los Angeles, but it was too late to help much. McCarthy did brave the Kennedy territory of Watts to speak at a rally in a public park. The few hundred people who came were clearly influenced by the

138

offer of free hamburgers, cokes, and hot dogs. One large lady, smothered in McCarthy buttons and doling out food, said cheerfully: "I'll still be voting for Bobby on the day. I don't know why, but I will."

Everyone knew the problems, but who knew how to solve them? One of the more repulsive experiences for the visitor in 1968 America was the spectacle of white liberals retreating into self-denunciation. At coffee klatches and social-welfare meetings they could be heard covering themselves and their fellows with verbal sackcloth and ashes, as if this self-accusation would solve the problem or absolve them from responsibility for further efforts. Of course, it did neither.

Segregation, though outlawed, remained a reality in much of the South in 1968. The Southern states had just over 50 percent of the total Negro population, whereas in 1940 they had had 77 percent. There had been a natural drift from the cotton fields and small homesteads to the steel plants and auto factories, suggesting one basic fact about America's Negroes. The militants and the liberals could talk all they wanted about pride and dignity, about integration and "not thinking of a Negro as being a black man." But the first step was to ensure that the Negro was receiving a decent slice of the American cake.

By 1968 many corporations had begun to realize that they could not leave the economic elevation of the Negro entirely to the efforts of the Federal government. Several schemes to give jobs to Negro Americans, particularly those who seemed unemployable, had been introduced.

The Chrysler Corporation was one of the first big companies to involve itself in this problem, and in June 1968 its president, V. E. Boyd, gave a fascinating account of its experiment. After the Detroit riots, the three big automobile manufacturers recruited thousands of people from the ghetto and gave them jobs. Many of them were considered hard-core unemployed. Mr. Boyd explained what "hard core" meant.

> "Hard core" refers not to those without steady jobs but to those who are not equipped for any job, not the unemployed, but the unemployable—those who are unable to fill out even a simple job application.
>
> We decided to take some 750 of these people and give them whatever training was required to make them able to work. This didn't mean instruction in operating a lathe or a drilling tool. These people, who had been pushed into the backwaters

of our society, couldn't read simple words such as "in" and "out" on a door. It came right down to blackboard drills, teaching the letters that spell common colors, so they would be able to read the instruction card that tells what color seat belt or steering wheel to put on a car as it comes down the assembly line. It entailed teaching simple addition, so that they could count boxes of parts they took off a supplier's truck.

After explaining to the recruits that they would be paid while being trained and showing them were to report, Chrysler executives found that many never bothered to come back. Mr. Boyd commented, "Naturally, a lot of people in my company—just as in many other companies—quietly nodded their heads because it seemed to reaffirm everything they had always known to be true, that people who aren't working just don't want to work."

But Chrysler did not leave the matter there. The company got in touch with every missing Negro, and, in almost every case, the reason for his absence was the same. Being unable to read, he had simply been unable to transport himself across the city to the plant. Patiently the men were taught how to read the bus signs and where to make the transfers. Once they were mobile, they came to work —but rarely on time. Once again, the image of the feckless Negro arose to support old prejudices. Once again, the men from Chrysler started checking. The reason the Negro workers were late, they discovered, was because they did not own alarm clocks. As Mr. Boyd said, the explanation was simple:

> Never before in their lives did any of them have any reason to be in any particular place at any particular time. So we took them into the plants and showed them men, just like themselves, who owned cars and clothes and houses. And it became clear, without our pointing it out, that these workers owned cars and houses because they lived within the rules of an industrial society and showed up for work on time every day.
>
> And this is the point at which some of our established, competent people began to revise those things which they "knew" to be true. They changed their thinking because once these hard-core people knew how, and why, to come to work, their attendance and tardiness record was *500 percent better* than the average of all our employees.
>
> Our people began to reexamine the facts and *they* became as much learners as teachers. They found one out of five hard-core job applicants was rejected for physical reasons and that 40 percent of these were rejected because of poor vision. And,

after these rejects were sent to the proper agencies and tested and fitted for glasses, our people found that many of them could very quickly pick up the elementary reading skills required for simple jobs.

Further, we found that, while the majority of the hard-core people had only a third-to-fourth-grade reading ability, they also fell within a very acceptable range of I.Q. And, given sufficient motivation and direction, they performed at the average level within a relatively few weeks.

To put it bluntly, our people found far fewer "hopeless cases" than they had expected. The nonperformers are now performing and performing well. . . .

We have made an important discovery and a change in attitude that is critically important to the resolution of the urban crisis. We have recognized that it is not only possible but definitely to our advantage to help the chronically unemployed and that with a lot of help and some patience they will help themselves.

Just how much a change of attitude is needed is indicated by the realities of 1968. While laws were being passed to banish the last traces of legal discrimination more than 80 percent of Negro children in the South were still attending all-black schools. In Detroit the percentage of Negro children in predominantly Negro schools had actually risen between 1961 and 1966.

Perhaps the saddest aspect of discrimination lay in the way that the unions continued to exclude Negroes, even those who had high qualifications, from the better-paid jobs and trades—a technique that was already being copied in Britain. From the electrical workers to the steelworkers, from the builders to the garment workers, fierce discrimination either kept the Negro out or at a menial, low-paid level.

After shopping in Bronxville, one of the exclusive New York suburbs, the visitor was shocked to find that the same things cost more in Harlem. Packaged goods were always 3 or 4 cents more. Perishable goods were always inferior *and* more expensive. Some of the smarter Negroes in Detroit, Los Angeles, and New York shopped in white areas, but the majority still bought in the ghettos and paid the most for the worst.

The freeways were another irritation. The John C. Lodge Freeway in Detroit was a good example. It had been constructed to relieve traffic jams among white commuters to the suburbs. A main reason these whites had moved to the suburbs was the Negro influx into the central part of the city. But, in order to build the freeway, the government had to tear down the homes of 80,000 people, mainly black people. Those homes were never replaced. Three familes had to live in the ghetto where one had lived before —or else the Negroes too had to spread beyond the central city. Obviously, in a few years more freeways would be needed for the same reasons, and the cycle would begin all over again.

Similar distress was caused by what was euphemistically called "urban renewal." To the Negro the term usually meant tearing down a block of twenty houses to provide something like a parking lot for white-owned stores. The houses were often not replaced.

In 1968 more than in any other year, perhaps because of the deadly evidences of what racial civil war could be, perhaps because of the additional impact of Vietnam, many Negroes in America had decided that mere promises must stop. Action and only action would do. All politicians were greeted with skepticism, and there were even those who thought that Robert Kennedy was merely using the Negro for his own ends.

President Johnson had actually done a great deal of constructive work on behalf of civil rights, pushing the Civil Rights Bill through Congress in 1964, pressing for open-housing legislation, and so on. Yet—because of his involvement with the Vietnam war, in which Negroes seemed to be carrying more than their share of the fighting and casualties—and also perhaps because he was associated with a period in which there had been so much overt racial disorder—he had lost their sympathy.

Humphrey was regarded as very much a front man for organized labor, which had continuously given the black man a bad deal. McCarthy was virtually unknown among Negroes, in spite of an excellent voting record on civil rights (Humphrey had a similar record).

Nixon stood for the interests of big business, and the Negro could hardly identify with those. Rockefeller, paradoxically in view of his vast wealth, did have a reputation for sympathy with black aspirations, though, as with Kennedy, there was suspicion of his motives. Reagan had discarded the liberalism of his early years and was clearly *not* for the black man.

Nevertheless, all these men needed Negro votes. They made a great number of the right noises for their black audiences.

Kennedy was most successful at illuminating the Negroes' problems, though his listeners often wondered how he proposed to solve them.

142

McCarthy demanded solutions. But he did not say what was to be done, though, to be fair, he refused absolutely (often against the advice of his aides) to capitalize on the Negroes' plight. After King's death, he resolutely refused to make any dramatic, vote-pulling public statement or gesture and, when his wife Abigail, an old friend of Coretta King, went to comfort her, he actually appealed to the three newsmen who knew of the visit not to publicize it.

Even Richard Nixon had to rationalize his conservatism in relation to Negro aspirations. In December 1967 he said: "Under the illusion of the government's unlimited power to remake society, extravagant promises have been made to the Negro. Much of the bitterness of the Negro slum dweller is the result of these false promises. The urban Negro is the chief victim of urban violence."

It was easy for the Briton to feel disgust at the society that allows its Negro citizens to exist in ghettos and rural shacks. But he was like the northern liberal a few generations ago who felt strongly about the way Negroes were treated in the South and who could afford to sympathize in the security of his trouble-free suburb.

Since then Britain had found itself with a colored population that had grown up in less than two decades. It was clear that racism was as likely to be present in the British soul as anywhere else. But the British had the advantage of seeing what had happened in the United States, and they could say, "It mustn't happen here." With a touch of smugness they added, "We cannot allow an American-type racialistic situation to develop in Britain."

A journey through black America thus made an English visitor think of home, where the problems—bad enough—were so much simpler and could still perhaps be solved. In the United States in 1968 so strong were the feelings and so intense the hatred between extremists of both races that the gap seemed unbridgeable. The overwhelming impression was of hatred, fear, and despair that were destroying America from within like some strange, fatal malignancy. One felt great sadness for both white and black Americans gripped by this curse. At times in conversation with militants, a sense of angry futility would overcome the interviewer. At other times, as he observed the effort and sacrifice aimed at easing this terrible problem, all his old admiration for and confidence in America returned. Perhaps the election could be a turning point. Perhaps this problem, a world problem, would first be solved by Americans. The observer waited, as did millions of Americans themselves, to see what the politicians would suggest to ease a situation that all too often seemed hopeless.

Bleak though the picture was, 1968 provided an inspiring chapter in the story of one remarkable politician from Brooklyn's tense black ghetto. The story began four decades ago.

The liner *Vulcania* nosed down the Hudson River. She passed the Statue of Liberty and picked up speed as she came out into the Atlantic and turned south for her run to the Caribbean. On board was a three-year-old girl, Shirley Anita St. Hill, and the ship was carrying her away from Brooklyn where she was born. Forty years later, as Mrs. Shirley Chisholm, she would be back in Brooklyn and making history as the first Negro woman ever elected to the United States Congress.

On that gray day in 1928 Charlie St. Hill and his wife Ruby were heartbroken. Immigrants from the West Indies, they had been drawn to New York as the mecca of riches. But his wages as an unskilled laborer in a burlap-bag factory and her occasional earnings as a cleaning woman could not keep pace with the inflation of the pre-depression years. So, to ease the problems of household management, Shirley and her two younger sisters were going to live with their grandmother in Barbados. With them went four other children, their cousins, for whose parents also the American dream had turned into a nightmare of hardship.

To the deported children the new living arrangement was an exchange for paradise. From the gray tenements and dirty streets of Brooklyn, from freezing winters and broiling airless summers, they went to a tropical island cooled by breezes from the sea. Gone was all uncertainty about where the next meal was coming from or whether there would be enough to eat. Their grandmother, a pastry cook who sold her cakes at a profit, also ran a farm that provided enough eggs and poultry and vegetables to feed the seven new arrivals better than they had ever known.

Nor was Emmaline Seales, the grandmother, in her mid-fifties with no man about the house, fazed by the acquisition of an instant family. She taught the children always to have confidence and courage. If they were naughty she chastised them, sometimes hitting them with a strap or the back of her hand, but she was never unfair in meting out punishment. Attendance at Sunday school and church were mandatory and every Sunday she led her small brood on the two-mile walk over the hill to the Parish Church in the

144

village of Vauxhall. Barbados was then a British colony and English influences were strong. On Sundays Shirley wore dresses with flounces, frills, and ribbons and, in her broad-brimmed boater, she looked exactly like little girls in Victorian England except, of course, that she was black.

British rule gave Shirley a benefit that stood her in good stead forever. She was exposed to all the advantages of the British elementary school system. There in the Vauxhall Parish Hall with two classes in the same room she learnt almost nothing about the outside world but she was given a thorough grounding in how to read and write and do sums. By age four she could read, at five she was linking up her alphabet in the copper-plate English style and by six she was listening to the more advanced class and understanding all that she heard. She was later to contrast her marvelous early schooling with that in the ghetto schools of New York City where even now some teenagers still leave unable to write their names and where many cannot read before they are nine or ten years old.

When Shirley was ten and had been in Barbados seven years, her mother came to reclaim her children. Grandma argued that Brooklyn was no place to bring up a family, but Mrs. St. Hill ached to have her girls around her and by now enough money was coming in to feed and clothe them. Also, another daughter had been born while the older girls were in the West Indies. They sailed for New York.

Coming back from Barbados, Brooklyn was a disheartening change for the three St. Hill girls. No more sea bathing every day. No more playing in the fields. Paradise no longer was theirs. Already Brooklyn was racing toward its eventual population of three million with a concentration of Jews which made it the biggest Jewish city in the world. So much of the surface was paved with asphalt that a book title, *A Tree Grows in Brooklyn,* seemed ironic. Although the girls had difficulty readjusting to city life they were greatly aided by their British education. It meant they were a lot more advanced than their classmates, first at Public School 28, then at Junior High School 172 and eventually at Brooklyn Girls' High. Indeed, they were so advanced that they were assigned to classes a full year ahead and still outpaced their fellow students. By her teens Shirley knew that she was more than commonly intelligent and with this realization came the first full flowering of the aware-

145

ness of self-worth which she bears now as proudly as a family coat-of-arms.

Brooklyn's schools at that time were integrated far ahead of the rest of the nation. They were two-thirds white—largely Jewish—and one-third Negro. Today they are almost 100 percent Negro and Puerto Rican. Then there was no hostility between the Jews and the Negroes as both groups saw themselves joined in a fellowship of humiliation at the hands of white Christians.

Upon graduating from Girls' High, Shirley was eligible for four scholarships, a remarkable number. Reluctantly she settled for Brooklyn College, the one nearest home, because it would mean the family would be spared the expense of maintaining her in a dormitory. At college she studied sociology and there she began to learn for the first time something about the aspirations of black people. She joined the Harriet Tubman Society, a social concern group, which was named after an escaped slave who became a noted conductor on the underground railroad system which helped other slaves to escape from the South to the North and freedom. She joined the debating society and plunged into arguments with relish. But she was also a good mediator and could help others to see both sides of a question.

Professor Louis Warsoff of the Political Science Department, with prophetic foresight, urged her to go into politics. She laughed off the suggestion. She explained: "The idea was far from my mind because even today the word 'politics' in America has a connotation of corruption. In addition to that I was black and a young girl. It was impossible at that time for blacks to make progress in politics on the local scene and that is where you must start."

Meanwhile, the teenaged Shirley was showing a streak of rebellion against her mother. Mrs. St. Hill, who wanted to bring up her daughters by the standards of Barbados, did not approve of the social and cultural temptations of the big city. She particularly disapproved of dances and if her daughters went to a dance they were always ordered to be home early. This bothered Shirley. "We were a laughing-stock, always the first to arrive at a party and always the first to leave. I remember one time dancing with a boy and trying to be ever so sophisticated until my sister Muriel came over pointed at her watch and said 'Remember what time Mummy said we had to be home.' I wished the earth would open up and swallow me."

Shirley became an expert dancer, undoubtedly as a direct reaction

146

to her mother's dread of dancing. She won prizes for the lindy hop, the applejack, jitter-bugging and her particular favorites, the rumba and tango. She said: "I come alive on a dance floor. I'm very creative. I use my hands and my body. Even now I amaze people when I dance. I suppose it's part of my cultural heritage as a black woman. But my mother hated it. She thought I would go to work in a nightclub. She bought me a piano, I think simply to curb the surging activity she thought would lead to a theatrical life."

In 1945 when she was 21 the family achieved a lifetime ambition. Mr. St. Hill plumped down $10,000, a great chunk of his life savings, to buy a house in Brooklyn. The family moved into the grandest home they had ever had, a three-story house which was one of a row of terraced structures on Prospect Place on the edge of the district known as Bedford-Stuyvesant. There was a basement and a front garden with railings and an imposing flight of steps up to the front door. The St. Hills were only the third Negro family to move into the neighborhood. Now all the whites have fled and Prospect Place is solidly Negro and Puerto Rican. But old Charlie's house would fetch more than $30,000 today. He had invested well. His widow and two of his daughters still live there.

In buying the house Charlie indisputably lifted his family into the lower middle class. Mrs. Chisholm cites his achievement proudly. "It was really remarkable to bring up a family of four daughters on a laborer's pay, give them all an education and then buy them a house. My parents were obsessed with making sure we would not have to struggle as they had. This is something I have noticed about West Indian migrants compared with American Negroes. They are more ambitious and more prepared to make sacrifices for goals they consider important. They strive for home ownership and good schooling while American Negroes do not always have these priorities. I think the explanation lies in our history. We had slavery in the West Indies but it was not so brutal as in the deep South and it did not break up families in the same way. For 300 years in American slavery there was no family life after the day's work was over and we are still suffering the consequences."

After she had earned her B.A. degree at Brooklyn College, Shirley St. Hill still thirsted for more education. And when she took a job as teacher in a Harlem day nursery, her evenings were devoted to studies for her Master's degree at Columbia University. During these years she allowed herself few distractions. Boy friends were useful as dancing partners but that was all. "I had no time for them because all I wanted was to get an education. Besides, boys shied away from me because I was too brainy. I dominated the conversation. One boy danced with me only on condition I never talked to him about my lectures."

One young man, however, was not inhibited by the fiery young woman who rushed from job to class to civic group without appearing to pause for breath. Conrad Chisholm, a sturdily built graduate student from Jamaica, watched her for several days before asking if she ever stopped to have any fun. "I thought he was terribly fresh. He said there were other things in life apart from work and that he was going to take me out to dinner. It wasn't so easy for him to get me to agree because I had all kinds of reasons why I shouldn't go. But he just said he would never take no for an answer. Up to then I had always been in control of a situation and this was the first time I wasn't. This interested me more than the possibility of becoming his girlfriend. Who was this man who could take *me* away from my vital day-to-day planning?"

They were married a year later when she was 25.

In 1953 the Negroes of Brooklyn established an historic landmark in their political development. For the first time they bucked the local political machine of the Democratic Party and managed to elect a Negro judge. It was a brutal battle. The party tried to impose a white attorney, brought in from outside the district. The Negroes rejected him as a "carpetbagger," preferring their own man, Lewis Flagg, who grew up on the spot. Flagg's candidacy was organized by the Bedford-Stuyvesant Political League, a new and independent organization put together to fight for Negro rights by Wesley Holder, a shrewd and innovative politician who had immigrated to Brooklyn from British Guiana.

After a campaign of bitter charges and counter-charges Flagg was elected by the slender majority of 123 votes. At the victory dinner Holder made a wild claim—that he would not give up the struggle until Negroes from Brooklyn held office at every level of government all the way up to the United States Congress. This was before the civil rights movement, even before the Supreme Court ban on school segregation, and Holder's predictions sounded like exaggerations.

But Shirley Chisholm, the woman who would make his ultimate prophesy come true, was jolted into political awareness by Flagg's success and Holder's challenging victory cry. By this time she was director of the newest and biggest day nursery in New York City. More than 150 Negro and Puerto Rican children attended her nursery near the stark and ugly blocks of publicly financed apartment houses under the shadow of the Brooklyn Bridge on the lower East Side of Manhattan. It was here that she first flexed her muscles as an executive and cut her teeth as an administrator. She was full of energy. She was the boss. And she insisted that things be done her way. Inevitably, her agressiveness upset some people. Sensitive feelings were trampled on. Feathers were ruffled. One woman colleague of those days recalls: "She was a first-class 'b.s.' artist. She was often unfair, but she learned from her mistakes. She's a shrewd cookie."

Politically, however, she was dormant until the election of Judge Flagg. Then she came alive with a flourish. She joined Wesley Holder's political League and within a year, became Vice-President, often challenging Holder on points of policy.

Bedford-Stuyvesant was in a state of flux. Jews were streaming out to the new suburbs of Long Island. Their places were filled by thousands of Negroes and Puerto Ricans who in the years following World War II were attracted to New York like dazed fire-flies rushing towards a searchlight. Eventually nearly half a million people were herded into Bedford-Stuyvesant alone, filling the once-graceful homes with many more occupants than they were built for. There were a quarter of a million Negroes, 95,000 Puerto Ricans and only 100,000 whites, most of them poor. In the equally crowded areas around Bedford-Stuyvesant there were another 125,000 Negroes and thousands more Puerto Ricans. It all added up to one of the biggest, filthiest, most depressing slums in America.

Streets in Bedford-Stuyvesant are choked with stinking garbage, resembling British towns in the Middle Ages. Prudent shopkeepers have thick iron shutters over their windows at all times. On warm days people looking as derelict and unwashed as many of the buildings lounge in the gutters and stare at the stranger with mute hostility. Wrecks of old cars litter the thoroughfares. Scrawled obscenities adorn the walls. A large number of the women are pregnant. Mongrel dogs prowl the garbage heaps. Strangers should not go there at night for to do so is to risk being mugged. Yet from the rooftops on a clear day you can see across the East River to the towers of Wall Street and the biggest concentration of wealth and commercial power in the world. It costs twenty cents to get there from Bedford-Stuyvesant on the subway. But one need not make the journey if he has no skills. For there will be no jobs over there for the unskilled any more than there are in the ghetto.

Bedford-Stuyvesant was the sullen arena into which Shirley Chisholm strode like a tigress, suddenly conscience-stricken at how lucky she had been and determined to try to help less fortunate black folk. "I realized I had a good home, a well-paying job and a fine husband. All this had come because of my good education. I had escaped. But all around me was suffering and, even worse, ignorance. I had to do something."

She was thirty-one and all exuberance. Her figure was lithe and slender. She weighed 117 pounds and was only 5 feet 4 inches tall. Her skin was very dark brown and her hair was short and becomingly styled. She laughed a lot but she flared up as readily. Her voice still had traces of a British West Indian accent. Someone called her "Mrs. Dynamite."

She and Holder seldom used the word "politics" in the early days. It frightened off the people they wanted to help, who thought of politicians as overweight white men with big cigars, with rings on their fingers and with the Democratic Party machine at their fingertips. So the phrase "civic action" was employed instead. Evenings and weekends she was out in the streets, organizing classes in Negro history, seeking jobs for the unemployed, helping them find ways to get the welfare services to which they were entitled from the city. Holder said: "Our people are not the most intelligent. We had to tell them and show them where they could be helped. It was hard work with long hours, often unrewarding, but it gave Shirley her political indoctrination."

Over the years she worked in several campaigns and saw some of Holder's predictions come true. Negroes moved into more judgeships and positions on local councils. By 1964 she herself was ready to seek election to public office. She decided to run for a seat in the Assembly of New York State. Her constituency was an area of Bedford-Stuyvesant with roughly 40,000 residents. In the primary she ran against the machine candidate, beat him and went on to an easy victory in the general election. Her opponents from the other parties were so insignificant that neither she nor Holder can now remember their names.

Assemblywoman Chisholm gave up her job as Chief Educational Consultant for all of New York City's day nurseries. She would be spending four days a week in Albany, the provincial town in the foothills of the Adirondacks that is the Capital of New York State and far removed in fact and spirit from the stench of the city slums. But Shirley did not intend to let them forget; nor would she display the normal timidity of a freshman in the Assembly. "I quickly made my maiden speech. I could hear the men around me making jokes. 'Hey, she's pretty,' they said. But I gave 'em a fighting speech and when I'd finished they came over and said 'Sister, where did you learn all that stuff?' "

In Albany she soon built up a power base and in four years she sponsored six new bills, three of which were passed—an astonishing record. Her failures included efforts to expand the state's kindergarten program, to bring in a state-wide minimum wage of two dollars an hour and to start a slum insurance pool. She hopes, in time, to get back to all of these ideas.

The first of her successes was to get more money for the day nurseries where she had spent her working life. The second was a bill to secure unemployment pay for domestic workers. She explained: "Every black woman in New York City including my own mother has done cleaning work at some time. But whenever they were out of work they got nothing. Thousands of women have felt the benefit of this bill."

Her best-known bill and her proudest achievement is called the SEEK program. The initials stand for Search for Education, Elevation and Knowledge.

She said: "I am so pleased about it. The bill gives funds to young Negroes and Puerto Rican students who have potential. It gives them the opportunity to go to college.

"A lot of these children come from so-called ghetto schools which only give them a dead-end vocational diploma. They are not able to compete with white children for scholarships.

"They are the victims of a system of discrimination and segregation. I know because I visited 26 schools in black and white areas of Brooklyn—never telling them I was an assemblywoman—so I could make valid comparisons.

"Four things stood out. One, the large number of substitute teachers in the black areas. Two, the lack of a good curriculum in the black schools that would give black boys and girls the chance to compete with whites. Three, the attitude of many of the teachers indicating they thought black children were inferior. And four, the inability of black parents, in many instances, to have a full voice in the Parent-Teacher Association."

Under SEEK Negro and Puerto Rican youths who feel they

151

can do better despite shortcomings in their secondary education are encouraged to take a test administered by the SEEK counseling service. If they pass the test they are accepted for a college course provided they do extra work during the first year to catch up with their classmates. In two years nearly 8,000 youngsters have joined the program.

Shirley Chisholm spoke enthusiastically about the scheme: "I held a series of public hearings about SEEK up and down the state. Many of the young people said that without it they would never have dreamed of becoming anything in America. The kids showed they knew there was hope for them in this land, even though they were black. I remember a boy of 15 who had been taken out of a dead-end school because he wanted to be a surgeon. I looked at his fine hands and I kept thinking that one day those hands would save both black and white lives. I thought back to my own youth. I was a near genius so I was able to make it in spite of being black. But some of my peers never made it because of the system. It makes me sick and angry to think of the hundreds of thousands of brains which have been lost to America."

An elderly Negro woman knocked on Shirley Chisholm's door in Brooklyn on a cold day in February 1968. She was invited inside and timidly came to the point of her visit. She was one of a group, all housewives, all black, and they had been holding coffee klatches and tea parties and . . . well . . . it wasn't much . . . but would Shirley please take this envelope as a campaign contribution towards running for congress. Inside was $9.69, all in coins. Tears streaming down her face, Mrs. Chisholm wrapped up the money and put it in a drawer where it stays to this day. At that moment she says she knew she had to try to become the representative of Bedford-Stuyvesant on Capitol Hill in Washington D.C.

She also knew that the democratic machine would not want her. "You see, I cannot be manipulated. I have a fiery, independent, fighting nature. I'm not a machine or a hack politician. I'm part of the new breed of politicians that has emerged in the last four years. I cannot be bought and I cannot be bossed. As a result, professional politicians respect my ability but they don't like me. I'm a maverick and they don't know what I'm going to do next. I even walk out of caucuses. Politicians are not supposed to do that."

Her opponents in the primary were two Negroes, William Thompson, who was a New York State Senator, and Mrs. Dollie Robinson who had been with the New York State Department of Labor. Willy Thompson was the one to worry about. The district had ten party leaders and of these the eight white leaders were all backing him. In addition he had pledged his convention delegates to Bobby Kennedy who in return promised to come into Bedford-Stuyvesant to campaign. Shirley Chisholm was well aware that Bobby's appeal to the Negroes in the area would give Thompson a big boost.

Her counterstroke would take the form of bringing McCarthy into the district after Kennedy. Tragically, this ploy was never needed. On the day Kennedy was scheduled to have been in Bedford-Stuyvesant his body was lying in state at St. Patrick's Cathedral and all campaigning had been suspended.

Chief strategist of the Chisholm candidacy was her old partner, Wesley Holder, by now 71 years old but still spry and committed to seeing his prophesy fulfilled. He recalled: "Shirley had a lot going for her. There are more women than men in the district so that gave her an edge. And she speaks Spanish fluently from her days with the Puerto Rican children so she was able to talk to the Spanish voters in their own language. But Willy Thompson had backing, money, resources, and a good image. My job was to tarnish that image. I had to be careful not to get a white backlash but in my last brochure to the voters I implied that Willy Thompson was being backed by the whites. I made it clear that the Negro leaders had not chosen him. It worked."

In a miserably small turnout Shirley Chisholm polled 5,680 votes. Willy Thompson 4,907, and Dollie Robinson 1,848.

In the general election the Republicans picked a heavyweight to oppose Shirley Chisholm. Their choice was James Farmer, a nationally-known Negro leader and civil rights worker who was once director of the Congress of Racial Equality. As he announced his candidacy, Mrs. Chisholm entered a hospital for an operation that removed a nonmalignant tumor from her stomach. One medical source said the tumor could have been caused by nervous tension. While she convalesced Holder devised a plan to beat Farmer. He said:

Farmer's strategy was that Shirley was a gracious lady but we needed an experienced man for the job. I told Shirley that Farmer would appeal to the one or two percent at the top of the pyramid, the intellectuals who had read about him. She was not to waste her time with them but to concentrate on

153

the broad base of the pyramid which had all the average voters who knew her as a local figure.[*]

In August 1968, however, Shirley Chisholm's standing as a bonafide national figure was certified. At the Democratic convention in Chicago she had been elected the first Negro National Committeewoman of the Party. And now that she could almost certainly be the first Negro woman in Congress, television cables snaked through her home and applications for interviews flooded in from newspapers.

What would she do in the House of Representatives? It was an inevitable question. She replied firmly:

> I won't be a freshman who says nothing, I can assure you of that. First I want to get my SEEK program on a national basis. The American dream has to recognize that it must compensate for what it has done to black people.
>
> Second I'm going to fight to revamp the anti-poverty program. It should be retraining people for jobs, giving them the skills to live in our automated society. At present it is nothing more than a band-aid. It isn't getting to the root of the problem for blacks. The program is badly run. High salaries are paid to officials who are taking kickbacks and putting their families on the payroll. It's almost become a pork barrel and in the meantime idle minds are plotting to burn down our cities.

In some ways, her ambition has proved costly. She has no children, and while theirs is a good marriage, she sees little of her husband because political duties often take her away from home for long periods. "People ask how can he stand being the husband of a prominent woman. He is marvelous about it. I can report my husband's ego is intact."

The Chisholm's home is two blocks away from her family's house in Prospect Place where her mother and two sisters live, although

[*] Farmer and Chisholm met for several face-to-face debates in the district. To this day Farmer is convinced that she was a machine candidate and a poor speaker. She is equally certain she demolished him in public. The final figures support her view: Chisholm 34,885, Farmer 8,923.

But the most significant aspect of both the primary and general election in Bedford-Stuyvesant would be that black fought black within the limits of the established system. Their divisions would be settled at the ballotbox and not by arson, sniping and looting. The low poll, however, reflected the dreadful apathy of the district despite all Shirley's enthusiasm.

the family has been split ever since her father died. Old Charlie St. Hill, recognizing this daughter's special political potential, had left a special trust fund of $11,000 for her alone and, according to the candidate, "the green-eyed monster of jealousy" had been quite busy.

Shirley Chisholm is aggressive and more worried about getting things done than being liked. She is in the vanguard of the new Negroes. She is a political leader who is compassionately concerned about the underprivileged but also has rapport with the smart, cool blacks who now swing down Fifth Avenue on Saturday morning, their lithe figures clothed in sharp, fashion-leading garments. She recognizes—and indeed partakes of—their pride in being black and being somebody. For her and for them black is beautiful and it was already being anticipated that soon she would be one of their most powerful spokesmen.

But she will have no truck with black extremists such as the Black Panthers and some spear-carrying agitators who once came to her door to urge her to be more "free-thinking." She condemns prejudice in white men and sees no reason for black people to perpetuate it in reverse. "I'm an angry moderate," she said, "against hatred in all its forms."

At forty-four, Shirley Chisholm reflected on her ascent to prominence and power:

> I have learned that independence and integrity are not the most desirable attributes in politicians—although they should be. Yet it is for these very two reasons that the people are pushing me. The liability has become a real asset in my case.
>
> My rise has been meteoric. In four years I have gone from the bottom to become the most powerful black woman in America today, not because of the professional politicians, but because of the people on this street. The people who say I have got to lead them.

Though Shirley Chisholm's story was far from typical, it was not completely exceptional. It proved that given sufficient drive and ambition the American Negro can crash through into the nation's power structure. It required total singlemindedness and a great deal of mental toughness. The amount of effort needed was more than a white American would be called on to expend in order to reach a similar position.

This was an inequity, for a significant truth was readily apparent. America had opened her arms to Poles, Italians, Irishmen, Jews and all the other downtrodden and oppressed minorities of Europe. These people arrived without money, without a word of the English language in many cases and yet, through work and determination, they made good. They faced the same problem that the Negro minority now faces, but there were two great differences: they were not black and they had come to America voluntarily.

Shirley Chisholm mad made it, perhaps because her family, too, came to America of their own free will. The vast majority of American Negroes cannot forget that their ancestors arrived in chains. This would be bad enough, but the national problem is that the vast majority of all Americans have been unable to forget that the Negro's forebears were slaves. Whatever they may say, this fact is built into the American subconscious, and unless it can be removed the color problem must remain.

Education and example were the two things which could exorcise this racial fixation. Shirley Chisholm and tens of thousands of successful Negro Americans like her, were setting the examples and the Federal government was making great efforts to provide the education.

Yet with the best will imaginable, the pace at which a country can move to right the wrongs of 22 million people can never be fast enough. America could only strive to improve the situation of its Negro people; it could not work a miracle overnight. The rate of improvement could be speeded up, however, and the visitor felt that there was a determination to do so. But it seemed a miracle was what the Negro wanted, in fact demanded. They were among the first arrivals in America; all the other minorities had come later, and had surpassed them and helped to suppress them. The Negro's anger was easy to understand, for it could be argued that the American Negro today was in the position of being the latest immigrant to America.

Today then, the Negro stood where all those other new groups stood a few years after getting off the immigrant ships—at the bottom rung of the ladder. But he had a new awareness of his power and saw his possibilities more clearly. Equality—full and true—could be achieved; but much depended on the means the Negroes would use to fight their way through to this long desired goal. And much depended on how powerful the opposition would be. White backlash was a potent force, a force that would be tested in the election.

.10.

"They Want Welfare: We Want Wallace"

Nine million people in America were drawing some kind of dole during the election year—more than at any time since the Great Depression. In that year it was also revealed that 30 million Americans were below the poverty line. The majority of them were white, simply because the majority of Americans were white. Few Americans realized this fact. The poverty and hunger of the Negroes could be seen, and as a group they were organized enough to draw attention to their problems. The rest of the underprivileged were hardly vocal. Indeed many white people were ashamed to admit their poverty, as if to be poor were to be un-American.

The real problem was the United States' inability to help its own poor. It sent millions of dollars abroad and with them thousands of highly trained experts. But, inexplicably, it could not end a national disgrace within its own borders. The President had declared a "War on Poverty," but it was being prosecuted with even less success than the war raging in Vietnam. Contrary to widely held belief, the United States spent billions of dollars on welfare

157

for its less fortunate citizens. Rather, it wasted billions of dollars. Seldom had a modern state created a more chaotic bureaucracy to provide for its poor, its sick, and its hungry.

In an office high in the romantic and gargoyled Chrysler Building, William Haddad pored over his plans for the rationalization of welfare in certain southern cities. Haddad, very much a Kennedy man, had been instrumental in founding the Peace Corps and later the War on Poverty.

He said:

> The anomalies of the welfare system can be seen by the example of the teen-age girl who dropped out of school because she was ashamed of the clothes she had to wear. It was forbidden to use welfare money to buy clothes or furniture. So for the lack of $10 with which to buy herself a new dress the girl ceased her education. But, as soon as she became a dropout, she was then eligible through another government department to have $20,000 spent on her rehabilitation.

While Haddad was at the Office of Economic Opportunity he had ordered a list prepared of all the Federal assistance programs which then existed. "The first draft was a foot thick. If we had published it, Congress would have gone up in smoke. So I ordered a fined-down version, with just the major programs in it." The book was cut to about 700 pages and only three inches thick. It listed no fewer than 459 different programs. Many appeared to duplicate the work that others were doing. They were administered by varying agencies—by the Department of Health, Education and Welfare, as well as by the Department of Defense; by the Department of Agriculture, as well as by the Equal Employment Opportunity Commission; by the Department of Labor, as well as by the Small Business Administration.

The overall impression reminded one of Rome on the verge of downfall, piling one law and one program on top of another in a hopeless attempt to stop up holes in a dam, rather than to build a new one.

On September 23 the Rockefeller Foundation announced an award of $200,000 to the New York Urban League for a street-academy program, in which groups of young men were to go into the streets in search of high-school dropouts whom they would attempt to persuade to stay in school. Just two weeks later the city's Human Resources Administration was rocked by revelations of corruption in its Neighborhood Youth Corps program. At least $250,000 were said to have gone astray.

It was by no means atypical of American welfare schemes that some should put in and some should take out.

Mary White, a welfare worker, sat in her small apartment in uptown Manhattan. She said that most of her colleagues were, like herself, in the field for the money:

> The only way they can get people to do this job is by paying them well. But I'm quitting soon. I don't like being sworn at and threatened when all I'm trying to do is to help people. I can't take much more of it. We have no real training. You learn on the job. But welfare is so complicated that even I don't know half the time what people are entitled to and what agencies they can look to for help.
>
> And it's getting worse. This summer someone got some information that they were entitled to help in furnishing. A basic list had been made out of all the things that were considered essential to a house, even down to the dishcloths, and how much they should cost. So all the people on relief went and sat in at the welfare offices until finally the authorities had to give them the money for this furniture. They were busy handing out $1,000 checks until the money ran out.

Richard Cloward is Professor of Social Work at Columbia University. He has written some of the most advanced papers on welfare in the United States and its attendant problems. In his quiet room overlooking a strangely un-New York backwater he discussed why many big corporations are trying to improve the situation in the cities:

> They went in, first because the riots are costing the big outfits a whole lot of dough. The big utilities have been hit very hard. That too is why the insurance companies want to help. So this side of it is purely self-protective.
>
> Secondly, they see the possibility of profit. In this country even work-training programs have got to have guaranteed profits. Robert Kennedy had a bill in progress to guarantee 17 per cent profits for work in the ghetto.
>
> Finally there are some who are genuinely concerned about

159

political stability in America, because only with political stability can they survive.

Professor Cloward had more pungent things to say about the welfare system:

The American welfare system continually cheats people. There are a whole series of laws designed to exclude people from getting aid. For instance, most states have a residence law, so that you have to live there a year before you are eligible to draw aid. This hits the migrant worker badly. Or again, a welfare officer can refuse welfare to anyone whose children are over three, if that person is deemed employable, and if it is deemed that there is full employment. But this does not take into account at all the question of whether the person is suitable or qualified for the sort of work he might be offered.

It gets worse:

Tennessee law says that a blind person can't go on welfare if there is any evidence that he has been begging. *Well,* if he needs to go on welfare, how *else* can he have kept alive? . . . Over the whole of the country the average family of four gets $1,800 a year in welfare. In Mississippi the average is $388, and the maximum permissible is $40 a month.

Senator Eugene McCarthy spoke to the visitor one night about poverty:

On the question of poverty I think the first thing is to get an idea of where we're all going. We are in the process of passing so many programs and bills that we can't possibly fulfill them all. Just recently we even passed a bill about round tires, that tires had to be round. Well, now, you'd really think that the weights-and-measures department could have taken care of that wouldn't you? It is when we've got our priorities right that we have the best chance of taking care of the poor people.

Dr. George Harrar sat in his beautiful office in the sky above New York and decided how to allocate giveaways of $40 million a year. In 1968 the money given back to society by the Rockefeller Foundation, of which he is head, totaled $1 billion.

Dr. Harrar, one of the world's experts on the problems of hunger, believed that private money *had* to form at least part of the welfare effort:

> We worry about crash programs because I feel they're always likely to crash. We prefer programs with a logically selected goal. I'd hate to be in a world where private philanthropy was stifled by a belief in governmental priority and responsibility.
> I believe the foundations should not be partners with the government but persistent pioneers. If we are successful, then the government can step in and take over, as happened with the Salk vaccine and the birth-control pill.
> We try to choose programs that might otherwise not get a chance, because they might be thought too much of a gamble with public moneys. This is how we achieved the "miracle" rice and wheat that have been so successful in combating hunger in Mexico and the Far East.
> But I do understand how confused people get with all the different committees and programs trying to deal with the various problems. Someone once said it took seventy activities to solve one problem. It's part of our national feeling of independence; everyone thinks they know how best to deal with a matter, and everyone therefore wants to have it their own way.

Charity plays a very big part in the American way of life. In some areas of the South, where landowners, even in the mid-twentieth century, made it their patrician business to see that "their" Negroes were well fed and clothed with reach-me-downs, it had almost feudal overtones. But in most of the country charity began in affluent suburban homes. Once again comparison with Victorian England was inevitable. Then good works were allied to a social status. For the middle class and the rich charity was a convenient basis for distinction within the social structure.

In 1968 charity dinners and dances occupied the minds of society matrons in cities across the United States. Instead of being presented at court, debutantes—America had thousands of them—were presented at pseudoregal charity balls. Pretentious as this custom may seem, charity did produce enormous sums of money in the United States. Most people in the middle and upper classes were conditioned to giving considerable donations to good causes, and the fact that they could deduct such sums from their income-tax returns helped to swell the total even further.

"The private citizen contributes $14.5 billion a year to charity,"

161

said Harrar. "All the money that we in the foundations [including Carnegie and Ford, which gave away $200 million in 1967] give away is only 8 percent of all charity."

To the undernourished, the underprivileged, and the impoverished, three supposedly well-intended programs were particularly intolerable. One was the Soil Bank. This idea arose because American agriculture had reached a pitch of overproduction. As a result, the government decided that farmers should at certain times be paid for *not* producing on parts of their land but for letting it lie fallow instead.

To starving Indians in Arizona this abundance was small comfort. Nor did they appreciate the farmers of Indiana who slaughtered tens of thousands of pigs and buried them in order to maintain the price of pork. In the eyes of the hungry, the Soil Bank stopped the production of food that would have made all the difference to millions of Americans and tens of millions in the rest of the world.

Second was the food-stamp program, in which poor people could buy stamps representing money for food purchase at much lower rates than their face value. For instance, $1 might buy $20 worth of stamps, which could then be spent at the food store. There was only one snag. In order to buy the stamps one had to have a dollar in the first place, and thousands of people were too poor even for that.

The government recognized this problem. Speaking in Chicago a fortnight before the 1968 Democratic convention, Secretary of Agriculture Orville Freeman said:

> To widen participation in the food-stamp program we have reduced the investment needed by the lowest-income people to enter the program from $2 a month per person to 50 cents. And, where necessary, welfare or other organizations will pay the 50 cents.
>
> Now, you might think this would solve the problem. But it doesn't. It doesn't because the Federal government can't do the whole job alone. It takes local government and local citizens if we are to reach the people most in need.

He went on to list three reasons why people were still going hungry when food was available. One was ignorance about the basic elements of good nutrition. One was a lack of transport to

162

distribute surplus commodities from central points to local distribution stations. The third was ignorance of the program's existence:

Millions of people in this country who don't read very well, including some who don't read at all and who don't have much access to radio and television, just don't know that these assistance programs are available. Or if they do, maybe they don't want to go downtown because they lack proper clothing or aren't feeling well or misleading information has left them feeling the aid they will get is not worth the effort.

The third program was Aid to Dependent Children (A.D.C.). Under this scheme a family could obtain welfare if, and only if, there was no able-bodied man in the house. The result, especially in big-city ghettos was that husbands often left altogether or appeared on the sly only for the few hours between midnight and early dawn.

This regulation was one of the sorest points of contention between welfare workers and recipients, for the former were supposed to report any signs of a man in the house and were therefore naturally regarded as akin to Gestapo agents. This requirement had a clearly disastrous effect on the family—and to a great degree on the Negro family, as in the city its plight was usually the direst.

On May 21, 1968, C.B.S. presented a shocking television program on hunger. Said reporter Charles Kuralt:

America is the richest country in the world, in fact the richest country in history. We spend a colossal amount of money— $1.5 billion a year—to feed the rest of the world. But this spring a private agency, the Citizens Board of Inquiry, consisting of distinguished leaders in many fields, released an exhaustive report claiming that serious hunger exists in many places in the United States.

Out of a total of 200 million, the report states, 30 million Americans are impoverished, with family income below $3,000 a year. Five million of these people are helped by two existing Federal food programs. Now a new figure must be added. Of the 30 million who are impoverished, 10 million Americans, whether or not they are reached by Federal aid, are hungry. That's just the arithmetic.

The documentary went on to show the terrible human effects of

163

malnutrition, especially upon children afflicted by "hunger diseases" like kwashiorkor and marasmus that leave a baby one year old looking like a miniature old man of eighty.

C.B.S. came under heavy attack from the Department of Agriculture because of this program. It was accused of numerous inaccuracies that could have been avoided by simply checking with the Department. "Checking" is often not quite that easy. On the same day that C.B.S. televised its report the Department had issued for correspondents a statement on food and hunger in the United States. It said: "Section 11 of the National School Lunch Act is designed to help needy children get free or reduced price lunches. In this fiscal year a peak of 400,000 children in 1750 schools will be so assisted." Six days later on May 27 the Department submitted to the House Education and Labor Committee its remarks on the C.B.S. program. Complaining that C.B.S. had suppressed or ignored facts, it reported, "2,280,000 needy children are receiving free or reduced price school lunches."

Particularly confusing—to a non-American—was how to determine precisely what "below the poverty line" meant. Poverty in America is very different from poverty in Bombay or Cairo, but starving is the same anywhere. Nevertheless, to be poor in the palace seems worse than to be poor in the woodshed. And deprived Americans were surrounded by affluence. The Gross National Product of the United States was expected to pass $846 billion in 1968. The median family income was almost $8,000 annually. Sixty percent of Americans owned their own homes. Americans possessed a total of 54 million cars, 70 million television sets, and 75 million refrigerators. Poverty in the United States must be measured against this background. Not to be able to own a car or a television set hardly meant poverty in the Middle East, but in America it did, particularly where a car was the only means of mobility.

The psychological reaction to being poor amid affluence has never been fully analyzed. In America every television commercial, every radio jingle, every newspaper page, held out the promise of a better life just around the corner. The peculiar tone of such advertising was an assumption that people were already enjoying the good life and would merely want to make it even better. When one was urged to switch to a new car, the implication was that he already had a car of some kind. If one had no car and could never hope to afford one, this technique must have been extremely galling.

164

The poor heard urgings to switch from bread to cake while they themselves were not even receiving the crumbs from the table.

From the sidewalk billboards of Los Angeles to the pages of *The New York Times*, American advertising and the glorification of the consumer society surpassed those of any other country. The New Yorker, rich or poor, could pick up his Sunday newspaper and next to the news, which was spread strategically through the pages (so that almost every advertisement could "touch copy" and increase its chances for attention), could read such messages as

Save $100 on an eight-piece suite. Now $995. Exceptional value.

Fanciful furs incredibly priced from $179 to $749.

Dynatone helps tighten weak facial muscles in just minutes a day. $69.95

Buy your own personalized sauna bath.

How about a neat little silver and gold paper knife set in crystal for a mere $650? Or dash along to the Marcus Jewel Galleries in Gimbel's for a ring that will please her so much ($3,100) or a brooch in diamonds and platinum ($12,800).

Small wonder that burglar alarms at $99 seemed a very good deal, indeed.

In the confusion over how many Americans were starving and how many were merely hungry, who was "deprived" and who was simply poor, it was understandable that the average person had no real conception of what welfare was all about.

The magazine *U.S. News and World Report* reported on April 22 that welfare payments had reached $9.7 billion annually and that 90 percent of this money went to Negroes. The figure would have seemed plausible to most Americans, but it was incorrect. Two weeks later the magazine corrected itself. Seven and a half billion dollars were being spent on welfare, but only 40 percent of the recipients were Negroes, it said. Despite the fact that *U.S. News and World Report* did correct misinformation for its readers, it would have taken a public-education campaign costing as much as the various welfare schemes themselves to convince the majority of Americans that Negroes were not the major beneficiaries of this wasteful and corrupt system of handouts.

For three decades southern Negroes had been migrating north to swell the urban ghettoes. They came looking for jobs, but, because most of them were unable to find work, they went on the welfare rolls. Then, as their political awareness grew, they began to organize themselves to extract all that they could from the authorities. In New York in 1968 there were 1 million people on welfare, and the majority of them *were* Negroes.

They formed an increasingly vociferous and demanding pressure group in every big city. The authorities for the most part responded with more and more welfare schemes, which in turn brought more and more Negroes north. To support welfare local taxes were increased, the usual device being a state or city sales tax. (Federal funds are given for programs assisting the disabled, the blind, the aged, and dependent children.) Everyone thus had to contribute to the billions for welfare, but the people who felt the pinch most sharply were those in the first stratum above subsistence—the blue-collar class.

One of the great myths that Madison Avenue has sold to itself and the world is that, although everyone works in America, there is no working class. The idea (always ignoring the Negroes, the poor, and the super rich) is that the United States is the first all-middle-class nation. Within this framework the bricklayer can drive a Cadillac (and often does) and the stockbroker a Volkswagen. There is, of course, television for all and increasingly the second set is in color.

The myth is so successful that most Americans believe it themselves. It is as if the working class were non-existent.

Unlike Britain where the working class, not only exists, but insists on being recognized, blue-collar America is all but overlooked. The proletarian worker seldom appears in novels, in plays, or even in those contemporary barometers of the social climate, the television soap operas. Television serials in the United States seem set in a sterilized middle-class wasteland, with none of the earthy vulgarity of such British shows as "Till Death Do Us Part." Nor would a serial like "Coronation Street," which is entirely about working-class life, have much appeal to American television producers.

The obscuration of the working class in American consciousness may explain the lack of vitality in the American theater. Working-class playrights come to the fore writing about the world they live in; but when movies and television companies raised an invisible barrier against this world, which they had persuaded themselves

166

did not exist, potential working-class playrights had to go on working at the factory bench, letting the loan companies repossess their typewriters. So America does not produce writers like David Storey, Alan Sillitoe, Arnold Wesker, and Shelagh Delaney, who in Britain contribute greatly to the national cultural vitality.

Nonetheless America has a working class. Living in the outer rings of the cities, between the stink of the ghetto and the deodorized perfection of the suburbs it was becoming extremely frustrated and angry in 1968. Close enough to poverty to fear it, this class increasingly felt the pressure of inflation as the Vietnam war developed. It resented higher taxation, which appeared to be spent in handouts to Negroes. It resented the fact that its sons went to fight while the children of the affluent could not only avoid the war (because they were lucky enough to be in college) but could also strongly criticize those who were fighting it. It resented the fact that crime in the streets was mostly in *its* streets and that there were never enough policemen to protect *its* women and children. In short, it felt abandoned by the affluent and threatened by the poor, especially poor Negroes.

The blue-collar Americans were materially better off than were their British counterparts. They had bigger cars, larger screens on their television sets, thicker carpets on their floors, and automatic washing machines instead of twin tubs. But they paid for this prosperity in insecurity. A man might rise faster in the United States, but he could also crash faster. And there was much farther to fall than in Britain.

If one lives in public housing, with rent subsidies (totally free should one lose his job); if one receives free medical care for all his family; if one has redundancy pay guaranteed by law; if one has the mental attitude that state assistance in bad times is a right and not a gift, then there is little cause for tension or fear in one's daily life. This attitude was common among British workers in 1968 and it is fair to say that it was not very conducive to ambition. But at least the worker could feel secure.

Affluence offered little security to American workers as 1968 progressed. They listened to the candidates, but the candidates had little to offer them. They were busy addressing the intellectuals and the young about the war, the businessmen about the economy, the Negroes about poverty. Everything they said seemed to promise higher taxes and bigger handouts.

Governor Nelson Rockefeller, who had increased taxes to finance public spending in New York, declared that America would have to spend $15 billion a year over the next ten years to end poverty. Robert Kennedy was almost guilty of racism in his approach. Knowing that he was the only politician popular in the ghetto and actively seeking the Negro vote, he tended to treat poverty as if it were a purely Negro problem.

"The Federal government has a job to do," he said. That task, he explained in his campaign, was to provide jobs for *all Negroes* who were out of work. The number ran into millions, and he never explained what kinds of jobs they would be. He went further than anyone else, even Rockefeller, in suggesting new taxes: "We must re-examine these provisions which allow many Americans to escape their fair burden of taxation."

He had a valid point. For more Federal money was allocated for welfare—or subsidies—for business than on the poor. Business subsidies totalled more than $6 billion annually. Two and a half billion took the form of oil-depreciation allowances and tariffs. Cotton planters collected almost $1 billion in subsidies. Most nations subsidize some industries and part of their agriculture, but America—archexponent of free enterprise—went further than some socialist countries.

The oil industry did extremely well out of the government, as the oil depletion allowance permitted the industry to avoid a great deal of taxation. In 1965 four big companies—Cities Service, Sinclair, Pure, and Richfield—paid no taxes at all.

It was such loopholes that Kennedy attacked. He wanted the depletion allowance dropped or radically reduced. He wanted death duties increased. He wanted a minimum income tax to prevent "many rich people from escaping tax completely." Anyone who earned more than $50,000 a year ought to have to pay at least 20 percent in taxes, he declared.

Hubert Humphrey—the old "New Dealer"—was perfectly at home with the problem of poverty. He proposed all the old remedies: increased welfare and local and Federal aid to mop up unemployment. Richard Nixon wanted big business to do more for the Negroes. They had to be given a chance to become capitalists, he said. McCarthy supported a minimum-income guarantee, by which the government would see that no one would fall beneath the subsistence level, which in 1968 was set by the Federal government at $3,300 a year.

What none of these campaigners realized was the depth of feeling against welfare among those Americans who kept above the poverty line only by hard work and skimping. To them it was outrageous that money should be taken from working Americans, whatever their station, and given to nonworkers. It is not difficult to understand why. Americans are brought up on a mixture of Calvinistic belief that the poor have only themselves to blame for their plight and a nineteenth-century free-enterprise philosophy that deplores interference by the state.

Poverty and hunger among 30 million people were the major domestic crisis facing America in 1968. The race problem, the crime problem, the problem of the cities all grew out of this one. If the distribution of American affluence could be equalized many other problems would disappear. But the will, the planning, and the logistics required were enormous. The candidates nibbled at the problem, but, even while it was being discussed, the issue was obscured in general resentment and backlash against welfare.

It was easy to understand why the working class became angry as it listened to every Presidential contender expounding views that were the opposite of what many had been brought up to believe. Yet the workers had no means of putting forward their views on the matter. No one inquired whether or not they even had views.

For years they had been whipped into line behind the Democratic Party's candidates; the unions made sure that they were told which way to vote. In 1968 once again party leaders were ignoring them while concentrating on other issues. But this time the resentment was too great. The unions themselves had lost touch, sacrificing as they did local issues to national agreements. This time blue-collar Americans were prepared to revolt. All they needed was the right man to come along and channel their frustration and bitterness into a potent political force. And this time there was such a man. His name was George Corley Wallace.

As the winter of 1967–1968 came to an end Wallace was already on the stump, speaking to small crowds in cities all over America. He had been making the same speech since before Christmas.

Now you take a big sack, and you put L.B.J. in there, and you put Hubert Horatio Alger Humphrey in there, and you put Bobby Kennedy the blood giver in there. Then you put

Richard Milhous Nixon in there, and you put that Socialist Nelson Rockefeller in there, and you put that left-winger George Romney in there. Then you turn that sack over, and the first one that falls out you pick him up by the scruff of the neck, and you drop him right back in again, because there's not a dime's worth of difference in any of them!

At this point there was always a roar of laughter that invariably turned into applause. George Wallace would raise his hands and laugh with the audience. But the humor never reached his eyes. The glitter there was not funny; it was dark with meaning and challenge. The small crowds listening to him had turned out expecting to see a southern curiosity, a racist redneck. But George Wallace never explicitly mentioned Negroes or segregation. He talked instead in a sort of code, using terms like "law and order," "hoodlums," "anarchists and Communists," "layabouts," and "good-for-nothings." But his listeners knew whom he meant. When he said that there was not a dime's worth of difference among the conventional politicians appealing for their votes, he expressed precisely what frustrated them. They went back to their homes, their factories, their workshops, and they told other men like themselves about what Wallace had to say. The crowds began to get bigger.

When Wallace began his campaign professionals within the Democratic Party treated him as a particularly obnoxious joke. "I don't think that he will round up many cattle," said Hubert Humphrey, using a western metaphor that almost certainly originated in the White House. There was a reason for this contempt. Third parties had never done very well in America, and Wallace had no organization, no money, no machine. His strutting bantam cock's manner, his southern accent, his very parochialism could never make him a national figure, said the pros. Either they had forgotten his impact in the 1964 Indiana primary, in which he polled more than 30 percent of the vote, or rationalized it, as Bobby Kennedy did: "Indiana is a border state with a good bit of the South about it. It's a special case."

The special case was not the state but the candidate. George Wallace was five feet seven and a half inches of political ambition, and he sensed as no one else had sensed the resentment, bewilderment, and prejudice (intensified by events since 1964) of the blue-collar American.

Incredible though it may seem now, early in his political career Wallace had been a moderate. His views had changed abruptly when he lost the 1958 Alabama gubernatorial election. Among the candidates was young, personable John Patterson, whose father had been shot to death in a notorious vice resort named Phenix City after launching a drive to clean the place up.

In the campaign Wallace's low-keyed segregationism ran second by 65,000 votes to Patterson's rabid racism, supported by the Ku Klux Klan. Wallace, after some hesitation, had issued a statement denouncing the Klan, although he added that some members were acceptable people.

Wallace was utterly stunned by his defeat and dropped out of sight for a time. A month or so later he reappeared one night at his old haunt, the Jefferson Davis Hotel in Montgomery. He looked almost like a sleepwalker, according to one observer, quiet, peaceful, and with a strange air of certainty. For a time he sat silently among the noisy local politicos and then he spoke words that must rank high in the annals of political frankness: "John Patterson out-nigguhed me, and, boys, Ah'm not goin' to be out-nigguhed again."

Wallace was a southerner to the end of his brilliantined hair. To visit the small-town South of the United States in 1968 was to travel back in time. There was racial tension, of course, but very often it was less apparent on the surface (and less dangerous because of the compliant attitude of southern Negroes) than it was in the North. The atmosphere was also rendered curiously old-fashioned by physical appearances. There was a dated feeling, as if one had crossed into the 1930s. This impression was heightened by the behavior of the people.

Southern courtesy may have seemed exaggerated because its standards were prewar (and in the 1930s its standards were Edwardian), but it was practiced with skill. One of its greatest exponents was George Wallace himself. He received visitors, even when he knew that they were violently opposed to him, with courtesy, humor, and even flattery. "You're British," he said to one visitor in Montgomery. "Then you all should know about us and be sympathetic to our problems down hyah, because you see"— and his glittering eyes looked straight at his guest—"we're all of British blood here, most of us." He picked up a telephone directory. "Just look at these pages," he said. "All British names—English or Scots-Irish. We're your people. A fine people."

Wallace is a good Scots name. The Wallaces had been in the South for 200 years, having come to the Carolinas originally from Ulster. George Wallace's forebears moved to Alabama in the nineteenth century. Many men from Barbour County, Alabama, carried the first name Wallace because they had been delivered by Doctor George Oscar Wallace, the local physician. His son "Sag" was a poor farmer, who showed more talent for politics than for agriculture. Sag's son George inherited and developed that talent.

Although the legend was that he was a "poor country boy from Barbour County" and many people pictured those distant days in Huckleberry Finn terms, George Wallace never had any time for country pursuits. Power was his goal from the first, and he had never taken his eye off the target.

While he was serving in the air force during World War II "the folks back home," including "folks" who had barely known him, were puzzled to receive a flood of pleasantly worded Christmas cards from him. The cause became clear when he was demobilized. He came out of uniform and began his political career the next day. In 1946 he won his first election and went into the Alabama State House of Representatives.

After his 1958 defeat, he campaigned for the governorship again in 1962 and won. It was during his term in the governor's mansion in Montgomery that he became a national figure with his grandstand play in defiance of school-desegregation orders.

Wallace was a nominal Democrat, but the term was meaningless. In 1964 he proclaimed: "Ah'm an Alabama Democrat, not a national Democrat. That's like the difference between being a Communist and a non-Communist." He had more or less supported Barry Goldwater in the Presidential election of 1964. At that time he was already toying half-heartedly with the idea for which he went all-out in 1968: the creation of a third party. But in 1964 it became clear that if he managed to attract a large vote, he would anger conservatives by damaging Goldwater in a part of the country where he was expected to do well. So Wallace dropped out of the race.

In 1966, at the end of his four-year term as Governor, an annoying snag presented itself. Alabama's constitution, like those of most southern states, does not allow a governor to succeed himself. Wallace sought to brush aside this nuisance and asked the Alabama legislature to amend the constitution to allow him a second term. The legislation was blocked by a filibuster on the part of anti-

172

Wallace state senators. Then rumors that most people could hardly countenance at first became official: Mrs. George Wallace was going to run for Governor!

This crude piece of power politics caused a furore. Even the most naïve observers were unwilling to believe that Lurleen Wallace would be more than a puppet of her husband. She was on record as having said, "I used to hear Daddy talking politics with his friends, but he never talked politics with me."

He never had talked politics to her. She had devotedly and happily remained in the background of George Wallace's life, giving him four children, never getting in his way, but always being ready to assist if and when he should call her. In 1966 at the age of 39 this pale, modest, former dime-store clerk was called.

Running would be a sacrifice. She hated the limelight, and she knew the sneers that she would have to face when she went on the road. Even more she knew the physical hardships the campaign would impose. Only a few weeks earlier she had undergone major surgery for cancer, and the prognosis had not been encouraging, but she was ready to play her part without question. She would do what her husband wanted.

She made dozens of appearances, reciting a set speech as if she were valedictorian at a high-school commencement. It always seemed to give her great relief to reach the closing sentence: "And now my friends I give you my husband, and your Governor, who will be my number-one assistant in the next administration—George C. Wallace."

This shy, already-dying woman became Governor of Alabama, but her career as political puppet was brief and somber. Jests about her were usually muted, but her governorship was regarded even by Wallace men as a cynical comedy. She became known in Montgomery as "the automatic pilot"—a device which pilots call "George." When it was put about that she and George had sat up all night agonizing over a decision whether or not to reprieve a murderer, nobody imagined that the agonizing (if indeed there had been any) had been done by more than one person.

As cancer led to further surgery, Lurleen Wallace's condition became all too obviously hopeless. Her eyes stared pathetically from dark circles, and she became so weak that she was barely able to go through the motions of doing her job. She carried her personal sacrifice to the end and in doing so hastened it. In April she went into hospital for the last time and on May 7, 1968, she died.

173

George Wallace observed the proper interval of mourning. Then he pressed on with his task, which was now clearly defined: to harness the forces of discontent at one extreme of the Democratic Party, just as Eugene McCarthy had harnessed them at the other. George Wallace had a constituency. All over the country groups of men, mostly workers and sometimes led by local union secretaries (who had been ordered by headquarters to organize for Humphrey), were spontaneously forming "We Want Wallace" clubs. Whatever the motivation, here was American grass-roots politics in action. With little money and no paid campaign staff, George Corley Wallace was nevertheless able to collect hundreds of thousands of signatures to put him on the Presidential ballot in every state in the union.

At last he was breaking out of Dixie. It remained to be seen whether or not he was strong enough to smash through into mainstream politics. In any event, third-party politics could no longer be taken lightly in America in 1968.

.11.

THE REPUBLICANS: NEW IMAGE VERSUS OLD FORTUNE

THE LAST TIME RICHARD NIXON HAD RUN FOR PRESIDENT, HIS CAMPAIGN had been dogged by such ill luck that many of the reporters assigned to him became convinced that they would inevitably be killed in a fatal crash of the Nixon plane. Others, who did not believe in fate, simply became fed up with the inefficiency of the Nixon staff and the grueling schedules necessitated by his promise to campaign in all fifty states.

Indeed, all the men around Nixon, whether staff or reporters, became irritable from exhaustion. Nixon was no exception, and it was this exhaustion that helped to make the bad luck. First, there was an accident to his knee, which led to two weeks of enforced hospitalization. Then came a series of colds, culminating in an attack of flu that left him weak and almost speechless. Finally, there was the devastating miscalculation over the television debates, which almost certainly lost him the election.

Now, eight years later, eight years older, and eight years wiser, Richard Nixon was trying again, and this time luck seemed to be on his side. The Democrats were in the middle of a cannibalistic struggle. His Republican opponent, Nelson Rockefeller, was challenging him with all the decisiveness of an Egyptian general. And the Nixon machine, carefully constructed during his years of exile, was running faultlessly.

Of all the characters in search of the Presidency, Nixon was unquestionably the most intriguing. Born into a classic American lower-middle-class background, he was impelled from an early age to devote every energy to seek the success that is apparently a necessity to Americans from that background.

But his achievements—as a congressman, senator, Vice-President, party leader—had never seemed to give him the poise and maturity that others gained from such successes. A nervous uncertainty seemed always to be near the surface. It was partly this uncertain quality that made people distrust him. Not only his personality seemed elusive; his views on policy were vague as well. He could change course more swiftly than a hounded fox. The label "opportunist" was glued to him in his early appearances, and it had never come completely unstuck. People asked: "What *does* he believe in? What *does* he stand for?"

He was called "the man with the built-in smile" by hostile writers, yet cartoonists always drew him with a permanent, unshaven scowl—a funny contradiction. Whoever looked at Nixon—whether friend or enemy—saw only the image and never succeeded in penetrating through to the man underneath.

David Broder and Stephen Hess, in their acute study of the G.O.P., *The Republican Establishment,* relate the following anecdote, which illustrates Nixon's image problem. A series of disastrous brushfires was sweeping southern California in November 1961, leaping from one luxurious home to another in Bel Air and Brentwood. Nixon, at the time, was living in a Tudor-style house on North Bundy Drive, rented from a film director. Across the street flames had already destroyed the residence of comedian Joe E. Brown.

> As the first press photographers reached the scene, the former Vice-President was hosing down a small fire. "He got a true action photo," a Nixon aide later commented. But true to the code of the paparazzi, the photographer insisted that Nixon re-enter his house and pose at the door with a suitcase. The next day almost every newspaper in the country

showed Nixon with suitcase instead of Nixon with hose. *For the real Nixon looked posed and the posed Nixon looked real.*

One of the major discussions of the 1968 campaign—beginning with reporters, amplified by television commentators, and finally echoed across all fifty states of America—was whether or not the *new* Nixon was the *real* Nixon. In other words, which Nixon was the phony? Had he changed or merely learned? Or both?

The disastrous slogan, "Would you buy a used car from this man?" which had helped to defeat Nixon in 1960, had always seemed curiously inapposite. Perhaps American used-car salesmen are different from their British counterparts, but Nixon never appeared to have the flashy transparency of the traditional dealer in second-hand cars. His personality was more unctuous, a bit too ingratiating, more that of an undertaker.

Watching him in 1968 the visitor found that Nixon—when he was not campaigning in public—still reminded him of a mortician. Maybe the fault lay in his clothes; he wore dark suits and ties, the suits usually dated in cut and badly fitted around the shoulders, where he developed a peculiar slouch. He is five feet eleven inches tall and stoops deferentially when greeting people. Perhaps a lifetime of political greetings had given him a hunched appearance. He tried hard to please when he was on show, and one could see that it was not easy for him.

In physical appearance he had changed very little. His face was perhaps a little fuller, though the jowls were just as dark, in spite of relentless scraping twice a day. He was always tanned, which made him look better, and the bitterness around that rather tight mouth was gone. His smile reflected genuine humor, whereas before it had been merely a muscular contraction, programmed to exhibit his teeth in response to a given set of stimuli.

There was a new air of easy confidence too. Perhaps New York had done that, for there he had been forced to move outside the Washington political stockade and to meet with men whose interests—both personal and professional—extended well beyond the range of Nixon's former world. Some of their sophistication had rubbed off on him.

He had also become richer. When he closed his Washington home in 1961 his net worth had been $45,000, according to his closest friend, Bebe Rebozo. It was the dividend of eight years as Vice-President. But then no one, even his bitterest opponents, had

177

ever accused Nixon of feathering his own nest; he took money from sponsors for his campaign, but it was all spent on the main purpose of his existence, getting elected. And, once elected, Nixon ceased to worry about money.

When, in 1963, he became a senior partner in the law firm of Nixon, Mudge, Rose, Guthrie, Alexander, and Mitchell (as the "headliner," to attract business) his salary was put at $250,000. But Nixon did more than simply headline the firm. He proved—more to his own surprise than to anyone else's—to be a first-rate litigation lawyer and a near genius in coaching young attorneys. He moved into the same Fifth Avenue apartment building in which his millionaire Republican rival, Nelson Rockefeller, lived. His daughters went to the best schools and made their social debuts.

And so the classic success story was now complete—in financial terms. Richard Milhous Nixon, millionaire and successful Wall Street lawyer, had finally joined the establishment. But some deep instinct still prevented him from letting himself be fully absorbed within its ranks.

His scramble for power and success in the political arena had never been dignified. He had always been too much in a hurry. His naked ambition had been a source of embarrassment to him, and he knew it. Now, however, he had what had eluded him before: dignity.

The lemon grower's farmhouse in which Richard Nixon was born in 1913 made a romantic scene for the beginning of his story. But there was nothing romantic about it at the time. The Nixons were honest, hard-working, devout Quakers—and poor. Sickness ran in the family. Frank Nixon, permanently troubled with ulcers, lost two of his children before their tenth birthdays, one from meningitis, the other from tuberculosis. Richard Nixon remembers those days very vividly.

> Mother took Harold away to Arizona and more or less lived at the nursing home where he was for two years. She was able to keep him there by working on the staff. She did everything, cooking, scrubbing, cleaning out furnaces or anything she was told to do. While she was trying to save Harold's life, my little brother Arthur died of meningitis. He was seven.
>
> When Harold came back he was still sick but we believed he was going to get better. One day he asked me to take him into town because he wanted to buy mother a present. . . . So I took him downtown and he bought [it] and we went back home and I went to school thinking how happy he was

that he had got the present. I hadn't been there a quarter of an hour before a teacher came and told me to go home because my brother had just died.

It was a hard time and the Nixons did not have a great deal of luck. Frank Nixon had bought a small general store with a gas pump but he only just made a living, and was often owed more money than he made. He accepted his luck as a loser and that was that. But these experiences helped to form the character of Richard Nixon, the man who would never accept the role of a loser himself.

This determination is the clue to his drive. The social graces were given to him neither by birth nor by environment, and success was the necessary—and indeed the only—substitute for them.

The 1952 "Checkers" telecast was perfectly understandable against this background. When his career was jeopardized by the charge that California businessmen were backing him with an illegal campaign fund in the 1952 election, Nixon abased himself before the television cameras. He sacrificed all dignity as he twisted, pleaded, and finally begged for sympathy. His wife, his children, even his daughters' cocker spaniel were invoked in his plea for absolution at the altar of American sentiment.

Absolution was granted, but at what a price!

One wondered if such a man could have made the political scene in Britain. Could a Nixon survive the Commons with its ritualistic blood letting, its suave and subtle savagery? Would it be death by a thousand cuts, or would it be the making of him? The inescapable conclusion is the latter. Half a lifetime in politics had made him rather than destroyed him, but it took defeat to give him dignity. It was only when he became a loser and found that he could live with it that he came to terms with himself.

In 1968 past political insults and humiliations were no longer so important. He had marshaled his talents and started again. And this time, because he was older, wiser, and cooler; because his ambition was not so naked; because he had learned that one does not necessarily win even when he sacrifices everything, he chose to drop the phoniness and be more himself. As a result, he was more attractive than he had been eight years before.

The crowds that turned out for him were enthusiastic, though lacking the frenzy of the Kennedy crowds or the devotion of McCarthy's. Nevertheless all through the spring they grew bigger and bigger. In small town after small town, Nixon would come on the platform to applause, smile, and start immediately with a stream of gags: "Everyone's in the Democratic race. McCarthy's running for President. Now Bobby's got in there. He's running for King, and Hubert, well, he's running for the foreman's job down on the ranch."

Then to serious things. The war? He refused to talk about it because negotiations were taking place and no responsible American would want to embarrass the President at such a time. The economy? It was facing one of its biggest crises in American history. The cities? There was a breakdown of law and order: "Some courts in America had gone too far in weakening police forces." Vast sums of money had to be spent on the cities, but it simply was not available at the moment. The "law and order" theme, which was to become one of the big issues in the election, figured prominently in Nixon's repertoire right from the beginning. But he had other things to say, and many members of his audience (and most of the press corps) felt strongly that they were things the old Nixon would never have said.

The most important statement of all was about Negroes:

> For too long white America has sought to buy off the Negro —and to buy off its own sense of guilt—with ever more programs of welfare, of public housing, of payments to the poor, but not for anything except for keeping out of sight—payments that perpetuated poverty and that kept the endless dismal cycle of dependency spinning from generation to generation.
>
> Our task, our challenge, is to break this cycle of dependency, and the time to begin is now. The way to do it is not with more of the same but by helping to bring to the ghetto the light of hope and pride and self-respect. . . .
>
> Much of the black-militant talk these days is actually in terms far closer to the doctrines of free enterprise than to those of the welfarists of the '30s. What most of the militants are asking is not separation but to be included in—not as supplicants but as owners, as entrepreneurs—to have a share of the wealth and a piece of the action. It ought to be oriented toward more black ownership, for from this can flow the rest —black pride, black jobs, black opportunity, and, yes, black power.

It was a great speech, a brilliant speech—compassionate, far-sighted, and hitting precisely a point that many liberals seemed not to have observed. The Negroes did not want patronizing sops, not welfare and handouts, not even "made" work. America was a capitalist society, and the Negroes wanted to be capitalists.

180

Afterward the visitor questioned Nixon on how he thought his conservative supporters would react to this radical speech.

Well, I think they understand, and I believe they'll accept the whole thesis. It's very difficult for them to be against private enterprise. How can they possibly adopt a stand against that? Anyway not many of those people like being called "racists." They want to escape that tag if they can.

The "bridges to human dignity" speech, he believed, would give them an opportunity to do so.

The pressmen assigned to the Nixon campaign in the cold winter days of the early primaries at first adopted their traditionally hostile attitude toward him, taking up where they had left off in 1960. Nixon worked and held private meetings in a compartment at the back of his chartered Lockheed Electra. He spent much of his time there while the press sat in front.

The visitor asked a well-known American correspondent whether or not it was possible to wander into the rear section to talk with the candidate. He received a short, barking laugh and the reply: "You Limeys kill me. Do you think they're going to let you walk in back there and actually see Dracula resting in his coffin?"

Within a few weeks the attitude of the traveling press had changed from hostility to grudging admiration and then to something like affection. Several factors contributed to the change. First, this time the Nixon organization was infallible. Hotel rooms were always arranged, and they were usually the best. The baggage always arrived exactly on time. Everyone was called at the correct hour, cars were never missing, and everyone was always kept informed. The campaign was much more leisurely. Instead of the frantic dawn-to-midnight schedules of the opposition, Nixon kept up an unhurried, almost gentlemanly, pace. Breakfast could be taken at 10:00 A.M. because, as N.B.C.'s Herb Kaplow observed, "We're all geared up to get started at the crack of noon every day."

In the plane, the atmosphere was even more serene. Nixon showed no tension and made a habit of talking at length with the men assigned to him. He was more relaxed talking to individuals than to groups, and he seemed more at ease with foreigners as he felt foreign affairs to be his forte.

On one occasion he talked about his life in politics and the events that had led to his position as front runner among the Republican nominees:

181

I was always in politics in the broadest sense. After California in 1962, I moved to New York and took a trip around the world. I was not in politics then—I was out—but that trip had a political significance. Then in 1964, 1965, and 1966 I made trips around the country. My firm decision to try again was made after the 1966 off-year elections. I mean, after 1962 and California it was a thousand-to-one chance I'd be a candidate again. There was some talk in 1964, but I had no illusions about it.

I mean, hell, my philosophy has always been that you do the job no matter how grubby or irrelevant it is or because of your personal ambition. Inevitably your mind will adopt a certain fatalness—not predestination; I don't mean that. A man must be in the arena if he is going to fight. I stayed in that arena without the expectation of ever being a candidate again. But should the occasion arise I would be there. It did, and I was.

Nixon was often carried away by his thoughts. He was a man who rarely thought of anything other than politics and its practical applications. "There are two classic examples, perhaps three, of this," he went on, staring out the cabin window at a desert of white cloud. "Adenauer, De Gaulle, and Churchill. Who ever thought De Gaulle would come back? Churchill suffered defeats in the '30s, and no one saw a future for him. Adenauer was a very obscure mayor who was initially arrested by the British. But all three of them were there when needed."

Richard Nixon had a penchant for sporting metaphors. Indeed one suspects that he deliberately injected slang phrases into his speeches in order to jolt his audience. ("It also injects the idea that he identifies with them," said one aide, "but then of course he does.") He slipped into sports phrases to describe his emotions.

A man can't sit in the bleachers. You've got to do the grubby things like fund raising in miserable congressional districts. But then, when you are called on to lead, you can honestly say, "I was there."

You know there's a lot of bull written about collecting political I.O.U.s. The game just isn't played that way. Sure they remember and appreciate it. But then, towards the end, even the ones who don't like you say: "We're stuck. We've got to take the old S.O.B." And they go with you for the party—not because they owe you anything.

But I rock with the punches. I don't mean grin and bear it either. I mean grin and like it."

What went through Nixon's mind when he decided to run again? Looking back on it, 20,000 feet above the heartland of America in April 1968, he recalled that he too had written himself off:

But then in 1966 the party was on the ground, and we all, as individuals, had to pick ourselves up in order that the party as a whole should pick itself up. So I decided that I would have another go.

I took my decision to Florida after Christmas 1966. Of course, there were family considerations, more now than in the past. And I say now that I would not have done it had my wife and daughters been against it. And—you may find this curious—the strongest advocates of my political life are my daughters.

My wife, Pat [Nixon had a strange habit of always naming his wife in conversation, as if he had to identify her] knew the struggle. Frankly she was not keen. But the girls worked on her. Both are history majors. Both are very bright, no, reasonably bright. They are very idealistic.

Well, the kids said the country was in trouble and you, meaning me, can save it. Had they opted against it I would not have tried again. Women in politics are historically more idealistic than men. They tend not to ask the question "Can he win?" And I knew it was a long shot. The party was terribly divided.

One summer at Duke University [where Nixon studied law during the Depression years] I needed money, so I ran a hand-operated mimeograph machine. It was dreadfully boring, and this terrible assignment sometimes took ten hours a day. I think of that awful summer frequently because, when you're campaigning for the Presidency, you have to do a lot of boring political things.

During those leisurely spring days, as the nights grew longer and warmer, the crowds bigger, and the hopes greater, Nixon's thinking often outpaced his words, producing a stream of consciousness in which past humiliations mingled with future aspirations. The words would flow jerkily from multidimensional thoughts, slipping through time barriers, so that the man talked about the politician, the politician about the man, and the man about the boy. One day, as the plane headed for Miami after a week of campaigning, Nixon set off on another of his verbal voyages:

Once you are in the race you do it well. I mean the small things, as well as the big ones. I'm not a complete perfection-

183

ist, but anything worth doing is worth doing well. In 1960 both camps worked too hard and too long. Jack Kennedy told me afterwards he was exhausted for one full month after the election. Well, I was just as bad, and I think we both knew then that it was the wrong way to fight.

"You must think of the big play, and you must make the big play," he went on, dropping into sporting metaphor again.

A man must be emotionally and physically at his best. Saturate the mind, and ideas grow and expand. The brain is like a big muscle. You've got to exercise it.

We are at a time when we need a new imput of ideas. The idea that all nations will be friends forever is bull. There will always be competition between strong individuals. The trick is to keep the competition peaceful. As close as we are to the British and the Canadians, regardless, there will always be competition. I understand the realities of power. I am strongly idealistic. That's why when you ask which American President is the greatest I must say Lincoln, but the one I admire most must be Wilson. He was a great idealist. He leavened his idealism with a practical, real recognition of the nature of man.

From that simple phrase "the nature of man," Nixon's mercurial mind switched to a completely different subject without missing a beat:

I'd like to see—I've been poor—people not having to worry. But getting a check for nothing is not the nature of man. There are saints who believe that everyone is like themselves. Everyone ain't that way. Take the Marxists. They've had to turn our way and introduce new economic theories to give people an incentive.

Now, take my family. We were poor for a reason. My folks were hard-working and saved money. My old man was so proud he wouldn't send his boys to public school.

We were poor because we spent money on being proud. There's no pride like the pride of the poor. It's a savage thing, you know, that kind of pride. As a kid I grew up with poverty. We had a grocery store, and all we served were poor people from poor families. It was tough for them; sometimes they didn't have enough money to buy food they needed. My father would always help them out. But he used to say, "You have to help without hurting"—no handouts, no insults to a man's pride. Not if you can achieve the same assistance in any other way. And you can.

184

The public man must have a heart as well as a head. All head and no heart is no good. A man who has that combination of heart and head has the potential for great leadership, for it means that he has a deep concern for people.

Here was a Nixon that few people had seen. His ideas were tumbling out at a ferocious rate. The question was whether he would stand by them the next day when talking to another person in another place.

From up ahead in the aircraft some reporters were singing, rather sarcastically, the campaign song "Nixon's the One," which had been performed for the first time during a $25-a-plate fund-raising dinner three nights earlier in Phoenix, Arizona. The dinner had been the scene of a delicate meeting between conservative Barry Goldwater and Nixon—and a comic disaster, in which the Old Nixon would have floundered but at which the New Nixon could afford to laugh.

First, the cost of the dinner given by the Trunk 'n' Tusk (the elephant is the G.O.P. symbol) had been reduced from $100 to $25 because California Governor Ronald Reagan had been there the week before, and it was feared that people would refuse to produce another $100 for roast beef congealing in cold sauce.

With the dessert came Frank J. Bright, a Welshman who had convinced the Republican organizers that he could sing. He dedicated his medley to the candidate; the first tune was "With a Little Bit of Luck" and the last "To Dream the Impossible Dream." But Bright's voice knew no key; the performance was painful. From a press table, John Sears, Nixon's 27-year-old political assistant, muttered, "He's got to be a Democrat."

Finally the master of ceremonies, Representative Jack Williams, stood to announce Goldwater: "There is no East or West at this table," he declared, referring to the fact that Nixon officially lived in New York. "No—this is a square table," he thundered and looked round for applause. Nixon's advisers cringed, and the press doubled up with laughter. It was that kind of evening.

Now, in the plane, as the reporters took up the simple tune, Nixon went up to talk to them about it. "Hey, how did you like that new song? It's a good one. It's a combination of the new music —I'm familiar with it because the kids listen to it—and the old-time revivalist music. I had a lot of that as a kid." He raised his arms like a revivalist and sang "Bringing in the Sheaves." He was elated. He was relaxed.

Several times during the year's campaign Nixon broke off to go down to Key Biscayne and stay with the man who is perhaps his closest personal friend, C. B. (Bebe) Rebozo.

Rebozo is just the kind of friend Nixon *would* have. He is rich—just barely a millionaire. He does not make headlines and when cornered by a group of reporters shows distinct discomfort. He is not a socialite but one of those easy-going Americans who made it up from the lower middle class to riches but who chose the stay in the middle class.

He started in business on his own with a one-pump filling station. After the war he went into self-service laundries, real estate and finally became the president of the Key Biscayne bank.

His one-story house on Bay Lane is pleasantly middle-class without pretention. This 55-year-old bachelor usually evokes a sadness in people he meets—except when he is around his adopted family, the Nixons. He had long been on the fringe of politics as a supporter and friend of Senator George Smathers of Florida. He met Nixon through Smathers. Although from different parties, Nixon and Smathers were elected to the House of Representatives together in 1946, and campaigned for the Senate successfully in 1950.

In 1948 Nixon made his name when, as a member of the House Un-American Activities Committee, he went after Alger Hiss—an urbane State Department official—demanding that he be investigated for Communist activities. Nixon's relentless pursuit of his victim split the nation, particularly after Hiss had been convicted and imprisoned. From that affair Nixon acquired a reputation that hardened people's attitudes toward him perhaps for a lifetime. They either admired him or despised him. One of the admirers was Rebozo. He had been unwavering in his admiration ever since.

"I first met Dick when he wanted a rest after the Hiss case," Rebozo recalled. "He asked Senator Smathers about a nice place to holiday in Florida. Smathers asked me to extend hospitality to Nixon, and I did so. Since then he's visited me regularly, sometimes alone, sometimes all four Nixons, Pat, Trish and Julie. After the '52 election, when he became Vice-President, they all came. I could say almost all his vacations have been with me. And I have traveled a lot with him."

Of Nixon Rebozo said:

> He comes down here to relax because he can get a little privacy. He just loves swimming in salt water, you know; he can't stand swimming pools.

186

I like him very much. I know it sounds corny, but I think he's a great man, a man who deserves to be President. It makes me mad when I hear him criticized for being shifty and opportunist. He's one of the most honest men I've ever met. He's selfless, he doesn't care about money, and he's generous.

Of course, he's not the easiest of men to know. He's very tense, a very deep thinker, and he likes to be alone. He mulls things over a lot. But, if you interrupt his thoughts, he lets you know if he's displeased.

Rebozo was surprised at all the talk of a new Nixon:

It just shows that no one knew him very well in the past. He's basically the same, just lighter. In 1960 he was, after all, the Vice-President and had to be more serious. There were important issues he had to master and tasks he had to perform. Nixon does not wear his brilliance on his sleeve. . . . People tend to think that Nixon is so tough that all the harsh things written about him just bounce off. They don't. They hurt; they hurt him a great deal. But he has amazing control and discipline for the most part, and so it rarely shows.

Nixon's routine, when he was not on the road campaigning, was to be in bed by 11:00. He would sleep instantly but invariably waken in the early hours. He always kept a tape recorder and half a dozen of his endless stock of yellow legal pads by the bed, and, as soon as he woke up, he would clear his mind by making quantities of notes on paper and tape. He would then go back to sleep without any problem.

"I've learnt to pace myself better, concentrate more, and worry less," he said during one reflective conversation in an Oregon hotel room. He had a habit of talking about himself in the third person, which was curiously inoffensive, whereas in Hubert Humphrey the same trick sounded pompous. "Nixon learnt a lot of things in 1960. For instance, John Kennedy would suddenly disappear and spend a couple of unpublicized days at the beach. Nixon never did that. He went the whole way without relaxing once, and it was both killing and unwise." He grinned. "Having a tan helps you, you know. Appearance counts for a lot. A good shave and a nice tan, they really help in our politics. I'm determined never to be without both if I can help it. I'm tired now, but give me the sun and the sea, and I'll come back fast. Also my voice is good. A politician's voice is vital, and Nixon's only had laryngitis three times in his life."

Nixon was fascinated with the techniques of campaigning, which perhaps explains his regard and liking for John Kennedy, the man who had beaten him so closely in 1960. It was a liking that was not reciprocated, a fact that Nixon accepted with equanimity. He repeated over and over that Kennedy's techniques had taught him a great deal, and the visitor felt that he was talking not only as a politician but also as a human being.

It is all in the pacing now. I must not stack it full. I want to do fewer things better. I want more time to think. Most politicians just get up and yak away, reading words they are not familiar with. With me it is a fetish to get into a subject, to feel it. And that requires time. There's so little of that.

I have also surrounded myself with another generation, a younger generation. They're faster. The old people are slower. Frankly, many people my age can't keep up with me. They can't stand the pace physically, and they can't move swiftly with ideas.

Why Rockefeller has 150 people around him, and Nixon has five. He uses the task-force technique, while Nixon prefers a few close key men. I wrote most of my own stuff. You've got to work like hell. This is not just a flashy thing.

Look at my small band. There's Leonard Garment. He's left of Nixon, a liberal. There's Pat Buchanan. He's right of Nixon. Ray Price is slightly left of Nixon.

It was growing late, but Nixon wanted to go on talking, particularly about the visitor's country. He understood the economic pressures that were restricting British foreign policy, he said, but the withdrawal from east of Suez was, in his view, a tragedy.

Had I been President, I would have subsidized Britain economically to stay east of Suez. Asia is the future arena. British brains and diplomacy are invaluable out there. I know these men. I feel British entry into Europe is essential both for the future of Britain and for Europe. From a defense point of view Britain must have a voice. I don't think this administration has done much to help on these lines.

"Britain is the blue chip of Europe," he said and tilted his head at his own spontaneous phrase. He must have liked the sound of it, for he repeated it. "Yes, Britain is the blue chip of Europe."

Richard Nixon's knowledge of Britain is extensive and affectionate. Perhaps it is sentimental, for Nixon comes of good Colonial stock.

Contrary to general belief that he is of German descent on his mother's side, Richard Nixon's ancestry is all British. The Milhouses were English Quakers who settled in County Kildare on an Irish land grant from the King of England. In 1729 the first Milhous from that side of the family emigrated to America and built a house in Chester County, Pennsylvania. Another kinsman is believed to have been living in Delaware in the late seventeenth century.

James Nixon, also of Anglo-Irish background, arrived in Delaware in 1753. Both the Nixons and the Milhouses are very much part of America. A Nixon crossed the Delaware with George Washington; another was killed in the Union army at Gettysburg. Eventually both families moved to the Midwest, where Richard Nixon's maternal great-grandparents ran one of the most effective stations on the "underground railroad" for Negro slaves escaping from the South.

Later in the nineteenth century branches of the two families joined the wave of American immigration to California. The Milhouses settled in the Quaker town of Whittier, where Richard Nixon was born and grew up. It is a distinguished family history, and many Americans—indeed most Americans—would be proud to claim such a lineage.

But, intriguingly, Richard Nixon is almost secretive about his ancestry. He is inclined to talk more of his boyhood deprivations than of his family's dignified background. Is it because Richard Nixon senses failure in his family after its impressive start? Many of the Colonists who came to build America made a great deal of money and acquired prestige. They were able to provide their descendants with land, money and position. Yet when Richard Nixon was born his family, with almost two centuries of opportunity behind it, was able to bequeath him nothing. One must accept that this sense of almost shameful failure is what makes Richard Nixon so secretive and is responsible for yet another contradiction in his complex personality.

One often felt that Richard Nixon craved the urbane, detached arrogance of an archetypal British Tory politician. Certainly his loner instincts propelled him toward coolness. Yet he did not have the confidence to carry it off, and so he overcompensated by adopting a lower-middle-class, almost rural, coarseness in his speech.

No European leader would ever talk so openly about his personal habits as Nixon did: "I need a lot of shirts when I campaign. I'm a sweater you know. I had several dozen shirts run up in Hong

189

Kong last time I was there. But don't ever get a suit there; they fall apart on the first cleaning! I make my suits last, mainly by keeping my weight level." He weighed 160 pounds. "I have to eat very little because I have a real weight problem."

British politicians do not discuss this kind of thing. Nor does it occur to anyone to ask them to do so. But trivia about a candidate's personal life were swiftly digested by American crowds, and they came back for more. In Oregon Nixon went on statewide television to talk about his policies but ended up discussing his weight. He never ate potatoes and bread, he said, because he had such a problem.

It isn't easy for me to keep my weight down. But I have very strong arms, you know—I just push the food back. I wish there was another way. Exercise? Yes, for physical fitness, but let me tell you what it does to me: The more I exercise the more I eat, and then I gain more. As for foods, I do without the usual things, starches for example. I don't eat any desserts, and I love desserts. I eat proteins. And cottage cheese; I eat cottage cheese until it runs out of my ears. But I've learned a way to eat it that makes it not too bad. I put catsup on it. At least that way it doesn't taste like cottage cheese. My grandmother lived to be 91, and she always mixed catsup with her cottage cheese.

"Wasn't that great?" exulted a Nixon aide after the broadcast. "It was really human."

When one asked whether or not it was profitable to spend expensive television time talking about weight problems and cottage cheese, the answer was pat: "There are more men and women worried about their waistlines than there are worried about our fiscal policy. Dick *identified* with those people. It was a great program."

One morning, when the Nixon plane was en route from Texas to Atlanta for an important meeting with southern Republicans led by Senator Strom Thurmond of South Carolina, the candidate came up front to congratulate Ward Just of the *Washington Post* on publication of his book on Vietnam.

"Excellent book, Ward," said Nixon, "especially the foreword." (Later the astonished Just remarked that, if Nixon had really read the book and liked it, his Vietnam policy was a total mystery.) The foreword included a quotation from playwright Harold Pinter: "The more acute the experience the less articulate the expression."

190

Nixon was obviously eager to get into a discussion along these lines.

"That certainly is a correct observation," he said, moving his big hands in circles. "I have never been able to describe my war experiences." Nixon had enlisted in the navy early in World War II and had been commissioned as a lieutenant (junior grade). "It's again the question of style versus substance," he went on, his mind quite literally three phrases ahead of his tongue. "Jack Kennedy had true style. Johnson's troubles stemmed from the fact he wasn't being himself. All along during his Presidency he should have been more like he has been since he withdrew from the race, not so damned sanctimonious."

Ward Just remarked, "Yes, Johnson is like a 'Hud' figure," referring to the amoral Texas character played by Paul Newman in the film of the same name.

"I'm not familiar with that person," Nixon said and then admitted that he did not know who Pinter was. Either admission was clear evidence of his detachment from the world outside politics. Nixon was not bothered by his lapse. He maintained that it took all his time just to keep abreast of world events. As he talked, it was as if he had decided to make a tiny speech in order to clear up his thinking on the style-versus-substance issue. He was rambling, not really paying attention to what the rest of the group was saying.

> Now Woodrow Wilson was one of our greatest speakers, a rare combination of a man of action and a man of thought. Look at Eisenhower after his heart attack. *Time*—or was it *Newsweek?*—said he stuttered in a speech about sixty times. I got mad as hell. But later I realized that the people admired him much more because they saw him struggling to be understood. People who stutter *can* have more value.

Nixon frequently argued that one could reach and impress the people without "style."

"I like my news once removed," he added with a nervous smile. "You of the press are a kind of buffer for me. The press has a job to see through style to substance. There's a lot of intellectual snobbery around. Many intellectuals are becoming absorbed with style. They seem to feel that it is the delivery rather than the concept that matters."

This preoccupation with style really bothered him. "It's a pretty obvious thing to quote the Bible. In 22 years I've never quoted it

191

because I am an introverted Quaker. But that doesn't mean I don't read it. I would have liked to have read much deeper into history. But, since entering public service, I've only had time to read current history. There's so little time."

Nixon talked on about the moderation of his foreign policy compared with his more conservative domestic attitudes. His historical grasp was impressive, and finally someone said, "You know you're an intellectual, Nixon; why don't you admit it?" Nixon laughed awkwardly.

"I'm a sort of egghead in the Republican Party. I don't write as well as Adlai Stevenson, but I work at it. You know I'd really like to write about two or three books a year and go to one of those fine schools—Oxford for instance—just teach, read, and write."

This then was the man whose very name made millions of Americans grimace in disgust, as if he were not a human being but some terrible, contagious disease. And they were still doing so. "If that man wins the election and becomes our President," said a Bronxville lady to the visitor, "I shall leave America and settle in Britain for good."

It seemed a strange thing to say, unless one considered that Republican intellectuals and East Coast socialites were ashamed of Richard Nixon's very Americanness, of his square suits, of his joyless diet drenched in tomato catsup, of his too obvious ambition. These Republicans could not accept Nixon, but throughout the country, as he campaigned at his new leisurely pace, the votes in the primaries spoke for themselves. He won New Hampshire with 84,005 votes, Wisconsin with 385,052 votes, and Indiana (where the law banned write-ins) with a half-million votes in an unopposed fight. As he moved casually from triumph to triumph, the anxiety of his opponents within the Republican Party mounted almost to the level of hysteria. It was not just that Nixon was so obviously making a comeback that so disturbed them. It was the reluctance of their own St. George to mount up and rescue the party from this upstart dragon.

It was only on May 1, after much agonized indecision, that Nelson Aldrich Rockefeller finally decided to challenge Richard Nixon for the Republican nomination. Rockefeller's ambivalence was one of the most curious aspects of the whole campaign.

Since Romney's withdrawal, Rockefeller had alternately raised and dashed the hopes of his supporters. Only at the last minute did he officially fling down his challenge. But how much of a challenge was it? Rockefeller not only had to overcome Nixon's commanding lead and more extensive organization. He had also to overcome the party's suspicions of Nelson A. Rockefeller. Local party officials, whom Nixon had cultivated so assiduously, had little time for Rockefeller charm at the eleventh hour.

"He's coming round now because he wants us," said Ralph Kenney, an Oregon Republican. "But who the hell is he? Just a face on television. We don't know him. But we do know Nixon."

To thousands of Republican Party workers throughout the United States, Rockefeller seemed an aloof eastern aristocrat with heretical ideas about planning and state financing, who was launching for the third time a campaign of personal aggrandizement that would split the party. To his supporters he was still a question mark. Was he really going in for the kill? Had he not left things too late anyway? Why had he not made up his mind earlier?

Rockefeller's indecision reflected a mixture of his personal ambivalence toward the prize at stake and conflicting advice on how he should seek it if he did want it. His mood seemed to change from day to day. On some occasions he seemed to live up to his driving, ruthless, ambitious image. On others he seemed to expect to come in second—and even determined to make sure that he did.

There are some politicians (Britain's George Brown for example) who, because of pressure, emotion, fatigue, conducive ambience, or sometimes all these things, will talk with astounding frankness about their problems, their fears, their hopes, their plans. Nelson Rockefeller never did. He said only what he planned to say, and in any conversation he *always* preserved something of his inner self.

This fastidious sense of privacy extended particularly to his personal life. Early in the year, in a lengthy conversation with the visitor, he had revealed his indecision. He hinted that the demands of the campaign on his personal life might be a higher price than he was prepared to pay. Like an Olympic runner who has three times won a silver medal, he was debating whether or not it was worth trying once more for the gold.

He had, in his sixtieth year, found great happiness in his second marriage. His elder son by Happy—four-year-old Nelson, Jr.—was a total delight to him. His devotion to his wife and children was fierce; he spared for them every moment he could from his public life. The only other activity, outside politics, that occupied him was his trusteeship of the Museum of Primitive Art in New York City. This work constituted a kind of homage to his son Michael, who had been drowned off New Guinea during an anthropological expedition. Michael's death had been a profound sorrow for Rockefeller, but he had come to terms with it, and through his interest in primitive art he kept his son's memory properly alive.

But there were no other distractions from domesticity. It was Rockefeller's habit, when accepting dinner engagements, to arrive before or after the meal to make his speech but to excuse himself, on the pretext of "urgent business," from sitting through the whole function. The "urgent business" was invariably Happy and their two children. He could not continue this practice if he decided to aim seriously at capturing the Presidency. So why bother? Well, not all the old competitive spirit had evaporated in his glow of contentment, and there was always that call to duty.

If the moral and political pressures in and out of the party were strong enough, said Rockefeller, they would decide the issue. "I would not have the right not to make myself available. If the party think they can win anyway, they will do it with Nixon. They would rather have Nixon. And I will not force myself into dividing them. If they do not think they can do it with Nixon—well that is where I come in."

He insisted that, in spite of his 1964 experiences, he was not afraid of the job—or the struggle to win it. "I enjoy campaigning. I enjoy meeting people. I enjoy fighting." Why then this insistence that the Presidency was a job he really did not want, particularly in a year when many pundits were telling him that he was closer to it than at any time in his 27 years of active public life?

This is my problem—one of the ironies of life, I suppose. This was a contest in which I was no longer really interested. In politics, if you try hard for long enough and you do not get there, you quit trying and accept it. But, when George Romney's support began to slip around the beginning of the year, I had to recognize the fact that I might have to become involved again myself.

Frankly, if the international and domestic situations were not as serious as they are, I would not feel that sense of responsibility. I would be happy to stay out. But we are facing the most serious situation perhaps ever in American history. I do not say I have the answers to that situation. But I have no doubt I could find them. I have confidence that, as you get closer to a problem, you plan steadily step by step—you make *this* move, which leads to *that* move, and at last you see how to unravel it.

194

I started working with Roosevelt when I was 32, and in those days when something would break I would get upset inside. That was 27 years ago, but today I have learned that, though I do not necessarily have the answer, every problem has a solution if you have the best minds, goodwill, and proper handling.

It was the philosophy that had carried Rockefeller to repeated triumphs in New York. Why not now in Washington? When had the urge faded? He hunched his broad shoulders and spread his elbows on his desk.

There's a book called *What Makes Sammy Run*—it's the story of a young guy who works night and day to fulfill his ambitions—well I have worked night and day for 35 years, and finally you reach a point—and here we reach the area of psychology where I am not at all qualified—where you begin to wonder what are the motivating forces in people that rule the things they do.

With me there were two turning points. One was the culmination of that convention four years ago. I went against the party, and it really was a terrible thing to do, and I got booed for fifteen minutes.

I did it because I had to make a point. I was concerned about extremism and the dangers toward which we were advancing. I thought the time had come to tell the truth. And, as all those little old ladies stood there and screamed abuse at me, I just pointed straight back and said, "Yes, it's you that I'm talking about."

For a moment, he was out there again fighting, and then he continued:

The other was in 1966. The polls and everyone else told me I was finished, that I could not stand again and hope to win a third term as Governor of New York State. But I believed I could—and I could do it not on who I was but because I had done a valid job for New York. And I went out, and I froze those other people. That was a tremendous satisfaction. For the second time I had had the courage to stand in the face of total opposition for something I believe in. I had justified myself to myself.

But would he again be ready to risk the unity of his family in a new bid for the White House?

"I know the tremendous sacrifices involved for a family," he replied. "I have worked for three Presidents, and I know something of the heartache, and the lonely hours, that go with the responsibility of decision that will change the whole course of events. But these are sacrifices I will accept if I am wanted." For the moment, he said, the problem was to know, to judge whether or not the "sympathy" for him among the people was sufficient to force him to make an open run for the Presidency. "If I decided it was, then I should announce myself a candidate; it is the only clean way to do it."

There was sympathy, but how much "sympathy" in an American political campaign is genuine, and how much as artificially stimulated? When there is no limit to how much money can be spent, it is possible to manufacture "sympathy" as easily as instant coffee. In March advertisements were appearing across America either calling for support for Rockefeller or urging him directly to declare. They were so contrived that the visitor had difficulty in believing that they were placed spontaneously; they looked like products of a highly centralized organization, an organization controlled by the Rockefeller machine.

One such advertisement spread across two pages of *The New York Times*, pleaded with Rockefeller to announce. It intrigued the visitor sufficiently to make him seek out the man who had placed it. He was Stewart Rawlings Mott, son of the senior member of the board of General Motors, the biggest corporation in the world. Mr. Mott was young, handsome, and rich. With that engaging American readiness to be interviewed, whatever the inconvenience (he had just gotten up and was dressed only in a crumpled pair of shorts), he not only welcomed the visitor but also immediately handed him a printed "fact sheet" about himself.

The visitor digested it while Mr. Mott made "bloody marys." It revealed among other things that his blood group was AB+, that he was a bachelor in good health, and that, despite considerable experience as a management trainee with General Motors and other companies, he had achieved his real ambition only in 1965, when he had founded the Spectemur Agendo Inc. Foundation.

"It means 'let us be known by our deed,'" he said. "That is my credo."

This credo directed the wealthy Mr. Mott ("I give away 41 percent of my income, pay tax on 49 percent of it, and live on about

10 percent of it") into leading a pressure group for reform of the abortion laws in New York State, a crusade in which he hoped to win some success in 1968. What he hoped for from his $25,000 advert, which called for financial support of the Governor, was at least 5,000 direct responses and a quarter-million dollars in pledges to a Rockefeller-led "peace in Vietnam" campaign.

I'm trying to say, "It's your move now Rocky." I want to see him put his candidacy forward at the latest by March 22. If we get this sort of response, then I think we may well succeed in pushing him in. I half thought that he might have called me up this morning and said, "Come over, and talk it over," but he hasn't. I do not think he is displeased. Before I put the ad in I discussed it with Irv Barash, the executive director of the Citizens for Rockefeller Group, and I let the Governor know through one of his aides what to expect. If Rocky had wanted to stop the ad, he could have done it by getting on to the publisher of *The New York Times*. He didn't. I have a notion he is really tickled pink.

The attitude of Mott's father, Charles Stewart Mott, from whom the money spent on this effort originally came, was much less clear. "I told Mother in a phone call on Friday what I was up to," said young Mott. "Since then there has been silence from home. I do not know how Father is taking it. But he is a Goldwater man."

It was clear that Mr. Mott's actions were his own and probably as inexplicable to Nelson Rockefeller as to Mott's own parents. Similar actions were being repeated across the country, as groups or individuals bought space in newspapers and time on television to boost the demand for Rocky. They had taken him at his word. If there was a demand for him, if the people really wanted him, then he would run. Into Albany thousands of letters and telegrams flooded. According to Leslie Slote, 90 percent of them urged the Governor to run.

Walter Lippmann, aging doyen of American political columnists, championed Rocky for President in his widely syndicated column and urged Republicans to nominate him. "I regard Nelson Rockefeller as the most qualified man available for the supreme task of reconstruction. I believe that Lyndon Johnson has disqualified himself," wrote Lippmann. He was joined by a growing chorus of editorialists in daily papers across New York State and in the Midwest.

So fierce was the groundswell that few Americans doubted that Rockefeller would "have a go." National headquarters for the Draft Rockefeller for President movement was set up in Annapolis, Maryland, and headed by Republican Governor Spiro T. Agnew.

It was announced that Rockefeller would make a television broadcast to the nation on Thursday, March 21. It seemed a foregone conclusion that he would announce his candidacy. *The New York Times*, in a front page story, declared that he had made up his mind to run. Governor Agnew invited reporters into his office to watch the telecast, telling them, "You may as well be in at the start." And, as Rockefeller arose in the west ballroom of the New York Hilton Hotel—packed to capacity with reporters, cameramen, and correspondents—one radio commentator said, "And now the Governor is stepping up to the platform to announce his candidacy."

The Governor did no such thing. In flat, even tones he delivered the third shock in a campaign that was to become memorable for its unprecedented upheavals. He did not propose to enter the race, he said. Everyone was staggered by the announcement. Newscasters went into reverse; newspapers had to reset headlines at the last minute.

In Oregon, where Rockefeller had won the primary in 1964, his supporters, who had called their own press conference to welcome his candidacy, tore up their statement in a fury. In Annapolis, the National Draft Rockefeller headquarters closed down that afternoon. Agnew, who had been humiliated before the top political reporters in his state, was furious. "This is obviously as big a surprise to you as it is to us, Governor," they had said. "Don't you think it's rather curious that Mr. Rockefeller didn't take you into his confidence?"

All the Maryland Governor could reply was that he was "tremendously surprised."

"That's obvious," said a reporter, salting the wound and thus ensuring Mr. Agnew would not forget Rockefeller's offhand treatment.

At La Guardia Airport, leaving for the Wisconsin primary election, Richard Nixon said that he was surprised but with commendable restraint declined to admit that he regarded the party nomination as his. In Wisconsin, where he was already campaigning, Senator Eugene McCarthy issued a special statement calling on Republicans to cross over and vote for him in the primary because Rocky's withdrawal meant that Wisconsin Republicans had "only one alternative to the present policies of mounting conflict in Vietnam."

Between planes in Alabama, Senator Robert Kennedy said he was sorry: "It is unfortunate the Republican Party will not have a choice. Obviously we in the Democratic Party will."

In Washington, Senator Hugh Scott of Pennsylvania said Rocky had telephoned him after the announcement to say that he "kind of felt he had let us down." Scott promptly dropped plans to found a draft-Rockefeller group.

In Oregon Governor Tom McCall was "shocked and dismayed. America is definitely the loser."

Only in California was there a glimmer of delight, and it came from a suspect quarter. Former Arizona Senator Barry Goldwater, with whose forces Rockefeller had so violently and bitterly clashed for the nomination four years earlier, wired congratulations to the Governor on his "courageous and intelligent decision," which would "contribute immeasurably to a 1968 victory for the Republican Party."

What exactly *did* the decision imply? How was it reached—and why? Had Rocky truly lost his ambition, or was he playing a waiting game, which few believed could win him any prizes? These questions buzzed through the nation.

After his reelection as Governor of New York in 1966 (a contest in which he ran without the support of the Republican Party and that he had not been expected to win) Rockefeller had remarked, "The Republican Party has to decide that it wants to win." This statement summed up his view of the whole dilemma facing the Republican Party then as later: how to persuade the reluctant party chiefs to steer a moderate candidate through the convention to the nomination. In 1968 he thought the solution was to back George Romney's candidacy; some said his idea was that, should Romney prove unequal to the convention challenge, his delegates would turn to Rockefeller.

Any such hopes dissolved with Romney's premature retirement from the race, which left a nasty scar on the prestige of the party's moderate faction. Some rapid reassessments and fresh strategy were now required. But the Governor's intimates were struck by his rather lethargic approach to the issue, his evident unwillingness to launch himself with his old fire and conviction into the Presidential campaign.

The reticence was partly the result of Rockefeller's conviction that a mud-slinging campaign with Nixon could only wreck his chances and expose him to the bitter attacks of 1964. It was also partly the result of reluctance to involve his wife and two children in another acrimonious campaign. (Mrs. Rockefeller was personally against his candidacy but ready to campaign with him to the end if asked.) There was another even more valid reason. During the Republican governors' conference in Washington immediately after Romney's withdrawal, it had been widely reported that probably 18 of the 26 governors were ready to back Rockefeller. The truth was that only two—Agnew of Maryland and Raymond Shafer of Pennsylvania—were actually ready to pledge support for a Rockefeller campaign. The rest, though sympathetic, preferred to remain uncommitted. On March 10 Rockefeller invited to his duplex apartment in Manhattan—at 812 Fifth Avenue, only a few floors above Nixon's home—a group of Republican leaders from across the nation. The sentiment that emerged from this meeting was similar to that of the governors; everyone thought Rocky should run, but few were ready to endorse him. The reticence no doubt arose from fear that anyone who stuck his neck too far out for moderation could very well lose his head if Mr. Nixon were (as seemed likely) to win the nomination. To the Republicans in 1968 "splitting the party" was about the most serious charge that could be leveled. It was clear that, whatever the "call from the nation" might be, the Republican Party itself would ignore it.

On this basis, Rockefeller's top political adviser, George Hinman, who had been urging the Governor to declare his candidacy and enter the coming Oregon primary, had second thoughts. During the next few days Rockefeller talked the problem over with his closest advisers. In particular he had a long session with Emmett J. Hughes, a *Newsweek* columnist and former public-relations man in the Rockefeller organization, whose advice was highly valued. Hughes was also against Rockefeller's candidacy.

And so the decision was taken to stay out.

There was a possibility that the situation might change, but few people around Rockefeller believed it. They went back to the 1960 strategy. Rockefeller might still be strong enough to influence party policy; he announced that he would address himself to the major issues in the coming months, and it was possible that he could arrange another compact with Nixon on various planks in the platform. But, as for the main prize, he decided to let Nixon have it.

It was ironic that the only man that the polls at that time showed to be capable of winning the election for the Republican Party was to be prevented from winning the election—by the Republican Party.

Nelson Rockefeller went back to Albany, to his concentration on Happy and their children, and to a multitude of state projects; Richard Nixon was left to walk a solitary, victorious path through the Republican primaries.

Forty days later Nelson Rockefeller publicly changed his mind. The situation had forced him "to reconsider," and he declared himself an active candidate. By changing his mind yet again Rockefeller was taking a huge risk. He had at last resolved the conflicting advice that had been pouring in on him. During all that time the atmosphere in the Rockefeller entourage in Albany and New York was reminiscent of that in the Rhodesian cabinet during the final weeks before Ian Smith declared U.D.I. [unilateral declaration of independence]. The Governor had been battered and bewildered by conflicting advice while Richard Nixon blithely campaigned his uncontested way through the primaries.

But meanwhile a significant event had occurred: Lyndon Johnson had withdrawn. The situation that had led to the March 21 decision had changed, according to Hinman and Hughes. They argued that the party had been convinced that Nixon could beat Johnson, his likeliest opponent. But they felt certain that Nixon could not beat Kennedy, whom they were equally sure would win the Democratic nomination.

Rockefeller was inclined to agree. One night, while watching Nixon on a national telecast, he suddenly exploded to those around him: "There's no new Nixon. It's the same old guy. He always seems as if he's looking at someone in the corner of the studio. Look at the way his eyes keep going sideways."

The policy Rockefeller had chosen, of leaving himself free to speak out on major issues, and to influence party policy, had not worked. Those in the party who were suspicious of him read every speech as if it held some hidden clue to his own intentions that summer; those who supported him thought that speeches were pointless unless he were going to take the issues to the people.

Now Republicans around the country began to press Rockefeller more strongly. Those in his own camp kept up the persuasion, and the draft-Rockefeller movement was revived by Kentucky Senator Thruston B. Morton, a moderate who opposed increased American involvement in the war. These people had come to one conclusion: The Governor must be persuaded to run.

Toward the end of April, Morton and William Miller, a former New York congressman and Barry Goldwater's running mate in 1964, went on a whistle-stop tour of the Midwest, talking to party leaders. They reported to Hinman that there was a lot of support for Rockefeller. All kinds of political feuds can be buried in the necessity for reelection. When America holds a Presidential election, it does more than select a man for the White House. In 1968 there were also 21 state governorships, 34 Senate seats, and 435 congressional seats at stake. In addition, thousands of state and local contests had to be decided.

In the great drama of the Presidential contest the rest of the world tended to forget this. But those other elections were vitally connected with the Presidential election in the United States. It was the habit of many Americans to vote a straight party ticket. That is, if they preferred the Republican Presidential candidate, they were likely to vote Republican for every contested office down to that of local dogcatcher. Morton and Miller cited this fact in talking to midwestern politicians. The party wanted Nixon, but was Nixon the right man to beat Kennedy? Obviously not. Only one man could beat him—Rockefeller. What was the situation locally? they asked; who could carry the ticket right down the line—Nixon or Rockefeller?

The answers they received were encouraging. Morton quoted one extremely pro-Nixon politician as having said: "I love Dick Nixon, but, if you want to know, my candidate is Nelson Rockefeller. We need people to vote the straight ticket."

The reports flowed back to Hinman, and in New York enthusiasm rose. Hinman and Hughes agreed. The Governor stood a chance, but he had to announce at once. So the decision was taken. The curious thing was that it paralleled events in 1960 in an almost eerie way. Then Richard Nixon had been the Republican front-runner, destined to meet either Kennedy or Humphrey. Rockefeller had been indecisive and had entered only at the last minute. His strategy had failed miserably. So why try it again? The answer lay in the opinion polls. Almost weekly in 1968 the two great oracles of American public opinion, George Gallup and Louis Harris, unveiled sample findings revealing that Rockefeller was more popular than Nixon.

Then, as if in omen, on the very day of his announcement,

Rockefeller won a spectacular victory in the Massachusetts primary. It was as big a surprise to Rockefeller as to everyone else. He had not campaigned; he had not even been a declared candidate. But the results confirmed what the polls were saying: He was the most popular Republican. Actually, the only Republican on the ballot in Massachusetts was Governor John Volpe, running as a favorite son, a position he hoped to trade for a Vice-Presidential spot. Rockefeller forces were entirely unofficial and had no headquarters or funds. The total vote was low. Volpe received 30,252 votes. Rockefeller received 31,344 write-in votes and Nixon 26,422.

The trend toward Rockefeller continued nationwide—buoyed up by his official participation. A Gallup poll released on May 13 showed that Rockefeller was more popular than any other contestant for the Presidency and could beat any Democrat, Humphrey, McCarthy, or Kennedy.

The Governor took to the road. He would not risk a battle in the primaries, but he would talk to the party leaders. The approach was simple. He would ask each state delegation not to support him outright but simply to remain uncommitted until the convention. Between May and convention time his strategy would be to undermine Richard Nixon, to reattach the "loser" label that the "new" Nixon had succeeded in glossing over and to build up his own standing in the public-opinion polls. To this end he was to spend $4 million, much of it his own money.

There was, however, a third contender, whom both Richard Nixon and Nelson Rockefeller found it difficult to assess. Ronald Reagan, B-picture actor turned politician, elected Governor of California in 1966, and a favorite of the right wing, was indeed difficult to pigeonhole. Was he a threat or a joke? Was he a serious contender? Although he had not announced his candidacy, he was clearly available. And he was making his views of current affairs as public as possible in a series of "position papers." Reagan's appeal was geared to the right-wing hawks, the remains of the Goldwater movement within the party. He called Lyndon Johnson a "weak man" who had undermined America's world position by following the example of President Kennedy. These two Presidents, he said, had not only been responsible for the Vietnam disaster, but had also "ruined NATO" through their feebleness and irresolution. They had "wrecked" Britain's plans for modernizing the Royal Air Force by canceling the Skybolt-missile program. Their general policy—or lack of it—in Europe had infuriated General de Gaulle.

According to Governor Reagan the United States in mid-1968 was "lonely in the world" because for the past seven years its leaders had countered international Communism with "timidity and petty improvisings."

The man behind Reagan was Clifton White, the neat, middle-aged political professional who had run Goldwater's nomination campaign in 1964. That had been a traumatic experience, but even though White's nervous system had taken a beating his reputation had not suffered from the Goldwater fiasco. In April he had flown to California at the invitation of the state Republican Party. They had asked him to "guide" the Governor through the next few months and to secure his nomination as California's favorite-son candidate for the Republican convention. He could then go to Miami as the best-supported alternative candidate to Nixon. White accepted the task with enthusiasm. "To have been out of the campaign would have been agony for a man who lives for politics the way I do," he said, "and the strategy required for Reagan was something entirely new."

The first problem was that the Governor's name had already been placed on the primary ballots in Wisconsin, Nebraska, and Oregon, thanks to an excess of right-wing enthusiasm. "This was the last thing I wanted," said White, "but legally there was no way to get his name removed." Wisconsin came and went before White's work could have an effect, except to warn Reagan not to campaign in the state. The California Governor polled 12 percent of the vote.

By May the Reagan position papers were being discussed by Republicans across the country. White took the film star-politician on a national tour. His face, already recognizable from television reruns of old movies and from newsreel appearances, became even more familiar to his fellow Republicans. It was an extraordinary face, very Californian and still extremely boyish, despite the middle-fiftyish lines, which looked as if they had been put there by a Hollywood makeup man. It was marred only by the petulant mouth, too small for the rest of the features.

Reagan had a simple direct approach. His right-wing stance found plenty of echoes. His simplistic solutions eased plenty of worries. Soon the results began to show. In Nebraska—on White's orders Reagan never set foot in the state—he polled 25 percent of the vote against Nixon's 70 percent and Rockefeller's 5 percent.

In Oregon, where Rockefeller had triumphed in 1964 the Reagan forces spent $110,000, far less than the amounts spent by Nixon and Rockefeller, whose combined expenditures exceeded $1 million. Yet Nixon received 73 percent of the Republican primary vote, Reagan 22 percent, and Rockefeller just under 5 percent.

Both Richard Nixon and Nelson Rockefeller prudently stayed out of California and left it to Reagan, who was duly selected the favorite-son candidate.

When the primaries were over, Richard Nixon had won every state that he had contested. Massachusetts and California had been lost by default.

There was little that was inspirational or original in the way that Nixon had won. He had run a flawless campaign and had kept his cool. Apart from the one brilliant speech on Negro capitalism, he had spoken in platitudes and generalities. In Britain he would have been cut to ribbons by questioners, but few questions were asked at American political meetings. When Richard Nixon did face questions on television programs (the public was asked to telephone queries), his replies were skillfully vague. To questions about the war he replied, "This country is united in its desire for an honorable peace, but at the same time we will not yield to any blackmail for a dishonorable settlement." He called the capture of the *Pueblo* by North Koreans "a national disgrace" and said that he would take action to bring the ship and its crew back unharmed.

But Nixon was no worse than either of his two Republican opponents in this respect. All had been dealing in generalities. Reagan had launched a conventional right-wing attack upon the two previous administrations; Rockefeller's attack had been on Nixon himself.

But Richard Nixon had little need to fight. He had a head start in the primaries, and he knew that he could keep it. All he needed was a mopping-up campaign.

.12.

From the Granite to the Gold

EXACTLY FOUR WEEKS AFTER THE ABDICATION, THE HEIR APPARENT officially announced his candidacy for the throne. On April 27 1,700 United Democrats for Humphrey (an all-embracing title that had been adopted only a week before) gathered in a Washington hotel for lunch.

With the television eyes of all America (and eleven European countries) trained upon him, ebullient Hubert Humphrey declared his entry into the race for what vaudevillians would call the "number-one spot." Said, or rather gurgled, the Vice-President, "I intend to fight hard for my nomination, but I do not intend to divide my party or my nation."

The theme was to be unity all the way. Instead of the New Politics, Humphrey offered the New Patriotism, "a new American patriotism to keep alive the vision of what America can be."

About the troubles that so divided the country, Humphrey preferred not to talk:

Here we are, the way politics ought to be in America, the politics of happiness, the politics of purpose, the politics of joy. The time has come for those who share a deep and abiding belief in the purpose and potentialities of this nation to say, "I love my country."

The man who wins the nomination must be able first to unite his party, and the man who unites his party must above all be able to unite and govern his nation.

Humphrey's plea for unity had the opposite effect. Politicians can be incorrectly tuned and thus insensitive to the state of their nation, and Humphrey's "politics of joy" speech was particularly inappropriate in 1968 America. Robert Kennedy was quick to draw attention to this disparity: "I do not believe that 1968 is the year for talking of the politics of happiness or the politics of joy. I believe there are too many great problems which concern us to speak of happiness and joy."

Senator McCarthy observed: "The announcement of the Vice-President's candidacy comes as no surprise to me. I could have predicted it in 1952, when he first made it clear he wanted to be President. Four years later I proposed him for Vice-President, and then in 1960 he ran for President again. In 1964 he ran for Vice-President, and this time he made it. So I knew that 1968 was his year for running for President again."

In different ways both men made the point that Hubert Humphrey could hardly be treated as a serious political candidate. America was in a parlous state, economically, socially, and militarily—which was why McCarthy had entered the race at all. It was why Kennedy also claimed to have entered. They preferred to reserve talk of joy and happiness for a time when those twin blessings had been more clearly achieved.

Humphrey, however, could not be forced to a direct confrontation over his opinions. Kennedy had announced his candidacy on March 16, early enough to enter the main part of the primary trail, but Humphrey had delayed his announcement until it was too late to have his name put on the various ballots. His delay may, of course, have been a courtesy, to avoid charges of unseemly haste in trying on Johnson's boots. Or it may have been a purely tactical delay to ensure his own support. Finally, it may have been the result of a decision to win in the back-room caucuses.

Whatever the thinking behind the tactics was, the tactics themselves were good. Humphrey could let his two rivals fight it out in the primaries although they could not directly challenge him on his apparently blind devotion to the Johnson-Rusk-Rostow line on the war. In any case Humphrey had to reassert his campaign personality. Even the most dynamic of men fade in the twilight zone of the American Vice-Presidency, and Humphrey had been a faithful Vice-President, always as loyal and as unobtrusively helpful to Lyndon Johnson as he could be. Now he had to repolish his image, which, judging from the response to his declaration speech, was sadly tarnished.

While Humphrey was turning that Washington lunch into a laugh-in Kennedy and McCarthy were entering the last ten days of the Indiana primary campaign, the first of a series of battles in a war of attrition. And attrition it was. The Irish are deadly fighters, particularly among themselves. Clearly no quarter would be asked or given. Both were Roman Catholics, both were liberals, both were against the Democratic Party establishment for the same reasons. Yet there could be no question of their working together, and there was only one way to decide which of them would carry the flag of revolt: the primary way.

McCarthy, who bitterly resented Kennedy's intrusion—especially after he had announced that he would not enter—set out to link Bobby with his brother's responsibility for sending the first U.S. Special Forces to Vietnam. Kennedy responded with a display of that old-fashioned political "muscle" that had helped to carry his brother to power in 1960.

It is probable that neither man was ever to stand as high as he did before those last ten days in Indiana. While Humphrey caucused McCarthy and Kennedy flailed at each other rather than at the main enemy.

Kennedy was then at a peak in the popularity polls. There was a vast segment of the electorate to whom the mere mention of his name could bring delirium. But every day of the primaries, it seemed later, eroded a little of that support.

McCarthy, surrounded by supporters yelling "We Want Gene," also stood at a peak, as he wryly dissected the pundits who had belittled his successes. At one dinner in Fort Wayne he remarked: "I got 42 percent in New Hampshire, and they said I won. I got 58 percent in Wisconsin, and they said I lost." Just after the Massachusetts primary, he said at an early breakfast in Evansville that he did not understand how they could say he had lost when he had won 51 percent of the vote.

His success in New Hampshire had been overshadowed by Kennedy's entry, but it seemed that nothing could darken the victory that experts had predicted in Wisconsin. But something did: President Johnson withdrew, once again pulling the rug of satisfaction from under McCarthy's feet. McCarthy contented himself with wry remarks and pushed on into beautiful rich Connecticut, where he won 44 percent of the Democratic vote. He took all these primary victories in stride. His was the only name on the ballot in Pennsylvania, but write-ins were allowed and the names of Kennedy and Humphrey were better known than his. Yet he polled 410,000 votes, seven times the write-in figure for Kennedy and ten times that for Humphrey. Unfortunately, Pennsylvania was one of those states whose delegates were not bound by the primary vote, so his victory there merely demonstrated his popularity rather than strengthened his political muscle.

But a week later, as April turned into May, Massachusetts, land of the Kennedys, went to the polls. Some experts said that, with Robert Kennedy in the race, McCarthy could hope at the most for "a good loss." Kennedy won 28 percent of the Democratic vote and Humphrey 19 percent, but McCarthy's "good loss" turned out to be a 51 percent majority. He topped John Kennedy's 1960 record of 91,607 votes by 25,000. A nice irony of this victory was that Senator Edward Kennedy, Bobby's younger brother and a Massachusetts delegate-at-large, would, along with the other 71 delegates, be forced to vote for McCarthy on the first convention ballot.

From then on there were no walkovers and no excuses. The battleground was Indiana, self-styled "crossroads of America." Indiana's landscape was exactly as pretty as a picture postcard. That spring it was all light green and purple. On the tree-lined streets of its neat little towns, which, with their neat little blocks of neat little houses, were all virtually indistinguishable, the lilacs vied for attention with a profusion of lighter-red crab-apple trees.

From the air, the vast checkerboard countryside seemed curiously dappled. No one could explain this phenomenon until McCarthy characteristically came up with a brief rundown on Indiana's glacial prehistory. The roads ran straight and flat, seemingly forever, through cultivation broken only by farmhouses, uniformly built of white-painted weatherboard, whose porches occasionally had pretty carving on the gable ends and always had ready rocking chairs.

The people, known as Hoosiers, were not, however, as pleasant as their environment. Nobody quite knows what "Hoosier" means.

It has been suggested that the name comes from a Cumbrian dialect word meaning "Whig" or perhaps it is derived from the English "hoozer", meaning large of its kind, or maybe the Hoosiers were members of a Dutch-German religious sect. At any rate it is comparable to "Geordie," a slang term for a man who comes from the Northumberland-Durham area, particularly from near the River Tyne. "Hoosier" implies all the pride inherent in the name "Geordie" and equal distaste for those who do not find its ambience congenial.

Whatever the term's origin, the Hoosiers are tightly knit, conservative, parochial. The local Democrats put up their own favorite-son candidate, Governor Roger D. Branigin, who was always being photographed on street corners in a gangsterish turned-down hat. He was taken by most to be a stand-in for Hubert Humphrey and was supported by a vitriolic local press that called Kennedy an upstart trying to buy the voters of Indiana.

Kennedy hurled some charges of his own at McCarthy, inserting advertisements in college newspapers that implied that McCarthy was not really as liberal as he made out. And McCarthy replied with the sly question of why, if Kennedy were as much against Vietnam as he said he was, had he in January supported the renomination of Johnson? The battle was very cutthroat, and when Indiana went to the polls on May 7 Kennedy received 42 percent of the Democratic vote, Branigin 31 percent, and McCarthy 27 percent.

First blood had been drawn, and on the same day Kennedy easily won the District of Columbia from Humphrey. Kennedy's victory, though regarded as sufficient, was by no means overwhelming. The fight rolled across the plains to Nebraska, the Cornhusker State, flat and full of corn of all kinds.

Nebraska stretches almost 500 miles from Iowa in the east to Wyoming and Colorado in the west. It has 1.5 million people, 40 percent of whom lived in the cities of Omaha and Lincoln. Omaha, the biggest cattle market in the world, was the nearest city to the headquarters of the Strategic Air Command, the deadliest striking force in history. The cattle pens ran beside the legendary Union Pacific Railway, which was built by Irish, Poles, and Czechs, who also ran the stockyards, so that in 1968 there was a large ethnic and Roman Catholic vote in this Nebraska city.

The people of Nebraska, tall and rangy, gave the impression of being not much in touch with the outside world. In New York the response to "thank you" was "you're welcome." In Indiana the only response was a noncommital "Uh-huh." In Nebraska it was "You bet," which seemed to mean that Nebraskans really had not expected anything but thanks.

The campaign meandered around this wide state in a series of short plane hops. The whole affair seemed a digression from the mainstream of politics, though both candidates were anxious to win. For McCarthy the most delightful day was spent in Nebraska City, though there was no string quartet to greet him, as there had been in one small Indiana town. Nebraska City sounded far grander than it was. In the middle of the square stood the Otoe County Courthouse, built in 1864, the oldest public building in the state. It was of red brick with white trim, and above the door was inscribed: "Oh Justice! When driven from other habitation, make thy dwelling place here."

Beneath that inscription Senator Eugene McCarthy addressed the citizens. Thousands of such meetings took place in the campaign year. The styles and atmospheres varied from region to region. This one, in the heart of the Great Plains, had a timeless quality about it, not least because of the lengthy introductory speeches. But it was typical of what went on along the primary campaign trail.

First the Mayor spoke for twenty minutes or so and made Senator McCarthy an honorary citizen of Nebraska City. Then the chairman of the local Chamber of Commerce made an even longer speech and ended by making the Senator an honorary member of the Chamber. Then came Father George Heinzen, a Roman Catholic priest from St. Mary's Church on Sixth Street, who gave the invocation:

> O God of wisdom and understanding, if your servant, the Apostle Paul were here this morning and would have been privileged to give this invocation, he would have repeated an encouraging portion of his Epistle to the Corinthians: All the runners in the stadium take part in the race, but only one wins the prize. So I do not run like a man who doesn't see the goal. I do not fight like a boxer who punches the air.
>
> There have been, O Lord, those who through many media have sensationally expressed complete cures of the nation's cares, but many of these would lead to more seeking of power rather than entrusting the democratic concern of our nation to the people themselves. There have been cases of boxers

211

punching the air, of not seeking the goal. We ask your help, O Lord, that we concern ourselves here and in the future to seek and retain the wisdom of our candidate who through a maturity of public service to the Midwest and the nation has proven that he is serious runner and who sees the true goal, saying, "Let the thinking people decide."

We pray that we may see the wisdom in the quality of the character and mature experience which can provide needed leadership. O Lord, we need a great deal of reconciliation in our nation: that of the young with the old, that of race with race, of Congress with the Presidency, but principally of the thought and spirit and the best traditions of America with the pressing need for action. These requests we ask in the name of your Son Our Lord, so that the future will see Senator McCarthy and his family in the White House. Amen.

After a suitable pause, McCarthy replied, "That's the first time that I've had an invocation asking for help right down the line." It was a hot day, and he said that for a start people should consider the merits of those other candidates who had declined to run in the cold-weather primaries (New Hampshire and Wisconsin); a little later he remarked that Selective Service chief General Lewis Hershey ought to retire as he was 74 and (he turned to Father Heinzen) they were even asking cardinals to retire at 70 nowadays.

While McCarthy gently wooed the farmers, Kennedy conducted what *Newsweek* aptly called an "in-person Blitzkrieg." Originally his campaign managers had not wanted to risk entering Nebraska, which had always been regarded as a maverick state. But Nebraskan Ted Sorensen had won the argument against Teddy Kennedy, and his brother Philip Sorensen had gone off to "put it together" in the Kennedy jargon. To round off the campaign Bobby delivered some scathing attacks on Hubert Humphrey's "politics of joy": "If we have to bring 12,000 troops into the capital of the United States to protect it, if 14 million Americans are going hungry, how then can we talk about the politics of joy?"

His organization was far better than McCarthy's, he spent far more money, and—more important—because of the availability of cash, he was able to buy the best television time. His advance men made sure that wherever he went the crowds were big and lusty, compared with the driblets that turned out for McCarthy.

Tuesday, May 14th dawned very hot and rather windy; the corn and the wheat were still green. Kennedy stayed at the Sheraton

212

Fontenelle in Omaha and McCarthy at the Cornhusker in Lincoln, the state capital. Soon after 8:00 P.M. the returns started coming in. By morning Kennedy had 51 percent of the Democratic votes, against 31 percent for McCarthy, 8 percent for Humphrey (for whom there had been a lukewarm write-in campaign, and 6 percent for President Johnson. The President had announced his decision not to run again too late to have his name taken off the ballot in Nebraska.

Kennedy went on television that night and told the nation delightedly that he and McCarthy should thenceforth work together, a clear suggestion that McCarthy was finished and should join the Kennedy camp. McCarthy, before the faithful gathered in the Georgian Room of the Cornhusker, admitted that Kennedy had won a "significant victory" but told his troops: "One thing about this campaign has been that we're always better when we're challenging someone. So now we come to the difficult part. On the old Oregon Trail it was always easy enough to get the wagons to the Missouri River, but it was those that made it right through to the West Coast that really proved they had it in 'em." It was an analogy that he used many times in the next few weeks; he intended to fight to the end.

The last leg of that journey to the West Coast was one of incredible beauty. God help America if she manages to pollute the waters of the Columbia River Gorge, or to despoil the coniferous forests at the base of Mount Hood! The coastline was rugged and strong. The people of Oregon were strong too. There were few of them for such a huge state, but they had a natural independence. They were good people, the sort one would like to know, with few prejudices. They worked hard, as befitted residents of "the Beaver State."

One knew what Oregon would be like as soon as the plane touched down. After the uniformity of Indiana and Nebraska, each little garden seemed different, bright and with a profusion of summer color fit for an English flower show. Kennedy, having failed to knock his rival out in Nebraska, confronted a difficult task in Oregon. There were no ethnic minorities on which he could count for solid support. McCarthy perhaps had an inkling of what would happen in Oregon. His technique altered hardly at all, yet this time he was talking to the people who had elected liberal Wayne Morse to the Senate and were certainly not going to kowtow to anybody's "machine." "We'll do better in Oregon," McCarthy had said.

213

"We'll be satisfied with a lead around 5 percent," the Kennedy people said. But, when Kennedy visited the Portland zoo, he found a McCarthy crowd, and at the Portland rose gardens he had to run to avoid bumping into McCarthy and suffered the mortification of being booed by those who watched.

His people were sure that he would win, for Kennedys always did. Kennedy felt sure enough of himself to remark that if he did not win Oregon he would not be a very viable candidate. Because his strategy was to demonstrate his popular appeal by winning every primary, as his brother had done, this remark was clearly true, but only a confident man would have made it.

On May 28 in was put to the test. In the old Elks Lodge in Portland, the McCarthyites gathered before their television sets to put the final touches to the resurrected hall for their candidate's appearance. In growing excitement, which finally erupted into a sort of mass delirium, they watched the votes pile up until the results were revealed in all their glory: McCarthy 45 percent, Kennedy 39 percent, Johnson 13 percent, and Humphrey 4 percent.

For the first time in 22 years and 27 elections, a Kennedy had been beaten. The legend was well and truly shattered. Kennedy stated with a great deal of accuracy. "I am not the candidate that I was before."

Almost exhausted, the two Irishmen, the Poet and the Politician, as someone had called them, prepared for the final round. But Humphrey, undeterred by the miserable percentages of people who had cared to write his name in on the ballots, blithely continued his journey round the caucuses, collecting promises, shifting bead after bead on the political abacus toward the magical total of 1,312 votes in Chicago. For, whatever the voters did, the party machine was still there, and the nonprimary states had more delegate votes than did those with primaries.

No man could win the nomination only with votes won in primaries. Primaries could be conclusive only if they could demonstrate that one man was overwhelmingly a winner, as Jack Kennedy had proved in 1960. But the Kennedy-McCarthy fight in 1968 had been inconclusive, and it left the way open for Humphrey to politic through the back doors, talking to the state bosses, addressing hand-picked delegates, and sewing up support. And the system was working for him.

One of the first aides to speak to him after Johnson's speech had begged him: "For heaven's sake, Hubert, don't jump into this thing without knowing what you're doing. You got clobbered before." Humphrey, remembering his humiliating West Virginia defeat by John Kennedy in 1960 (he had had to mortgage his house to pay the campaign costs) was only too ready to take the advice. His people spent four weeks in ensuring solid support, from the South, from the unions, and most of all from the Democratic rich before Humphrey announced his candidacy and set off on that round of cozy talks with all the local Democratic leaders for whom he had put himself out during his four years as Vice-President. In that capacity he had traveled 600,000 miles around the country, speaking in half a thousand towns and patching cracks in the political plaster of every state in the union. Now the handyman was coming round with the bill, to be paid not in dollars but in convention votes. The Democrats paid up.

Later many analysts tried to determine whether Eugene McCarthy had really been what he seemed or whether, through some Olympian conjuring trick, nothing had been made into something. With Humphrey many people began by asking the question in reverse. Could something have been atomized into nothing? For Humphrey's record, his history, his reputation had been those of a firebrand, a fighting liberal, an opponent of reactionary convention, a wooden horse within the senatorial Troy, a respecter of no person or institution.

But in 1968 the liberals, the New Left, even—the hardest pill to swallow—the Americans for Democratic Action, a radical group that he had founded, were all reviling him with equal fervor. They called him a conservative, a reactionary, a mouthpiece for the administration, an apologist for the war, a Johnson hack, a nothing.

Which view was correct? Or had he actually changed? Or was he simply a mirror reflecting his master's image? The last seems unlikely. Hubert Humphrey was nothing if not an extrovert and an extremely irritating one at that. The huge cupola of his forehead curved back to dyed hair—a giveaway to his vanity, the strangely pink cheeks lent an air of clownlike effeminacy; and that tiny, constantly working mouth, which pecked at words like the beak of an energetic capon combined to give him an unenchanting facade.

But what he said was worse. An acute observer remarked that McCarthy was a very private man in public and Humphrey was a very public man in private. No matter where the place or what the time Hubert Humphrey could not stop being the optimistic politician. Inflated rhetoric was his natural mode, and euphoria his natural temper. He was a trying man to be with yet difficult to dislike. He was a man of his time, but his time had been the America of the Depression and the years immediately following. His biggest appeal, according to one poll, was among people over fifty. McCarthy's biggest voter appeal was among the 33-to-50 age group and Kennedy's among the 21-to-35 age group.

The young, particularly the radical young, had no time for Hubert Humphrey. Yet, ironically, he had pushed through more liberal legislation than most of his detractors could name. That was why liberals were so bitter. How could such a man have turned into a nonstop cheerleader for the policies of Lyndon Johnson? How could he have betrayed everything for which he once stood?

"Hubert's tragedy," said a friend who had known him for more than twenty years, "is that whatever he does he has to do with enthusiasm." And in no way was he more humiliatingly enthusiastic than in his rapture over Johnson's Vietnam policy. Hubert Humphrey became the archenemy of the left because he spoke as the archapostle of the great American blunder. But he never flinched. The President demanded his loyalty, and Humphrey did his job.

He had blown into the Senate in 1949 like a midwestern tornado. He flouted Senate rules and deflated senatorial egos. He was so brash, so enthusiastic, so intemperate that dislike for him became universal in the upper house. Whenever he rose to speak there was a pointed exodus. Only when Senator Lyndon Johnson took him in hand and explained the art of political compromise, showing him the footwork necessary to be really effective and finally placing him on the right committees, did Humphrey become a force in the Senate. Humphrey owed Johnson a great deal: for his advice and support, for his teaching and help, for his choice of Humphrey as his Vice-Presidential running mate in 1964.

It was to Humphrey that Harold Wilson had gone for instruction in the art of pleasing the President. Humphrey told him what he had learned himself, that the best technique was to give unquestioned support to the President's Vietnam policy.

This was what politics was all about. Following these rules could lead a man to the Presidency someday. And Hubert Humphrey, as McCarthy observed, had always wanted to be President, a fitting ambition for a child of the Depression who had used his own emotional brand of morality to become a national figure. Now this homespun hero, this political relic of a fading America, would have his biggest chance. He had been loyal to the President, and, although he would never snap at his master, he was at last off the lead and able to speak in his own cause.

To watch him in action was like watching a rerun of prewar American movies. Mr. Deeds was really coming to town again: "There you are my young friend," he would say to a bewildered small child. "Here's a badge for yourself and another for your Mummy; don't forget to give it to her. Here's one for you; by golly we can't leave you out. God bless you. You want one too; this is my lucky button—you'll wear it for me. You know what that means, don't you? It means that you and I are going steady."

When his campaign staff advised him of the dangers in the primary route, his reply was, "by golly, you're right." Most of his sentences began with "by golly" or "good grief"—like the captions in Batman or Captain Marvel comics. A constantly recurring remark on and off the platform was, "By golly, it's great to be an American." The overall impression, beside being totally dated, made even Lyndon Johnson sound sophisticated.

Early in May Hubert Humphrey spoke to 3,000 delegates of the powerful United Auto Workers' Union. The unions were important, for they had long formed a solid bloc of Democratic Party votes. On this auspicious occasion, when he was bidding for endorsement as a candidate for the world's biggest job, Hubert Horatio Humphrey opened with, "It's great to come here and see all the lovely brothers and sisters; it's just great." To another audience he remarked, "Oh my, what a rascal I was in those days," and in a different setting, "Oh boy, we Americans are a bunch of doers."

He told a television audience in West Virginia: "I am my own man. I am my own personality, with all its limitations." His limitations were there for all to see, and they were so consistent that no one, even his nearest and dearest, could be blind to them. On one occasion when he was in the midst of an apparently endless peroration, his wife Muriel, who was on the platform, passed him a note: "Hubert! A speech does not have to be eternal in order to be immortal."

But in fairness one must examine his actions, as well as the depressing flow of words. And there is no doubt that, from very humble beginnings, Hubert Humphrey had fought against great odds and finally won a great many advantages for his fellow Americans. He was born to a corner druggist in Doland, South Dakota (population 550), on May 27, 1911.

During the Depression his father suffered setbacks, and Hubert dropped out of the University of Minnesota. But by the time he was 25 he had earned enough to return and take his degree, after which he practiced pharmacy for a few years.

In 1943, having been rejected by the army because of color blindness and a double hernia, he was beaten in the election for Mayor of Minneapolis, but two years later he won. He achieved great distinction in ridding that city of gangsters, corruption, and most of the other ills to which the American metropolis appears to be a natural prey. Three years later he became the first Democratic senator from Minnesota in ninety years.

In 1948 he fought for inclusion of a civil-rights plank in the national Democratic platform. In 1964 he was instrumental in writing and pushing through the Civil Rights Act. In 1948 he had proposed measures along the lines of Medicare. In the end he saw his lone efforts—and they *were* lone—vindicated when Medicare became effective in 1966. On an international level he was co-author of and rallied support for the partial nuclear-test-ban treaty of 1963.

So in 1968 he campaigned in safety, taking trips down memory lane with audiences of middle-aged Democratic supporters and dealing in smoke-filled rooms with the agents of the machine he had once challenged so brashly. He was, and he knew it, the organization candidate, however the rank and file felt about him, and he would play it the organization way.

But, whether he was romping with his grandchild on his Triple H Lakeside farm in Minnesota, dining with Muriel and his four grown-up children in the apartment overlooking the Potomac, or speaking on television before millions of people, no matter which way Humphrey turned, he could not escape the man in whose steps he trod. In Paris that May the first direct conversations between Hanoi and Washington had begun. Progress was infinitesimal, but from those talks could come the key to victory at the polls.

Lyndon Johnson had embarked on a determined course to bathe his five years' leadership in a golden glow that would illuminate the pages of future American history books. All the Federal agencies had been ordered to compile a record of his administration and its great works. Blocks of filing cabinets were being shipped to Texas, where they would provide the material for the Presidential memoirs. But to achieve his statesman's crown Lyndon Johnson needed a spectacular coup. If he could end the war that had brought his downfall, he would have achieved the most splendid and surprising of finales.

Secretive as ever, the President was engaged in efforts to enlist the support of the Soviet Union to ensure the success of the Paris talks. A secondary triumph would be to secure for the Democratic Party, and incidentally for Hubert Humphrey, another four-year tenure in the White House.

Against this background, there was no way for Hubert Humphrey to quit the Vice-Presidency and campaign as his own man. Wriggle as he might, he could not abandon the master who had politically emasculated him. For Humphrey knew that Johnson's wrath was awful and his vengeance swift; equally, Johnson's gifts could be great. Hubert Humphrey had waited too long to risk the former or squander the latter.

While Humphrey waited and watched the polls (where his popularity now showed a steady decline) and kept in touch with the President (who told him very little), Kennedy and McCarthy were coming out for the last round in their own battle.

It was to be fought in California, where the winner really would take all: 172 first-ballot votes.

Like a boxing match the primaries provided fifteen rounds in all. Everyone knew that there could be no decision on points. Robert Kennedy needed a knockout in California. After Oregon, he had to have a totally decisive victory. With anything short of that he was finished.

In their respective jets the two men and their followers flew south to the Golden State.

.13.

CALIFORNIA: SHOWDOWN IN A PLASTIC PARADISE

ANYONE WHO SPENDS ANY TIME TRAVELING THROUGH THE BIG INTERnational airports of Europe knows the fascinating game of "spot the nationality." Is that traveler with short blond haircut and lightweight luggage German or Dutch—or Finnish? The long-haired, languid fellow in tweeds—can he be British or a frightfully mod Italian? The game involves checking one's guesswork by getting close enough to hear the "object" speak, but it is one of the best ways to pass the time in those cavernous interchanges of our jet age. The airports all look alike, but at least the people are still somewhat different.

Playing the game in America was better still because one did not have to be in an airport to do it. One could set out to guess the ethnic backgrounds not only of immigrants but also of their descendants. To find the answers, one had only to strike up a conversation—never any problem in America.

The one place where people defied the game was California. There the British visitor really felt as if he were in a foreign country. The East—New York, Boston, and New England—was still linked to Britain and Europe in its manners and attitudes. All America was created by immigrants, but California was created by *American* immigrants. In a curious way the rest of the United States might only have been a staging ground for the development of the true American personality. Immigrants came from all over the Old World and implanted their seed in the eastern and central parts of the New World. That seed developed over generations and was then transplanted to California. There as elsewhere, of course, the Negro was still an exception to the process of homogenization.

Daniel P. Moynihan and Nathan Glazer, in *Beyond the Melting Pot*, a study of the American people, concluded that "the American nationality is still forming; its processes are mysterious and the final form, if there is ever to be a final form, is as yet unknown."

There were clues, however, in California. There the ethnic break with the Old World was almost complete. Californians were a new people. Their charm, their blandness, and their warmth were as American as the premixed cocktail. Within minutes of first meeting, they behaved as if they had known one all their lives, and one felt that, within seconds of his departure, they would have totally forgotten his existence.

It was strange to be with them, for, although they spoke the same language, they did not seem to mean the same things. Although they might be of the same generation, they did not seem to be of the same era. Perhaps they were the first of a new breed and the twenty-first century was already beginning in California.

To visit California then was to see the future—and to wonder whether or not it would work. California was dominated by Los Angeles County. One third of the state's 19.5 million people lived there, yet Los Angeles was probably the most distasteful city in the United States, if not the Western World. It was a terrible warning of what could happen to the whole world in the third millennium. Its interminable yet pointless boulevards—each indistinguishable from the next, each vulgarized by the wanton search for profit, each in a way a self-parody—stretched for 25 miles at a time, connecting what were separate cities but seemed to be merely gobules in one great oily mess. It was not only a city without a soul; it was also a city without character, without charm, without style. It was the ant heap of affluence.

One understood why Californians, particularly "Angelenos," sought refuge in churches, of which there was no shortage in the

221

state. The rush to Sunday absolution in a clearly amoral society again reflected the curious parallels between modern America and Victorian Britain. Religion had its commercial overtones in Victorian times, and in California in 1968 it was actually sold. God was packaged and projected in the same way that a new Hollywood personality was put across.

Two whole pages of church listings in the *Los Angeles Times* proclaimed this truth in 1968. They offered every flavor of religion, from the Independent Lutherans to the Pillar of Fire, from the Covenant to the Foursquare Gospel Church. One could go to the Temple of Tarot and Holy Qabalah and hear the Reverend Ann Davis preach on "The Cosmic Polarity Behind Evolution" ("develop spiritual power thru color and sound"), or one could visit the Church of the Open Door and hear Dr. J. Vernon McGee teaching "Action in Acts."

An advantage of the latter was "free parking and nursery facilities for all services." One could even dial "Share-a-Prayer." Or one could attend the annual convention of the Full Gospel Business Men's Fellowship and hear Dan Machaluk, chairman of the "FGBMF charismatic seminar committee."

That was one side of the scene. On the other were the benches for any weary nondrivers who might brave the boulevards. These benches were used for advertising and seemed to concern themselves almost exclusively with death and burial. Advertisements for "Westwood Village Mortuary," "Groman's Mortuary, Jewish Funeral Directors," "Malinow-Silverman, Jewish Funeral Directors," were interspersed with a few like "Raymond C. Jones, Exterminator" and "Brentwood Hills, Homes from $55,000 to $85,000."

California, surprisingly, appeared to have no greater proportion of people known to be mentally ill than did other parts of America: Eleven percent of its citizens were receiving treatment at psychiatric hospitals. This figure did not include those who were mentally retarded or in private analysis. On the other hand, it found itself the center of the flower-child, or hippie, movement— that incoherent, apparently sincere, but aimless form of unwashed protest.

Too, California placed an enormous and surely unhealthy emphasis on the dream of youth. Everyone had to be young. Young females had to have forty-inch bosoms and blonde hair down over their shoulders. If God had not provided the said prerequisites they

222

could be produced artificially with the aid of chemicals. There were "bust shots," injections of silicone into the breasts, although it was understood that they could lead to cancer.

Equally strange, was the general pollution of the air. The atmosphere of the Los Angeles basin was perpetually thick, partially, it was said, because of the surrounding low ring of hills. Doubtless motor vehicles also played their part.

Late at night, on one of the dozens of Los Angeles radio stations (could they *really* have all been necessary?) there was a popular show called "Private Line," on which a sort of tame psychiatrist spoke to people who telephoned him about their problems.

These people, who remained anonymous, said things like "I got divorced for the third time last month, and I feel very lonely," to which he replied, "Well, what did you expect to feel?" He then advised them to read certain books. It was very, very funny and very, very sad. But in California it came as no surprise that such appalling programs should appeal to the broadcasters, the callers and to the listeners.

The technological imperative was at its strongest in California, the home of the aerospace industry, computers, and cybernetics. These industries needed millions of trained workers, who had to be able to move freely on an amazing network of roads. The state was traversed in 1968 by 2,993 miles of expressways. By the early 1980s this figure will have grown to 12,500 miles. Already, one was gleefully assured by the authorities, freeways covered 2 percent of the total land available in greater Los Angeles. In central Los Angeles streets, garages, and parking lots took up an unbelievable 55 percent of the space.

California had 12 million vehicles, more than any other state or country in the world—except the United States itself. The prime preoccupation of the Californian 24 hours a day appeared to be the parking, servicing, fueling, polishing, buying, and selling of his motor car.

This California had all been developed in 120 years. The territory's population had been a mere 14,000 in 1848, the year it was annexed by the United States after victory in the war with Mexico. That war had started over Texas but had ended with the acquisition, for $15 million, of New Mexico, Texas, western Colorado, Utah, Nevada, Arizona, and California.

Traditionally, the ideas and trends that shaped American be-

223

havior patterns started on the East Coast and rolled westward until they took root in California. But in the 1960s California itself was setting the pace. Way-out things began there, and serious things started there.

Although most students in other parts of the country paid for university education, the idea of free higher education for everyone flourished in California. The state had 182 establishments of higher learning, constituting the "Megaversity," and every California child who wanted a degree was promised the opportunity to earn one. Billions of dollars were spent to provide the best possible conditions in which students could learn.

Then, to the astonishment—and subsequent fury—of the older generation, a student revolt broke out in Berkeley, where the main campus of the University of California was located. Only a few years later, students all round the world were rebelling against educational machinery that they believed was merely processing them to be fed into a soulless industrial complex. But the genesis of the revolt was California.

Nevertheless, the industrial complex had made California the richest state in the union. The world's biggest bank—the Bank of America—was there; its assets were $21,267,639,000. J. Paul Getty, a Californian, was estimated by *Fortune* to be tied with another Californian, Howard Hughes, for the title of richest American. Getty's worth was put at $1,235,584,504.

But California's wealth (its G.N.P., at £37,035,000,000 was 8 percent higher than that of Great Britain) was not shared equally. The underprivileged groups included urban Negroes (who showed in the Watts riots the length to which frustration could drive them) and the Mexican-Americans, many of whom worked for pitifully low wages in agriculture, in which the state leads the nation.

Kennedy appealed to these people, McCarthy to the huge academic community. But what of the average Californian, the rootless, restless individual reputed to change his home every three years and his job more often than that? Who would capture him? Considering the importance of California, the two candidates had little time to campaign. Though they had both made previous forays into the state, the effective down-to-the-wire battle lasted only one week from May 29 (the day after the Oregon primary) to June 4.

Only three weeks before Primary Day things looked bad for Mc-

Carthy. Opinion polls—several, like the Field Poll and the Quayle Poll, dealt solely with California—showed him running 15-18 percent behind Kennedy.

There were probably three reasons for this showing. First, Kennedy's name was known already. The only way to counteract this factor in a state as large as California was through massive television exposure, for which vast sums were needed. Just how vast could be gathered from a list prepared by KGW, one of Oregon's twelve channels, of the one-minute political spots bought during the campaign in that state. Nixon had bought 112, Reagan 104, Kennedy 58, McCarthy 46, and Rockefeller 17. The "prime time" cost of such advertisements was $400 a minute; that figure was just for one station in a state much smaller than California.

The second reason for Kennedy's early lead was that he was already well established as the supporter and champion of 1 million Mexican-Americans and 2 million Negroes.

Third, California was a state that thrived on glamor, that worshiped it, and that viewed the unglamorous as failures. Kennedy, with his retinue of stars, his family, and his motorcades epitomized glamor and was thus a "natural" for California.

McCarthy probably had two factors on his side. One was that the great number of university campuses in the state offered hope for support. Second, his supporters in the state had long been organized, thanks to Gerald Hill and Martin Stone. They had already set up McCarthy-for-President committees throughout the state. They had managed to get his name put first on the ballot by collecting 30,000 signatures between midnight and 9:00 A.M. on the first morning for filing ballot petitions.

And since he had won in Oregon McCarthy could hope for money from rich but previously hesitant supporters. It came: Within a couple of days his treasury had been swollen by $100,000. But it came too late. All the best television time had already been preempted by Kennedy. Television stations did not book shows on credit; they had to see the money first. To overcome this setback, the McCarthy campaigners sought free air time, which meant appearing on such "talk" shows as those of Les Crane, Stan Bohrman, and Joey Bishop.

The enormous amounts of money spent in American primary campaigns seemed almost shocking to an observer used to the parsimony of British elections (where candidates are forbidden by law to spend more than 9.5 cents per head of the electorate). The techniques used were even more extraordinary. A major ploy was to play upon the herd instinct. In California, this technique reached its apogee, as the candidates vied with one another for the most glamorous and impressive list of supporters.

The Kennedy forces ran two advertising layouts in the state's papers showing support from labor leaders and academic personalities. But their biggest blast came with a list of film stars. "Hollywood for Kennedy" included Gene Kelly, Truman Capote, Shirley MacLaine, Warren Beatty, Henry Mancini, Tony Franciosa, Peter Lawford (of course), Rosemary Clooney, Raquel Welch and Marlene Dietrich (an interesting duo of sex goddesses), Mike Nichols (director of the sensationally successful film *The Graduate,* whose star, Dustin Hoffman, was for McCarthy), Norman Mailer, Angie Dickinson, Rita Hayworth, Trini Lopez, Mahalia Jackson, Jerry Lewis, and Henry Fonda.

By what logic this list could have been expected to persuade people to vote for Kennedy was never explained. Instead, it was admitted that it was vote-getting on the level of sheer hucksterism. "That list could sell deodorants, cigarettes, zip fasteners, or bags of cement," said one Kennedy aide. "So why the hell shouldn't it sell a political candidate?"

Nevertheless, it was interesting that McCarthy also had an impressive list of Hollywood protagonists, though he displayed them less frequently. Apart from Hoffman, the instant folk hero, McCarthy supporters included Paul Newman and Barbra Streisand, author Arthur Miller and poet Robert Lowell, Jill St. John and Eva Marie Saint, Paula Prentiss and Jean Simmons, cartoonist Jules Feiffer and conductor Igor Stravinsky, sociologist Erich Fromm and singers Peter, Paul, and Mary.

McCarthy elected to hit hard on Vietnam with his advertising. One ad was headed "How Many More Vietnams?" It said:

> Eugene McCarthy was the first man to cry out "Let the killing stop." And he was the first man with the guts to ask "Why are we here?" . . . Both Humphrey and Kennedy (and Nixon, Reagan and Rockefeller too) are part and parcel of the kind of thinking about America's role in the world that is leading us on to catastrophe. . . . There is only one candidate who has no obligations to the present policies in Vietnam and who is under no pressure to defend old mistakes here. There is only one candidate who can win the election without mortgaging

himself either to the establishment or the special interest groups.

This ad showed right from the beginning that there was to be no quarter in the California battle. The McCarthy plan was to identify Robert Kennedy with his brother's decision to send the special forces to Vietnam. This approach would put Kennedy on the defensive and keep the Vietnam issue for McCarthy alone.

Kennedy was furious and hit back. Speaking at the Sheraton Palace on the last day in May, he alleged that McCarthy had "completely distorted the facts." He complained that he resented people who twisted the record and said that distortions demeaned politics. His backers prepared a set of advertisements attempting to prove that McCarthy had a poor liberal voting record. Kennedy also weighed in with a new list of personality supporters to fill a page, a mixed bag this time, and pretty impressive, ranging from composer André Previn to boxer Jose Torres, from author Terry Southern to cartoonist Charles Addams.

But the McCarthy knife had slashed deep. He had said in San Francisco near the end of the Oregon campaign, "Any man who played a prominent role in developing the policies of the early '60s can be called upon to explain his role in those policies." As he said many times privately, "We have to make Bobby run against his brother."

Kennedy ads answered McCarthy ads. The vitriol flowed fast. According to one: "The New Hampshire McCarthy wanted peace. The California McCarthy wants the Presidency. It seems to have made a difference." It pointed out that Bobby had spoken against Vietnam a year before McCarthy had, that McCarthy had been inconsistent in his attacks on the Johnson administration, and that he had contradicted himself over American intervention in the Dominican Republic in 1961. It ended: "Is this the heralded politics of conscience? Sadly, there was one Senator McCarthy in New Hampshire and a different one in California. We like the one from New Hampshire best."

This ad was gentle compared to the one headed: "Law enforcement and the Cities. How do Kennedy and McCarthy Stack Up?" On the left side of the page was a list of some of Kennedy's efforts at solving these problems. On the right was a huge blank space.

McCarthy replied to both in his usual dry way. Of the first he said that Kennedy had also changed somewhat: During New Hamp-

227

shire he had been for the reelection of Johnson and Humphrey. (But now he apparently felt differently about it. Of the second he remarked, "I hope the *Los Angeles Times* charges double for that or they give the space to me so I can fill it in."

The battle was also fought on the hustings. In many ways it was strange to British eyes. For a start, all the candidates were fairly limited as to what their actual policies could be. They were all very good at enumerating the problems, but one had the feeling that they were all holding back on solutions to allow maximum bargaining flexibility at the conventions and especially at official party policy-making meetings.

In Britain one knew the platform and made one's choice accordingly. In the American primaries, somehow, one made the choice first; the platform came later. Then again, American political audiences were on the whole very polite indeed. Whether or not the efficiency of the microphone arrangements was responsible one does not know, but at this stage the heckler was a fairly rare beast.

In general, the Kennedy technique in California was the same as in early primaries—to show that he could draw the crowds. Time and again he would throw himself into the mob, falling into its clutching, grabbing, pulling, pinching hands. It was the same technique that an ambitious pop star would use under the guidance of an old fashioned press agent. The whipped-up crowds were given Kennedy to maul, to paw, to engulf. But what did the adulation prove? "It proves," said Pierre Salinger, former White House press secretary to President Kennedy, who had joined Bobby Kennedy's campaign, "it proves that he is a winner."

This comment reflected the old conception of American politics. The primary voters were to select a man less for what he said than for his political Neilson rating. They were supposedly looking for a Democrat who would beat all Republicans. So, in those frenzied final days of the California campaign, Kennedy was trying to prove that he could outdraw anyone. In Watts, the still-unreconstructed ghetto of revolt, he unquestionably did. Thousands of Negroes turned out to welcome him, and they gave him the wildest reception of the campaign. They believed in Bobby, in him and in no one else.

Watts, if only because of its past, deserves special attention. It had a population of 225,000, 13 percent of whom were unemployed. At first sight, it did not look like a traditional ghetto. Many of the one-story houses there would have been welcomed by plenty of British citizens, as would the big cars parked on the streets. But after the first superficial appraisal, the ghetto atmosphere came through—the sullen defeatism, the faces of people with no discernible future, the alienation, the despair. Men who wished to find jobs suffered an extra disadvantage: A majority of all Watts males over the age of sixteen had been arrested at some time or another. Although the arrests were often for minor offenses and many never led to conviction, the peculiar American system allows the mere fact of arrest to remain on the record. This practice was bad. Enough mud thrown by a bad policeman would leave traces sticking even to the innocent, and this kind of mud naturally prejudiced a man's chance for a job.

The other statistics about Watts were just as depressing. The average family income in the black community was $4,200 a year, $2,500 below the California average and $1,400 below the national average. There were 106 doctors to serve the whole community; the doctor-population ratio was only a third of the average in the county. Twenty-two percent of the houses were classified as deteriorated or dilapidated. Only two of the eight hospitals satisfied state minimum standards.

McCarthy came into this area, but it was not his scene. His cool and aloof personality had no attraction for the soul brothers of Watts. He spoke at an open-air meeting in Will Rogers Memorial Park. The crowd of several hundred seemed listless and interested mainly in the free food: horrid-smelling hamburgers, over-roasted frankfurters, and the inevitable cans of Coca-Cola. The visit could hardly be called a success, though McCarthy did come out in apparent support of the Black Power movements, saying that, "No group in America has more reason to organize to get its rights than Negroes."

Earlier he had found an enthusiastic reception at his headquarters in Westwood, near Beverly Hills, where about 3,000 of his supporters and workers had cheered him as he told them: "None of us have in mind any compromises. I'm not taking or even making any offers of the Vice-Presidency. In fact, I think I may even run without one."

That afternoon he went to the predominantly Jewish Fairfax area of Los Angeles. He drew a huge crowd at the street crossing near Kantor's restaurant and bakery. One baker said that it was the largest crowd he had ever seen at the spot, a favorite stopping place for politicians. The official McCarthy press handout reporters said:

> The major issues in the area are . . . Israel (the area is Zionistic), Medicare and Social Security. Former Governor Brown was very successful in this area because on his walking tours he would stop in an Israeli import store near Kantor's and speak to the manager. Evidently this shows concern for Israel in the way the residents like it to be shown.

The unfortunate—almost jeering—tone of this handout and others like it was one of the great enigmas of the McCarthy movement. One never discovered whether his youthful helpers were being deliberately snide about the whole adult world or were simply inexperienced. The net result was that no newsmen ever missed reading a McCarthy handout while his opponents' offerings were usually scanned and often thrown away.

But even more interesting than the handout was McCarthy's own attitude at the Fairfax meeting. It was very, very hot, and McCarthy addressed the throng for 25 minutes without mentioning Medicare and saying almost nothing about social security. And, as the same baker pointed out afterward, McCarthy was the first speaker to come to the corner in twenty years and not mention the name of Israel once.

This omission was pointed out to him later. "Oh well," he drawled. "I guess I kinda covered it when I said we should honor our commitments around the world. I guess they woulda known what I was talking about." But he never actually said it, and his silence did not not seem to matter. This occasion was just one small example of how McCarthy deliberately and even arrogantly flouted traditions of politicking—and got away with it.

His big date on Wednesday was in San Francisco, where he spoke at a fund-raising dinner at the Sheraton Palace Hotel. A huge picture of McCarthy in typical half-turned pose on a blue background covered the wall at the head of the chandeliered ballroom, and big white balloons floated above the heads of the audience, which had paid $50 a head for the privilege of listening to him. He made a major foreign-policy speech. Its key point was that Red China should be recognized by the United States. He had long ridiculed Dean Rusk for pretending that China did not exist, while at the same time insisting that America would have to stand up to Com-

230

munism because very shortly China would have 1 billion people. "If they'll have that many," McCarthy would say, "I think we might figure they have 750 million now, so I don't see how 750 million people can't exist."

Our involvement in Vietnam had been to a large extent a product of misjudgments about the state of Chinese society and the capacities of Chinese expansionism. . . . For too long America has acted as if China did not exist. The time has come to find ways to include her in the community of nations.

His suggested methods of doing so included "abandoning the fantasy" that Taiwan would reconquer the mainland. The United States would have to stop assisting in Nationalist raids on the mainland. Red China would have to be given diplomatic recognition and there would have to be trade and cultural exchanges. Red China would also have to be included in disarmament and test-ban talks.

McCarthy also slammed into Humphrey for being more for the Vietnam war than the President himself was. "Those who want to please the King may be more for his policies than the King himself."

It was a good speech. Of poverty and racial prejudice, he said:

For one hundred years we've treated the black people and the brown as colonial subjects living in our midst. They had unequal education, economics, and health. There was a second-class citizenship. Now after the Second World War there was a demand that people shouldn't live under oppression. There is a genuine demand for equality and access to the better things of life. On moral grounds there is no time for postponement of that demand.

Of Robert Kennedy, he declared: "He admits he has made mistakes. But mistakes don't matter as much as misconceptions." Of Walt Rostow's conception of "internal aggression," as exemplified by the troubles at Columbia University, he remarked that the idea borrowed military phraseology, to which there was no limit once one began. "The language of poverty even is the language of war. We have a War on Poverty. Poverty does not yield to war. Ignorance was never reduced by war or the techniques of war. We have

231

a war on crime, a war on ill health. We need a new language, and I want to change all that."

And, finally, he said bitterly of Vietnam, "Like one of the women in the Judgment of Solomon, we seem to be saying, "Cut the child in two."

On Thursday Kennedy took off on one of his famous train rides. In Indiana he had hired the illustrious and noisy Wabash Cannonball. In California he took a slow train through the lush and fertile San Joaquin Valley. The old-fashioned caboose was draped with bunting, colorful in the withering sun as the train chugged from Fresno to Sacramento. Once again he was thrown to the crowds. Once again employed all the devices of old-style American politics.

At Thurlock, "turkey capital of the world," he and Ethel ate turkey for breakfast and then went out to tell the people how much they loved it. "I am running for President because my wife, Ethel, told me that I would have to come to Thurlock, turkey capital of the world, and that's why I'm here today," said Kennedy, drawing shouts of laughter from he crowd. He continued, "Do Gene McCarthy and Hubert Humphrey eat Thurlock turkeys?"

"No-o-o," screamed the audience.

Kennedy grinned: "Well my family does." Then came the great roar of applause.

Kennedy was said to be a withdrawn, introverted man. Could he have enjoyed these childish tactics? In any case he showed no signs that he was embarrassed by them.

His technique was more like that of Lyndon Johnson, than that of his brother. John Kennedy had attracted the crowds, but with style and without losing contact he always maintained that detached superiority that is the mark of a great star. Robert Kennedy seemed to be deliberately demeaning himself, lowering his standards, talking down to people. Only when one talked to advisers like Pierre Salinger and Theodore Sorenson did one come to understand the reason.

They were deliberately advising him, indeed directing him, into this pattern of campaigning. The warm, friendly, easily reachable Bobby was their answer to the "ruthless" tag which they feared could be used to devastating effect against him. There was hostility, in some cases bitter, among the crowds, but Kennedy always turned away insult with a smile and if possible a quip. It was revealing to

232

talk to people in a crowd after Bobby had passed among them. "I actually touched him," Los Angeles housewife Eileen Farris said. "I actually touched him, his arm."

Would she vote for him? "Gee, I haven't thought about that," she answered. "But I did touch him. You saw me."

Fred Shorter, shop assistant by profession, thought that Kennedy had "great charm." "He's very friendly, much more friendly than I expected, but he doesn't have the dignity of his brother. He's quite amusing. Do you think he writes his own gags? If he does, he's very good."

Mrs. Janet Cohen liked "his style." "You know, he's open, direct. He mixes with the people. I never actually got close enough to touch him, but I'm glad I came out here." Could she recall what the candidate had said? "Well, like he was the best man, and he spoke about his family and all," said Mrs. Cohen, "but I don't remember the details. You don't at these sort of affairs really, do you? You come to see the man and size him up for yourself."

If this random sample was indicative of anything, it was that the candidate did not give the people much detail to remember. When he did talk about issues, he spoke in slogans, and essentially vague ones: of peace with honor in Vietnam without reneging on American commitments in Southeast Asia, of law and order and replacing rioting with understanding, of cutting back on welfare by giving people what they want—jobs.

The performance was not impressive. Despite the mob scenes, the crowds, and the jokes, there was something lackluster about Bobby Kennedy's campaigning. Perhaps he despised the role in which his managers and scriptwriters had cast him. Perhaps the campaign brought back too many memories of the one in 1960, which he had organized with such flair and style for his brother. Or perhaps, like everyone else in those incredible American elections, he was simply exhausted. He seemed to come alive only when he was with the Negroes or the Mexican-Americans.

One could understand why. As Attorney General his record in the battle against the southern states was legendary. And another factor was important: Kennedy had a special magic with children. He was wonderful, not only with his own children, but with all children. In those ghettos he projected to adults in the same way that he did to children. And they—like children—reveled in the "chant and response."

While Kennedy went after votes in his "favorite" areas of Oak-

233

land, farther south at the San Diego naval base McCarthy talked about getting rid of Rusk, McNamara, and Hoover and issued position papers on pollution and the conversion of the economy from a wartime to a peacetime footing. Some of his facts on pollution were frightening. For instance, every day during January, 15,000 tons of filth had fallen on Los Angeles County. Every year 10,000 people or more were told by their doctors to leave the county because of dangers from air pollution. Annual damage to crops and forests ran into hundreds of millions of dollars. Lake Tahoe was turning gray with algae formed from sewer seepage.

Though Vietnam, race, and poverty caught the headlines, pollution was, in fact, one of the major problems of the United States in 1968. McCarthy blamed much of the dirt in the air on the motor car. He advocated large spending on developing rail or subway systems:

> Mass transit would serve not only to reduce the direct discharge of contaminants into the air; it would help to change the very quality of life in our cities by reducing congestion and preserving homes and parks from the encroachments of new freeways.
> More freeways lead only to more pollution. By preempting space and poisoning the atmosphere, they drive more people out of the city and create more traffic. Thus our cities are caught in a vicious cycle of more traffic, more movement, more freeways, and more pollution.

This analysis was an example of McCarthy at his best, of the clarity with which he recognized that the dangers of unplanned escalation could be even more dangerous in America than in Vietnam.

On conversion of the economy, he said that war resources could be used to solve domestic problems. For instance, with those resources alone the nation could build 6 million new houses within five years. He added, "The final conversion problem, however, will not be economic; it will be moral and political."

After a day's campaigning McCarthy sat on his hotel balcony with a visitor, surveying the sprawling mass that was Los Angeles and talking about this problem.

> I feel so sorry for those people down there. You see that section over there. That's a middle-class area, mostly Jewish.

234

And there are all those nice Jewish ladies thinking of nothing but ordering their groceries quickly so that they can get out to the country club. There's nothing else to their lives. And the idea is that everyone should live like that. In the end it's much harder to stop this kind of escalation than it is to stop the war.

The California campaign ran through the last week in May, as the red poppies were already losing their opulence under the dust mantle thrown over them by passing cars. The climax was planned for June 1, three days before the vote. The big debate was finally on: the television confrontation sought since March that would finally decide the champion to be fielded against Hubert Humphrey.

It had been on Wednesday, May 29, the day after his disaster in Oregon that Kennedy had finally agreed to this meeting. For weeks McCarthy had been goading him to a television debate, and Kennedy had continually refused, saying that he would agree only if Humphrey also appeared. The whole thing had been a kind of game. Everyone knew that it was to the benefit of the back marker to appear on television with the front runner. Equally the latter wanted to avoid giving his opponent free publicity by such a confrontation. By agreeing at last Kennedy was implicitly admitting that California was by no means certain for him, that McCarthy had the momentum, and that Kennedy might even benefit from the debate.

There was much jockeying among the various television companies for the show. In the end the two candidates settled on A.B.C.'s "Issues and Answers" program. McCarthy was a little upset that there was not going to be an actual debate, but there was little that he could do about it. Three newsmen would question the two in turn, and each candidate would have a chance to reply to the other's main statements. But there would be no direct conversation between them.

That afternoon both candidates returned to their suites in San Francisco's Fairmont Hotel to rest. The Fairmont, a vast and ornate palace "atop Nob Hill," made its name on exclusivity, and its attraction for the elite depended mainly on its view. Kennedy, having canceled his program for the day, including a massive meeting with 600 of the state's top labor leaders (a never-explained tactical error), arrived first. As he entered the elegant Fairmont

235

foyer, his spaniel Freckles, whom McCarthy had so often derided as "not really bringing much towards the issues in this campaign," took a fancy to the deep pile of the carpet and piddled lustily upon it. It was the best performance of the day.

The news raced through the hotel. It was known on the fourth floor within about 65 seconds of the occurrence. Shortly afterward McCarthy came in with his party. He was instantly informed of the development. "Yeah, the center pillar I believe," he said, looking cautiously around. The thought must have cheered him because he spent the next two hours with his young helpers singing Irish songs and telling Irish jokes. Kennedy and Freckles spent the afternoon with a few intimate friends.

For months the American press, itching for scalps in a race that it apparently found almost impossible to understand, had longed for the debate. Now, scenting blood in living color, 300 journalists thronged the studios, a five-minute cable-car ride down Nob Hill. One hundred fifty newsmen, mainly those who had been following Kennedy, crowded into one studio. The McCarthy following of 150 squeezed into the adjoining one. Coffee was provided, and the newsmen sat at long desks studying the screens. A group of eight reporters sat in the studio itself, as did Ethel Kennedy and four friends. The reporters were to record such fascinating details as who crossed his legs when and how many sips of water each candidate took. Meanwhile, as they waited for the confrontation, they were kept breathlessly informed by one of the instant-trivia men that a cushion had been placed on one of the chairs so that, sitting, Bobby would seem to be the same height as McCarthy.

This morsel turned out to be instant error; the cushion was for Frank Reynolds, the "anchor man" of the program, who had a bad back. Finally, at 6:30 P.M., after sheepish handshakes and grins, the famous battle commenced.

Battle? It was little more than what McCarthy had predicted it would be, a sort of nice tea-party chat. This atmosphere was as much his fault as anyone's. It was he who had insisted on the show. It was he who had insisted that there were great differences between him and Kennedy. It was he who had said that the people should be given the opportunity to make a choice. The 30 million who were said to have watched the nonevent could have been forgiven for sleeping; never mind choosing.

If the two men differed at all, it was on three minor counts. McCarthy thought that the National Liberation Front in Vietnam

236

should be brought into negotiations and promised a part in a coalition government right from the beginning. Kennedy believed that the United States was wrong to impose any group into the government of Vietnam, that the decision should be up to the Vietnamese people. On the race issue, McCarthy put forward the view that Negroes should be moved out of the ghettos and into the suburbs; the ghettos would thus disappear. Kennedy said that this solution would be catastrophic. The third and final battle came over personalities. McCarthy said again that he would remove J. Edgar Hoover from control of the F.B.I. Kennedy refused to say what he would do about Hoover. Would he keep Dean Rusk as Secretary of State then? McCarthy would not. Kennedy answered, "I won't say." Did he think Rusk was a good Secretary of State? Kennedy replied: "I think he has been a very dedicated American, committed to perform his service for the United States. I happen to disagree with the policies that he is espousing in very important areas of this country. But he is entitled to his opinion as I am entitled to mine."

This evasive answer was typical of the totally frustrating blandness that the American primary campaign produced. But it gave McCarthy an advantage, and in his rebuttal he produced the one spark of the entire confrontation:

> I think we give Cabinet members too much protection. You say, "He is a dedicated man, and he is serving the country," but I say he ought to be answerable for policy mistakes and for position mistakes. I think your brother was too kind to a number of people after the Bay of Pigs. I think this binds a certain weakness into the government. You say, "Well this is a man who was appointed; therefore we have to protect him." I think Cabinet members ought to be more expendable than senators, like the British cabinet system. You make a mistake, if a man makes a mistake, now, you let him go. They say: "You have been a great Secretary of State. Goodbye."

At the end of the hour, in an extraordinary conclusion that was rather like a sixth-form oral exam, each was asked to say why he should be the next President. Each recited his credentials, and McCarthy probably sounded a little more impressive because of his twenty years of congressional service.

The debate was over. The newsmen asked one another: "How

237

did you see it? What did you make the score?" They also asked these questions of the candidates. Said McCarthy: "It was a kind of no-decision bout with three referees [the three A.B.C. questioners]. We were wearing sixteen-ounce gloves."

Said Kennedy: "I thought it was fine. It's up to the voters to make the judgment."

McCarthy, when asked whether or not he would like to debate again, replied, "No, we'd get tired of each other." So, probably, would the watching Americans. The newsmen compared all their notes, with the inevitable result that every paper across the land the next day called the debate a draw.

A draw it probably was, but a poll taken 48 hours later showed that, although most people could not remember a thing that either man had said, a great majority thought that McCarthy "looked more like a President." The day after the debate A.B.C. proudly announced that it had topped the national viewing charts. It had been watched by 32 million people, or 38.8 percent of the total viewing audience. Cary Grant and Doris Day, who had started half an hour earlier with *That Touch of Mink* drew only 31 percent and "Petticoat Junction" 23 percent.

On Sunday, apart from television appearances, Kennedy relaxed. He went to Disneyland. It was a jaunt for his children, he said, but it was also good public relations to show that he was a good father, a family man with great-looking kids, and not a bit ruthless. Despite the contrived air—it was hard to have a family outing with a couple hundred newspapermen along—Kennedy was relaxed. With children he was always happy, and on that last Sunday of his life he seemed very happy indeed.

He went for a ride in a big old open car with the press all clinging to the ladders of an ancient bus that preceded it. Then there was the dark ride on the water among the caves of the "pirates of the Caribbean." The visitor found himself in the boat with the entire Kennedy family. Bobby sat in front with three of his small children. We shot down steep waterfalls and into marvelous gun battles between pirate ships, villages in flames, and randy brigands chasing feckless maidens in a never-ending romp. He loved it. "Now we're pirates properly," he told the children; when we emerged he fed them popcorn. John Glenn, who accompanied him, grinned happily and bought a bag himself, saying, "Nothing free for an astronaut—15 cents same as anyone else."

The party rode on a replica of an old river steamer, which

chugged round a huge island with model deer and elk turning their heads at our approach; the visitor stood by Kennedy at the rail and asked about the battering to which, even on a day off, he was exposed. "I can't see Harold Wilson giving himself to the people like that," said the visitor.

Kennedy grinned. "I guess we do it differently." Then, as he walked down the steps toward the landing stage, he turned and asked, "How would Harold Wilson get from here to there?" What he meant was that, confronted with any one problem, there was only one best way to solve it.

For everyone it was the pleasantest afternoon of the campaign.

On the Monday before the vote, McCarthy made a major speech at the Ambassador Hotel in Los Angeles, where Kennedy had made his headquarters in the Coconut Grove Room. He told an attentive audience from the Los Angeles Chamber of Commerce:

My purpose in running for President is not, essentially, a personal one. I would not have run if I had not sensed the will of the American people for a redirection of the basic processes of American government. The American people have already passed a judgment in this campaign. They have rejected not only the political decisions which have escalated the war and neglected our cities, but also the methods by which these decisions were made. I am, I believe, the only candidate addressing himself to causes as well as results, to institutions as well as programs. . . . One of my purposes in running for President is to clarify the functions of the various institutions of government, to restore Constitutional processes, and, in so doing, to bring the Presidency closer to the people. Neither Vice-President Humphrey nor Senator Kennedy have indicated any interest in these relationships, nor have they made any proposals for changing these policies. I submit that the old politics is finished in America.

Later in the day he went further, claiming that his voting record in Congress had been consistently distorted by the Kennedy campaigners. "Kennedy's denial that he knows anything about these distortions is a bit like his knowledge of wiretapping."

On that last day of campaigning, Robert Kennedy was in San Francisco, where he attacked McCarthy but without conviction somehow. The men around Kennedy also seemed tired and dispirited. An air of resigned bitterness surrounded the whole Kennedy camp. "All we have done," said one Kennedy man, "is give the thing to Humphrey." They had started in March with enthusiasm. The old professionals squeezing into harness to recapture the glories of 1960. But it had proved to be a venture in disaster. The campaign was badly coordinated, and in that it reflected the out-of-condition reflexes of its aging warriors.

The Kennedy people, known variously by their opponents as "the Goon Squad," "the Irish Mafia," "the eastern clique of the W.O.K.M." (the well-oiled Kennedy machine), feared that the necessary overwhelming victory was impossible. The night before Primary Day, looking at their battered, bruised, and terribly tired candidate, one wondered whether or not he really even wanted to win. Perhaps for the first time in his life, this man, brought up to compete as naturally as ordinary men eat and drink and survive, may have asked himself whether or not he *really* wanted to win.

That night in San Diego candidate Robert Francis Kennedy collapsed on the platform, at the finish of the last speech of the day and the campaign. "He is," said an admiring supporter, "like the perfect runner who is at the point of total collapse the second he strikes the winning tape." So, after a six-month primary campaign, in every kind of weather and over every kind of geography, it was time for the last big vote.

McCarthy rose early in his suite at the Beverly Hilton Hotel on June 4. After an early taping session for yet another television program, he flew to Phoenix, Arizona, in a chartered Boeing 727. There he spent the day canvassing the support of delegates from that arid state, returning to Los Angeles in late afternoon. His California campaign chairman, New York lawyer Tom Finney, and his brother-in-law, ex-C.I.A. man Tom McCoy, sat all afternoon at the Hilton watching the progress of the voting. Finney thought that the best possible result for them would be a loss to Kennedy by about 2 percent. Both men believed that if Kennedy were decisively trounced in California, their tasks of holding together all the anti-Humphrey delegates until August would be greatly increased.

Kennedy slept late. He was staying at the beach house of some friends, Mr. and Mrs. John Frankenheimer, with six of his children. There was one of those thick, polluted mists along the coast, but he and his son David went swimming anyway, and, when David was caught in an undertow, the Senator fished him out. All this activity was recorded because, despite the need for privacy, publicity could never be forgotten, and therefore selected newsmen were alongside. Pictures of that last day on the beach, planned to further Kennedy's campaign, were to appear with evocative poignance the following week.

By 3:00 in the afternoon the first reports had begun to trickle in. Early samples showed that Kennedy might win as much as a 49-41 percent majority over McCarthy. They gave him the confidence to take a late afternoon nap.

McCarthy had meanwhile returned to the Beverly Hilton, where during the evening he invited the visitor in for a drink. A loudspeaker went screaming down the road blaring last-minute urgings to vote for McCarthy. The candidate winced, and the visitor asked why he found it embarrassing. Was not it part of the political scene? "Yes, but it's part of the old political scene. It really doesn't do any good politically today. It merely gets people riled up. So it's embarrassing and ineffective, bad on both counts. It's too late to get people out to vote now."

At the other end of Wilshire Boulevard, at the Ambassador Hotel, the Kennedy supporters, in their boaters and bobby sox, clamored for the candidate. But it was not until about midnight, when it seemed clear that he was going to win a big victory (that in the end turned out to be roughly 46-42 percent), that he finally decided to greet his fans. At the time, the Kennedy advisers, because of a C.B.S. prediction, expected the victory margin to be much wider. Otherwise, Kennedy might have waited much longer and lived.

While McCarthy joined his followers at the Beverly Hilton in celebration of what seemed almost a victory to them, Kennedy; his wife Ethel; Jesse Unruh, Speaker of the California State Assembly; aides Rosey Grier and Rafer Johnson; and brother-in-law Steve Smith finally made their way down to the Embassy Ballroom. The supporters screamed for him among the brilliant lights and colors of the room. The television cameras rolled and recorded what seemed a great victory.

Kennedy cracked a few jokes aimed at himself, as they had so often been, and then repeated the message that he had carried across the United States: "I think we can end the divisions within the United States. What I think is quite clear is that we can work together. We are a great country, a selfless and a compassionate country. So my thanks to all of you and on to Chicago, and let's win."

The celebration was over. Ordinarily he would then have walked through the crowd, shaking hands, grinning, being mauled, losing

241

cufflinks and buttons, as he had done in countless towns. But this time the crowd was just too dense, and he had arranged to hold a press conference immediately after his speech. So, instead, he pushed through the gold curtains at the back of the platform and, with a throng of aides, pressmen, and supporters, walked through the double doors into the corridor-pantry that led past the kitchens. The time was 12:20 A.M. on Wednesday, June 5.

.14.

THE GUN IS MIGHTIER THAN THE VOTE

WHEN KENNEDY WALKED DOWN THAT GREASY LITTLE KITCHEN CORRIDOR
between the warming counters and the ice-making machine, he
had his three large bodyguards with him: Bill Barry, Roosevelt
Grier, and Rafer Johnson. He was also accompanied by representatives of all the mass medium, including photographers and television crews with their cameras working. But, in the event, the
guards did not prevent a little man half the weight of any of them
from shooting Robert Kennedy. And no cameraman recorded the
crime itself.

The events as they were immediately related by those present
were naturally tinged with the bias of each observer's recollection.
It was only weeks later that some sort of clear picture emerged as
to what happened in the seconds that made a small, wiry, 24-year-
old Jordanian Arab named Sirhan Sirhan a national figure.

Kennedy, it seemed, had been asked by Bill Barry not to use the
back corridor. But Kennedy had replied, "It's all right." Earlier,
Sirhan had tried to enter the Embassy Ballroom itself. But twice

he had been turned away because he had no ticket or press card. Finally he went around and into the kitchen area, where there was no check and no security. In his hand was a rolled-up Kennedy poster and, in the poster, a .22 caliber Iver-Johnson Cadet revolver.

He had had plenty of practice with it. Earlier in the day a college student named Henry Carreon had gone with a friend to the San Gabriel Valley Gun Club. When they arrived, Sirhan was standing among piles of empty cartridge cases. He had already used about 400 shots. They noticed him particularly because he was practicing rapid fire, which was not normally allowed. And there was another thing. Beside Sirhan was a box of special bullets that he was not using. Said Carreon later: "They are called the 'mini-magnum.' This type of bullet, when it penetrates an object, usually tears and splits out into different directions."

Inside the gun, as Sirhan waited in the pantry, there were nine mini-magnum bullets. It was at about 11:45 that Jesus Perez, a kitchen porter, first saw Sirhan standing there. Three or four times Sirhan asked Perez if Kennedy would be coming that way. Ironically, it did not seem at all unusual for an obvious member of an ethnic minority to be waiting to see the man whom minorities regarded as their champion.

As he waited, Sirhan talked to a pretty girl in a white dress with dark polka dots on it. Vincent di Pierro, a part-time waiter, saw him flirting with her. Said di Pierro: "Together they were both smiling. As he got down he was smiling. In fact, the minute the first two shots were fired, he still had a very sick-looking smile on his face. That's one thing. I can never forget that."

Kennedy came through the double doors with the hotel's assistant maitre d'hotel Karl Uecker and another employee, Edward Minasian, leading the way for him. Taped onto a wall of the corridor was a sign in hand lettering: "The Once and Future King."

Kennedy saw the kitchen staff lined up beside the hot-counters to his left. He started to shuffle sideways, as ever reaching to grasp the hand of anyone who wished a part of him. He came to Juan Romera, a seventeen-year-old busboy, and, as he took his hand, Sirhan stepped across the corridor. Then it happened. In a cool, deliberate, almost time-stopping act, Sirhan held the gun with its muzzle a bare three inches from Kennedy's head. Once, twice, he pulled the trigger. Someone later said that the shots were like popping balloons and another that they were like dry wood snapping.

244

Kennedy reeled backward. Uecker grabbed the gunman's arm and with the help of Minasian slammed him down onto one of the steel counters. But Sirhan's hand seemed locked to the revolver, and he went on firing. It finally took Grier, Johnson, and Barry to subdue Sirhan and a broken finger to make him release the gun.

It was too late. Apart from Kennedy, who was almost certainly doomed after the first shot, bodies lay all around in that crowded, stifling corridor. Five other people had been wounded, some seriously, by the random bullets. Blood was everywhere. People were screaming: "Look out. There's a madman in there, and he's killing everybody."

Juan Romera kneeled down next to Kennedy and gave him a crucifix. "Is everybody safe?" asked the dying Senator. "Yes, yes," said the boy. A priest appeared and pressed a rosary into his hand. One voice cried: "He doesn't need a priest for God's sake. He needs a doctor." When a policeman rushed in, shotgun in hand, the plea was repeated: "We don't need guns. We need a doctor."

Back in the ballroom, where the young Kennedy supporters were clutching one another and sobbing or on their knees praying, Steve Smith calmly stood at the microphone asking people to clear the room and appealed for medical help.

As Sirhan was held down, hands reached for his throat as if they would willingly rip him apart. With fantastic presence of mind the two Negro athletes managed to fend them off, as Jesse Unruh yelled: "Keep him alive! Don't kill him!" And another voice cried, "We don't want another Oswald!" Already, in the confusion of that total horror, people's minds were comparing the scene with that in Dallas. In a horrible, fatalistic sort of way, it was as if no one was surprised but everyone was determined that this time everything would be done properly.

Ethel Kennedy, who had been stuck at the edge of the crowd, was helped forward to where her husband lay. "Give him air; please give him air," she begged and once screamed at the photographers to get out. One yelled back, "This is history, lady." That was the real voice of the American press, and, cruel though it sounded, it reflected an attitude that nothing, however important, however personal, however terrible, could be censored in America.

The police arrived in a rush and hustled the defiant Sirhan out to the street. "I did it for my country," he said and then refused to speak further. Twenty-three minutes after the shooting, the ambulances finally arrived. Kennedy, with Ethel still clinging closely

245

to him and behaving at times with the same irrational protective-ness that had characterized her sister-in-law in Dallas, was taken to the Central Receiving Hospital.

There he was treated by Dr. Victor Bazilauskas, although, at first sight, it seemed as if the Senator were already dead. The doctor realized immediately that the only hope was for top-class brain surgery and alerted the Good Samaritan Hospital on Shatto Street, where attendants began to prepare the operating theater immediately.

Bazilauskas gave Kennedy heart massage, oxygen, and adrenalin and put him in a heart-lung machine. He also slapped the immobile Senator around the cheeks to try to get some response. As he said later, "We had to act quickly, and some violence was required." Ethel, distraught, begged him to be more gentle but, after twelve minutes, there was a reaction. Kennedy's heart picked up, and, in perhaps the most touching gesture of the whole terrible affair, the doctor placed the stethoscope to Ethel's ear so that she could hear it beating.

With a respirator attached to his face, Robert Kennedy was rushed to the great, gray Hospital of the Good Samaritan, or "Good Sam," as it was known. There a team of neurosurgeons, headed by Henry Cuneo of the University of Southern California School of Medicine, waited.

There were two main wounds to be dealt with. One was caused by a bullet that had entered under the armpit and lodged in the neck. It was not critical, and the surgeons decided to ignore it for the time being. The other wound was grave. The bullet, almost certainly the first shot Sirhan had fired, had entered the head just behind the right ear and had hit the spongy mastoid bone, scattering bone fragments through the brain. It was a terrible wound, and the surgeons operated on it for three hours and forty minutes.

Meanwhile Kennedy headquarters was not the only scene of grief. At the Beverly Hilton, where McCarthy had been resting, the seventh-floor corridor was filled with chatting aides, supporters, and pressmen. Suddenly there was a terrible hush. In every room the television set was already on, and as the news came through it was known immediately to everyone.

The election was forgotten as the three major networks, A.B.C., N.B.C., and C.B.S., switched from it to cover the drama at the Embassy Hotel. From that moment, for something like 72 hours, they were never to leave the subject of Kennedy, his life and death.

McCarthy, awakened with the news, registered what his campaign chief Tom Finney called "total shock and total disbelief." He had hardly heard the news before the hotel's four lifts deposited a flood of policemen on the seventh floor. Later it turned out that President Johnson on his own initiative had ordered Secret Service guards for all Presidential candidates.

Twenty minutes later, McCarthy went down to where his supporters had been singing "When the Saints Go Marching In" and where young Negro girls and bejeweled Beverly Hills ladies had burst into unifying tears. One onlooker said later, "When they heard what had happened this room turned stone cold." McCarthy, ashen, asked for a minute's silent prayer for his rival. Later he said:

I have a short statement to make. No words can fully convey the feeling that I have toward the Kennedy family in this time of their particular tragedy or the feeling that one must have for the nation in the face of this new tragedy. It is not enough in my judgment to say that this is the act of one deranged man, if that is the case. The nation, I think, bears too great a burden of guilt of the kind of neglect which has allowed the disposition of violence to grow here in our own land, or the reflection of violence which we have visited upon the rest of the world or at least a part of the world.

It was a sentiment that was to be echoed in editorials across the land during the next week.

At the hospital, the vigil started. The building stood at the top of Shatto Street, off Witmer Street. Some 200 yards long and ten stories high, the hospital had a large cross on top and its name picked out in aluminum on an aluminum-covered porch.

Over the road, up a short bank, is the doctors' carpark, which assumed a nightmarish sort of carnival glow as the television trucks rolled in. The banks leading up to it were covered with a carpet of pink-flowered rock cactus and a kind of yellow daisy, but daisy and cactus alike were crushed by media vehicles—vans of all kinds, growling diesel generators, and the obscene psychedelically painted trailer of KHJ-TV.

Police of every variety were everywhere, guns conspicuous on hips. Across all the access roads they planted rows of pink warning flares, and the light from these flares lit the faces of the little groups of people who huddled at the corners with their transistors and coffee flasks—Negroes, Mexican-Americans, Chinese-Americans,

247

Caucasians. Commentaries of one kind or another assaulted the ear on every side.

The American nation was shattered—but not American efficiency. In Britain reporters covering similar vigils after a great mining disaster or a train crash have to line up for solitary pay phones or beg or borrow official lines. But in America the phone company technicians arrived in the wake of the crowd, and within an hour an emergency battery of telephones had been set up opposite the hospital.

They waited through the night and the next day. By morning a local printer had rushed out some orange-and-black "Pray for Bobby" posters, which were given away. A Negro woman led a crowd in spiritual songs. Down the street a nameless coffee-and-doughnut shop was running out of supplies. The old lady who ran it hardly knew how to ring up $7.95 for a television man who came in and ordered 42 coffees and the same number of doughnuts.

The wait was a nightmare. Recollections became disjointed. Bill Eppridge, the *Life* photographer who had followed Kennedy throughout his campaign, seemed stunned and could only say: "I just can't believe it. What can I say?"

George Mitrovich, a Kennedy staff man, complained bitterly about the harassment the pro-Johnson Los Angeles Democratic machine had meted out to the Kennedys. "Our motorcade was given fifty citations for speeding. They cut them down to thirteen, but they have refused a police escort to us in Los Angeles. If the power structure in this country doesn't do something to change this, the students in the universities will do something. Assistance and protection have been denied us."

Throughout the day the family, friends, special Kennedy courtiers came and went, saying little or nothing, playing parts in some already-predictable drama. Those who had not been in Dallas felt almost as if they knew each step in advance except that this time it would go more smoothly for having had a rehearsal.

So the day of June 5 passed. The crowd stayed, silent into the night, and the television went on past midnight and into June 6, the anniversary of D-Day. Then authorities broke the news to the crowd. A moment earlier or a moment later would have made no difference. But the age of total information demands absolute precision: At 1:44 A.M. Pacific Daylight Time on June 6, 1968, Robert Francis Kennedy died of gunshot wounds received 25 hours and 22 minutes earlier in a hotel scullery passage. He died in the in-

248

tensive-care unit on the fifth floor of the Hospital of the Good Samaritan, in Los Angeles, California. He died despite the efforts of the best surgeons available. He died in the presence of his wife, Ethel, who had already borne him ten children and was carrying the eleventh. He died in the megawatt glare of total and absolute publicity by every medium known; he also died without ever regaining consciousness so that this very public death was never anything but very private.

There were no stars that night nor any moon, but there were rows of onlookers who seemed unsure whether they had come to a funeral or a carnival. When, earlier in the evening, Jackie Kennedy, widow of another martyr, had arrived, the crowd burst across the road past the sullen police, making the scene seem like some unsavory fun fair. But when, at 1:58 A.M., press secretary Frank Mankiewicz announced the news to the world, the street watchers fell silent in a kind of awe, and the silence dimmed even the stutter of the diesel generators. "It wasn't a question of sinking," Mankiewicz said. "It was a question of not rising. He needed a rally and a steady improvement from the wound last night and the surgery, and it simply did not happen."

Kennedy simply died, and in the street Charles Evers, the young brother of the murdered Negro civil-rights worker Medgar Evers, wandered aimlessly around saying: "He was our only friend among the whites. First Martin Luther King. Now Bobby. Who have we got left?" He found no answer.

At 4:00 in the morning Pierre Salinger, a chunky blue-jowled man who had had experience in handling this sort of thing, came into the hospital gymnasium, which had been converted into a press room. There had been a night and a day and then another night of vigil, and the place was a fearful clutter of the debris of mass communication: discarded wires and snapped pencils, junked beer cans and coffee cups, piles of newspaper and expended flashbulbs.

Salinger announced:

We are still formulating arrangements, but we estimate the body will leave between 10:00 and 11:00 A.M. A jet has been provided by the White House. We will fly it to New York, and the body will lie in state at St. Patrick's Cathedral between the hours of 8:00 A.M. and 10:00 P.M.

On Saturday there will be a requiem mass, after which we will go by train to Washington, then to the Arlington Na-

249

tional Cemetery where he will be buried. The route will pass the Senate office where he worked and the Department of Justice where he was Attorney General.

His words were heard directly by the millions watching television.

Upstairs the intimates had gathered, much as they had done the first time: sisters Pat Lawford and Jean Smith, Steve Smith, a Catholic priest from St. Patrick's in New York, Senator Edward Kennedy, the fourth brother now, through a process of grim elimination, the first.

"I expect," said Salinger, "that he will be buried in the plot with Jack. All local, legal formalities will be adhered to." The last comment referred to trouble in Dallas, where local authorities, claiming that paper work had not been completed, had attempted to prevent President Kennedy's body from being flown back to Washington.

The three eldest children—Kathleen, sixteen, Joseph, fifteen, and Bobby, fourteen, waited in another room. They had seen their father before he died. They were to travel back on the Presidential jet with the family and some of the staff and close friends. Mrs. Coretta King would also be aboard.

At 9:30 A.M. the hearse arrived. It was a long, pale-blue Cadillac with a top made of black material and lace-curtain trim around the windows. A purple drape covered the still-empty coffin, which was understood to be moderately priced and of plain mahogany—nothing flashy. On the back and sides of the hearse, neat aluminum signs proclaimed "Armstrong Family." In the passenger seat sat white-moustached Guy Armstrong, 72 years old, who ran the firm with his 70-year-old brother Burt.

He said, ". . . we have a very good class of clientele and do about 800 services a year. I understand someone recommended us. It is, of course, very tragic."

On the other side of the car, Burt's son Gordon was introducing the driver, a circumspect Negro who wore little blue jewels in his cufflinks to match his tiepin. "This is Mr. William Richard, and he is one of our funeral directors," said Gordon.

"And one of our very best, I should add," said Guy.

The Armstrongs said that the body would be embalmed in the hospital. First, however, it had had to undergo an autopsy to satisfy Los Angeles County laws regarding murder victims. The autopsy had begun at 6:00 A.M. and lasted until past 10:00.

Young Hugh Macdonald, a member of the Senate staff who had

250

acted as liaison with the press during the campaign, continued, in a sort of reflex action, to make arrangements to fly reporters to New York. He seemed close to utter despair. What would he do now? He shook his head and shook it again: "I don't know. I just don't know."

In the street the crowd took snaps of the hearse and listened to descriptions of itself on transistor radios. A Negro lady with an ancient face started a half-wail, half-groan: "Oh Bobby, oh Bobby, oh Bobby Kennedy, oh Bobby." It was a startling and horrifying noise that went all the way back to the Mississippi Delta.

Said the bulletins:

> The bullet penetrated the cerebellum, the part of the brain that controls balance and co-ordination and tore the superior cerebellar artery which feeds a portion of the cerebellum.
> The bullet had entered through the mastoid bone behind the right ear and it followed an upward diagonal path towards the center of the head.
> A fragment of the bullet lodged near the upper part of the brain stem. This was not removed in surgery because efforts to reach it could have further damaged vital areas of the brain.

Television sets poured out endless replays of what had happened and what people thought might yet happen. The 35 Los Angeles radio stations abandoned all other programing for massive concentration on a murder. Little men grew greater by their very presence at the event.

Down the plain, dull walls of the hospital, green ivy twined from the bronze window frames into a thick carpet on the ground. On the curb by the deep, litter-filled gutter, sat Mrs. Frances Castro, a plump Mexican lady with her daughter Carmen, thirteen, and son John, ten. The visitor sat next to her because that was the only place to sit. She said: "I think he would have found us work. I think he would have ended the war. I think, me, he was a good man."

Such was the death of a politician, American style.

After the death the other arrangements seemed part of a charade. There was the drive from the hospital to the airport, the lying-in-state at St. Patrick's, and the final, moving slow-motion, high-emotion train ride to Washington and Arlington Cemetery.

But what mattered most was how America would react. The first result was a wave of self-denunciation and a massive effort to pass tougher gun-control laws. Many commentators believed, with Mc-Carthy, that a nation that espoused violence had only itself to blame when violence occurred. There were admittedly a few who felt that the apparent motive for the crime (anger against Kennedy's support of Israel) was so pointless that the murder became almost a *crime gratuite*, but they were in the minority.

Most agreed with *Los Angeles Times* sports columnist, Jim Murray, who wrote:

> One bullet is mightier than one million votes. We quarantine the good, the reliable, the honest. We keep a 24-hour watch on the trustworthy but get a habeas corpus to let anarchy loose. Freedom is being gunned down. The "right" to murder is the ultimate in this country. Sloth is a virtue. Patriotism is a sin.

Wrote political commentators Rowland Evans and Robert Novak, after describing how McCarthy had used his invective far more strongly against Bobby in California: "Thus, in McCarthy's mind, he now shared in the general culpability for the insane state of American politics . . . to McCarthy, the result was escalation of the super-heated, irrational atmosphere conducive to a mad young man in Los Angeles firing point-blank at Robert Kennedy."

The general feeling was that American society was sick, that, quite apart from the ease with which guns could be bought, there was some streak in the American character that encouraged violence. The foreigner was inclined to agree. Violence lay at the very root of American values. The visitor remembered a young man in Fort Wayne, Indiana, who said quite seriously that the reason so many people were poor and starving was not because there were no jobs for them but simply because they were not aggressive enough. He was asked whether or not he was seriously suggesting that aggressiveness was a desirable characteristic. "Why of course it is," he answered. "It's about the best thing a man can have, aggression."

In America, nothing counts so much as financial success, certainly nothing else is more heralded. Since most advertising was geared to the premise that what is tangible is desirable, that sheer acquisition was an end in itself, winning a prize for poetry would not be much good if it were not backed up with a big cash prize or a visiting professorship.

Not only were people urged on in this way, but there was also the corollary notion of the loser. Somehow to be a loser in America was much worse than to be a loser anywhere else. Indeed, in Britain there was something rather noble, often distinguished, about being a loser. It is one of our curious national eccentricities that we not only prefer a good loser to a bad winner but we often prefer a good loser to a good winner. For years this built-in reflex has been said to be the cause of British failures in sport, where the British so often succeed in losing just in the nick of time.

Various American experts visiting Britain to diagnose her current economic ills have called for more aggressiveness in British business and commerce as the only solution. The last of these reports, prepared by the Brookings Institution of Washington, D.C., admitted that the British people might not care for this advice, for, if taken, it would almost certainly alter their pleasant and civilized way of life.

There was another important aspect in the different "aggression" levels in the two countries. If there is no stigma in being a loser, then he is socially much more acceptable and finds it relatively easy to return to his former position. The comeback is much more commonplace in Britain than in the United States, which is why, right from the beginning of the 1968 campaign, British political writers and their readers saw absolutely no reason why Richard Nixon should not become the President.

In the United States, it seemed to a visitor, the society was stratified by success. What is more, the successful lived to the hilt, enjoying and displaying their success. One detected an ever-present fear that everything would disappear should they fail and become "losers." It was a fear based on fact. The good life could be obtained more quickly in America than anywhere else. It could also disappear faster. There was no social cushion as there was in Britain. The banks foreclosed faster, the debt collectors moved in more ruthlessly, the unpaid-for Cadillacs were jacked up and towed away with remarkable speed.

So, if one was not to suffer in this way, one had to keep ahead. No one could afford to let someone else take his place in the winners' circle. And that was why aggression counted. One had to fight to get there, and one had to stay there at all costs, including someone else's expense if necessary.

People imbued from the cradle with such a notion did not find it hard to view with equanimity the fact that 6,000 people a year died of gunshots or to read the newspaper reports of how many

Americans had been killed in Vietnam or how many Vietcong had been erased, which appeared with the regularity of sports results. There was a natural belief that massive outpouring of money and power could achieve any object, and, of course, it could not.

As Professor Daniel Boorstin of the University of Chicago said in an interview

When people condone the use of force and violence to attain righteous purposes, it is contagious, and it is not at all surprising that other people with less righteous purposes also turn to violence. Lots of academic people and others these days, who are sympathetic to minority groups and poor people, seem to be very ingenious at finding justification for the selective enforcement of the law, for justifying the use of other than rational and civilized means. I really think this tragedy [Senator Kennedy's death] is just the beginning, unless we are willing to ostracize the people who advise others to use violence.

The obsession with guns of some Americans is one of the most incredible aspects of the country to a foreigner. They talk about their guns the way the British talk about their pets. Rifles, carbines, and shotguns are cleaned and polished and caressed with the same devotion that one grants to dogs and horses. This attitude was completely inexplicable to someone who had grown up in a gunless society like Britain. But Americans, even many who said they were opposed to the role that the gun plays in the American way of life, went to great lengths to explain why it should be so.

The main argument is that the Constitution provided that people should have the right to bear arms and that to stop them would infringe their rights. The Second Amendment to the Constitution, one of those first ten amendments which became known as the Bill of Rights, and which became effective on December 15, 1791, says: "A well regulated militia being necessary to the security of a free state, the right of the people to keep and bear arms shall not be infringed." It is quite clear that the latter provision is subordinate to the former, and, as the security of the United States is no longer in any sense whatever dependent on the militia it is very hard to see how people could imagine they were being done out of their Constitutional rights.

It was also argued—frequently by American suburban housewives—that a gun in the house was necessary in order to protect the occupants from attack. The statistic that no one could produce was how many times in a year housewives or their husbands actually used their weapons for this purpose as opposed to shooting each other in matrimonial tiffs or their neighbors in revenge or jealousy.

Fifty-four percent of all houseowners possessed guns, and they were buying more at the rate of 3 million a year, two-thirds of them through the post. One argument was that if criminals wanted guns, they would get them anyway. The facts seemed clearly to disprove this assertion. In 1962, for instance, England and Wales, with a quarter of America's population, had 29 gun murders. Japan, with half America's population, had 37. In that same year 4,954 Americans were murdered by the gun.

In 1967, 20,000 American citizens died by the gun (7,000 murders, 3,000 accidental deaths, and 10,000 suicides). It is arguable that a suicide would find another way, and it is arguable that accidents can happen anywhere, but it is not arguable that 7,000 murders a year are inevitable. The most frightening statistic of all is that, since the turn of the century, 800,000 Americans had died by private guns, more than 150,000 more than have died in all the country's wars.

Each year the situation grew worse. Crime increased, and so did the number of murders by guns. It seemed incomprehensible that the sheer weight of public protest would not immediately force a halt to this madness by insisting on legislation against firearms. George Gallup said that the very first poll his organization had taken thirty years before had showed that 84 percent of Americans wanted controls on guns and that a similar poll taken in 1967 showed that 85 percent took the same view. The paradox was that many of these people owned guns. They would be prepared to give them up, they said, if they felt that the controls could work.

In the postassassination shock, President Johnson went on television and tried to harness this feeling by appealing to Americans to put an end to the violence in their society. "Let us, for God's sake," he said, "resolve to live under the law. Let us put an end to violence and the preaching of violence."

Once again, attempts were made to introduce legislation for control and perhaps even banning of guns. These efforts failed as they had failed so often in the past. Within a few days of a move to legislate gun control, bumper stickers appeared on hundreds of thousands of cars throughout the United States: "If guns are outlawed—only outlaws will have guns." They were the work of the

National Rifle Association, and brilliantly illustrated the power that special interest groups could wield in the United States.

From its headquarters on 16th Street and Scott Circle in Washington, the 97-year-old association organized a remarkable campaign that successfully halted every attempt to stop the free sale of guns. The "gun lobby" involved a fascinating exercise of power and influence. As Congressman Richard McCarthy, a New York State Democrat, said: "The National Rifle Association is American efficiency at its best in support of the worst of causes. Any time it wants to it can arrange for a million letters to descend on Congress opposing real controls—even though four out of five Americans are in favor of those controls."

The N.R.A., however, insisted straight-faced that it did not lobby. William Gilmore, its chief public-relations officer, declared to the visitor, "We are a nonprofit-making, tax-exempt organization, and we are prohibited by law from lobbying." When the visitor expressed skepticism, Gilmore admitted, "Oh well, we do alert our individual members when we feel a point of view should be expressed, and they can exercise their individual rights as citizens by writing to their congressmen."

Said Gilmore:

> We simply do not regard the proliferation of guns as a threat to the social system of America. To be a bit corny about it, we think that this is one of the reasons why we remain a free nation and it would be very difficult to impose a dictatorship on this country for that very reason.
>
> Mind you, we frown on such devices as bazookas and machine guns, but rifles, shotguns, revolvers, and pistols are okay with us.
>
> You know, guns don't kill people! No, it's *people* who kill people! We see absolutely no reason not to have a proliferation of guns, and we certainly don't think it would have a beneficial effect to remove guns from the U.S. scene. Criminals will always manage to get guns, and there are 16 million persons in America who hold hunting licenses. What are you going to do about them?

Americans and Their Guns, the official history of the N.R.A. since its founding in 1871, starts off:

> The history of the National Rifle Association reveals the response of patriotic citizens to a national need; it reflects

essentially the rise, growth and problems of the United States during the past century. Within the span of the N.R.A.'s lifetime the nation has changed from a relatively new country with sprawling frontiers to a highly urbanized and well populated world power. Against this changing background, the gun as an instrument in shaping our destinies has had a vital role throughout and is today as important as when our country was wrested from foreign rule many years ago.

In our history books, we pay tribute to the man with the gun. He won the American Revolution and the War of 1812. He defended democracy in 1917–18. He fought the greatest global war in history in 1941–45. The American with a gun has been a great stabilizing influence in maintaining a balance of world power.

Psychologically, the campaign was perfect. It appealed to the hearts, if not the minds, of millions of Americans. The N.R.A. had also conducted another propaganda campaign through the years reminding Americans of what had happened under Prohibition. The Eighteenth (Volstead) Amendment to the U.S. Constitution, which became law in 1919, was a chaotic failure in the fourteen years of its existence. It sought, from the highest of motives, to ban all consumption of alcohol, yet it resulted in increased drinking, increased crime and gangsterism, and a general contempt for law, the consequences of which were still being felt in the 1960s. Gun supporters argued illogically that, if the banning of liquor had brought lawlessness, then the banning of private guns would be the equivalent of handing over America to the criminal. This entire attitude was summed up in their bumper sticker.

The world watched America after the second Kennedy death, convinced that there was no alternative to gun control. Even President Johnson was confident that he could secure action. But the President was losing his instinctive feel for the mood of Congress. Maryland Democratic Senator Joseph D. Tydings said so:

If he thinks that Congress will be galvanized into action on this matter he is wrong. Nothing is going to move the Congress; nothing is going to move the state legislatures except a tremendous outpouring of demands from ordinary citizens. Only the people can do it. The Congress is not going to change. We are not going to get a bill through the Senate unless people get themselves to a telephone and get through to their Senators and shout, "We demand action."

257

In the wake of the second Kennedy killing, the mourning rites—which have become all too familiar—included the establishment by the President of a top-level investigating committee. He told it to search for "the causes and control of physical violence," but, however sincere his concern, most Americans regarded the instruction merely as a way of locking the stable doors after the horses are stolen. However well-intentioned such a committee might have been, however intelligent and energetic its members, it could scarcely be expected to do anything practical in the way of tackling so formidable a national problem. Every time a new crime of sensational violence involving firearms took place, Congress showed a flicker of movement, like a man turning over in his sleep before settling down to unconsciousness once more. There were such flickers after Charles Whitman shot and killed fifteen strangers from a tower at the University of Texas in 1966 and again when the Reverend Martin Luther King was shot.

Now, in the aftermath of the assassination of one of its own members, Congress roused itself and passed another law, a law so weak and so meaningless that it could only be construed as no change. The new law forbade the sale of hand guns through mail order.

In a curiously distorted way the assassination of Robert Kennedy, instead of making the need for gun control one of the main issues in the campaign, had the opposite effect. It evoked once again the cry "law and order," and the average citizen was susceptible to the argument that the answer lay not in fewer but in more guns. The argument went that, if Americans surrendered their guns, the criminals and assassins would take over society. A vigilante mood gripped the nation. When the short moratorium after Kennedy's death ended, the question of "law and order" began to figure more and more in the candidates' oratory as the conventions approached. Their position on this subject became the prime question they faced, whether they were addressing public meetings or talking to groups of party delegates. George Wallace made it clear that he was for Americans' keeping their guns. Richard Nixon moved to the right and came out against Federal gun-control laws. Hubert Humphrey found the question embarrassing. In short, the death of Robert Kennedy, a liberal politician of the left, was one of the factors contributing to an American move to the right. And guns would stay.

Humorist Art Buchwald wryly compared the United States to a vast, beautifully appointed insane asylum where

the doors are open, the guards have gone and everyone thinks the other inmates are sick. The United States is a very special type of insane asylum in that all the inmates are allowed to have guns. These guns are sold right inside the asylum or can be ordered by mail because in 1775, when the asylum was built, the Founders wrote it into the rules. Every time someone wants to change the rules, the gun-loving inmates cry that they only want the guns to kill animals with during their recreation periods.

But Congress responded neither to satire nor to passion nor to common sense. Across the country some chain stores decided to stop selling guns. A few private citizens turned in their revolvers to the police. And in Los Angeles a number of film stars organized a petition on gun control.

Still many Americans continued to check the cartridges in their six-guns before going to bed. Clearly the attitude was similar to that toward lung cancer from cigarettes, or death from drunken driving: "It can't happen to me."

.15.

Miami: Love-In on the Beach

The republicans began trickling into miami beach toward the end of July. The city was, as it turned out, the perfect choice. The Republicans had selected it over half-a-dozen more traditional northern convention cities for two reasons: the $850,000 inducement the city offered the Republican National Committee and awareness that no city in the United States could be regarded as safer from the shock waves of civil unrest.

The British, indeed the rest of the world, have a filtered view of Miami Beach. They know it from aerial photographs in travel magazines or from technicolor films like *Tony Rome*; in this kind of exposure it seems staggering. The proud hotels stand in a thin, white line against the blue ocean, the epitome of affluence and of elegance too.

Not until one crossed the causeway from Miami and actually walked up Collins Avenue, Miami Beach's one main street, sweltering in the 90-degree heat and humidity, vainly looking for the ocean and finding instead the cracks in the precast concrete of hotel walls, did he realize, as the Americans said, that Miami Beach was "something else." *What* it was was hard for a European to define. At first, the city seemed a grotesque joke that America had played on itself. The hideous, hybrid achitecture crammed cantilever to cantilever, the monstrous menus and inedible food, the almost total extinction of the beach itself by the building boom and fat ladies in their mink shawls at midday was surely the ultimate in sick humor.

Not true. The humor in Florida was bawdy and blue, but it was also straight. Miami Beach was the home of the single entendre, and one did not have to look for sophisticated double meanings there. Miami Beach was not a parody. It was for real.

What Miami Beach was selling was the dream vacation, ultimate extension of Butlin's Holiday Camp. Its vulgarity passed beyond the level of nouveau riche into a new dimension of instant rich.

To walk through those bizarre hotel lobbies with their ludicrous fittings and furniture made one feel as if he were lost in a department store of next century's collectors items. The prevailing design and decoration looked like the creation of a Victorian computer.

The event for which Americans from all fifty states were converging on Miami Beach was itself totally Victorian. The political-convention system began in the middle nineteenth century and was swiftly fixed in tradition and style. It was a totally American exercise, a mixture of circus, political conference, patriotic rally, and dirty weekend.

Miami Beach was perfectly equipped to accommodate all these aspects. The city had only one industry: tourism. The resort industry in America was compounded of the package tour and the convention. Every conceivable business group or private organization had an annual convention if it could. It was a national pastime. Two Americans talking business at a bar between efforts to pick up girls were having a convention. This overwhelming desire for gregariousness, for combining business with pleasure, for being on the same team and having a great time was what Miami Beach catered to.

Even as the Republicans played out their particular drama, the National Funeral Directors and Morticians Association was holding its own macabre gathering. Other curious conventions in the Miami area at the same time were those of the Pollen Dodgers (allergy sufferers), T.O.P.S. (a dieters' group), as well as the Military Order of Ladybugs, the Society for the Preservation and Encouragement of Barbershop Quartet Singing in America, and the National Association of Fertility.

That was the Miami Beach scene. Several times it had been host to more than 500 conventions a year. Apart from "conventioneers" it handled 2.5 million tourists annually, and the 30,000 Republicans it accommodated the first week in August 1968 were far from the biggest single crowd it had seen. Nor was the 15 million they spent the biggest convention take ever handled by Miami Beach.

There was no need for the citizens to be overawed by its first national political convention. Nevertheless, the city's 368 hotels, with their 32,000 rooms, had to be kept occupied, and August was the slow season. Miami Beach was determined to show America what it could do. By July it was swarming with telephone and television engineers. The convention hall was receiving its third coat of new paint and the final wiring on 1,800 tons of powerful new air-conditioning equipment. The hotels were rewriting their menus, straining every p.r. man's imagination to dream up gourmet delights in honor of the convention—one restaurant came up with a G.O.P. omelet made with "fluffy fresh eggs and minced elephant meat."

New American flags were going up everywhere and—puzzling to the visitor—Israeli flags too. But he was informed with pride that Miami Beach was America's most Jewish city. Eighty percent of its 87,000 citizens were Jewish. It served the best Jewish food between Tel Aviv and New York, which perhaps accounted for its attraction. For its awfulness was overlaid with Jewish warmth and Yiddish good humor. Miami Beach may have been many appalling things, but it was never cold in either temperature or spirit.

Nor did it do things by halves. As July came to an end, the city's convention bureau was proudly pumping out hourly releases: 6,500 new telephones had been installed to serve the convention hall, a quarter-million miles of wire to connect the hall to each hotel, 4,300 feet of catwalk in the convention room proper.

Rocky Pomerance, a former footballer who was now chief of police, called in his 200-man force and lectured them about treating the delegates correctly. "Remember—at least within reason," he said, "that whatever they may be doing that's aggravating they're Republican delegates first and foremost and forever." He also issued a new item of uniform—orange-silk ascots to wear inside open-collared, short-sleeved white shirts—and checked on the additional weapons that the city council had allowed him to buy in case of emergency: 40 shotguns, 25 flack vests, and 400 cans of chemical Mace, a nerve-disabling spray used for controlling riots.

Pomerance exuded confidence that his men would be able to handle anything that came up with minimum trouble. The visitor was less sure when he discovered that, only a short time before, a Miami Beach policeman had dropped one of Pomerance's new guns in police headquarters without the safety catch on. In the resulting burst of fire a secretary and another policeman had been wounded. Nevertheless, the police were extremely courteous, not to say understanding and considerate, to delegates throughout the week. They reserved their spleen for the taxi drivers. Shortly after Chief Pomerance's lecture district sergeants were instructed to call in local taxi drivers for similar lectures on courtesy and cleanliness.

"They dragged me in for a long balling out about wearing socks and a clean shirt every day," part-time taxi driver Al Bernstein said. "That part was okay; then the sergeant says: 'If I see any of you bastards driving your cab in a goddam T-shirt, I'm gonna pull you off the road forever. The chief wants some class in this town.'" Mr. Bernstein, who was something of a philosopher, said he left the station and was held up in a traffic jam behind a dancing elephant painted orange. "I said to myself, 'What the hell is this, a circus?' and I thought for a moment and said, 'By Christ it is.' What a way to pick a national leader! Do you wonder we're in trouble?"

It was not a very original thought but one that would be voiced often before the end of the week. A convention was really a mathematical exercise. In 1968 1,333 delegates attended the Republican convention, and, in the balloting, the first candidate to receive a majority vote—the magic figure 667—would automatically become the party nominee.

But nomination was not quite that simple. Conventions in their time had become classic exercises in crowd psychology and mass hysteria. Delegates could be persuaded, hypnotized, even stampeded into giving their votes to an outsider just as experienced punters can be persuaded to plunge all their stakes on an unknown racehorse when sudden "inside information" sweeps round the track.

So the circus element—the big show to inspire confidence—was built into the convention by tradition. In the time of electronics

263

and instant communication, however, all the old parades, circuses, and pretty girls had become meaningless. Nevertheless they were part of the American scene, and Americans should not rush altogether to write them off in their anxious self-examination. For that matter, how many British or European traditions have any real meaning today?

There are very few. In London stock-exchange messengers still rush breathlessly through city streets with news of changed bank rates despite the fact that electronic impulses have flashed the information around the world before they have taken their first steps. The guards are still changed at Buckingham Palace. Black Rod stalks the Palace of Westminster. We keep these things up without embarrassment because they are part of our heritage.

America, aware of being a world power, has suddenly become embarrassed about things American. All over the country the visitor found Americans berating their own institutions and apologizing for them as gauche, unsophisticated, and terrible. But Miami Beach did not have doubts about anything, least of all the flashy extravaganza that was part of an American political convention. It made up its mind to provide the splashiest, gaudiest show ever— and nothing would stop it.

On Sunday of convention week the lobby of the Hotel Fontainebleau (which local residents pronounce "Fountainblue") was jammed with delegates and their wives, secretaries, and suit cases and with newspapermen and their secretaries and typewriters. A man in a red sports shirt, clutching a half-filled glass, stood in the center of this bewildered throng, an expression of fixed exhilaration on his face, bellowing: "Come on everybody, you're in Miami Beach. Let's swing like we've never swung before."

The delegates laughed back. "That's 'a boy," they said. Who were these delegates? Were they just front men, pliant instruments of the party power structure? Were they really in control of their own and their nation's destinies? Or were they just in Miami for a good time, the reward for faithful service? The role of the delegates was the most intriguing and puzzling aspect of the convention system. In Britain the people elect members of Parliament, and the members elect their leader, who, if his party is in the majority, becomes Prime Minister. But no party is likely to have more than 400 "members," and those members are tightly controlled by the executive. So, watching the opening of the first of the two conventions in 1968, it seemed to an outsider that the 1,333 ordinary

Americans there to select a man who would represent their party in the Presidential race, though old-fashioned, represented democratic process.

The median age of the delegates at Miami Beach was 49, and the median income was $20,000 a year. Most delegates were white middle-class business or professional men. Eight percent were women; fewer than 2 percent were Negro: 26 of 1,333 to be precise.

They had one thing in common: all were loyal party workers who had kept the machine going during the dull years between elections. The Republicans had fewer professional politicians than did the Democrats and virtually no support from trade unions. In this respect they corresponded to the British Conservative Party. The difference showed between elections, however. The Conservative Party's cohesive base is its continuous social activity, which can serve as a marriage bureau for young Conservatives seeking wives in their own class—and keeps the ranks at full strength.

In America, political activities did not duplicate the social functions of the country club. The devoted Republican worker required all his conviction to keep him plodding away while the voting machines stood idle; often his reward was to be named a convention delegate. The delegates were thus the hardest workers, which meant that they were disciplined and less likely to rebel against their leaders, but it also meant that they cared deeply about their party and its position in the nation.

The number of delegates from each state was based on a reward system for the most successful Republican state machines. The most active machine was therefore given a bigger say in selecting a candidate than was a moribund machine.

The figure of 1,333 delegates had not been set arbitrarily but was the result of complex arithmetic that could be understood only by delving into the fine print of the party's rule book and the records of an election that the Republicans would rather have forgotten. Each state was given four delegates as a start and then allotted additional delegates state by state, district by district, according to the number of Republican votes in the elections of 1964 and 1966.

Any state that had cast a majority for Barry Goldwater in 1964 or had elected either a Republican senator or a Republican governor in 1966 automatically picked up six extra delegates. Then one delegate was permitted for each congressional district that had cast at least 2,000 votes for Goldwater in 1964 or the local party candidate in 1966; if the votes had totaled more than 10,000, an additional delegate was allowed the district. Thanks to this scale, based on the party's fortunes at the ballot box, the convening Republicans included 25 more delegates in 1968 than in 1964.

The selection within the states was perhaps inconsistent. Those delegates selected as the result of statewide primaries came to support the men who had earned their support at the polls. Those nominated by party state committees, often behind closed doors, offered a less clear reflection of the electorate. The latter fact was at the root of widespread discontent with the convention system. The concept was democratic enough. As noted earlier, the state primary system seemed excellent to European eyes; indeed there was much pressure to copy it in modified form in British elections and thus enable all registered party members in each constituency to select candidates instead of leaving the decisions to a committee. But, in fact, the selection and makeup of a state delegation were usually guided by the state boss's views and thus designed to perpetuate his machine.

Not that all delegates were puppets; a considerable minority did speak their minds, did try to influence their colleagues. The youngest delegate was 21-year-old Paul Walter, Jr., of Shaker Heights, Ohio, a Cleveland suburb alleged to be the highest-income community in America. Paul's "biography" revealed that he had been

a member of the Boosters Club at Byron Junior High School and received scholarship keys at Shaker Heights High School for grades 10 through 12. He has been "homeroom" president through five grades and served on the student council and the safety council. During the 10th grade he received first prize for debating. He is a member of the United World Federalists for World Peace through World Law. He has been active in Republican activities through helping his father, who has been a precinct committeeman and campaign manager or chairman of the Robert Taft Senior and Robert Taft Junior campaigns . . . he attended the 1960 and 1964 G.O.P. conventions and has been a Little League umpire for four years.

Off-putting as his biographical notes sounded, Paul turned out to be far from square. He had come for the fun and eventually

266

reached the platform to second the nomination of Harold Stassen, the former whizz-kid governor of Minnesota who still pathetically believed that he could become President. Paul spoke for five minutes over a cocktail-party hum of indifference.

The delegates should have listened to what he had to say. It was impressive:

> It is often asked what is wrong with the half of the country under 28 years old. Let us answer:
>
> America is a great country with great ideals, but we are not living up to them. We are turning from a democracy to a hypocrisy. No one is for air and water pollution, and yet they surround us. The Thirteenth Amendment to the U.S. Constitution specifically prohibits involuntary servitude, and the government is supposed to be the servant of the people. And yet young men who cannot even vote are drafted to kill and die in a war that is never explained.
>
> We are taught, "Thou shall not kill, do unto others as you would have others do unto you, and love thy neighbor." And yet a huge percent of our Gross National Product is spent on war every year while hunger, poverty, and overpopulation abound both at home and abroad.
>
> The fault lies not in the black man aspiring for what is rightfully his or in Communist stars but in ourselves. For the true tragedy is we are not even trying to reach our ideals. And those few who do put principle above personal ambition are threatened with prison, such as Dr. Spock, the twentieth-century Sir Thomas More. Or ridiculed, as Governor Stassen, the modern Don Quixote.
>
> As Sancho Panza told Don Quixote, "don't die, Don Quixote; don't die. For the greatest guilt in this life is to die without good reason."
>
> Thank you for your inattention.

When he was later asked what he thought of the Republican platform, as far as his generation was concerned, Paul gave a succinct answer: "It's a lot of guff."

The oldest delegate came from Kentucky. He was 87-year-old Judge Charles Dawson, retired from the bench 32 years but still active in Republican politics. Judge Dawson, his voice still energetic, said: "I've attended every convention except two since 1920. This time we've really got a winning ticket. The Democrats don't

267

have a chance because they haven't any party unity. I had a fine time in Miami, as fine as the result itself, and look forward to the next convention."

In between there was a cross section of middle-class America. The Wyoming delegation, in big stetson hats, included four housewives, two small businessmen, a senator, a lawyer, two ranchers, and a civil servant. The Connecticut delegation comprised a manufacturing-company president, two insurance agents, one insurance investigator, two estate agents, a stockbroker, a housewife, a garage owner, a retired banker, a hotel owner, the head of a stationery business, a banker, and two lawyers.

Alaska's twelve delegates were immediately discomfited by Miami's awful heat. Mrs. Banfield, an accountant who also sat in the state legislature and the only woman delegate from the 49th state, said that the 94-degree heat outside and the 62-degree air-conditioned cool inside were "undermining" the delegation, which was suffering from colds and sore throats.

Conventions were typically prepared for this sort of thing. Almost every state brought as many "alternates" as it did delegates. The alternate voted only when a delegate was sick or absent. For the most part he could simply sit back and have a good time; the alternate system provided a splendid way to reward party workers, important state officials, and influential party supporters without entrusting them with too much responsibility.

Mrs. Banfield, who had left Chicago as a war widow and had built a new life for herself in Alaska was in perfect health. She was typical of the independent delegate. The majority of her state delegation was for Nixon, and she alone was for Rockefeller: "I am trying to get them to change their mind, and they are trying to get me to change mine. I don't know if anyone will succeed. You never should give in on principles. In politics the thing is to give your word and never go back on it." That is what she did. Alaska cast eleven votes for Nixon and one for Rockefeller.

The weekend of Saturday, August 4, was one of pleasure for most delegates. They settled into their hotels, located the "hospitality suites," took curious looks at the convention hall, and sampled Miami Beach's entertainment. But for the press and the professionals, who had been there for more than seven days, the weekend was only a brief half time in the political marathon. All during the previous week the Republican Platform Committee, under the chairmanship of Senator Everett Dirksen of Illinois, was holding hearings on the official policies of the party for the campaign.

Unlike British political conferences, at which policy motions are debated on the floor with some emotion and acrimony, those in the United States were held in closed committee, at which soundings were taken in an effort to find consensus—the most overworked political word of the day. There were extremes in the Republican Party that went beyond the political range of any of the three major parties in England. But a good platform chairman could write a policy statement acceptable to all factions. The platform has been called "an always worthless document," although it occasionally stirred intense fights, as in 1964, when Rockefeller and Goldwater shattered party unity beyond repair.

Dirksen, who looked like a nineteenth-century actor and had the stentorian voice to match, seemed born for compromise policies. He listened gravely as the various party leaders from "left" and "right" came forward to state their views or sent functionaries to read them, and he made notes, copiously and slowly, like an Old Bailey judge. Despite the testimony, Dirksen set out to write a moderate platform and thus, as it turned out, a Nixon document.

While Dirksen labored—and it seemed to one observer that no one *could* labor quite as heavily as Dirksen did—over the final touches, the campaign staffs of the various candidates checked their ammunition and equipment and prepared for the all-out last battle.

There was an increasingly powerful argument in America that conventions had become so cut and dried that they were no longer necessary. Recent history seemed to suggest that the view was correct. The last time a convention had gone past the first ballot and brought a real fight had been in 1952, when the Democrats had nominated Adlai Stevenson.

But there was always hope—particularly among outsiders—that the convention would flare into excitement at the last moment. It was up to the proponents of the convention system to keep this illusion alive, and in the last few years they had found powerful allies in the television networks, in whose view the conventions were spectaculars in human drama, instant history in the making. Television was absorbed, almost totally obsessed, with convention coverage. At Miami Beach the National Broadcasting Company had 840 workers and spent $4 million. The Columbia Broadcasting

269

System, N.B.C.'s main rival, matched it in both man and dollar power. The nation's television screens were preempted for endless live convention coverage.

Because of this investment—and the battle for ratings—the television companies had a vested interest in making the conventions seem more dramatic, more significant than could ever have been true. The fact was that most conventions were painfully tedious, planned, as Russell Baker suggested in *The New York Times*, by "six bores and a sadist." But through camera magic—and in 1968 coverage was entirely in that awful, garish, eye-torturing American television color so suited to Miami Beach—the big networks attempted to breathe artificial life into the moribund proceedings.

Television definitely had to work to create excitement at Miami Beach, for the Republicans had come to that city determined to play the convention according to the rules, in the same spirit in which the British approach a game of cricket. They were determined that there would *not* be any unseemly behavior. The American public watched on their television sets—because they had little choice—and they compared the Miami Beach convention with "Bonanza," "The Lucy Show," and even "The Late Night Movie." The convention did not have the pace, the script, or the drama of any of those shows, and there were great public cries for changing the convention system because of its dullness. Conventions had frequently been dull before television. Talking to Americans after Miami, however, one had the impression that they wanted to change the convention system not because of its political merits or lack of them but because of its dullness. One woman came up with a remark that best illustrated the general reaction: "I watched it from gavel to gavel and learned to speak French and play bridge. If the Democratic convention is anything like it I hope to read *War and Peace* and become a chess expert."

(Of course, as television showed the world, the Democratic convention was very different indeed. Even the networks were criticized for the way they covered the event. There were suggestions that television units had inflamed tempers, distorted events, and generally caused trouble all around. But nobody accused them of making things dull.)

Although the ritualized proceedings in the Republican convention hall were stupefying in their tedium, the frenetic activities outside were fascinating. There was a battle. What one had to decide was whether it was real or simply a very expensive war game.

Richard Nixon, everyone said, would win the nomination—and he did. His opponents tried to stop him and spent a great deal of money and activity in the attempt. Did they really believe that they would succeed?

Nelson Rockefeller of New York arrived, firmly convinced that he could stop Nixon. The professionals around him, who should have known better, believed it too. But in politics one had to believe in winning even when one did not know the strengths of his opponent fully. Rockefeller came with a substantial body of supporters: The New York delegation, 84 members strong, was the biggest at the convention. The New Yorkers took over the Americana Hotel at the north end of the beach, where the management welcomed them with the news that the supper-club show "Toujours Paris" was the "naughtiest, nudiest, sauciest show this side of Europe."

Undistracted by this promise, the Rockefeller campaign staff of 200, backed by unlimited funds and the most sophisticated communications equipment, faced the week with businesslike confidence. Governor Rockefeller arrived with "Happy" after an exhausting tour of 45 states, the price he had paid for procrastination and indecision at the beginning of the campaign. Nevertheless, he did not look tired. Showing his teeth, winking his wink and flexing his mental muscles in exchanges with political commentators and television reporters, the Governor exuded confidence. Happy, the non-political wife of a politician, looked as if she would rather have been anywhere—even Siberia—than Miami Beach.

Although Rockefeller had extended himself on his last-minute tour, his campaign force admitted that he had nowhere near enough delegate votes. He and his men had a triple job to do in the remaining days before the balloting. First, they had to win over any uncommitted candidates that were left. Second, they had to erode Nixon's delegate strength by persuading some of his supporters to vote for Rockefeller. Third, they had to make sure that their own delegates and those committed to favorite-son candidates held firm.

In effect, this job was what every candidate's staff would be doing up to the last minute. The executives around Rockefeller, like those around Nixon, all carried high-sounding titles—regional coordinator, floor manager, campaign director, national political director—but they were simply delegate hunters, poachers, and conservationists.

Heavily sprinkled among the whole Rockefeller organization of delegates, alternates, aides, secretaries, and girl supporters were the security forces—big, square-faced men from the well-known Wackenhut Agency's army of private detectives, Miami Beach policemen with their orange cravats, Secret Servicemen (ordered to protect all the candidates after the assassination of Robert Kennedy), and Americana Hotel security men.

On Sunday morning Leslie Slote, press secretary to the Governor, discussed Rockefeller's chances: "It will be close but we think—in fact we know—that if Nixon doesn't pull it on the first ballot, then he's gonna die. That's when we move in." The key to the Rockefeller strategy, according to Slote, was the favorite-son delegations. This device was one of the most curious political traditions in America. Favorite sons were usually state governors, senators, or congressmen nominated as Presidential candidates by their own states. They had no chance of winning, but they had the pleasure of hearing their virtues as "great Americans" extolled at length to the convention and through television to the nation.

But, beside indulging in boring ego massage, the favorite-son delegations—in this case the crucial ones were from Ohio, Michigan, and New Jersey—come to the convention with real bargaining power. They could sit out the early balloting to watch how things were going and then swing their votes to a likely winner. Or they could do a deal with one of the candidates before the first ballot was finished and declare at the eleventh hour that they would give their votes to him. Such announcements were of tremendous psychological advantage, and in the days before the nominations all three candidates would pressure the favorite sons either to declare or to remain firm.

During the week, sometimes several times a day, the state delegations would caucus. This verb, whose origin can probably be traced back to the Algonquian word *caucauasu*, meaning "elder" or "counselor," has been used in American politics at least since 1763, when it was mentioned in John Adams' diary. Although it is virtually unused now in England the word did cross the Atlantic in the nineteenth century. The Victorians loved it. The Birmingham Caucus, which controlled city affairs and permitted the Liberals to win consistently in the Midlands is a famous example of its everyday use. But in England it died out at the end of the century.

The point of the general caucus was to allow party members at a fairly modest level to select candidates for local office or delegates to conventions. The convention caucus permitted the uncommitted state delegation to discuss the merits of a candidate or to take a position on an issue. On occasion, a caucus would invite the candidates to address it, and, according to Slote, the Governor would attend 35 different caucuses during the week.

Two floors higher in the hotel, Rockefeller was getting ready for his first excursion of the day. He had already had several meetings with his aides, including New York Lieutenant Governor Malcolm Wilson and Leonard Hall, the bland former Republican National Committee Chairman, who had started the year running George Romney's ill-starred campaign. That morning they tested the radio transmitter, which broadcasted to some 900 friendly delegates and staffmen. Everyone of those people had been issued a one-way receiver that would give him the word from the Rockefeller headquarters up to the moment of balloting. The cost of renting or buying all this electronic equipment was more than $50,000, mostly paid by Rockefeller himself.

Phones were checked from the Americana to the front-line Rockefeller command post in the Octagon Towers Hotel, immediately across the road from the convention hall. While Hall received reports from aides in contact with every delegation, Slote made certain that press buses were available to ferry the press corps in Rockefeller's wake during the day and that his duplicating staff was running off enough releases on the Governor's activities.

Rockefeller's makeup girl, Mae Gold, a former television cosmetic expert, checked over his face before he exposed himself to the lights in the lobby; his physician, Doctor Kenneth Riland, made sure that he was provided with spare throat lozenges should his voice begin to crack. Finally, like a new-model car that has passed all inspections, Rockefeller was unveiled.

He went downstairs to begin a seventeen-hour working day, which included a full hour of prime television time on "Meet the Press." As he passed through the lobby, a shout went up from the "Rocky Girls," already forewarned to crowd round the elevator. They began to chant: "We want Rocky! We want Rocky!" The Rocky Girls were very superior for Miami Beach. Many of them seemed to be northerners, from prestige women's colleges like Sarah Lawrence, Bryn Mawr, Wellesley, and Vassar. They were long-legged, wore virtually no makeup except for eye-black, and had uniform golden tennis tans. Every candidate dressed his girl supporters in an easily recognizable uniform. Rocky's Girls wore blue-trimmed lemon-yellow dresses with Rockefeller's signature stamped on them and straw boaters. The dresses were miniskirted enough to stop spectators dead in their tracks—which they did—and to prevent the girls from overenthusiastic gyrations on behalf of their hero.

"The Rocky Girls were all volunteers. They haven't cost us a cent," said Slote. "They come from colleges across the country, and they paid their own way to Miami Beach. It's very different with the opposition," he added gleefully. "As far as I can tell, the Nixon girls are mostly mercenaries."

Rocky's girls were great. But Nixon matched them. He had his own flying squad of beautiful girls, the "Nixonaires"—one hundred hand-picked off-duty airline stewardesses. They wore white roll-neck dresses, sleeveless orange jackets, black-and-white jockey caps, white gloves, and gold badges in the shape of pilot's wings that spelled out "Nixonaires." But they were only the follow-up troops. The initial assault was made by the "Nixonettes," a group of 45 high-kicking dancers from New Orleans, who showed inexhaustible energy in Miami's heat. With their own New Orleans marching band, their miniskirts, white boots, and blue jackets, the plan was for them to grab the crowds, stun them with this routine, and let the Nixonaires move in for the kill.

Like so many other peripheral helpers at the conventions, the Nixonettes and their band received no pay for their hard work up and down Collins Avenue. Their travel expenses—$3,200—and their room and board in Miami were divided between the national Nixon for President Committee and the Louisiana branch of that organization. In return, they received television exposure and the goodwill of many local politicians and businessmen who promised them fully paid jobs later on.

The Nixonaires—who were certainly not mercenaries—were the inspiration of Mrs. Martha Ann Grubb, a former airline stewardess married to a Washington lawyer and a Nixon volunteer worker. Eight days before the convention opened, she had approached Nixon's headquarters in Washington and asked, "Have you got enough girl helpers for the convention?"

"There are never enough helpers, particularly good-looking girl helpers," she was told.

"How about one hundred of the most beautiful airline stewardesses in the country all strong for Dick Nixon?" asked Mrs. Grubb.

The Nixon staff agreed with enthusiasm. Mrs. Grubb had struck the right promotional and psychological note. In Britain airline hostesses are for the most part regarded as flying waitresses. But in the United States, perhaps because of the competition among different lines, advertising had invested the stewardess with an aura of glamor out of all proportion to her job. She had been given the kind of image a previous decade gave the showgirl. As a result, the word "stewardess" was synonymous with glamor and sex. The image was that of a beautifully groomed and sophisticated swinger. And, if Mrs. Grubb could deliver one hundred of these top American geishas to the Nixon camp, it would be a coup indeed.

Inside eight days, with help from Nixon's headquarters staff, Mrs. Grubb had designed the uniforms, had the badges made, flown to Miami (where 2,000 stewardesses live), sorted out Nixon supporters, recruited the hundred prettiest, explained that as a token of their devotion each would have to pay $10 towards the cost of a uniform while the Republicans would pay the other $15, taken their measurements, opened an office in the Hilton Plaza Hotel, arranged for the manufacturer to fly the uniforms in, and begun briefing her girls on their duties.

"These are young girls who want to know more about politics," Mrs. Grubb said. "I don't think there's one of them who has any idea about the issues involved," she added, "but they are trying to learn. And it is exciting for them to meet these really important people. It's glamorous too."

Among the girls she recruited was Jean Grosser, a 27-year-old Delta Airline stewardess separated from her husband and living in Coral Gables, Florida.

> I first heard about the Nixonaires when I read an appeal on the notice board. I had been reading about the election and I was rather ashamed that I didn't vote in the '64 election when I was 23. But I realized that I didn't know enough about the candidates or the issues. I felt I was Republican, and I liked Nixon, but I wasn't totally sure.
>
> It seemed to me that this would be a good way of getting involved, getting closer to the candidates, seeing the convention at first hand and finding out about the issues for myself.

Jean was accepted by Mrs. Grubb and began working for Nixon on the Saturday before the convention opened. Along with the other Nixonaires she was given a background briefing on the candidate and his policies on major issues. Each morning she reported to Mrs. Grubb on the fourteenth floor of the Hilton Hotel to be inspected with professional thoroughness. This inspection did not offend her; she was used to it in her job. "Mrs. Grubb insisted that we should be immaculate at all times," said Jean, "and she was right."

Among her duties for the week was to act as a receptionist at various Nixon information bureaus, escort visiting delegates to conferences with the Nixon staff, help at receptions given by the Nixon family, and work with the Nixon mobile task force at the convention hall, marshaling demonstrators and running messages. By the middle of convention week she was enjoying herself very much, and her earlier feeling that she was a Republican for Nixon was hardening into conviction, mainly because the Nixonaires were the center of television and press attention and Jean was asked for her views several times a day.

The Reagan forces were different. In the first place, California's Governor was not an official candidate but only a favorite son, a charade that was to end shortly after the convention opened. In the second place, the Citizens for Reagan, the right-wing group pushing him, was hardly composed of swingers. As a result, the Reagan girls tended to be older with the hard, glossy faces of unsuccessful movie starlets. Their smiles switched on when listeners showed appreciation of the Communist menace and Ron's ability to deal with it, but they had neither the gay abandon of the Rocky Girls nor the confident charm of the Nixonaires. They were wary, watchful, and reserved. Reagan girls could be spotted not only by their red, white, and blue dresses but also by their high-heeled pumps, in a style extinct in Britain for five years. Their elaborate hair styles were equally out of date, and their hemlines were, to say the least, conservative. Everything about the Reagan girls reeked of aggressive nostalgia for the unfashionable past.

Everywhere one turned there were girls. This phenomenon was the most striking difference between an American convention and a British political conference. In Britain there is nothing but middle-aged politicians. In Miami Beach one felt that youth was being exploited, for it was brought into the act only in a peripheral, exhibitionistic way. What would be the reaction, one wondered, if it rejected this role and tried to become seriously involved? The answer to that question was to be found with the Democrats in Chicago.

It could never have arisen in Miami. The young people there were content with their circus and show-business roles, with traditional casting. And the "go-go" atmosphere and pretty girls, although they were politically meaningless, turned out to be the most stimulating things at the whole convention for the millions watching on television.

A peculiar dichotomy in the American personality struck the visitor more forceably on each successive trip. Americans always seemed much more at ease conversationally than the British. The American could meet a stranger and launch swiftly into lighthearted or serious conversation without any self-consciousness. There was none of that dreadful inhibition, those awkward pauses that haunt British cocktail parties when strangers meet. Nor was the conversation necessarily cliché-ridden or devoted to trivia. In social gatherings the American spoke openly, said what he meant, and was interesting and direct.

But an American before an audience or, worse, a television camera, underwent the most astonishing personality change. He became stiff, pompous, and often terribly boring. If he were a politician, his oratory might thunder with hyperbole, with a totally anaesthetic result. If he were a scientist he might lapse into polysyllabic jargon that made one wonder whether or not the listener was even *supposed* to understand. The British, however, are the absolute opposite. They have no nerves in public, and before the television camera they blossom, which is why television discussion programs are so stimulating and full of unexpected delights in Britain and so overpoweringly predictable in America.

Such was the pattern of the convention. In the hall itself the speeches droned on and on, each sounding like the one before. In the bars, the hospitality suites, and the conference rooms, the exchanges were articulate, witty, and devastatingly direct.

And there, of course, was where the real work was done.

From the first day it was clear that the Nixon machine was incomparable at handling that side of the convention. Indeed, it was so good that Richard Nixon himself remained away from Miami Beach on opening day. While Rockefeller and Reagan leapfrogged madly up and down the beach seeking delegates, Nixon was at Montauk Point on the easternmost end of Long Island, 1,200 miles up the Atlantic coast. His aides reported to the press and delegates that he was preparing his acceptance speech, which was to be the most important speech of his life. It was a nice psychological touch, and all attempts by Rockefeller and Reagan to turn it to their own advantage rebounded.

Nixon's staff, from his brain trust down to his typists, numbered 200. Almost all were housed on the fifteenth, sixteenth, seventeenth, and penthouse floors of the Hilton. On each floor steel-mesh barriers were put up in the corridors leading from the bank of lifts. Armed private policemen from the ubiquitous Wackenhut Agency stood around, not quite sure what it was all about. Anyone who appeared in shirt sleeves carrying a sheaf of papers or wearing a lapel badge could breeze right through. But such lax security did not apply to the Nixon apartments themselves. There the strangely bland men of the Secret Service stood guard.

It was once common to laugh at the ease with which one could pick Russian secret police out of any crowd by their baggy trousers and grotesque square-cut coats. Something similar could be said of American Secret Servicemen. They too had taken on a haunting sameness: in dark business suits, slightly dated ties, heavy shoes, and young-old humorless faces. When, the visitor asked a senior Secret Serviceman how many agents he had watching Nixon during a grueling four-hour session of shaking hands with the public in the hotel ballroom, he replied with all the warmth of an activated robot: "Please contact our Public Affairs Division in Washington. I am sure they will be happy to speak with you."

When reassured that the matter was of little importance and that the figure would be made public only much later, in this book, he repeated the recorded message again in the same words, in the same tone. Of course, all one had to do was wander around the ballroom counting the men who wore tricolor Secret Service lapel buttons. Because these men came from Washington, Miami, or anywhere and did not know one another by sight they had to have recognizable identification badges.

One other security measure at Nixon headquarters was the regular visit of the Wackenhut guard carrying a trash bin lined with plastic. "Security call! Any security trash for burning?" Fifteen stories below on the sundeck, which was ordinarily covered with bikini-clad sun worshipers, two guards stirred the ashes of "security trash" that had been burned in an old oil drum.

Security became a mania of the rival camps during the convention and not without reason. Barry Goldwater, with that disarming frankness that his staff could never cure, said in 1964 that he had "bugged" the opposition. It was not the "bugging" that broke the rules; it was his open admission. In 1968 nobody mentioned bugging on the convention floor, but everyone was very careful about the olives in the martinis.

Jim Golden, the former Secret Serviceman who had become Nixon's personal bodyguard, spent much of his time warning everyone in the Nixon headquarters, "We have to be more careful." "What a rat race this is becoming," said Golden that preconvention weekend. "One of the girls on our switchboard has been trying to telephone outside the hotel and the voice on the other end kept saying, 'Rockefeller Research Staff.' We found out that the Rockefeller gang had wire-tapped right into our switchboard. Now we have to get the whole thing rewired."

And so, as the hot, humid Sunday wore on, the cocktail bars offered standing room only, and Rocky Pomerance's police paraded through the town, the whole cast of the spectacular—except for Richard Nixon—was on stage waiting for the overture, the proper opening of the convention on Monday at 10:00 A.M. The different personnel were easy to spot in the milling throng. The delegates wore medals with red and blue ribbons, sometimes with "campaign bars" signifying their local party rank. The news men were equally bemedaled: Daily reporters wore "gongs" with white ribbons; weekly writers had yellow ribbons; radio and television men had green ribbons. All this identification was essential for the series of giveaway bonanzas that seemed an integral part of the convention. Delegates expected to be entertained for the whole convention period. Much of the entertainment came from the candidates, but a great deal more came from various commercial companies.

The Pepsi-Cola Company flooded Miami with portable bars, at least one in every hotel and half a dozen in the convention hall itself. Pepsi flowed endlessly, dispensed by extremely pretty models or college students, whom the company had decked out in muted psychedelic dresses and scarves in the Pepsi colors of red, white, and blue. "Vote" toothpaste executives saw in the convention a heaven-sent opportunity to press their product. With a corps of beautiful girls dressed in shirts and what appeared to be skating skirts, they attempted to present every visitor on Miami Beach with a tin badge that said "use your vote" and a tube of toothpaste. After giving away 19,000 tubes, they ran out and gave away only badges.

Other companies took huge suites and dispensed liquid hospitality all through the day to key pressmen and politicians. Anyone who went to visit the Arkansas delegation's headquarters in the Ivanhoe Hotel was forced to eat a chicken leg before he could have any questions answered—and that included Ronald Reagan.

But the convention was not all take, however. On Sunday night 2,000 delegates and their wives attended the social event of the week, a $500-a-plate gala dinner in the Fontainebleau ballroom. The food in the Fontainebleau matched the decor, which was pillarbox red and tarnished gilt. *The New York Times* sent gastronomic expert Craig Claiborne to the hotel restaurant to sample the food. He came back with this report:

> It is my heartfelt contention that, if you are detached enough, dining can be a pleasure in circumstances that are less than perfect. A Martini at times may be summoned as a crutch and, indeed, one was on a recent evening at the Gigi Room of the Fontainebleau Hotel in Miami. It is a large, pleasant dining room, although much of it is decorated in shades of unrelieved red, tablecloths, carpet, fringes on the lamps. There is a seven or eight piece orchestra and dancing. . . .
>
> The captain made a fairly elaborate production of the project but the dish was cooked over the least possible flame and subsequently served lukewarm. He returned it to the same dish over the same flame and it was served again—lukewarm.
>
> As to the wine, oo-la-la! A bottle of Pontet-Canet listed as 1962 was ordered. A bottle of Pontet-Canet, 1964, was served. When this was pointed out to the wine steward, he shrugged stoically as though it was a circumstance too commonplace to be discussed. When it was pointed out to a waiter that a wedge of Camembert cheese was cold, he offered to run it under the broiler. Now I ask you. Isn't that worth the price of a meal?

But Sunday night the party's stalwarts in white tuxedos and long dresses trooped in for the dinner of capon and Pinot Chardonnay amid 500 orange trees. "This is the biggest social bash of the convention," said Mr. C. Langhorne Washburn, Republican financial director. "And do you realize it's given us a million dollars for our campaign chest, just this one night affair here?" Despite the careful arrangements the greatest disaster possible struck—the air-conditioning failed. Ornate hairdos collapsed. Antiperspirant sprays

280

failed, and elaborate orchid corsages wilted as the Republicans proved that they too were human.

It was understandable that the next day many of the party-goers were sleeping off the horrors of the night before and were unable to attend the convention's opening session. Yet precisely at 10:00 A.M. party chairman Ray Bliss opened the proceedings: "We have made history. This is the first time in my memory that we started on time." As planned, the session recessed exactly at noon.

The hall itself was a sprawling modern complex, circled by a chain-link fence, which was in turn surrounded by Florida highway patrolmen and Miami police, many of them carrying ax handles and looking as if they would like to use them. But inside all was sweet and light. The air-conditioning was perfect. The delegates—those who were there—sat and chatted as if there were no such thing as a right wing and a left wing. And they applauded all the speakers.

There was a prayer, the National Anthem was sung, and some welcoming speeches delivered. Then O. D. Huff, Jr., chairman of the Florida Citrus Commission, presented a gavel made of Florida orangewood to Ray Bliss. Later the gavel was handed over to the Senate's only Negro member, Edward Brooke of Massachusetts, who served as temporary convention chairman.

Florida's Governor Claude Kirk attracted considerable attention at this convention. He was reputed to have Vice-Presidential ambitions and was supporting Rockefeller, mainly because he was quarreling with Florida state chairman William Murfin. Murfin was a Nixon man. Because the rest of his delegation was for Nixon or Reagan, Kirk chose not to stay with them but remained with his bodyguards on a yacht flying the state flag. From time to time he gave a press conference on board, keeping the press waiting in temperatures of 100-plus degrees. In a macabre way it was worth the discomfort, for when he did appear Kirk usually wore a turtleneck shirt with a sweater on top and a cardigan on top of *that*. Despite the multiple layers of cashmere and lamb's wool, he neither sweated nor even looked faintly warm. It was uncanny. Was Governor Kirk a human being or an android? someone asked aloud. "I don't know what an android is," answered one Floridian, eyeing his Governor, "but he sure as hell ain't human."

The Governor had his moment of glory addressing the opening session, welcoming the delegates and informing them that his wife was expecting a favorite son or daughter. After that little bit of human interest the main event of the morning approached. It was an "inspirational address" by Hollywood film star John Wayne. Mr. Wayne, known as "Duke," was a primitive Republican who had stomped angrily around the right wing of the party for several years.

Age—he was 61—seemed to have mellowed him; he had become a comfortable Nixon man, but his moderation had not cramped his style. He came on wearing a broad-shouldered blue pinstripe suit and a high-collared blue shirt, and he walked like a sailor who had just set foot ashore after three years before the mast. For the first time the delegates watched the rostrum with real interest, as Wayne began his "inspirational address" with the drawling snarl that had sustained him through almost four decades of movies.

"Took me a long time to decide to stand up here," he said. "I'm about as political as a Bengal tiger." There was an appreciative roar. Then he went into high inspirational gear. "I'm here," he said, "because this is the party which cares. To use a good old American phrase this is the party which 'gives a damn.'" There were more cheers.

After paying tribute to America's fighting men and getting in a half-plug for his film about the Vietnam war, *The Green Berets,* Wayne turned and strode out of the hall to the cheers of the audience. The band burst into "You Ought to Be in Pictures," an unintentionally sarcastic thing to do, but Wayne liked it. He drove back to the bar at the Fontainebleau, where he ordered a screwdriver, which is made of vodka and orange juice, and announced, "I think the trouble with this country is that we've got just a little too much permissiveness in here."

Traditionally the candidates did not attend the convention until after one of them had been nominated. On the morning the convention opened, Nelson Rockefeller, staying in the $120 a day Peruvian Suite on the fourteenth floor of the Americana was getting ready for a hard day's campaigning. First, there was a 9:00 A.M. press conference at which he was in top form, insisting that Nixon would not win on the first ballot and from then on would keep going down. Then came a series of meetings in a conference room on the fifteenth floor: a talk with Governor George Love of Colorado and a group of Colorado delegates, then a meeting with seven delegates from Georgia led by Mike Eagan, a lawyer and Rockefeller supporter. Next Governor Dan Evans of Washington, the

282

convention keynoter, called to discuss his speech with Rockefeller. Before lunch there was another conference with Rockefeller's brothers, at which fresh reports of the delegate hunt were analyzed.

At 1:00 P.M. Rockefeller was due at the Sans Souci Hotel for lunch with the Maryland delegation; there he saw looming before him Harold Stassen, the one-time Governor of Minnesota, who still continued to "run" for President at 59. Stassen was the standing joke of Republican conventions, and, as he approached the Rockefellers, Mrs. Rockefeller showed some signs of social uncertainty. Finally, she put out her hand and with a swift nervous smile said, "I'm so glad to see you." Rockefeller turned the full force of his personality on Stassen and boomed, "Harold, you look great."

Perhaps touched by the meeting, Rockefeller rose to speak and hardly mentioned himself. Instead he praised the talents of Stassen: "There is no more brilliant man in the Republican Party." His aides looked surprised. It turned out that Rockefeller had heard some people, among them reporters, discussing what a pathetic figure Stassen had become. Angered, he changed his luncheon speech, and afterward he felt better.

The day moved swiftly on. Just before 2:30 Rockefeller arrived at the Fontainebleau for a meeting with Everett Dirksen, which was followed by a session with Governor Kirk and a drive to the Sea Gull Hotel for a meeting with about forty uncommitted delegates rounded up by Kansas national committeeman McDill Boyd.

At 4:30 Rockefeller drove 78 blocks to the Beau Rivage to talk to the Washington delegation. The delegates asked him about civil disorder. Rockefeller cited his own state, which he said could put 12,000 armed men into a riot area in less than half a day. The delegates looked impressed. Just before 5:45 the Rockefellers' light-blue Lincoln Continental returned to his headquarters. The Governor and his wife rushed upstairs to prepare for the big party that they were giving that evening.

In fifteen minutes both were back downstairs to receive some 5,000 delegates and guests crowding their way into the Americana's ballroom. The room was jammed. The delegates passed round hot and cold appetizers, drank endless cocktails, put away numerous plates of salad. Rockefeller made a brief speech ending, "Let's all have a good time, and don't forget Wednesday night." The party cost him $50,000, but, from the cheers he received, it seemed worth it. "Good old Rocky!" they shouted. "Rocky we love you!" But they were not going to give him their votes.

After the party Rockefeller went to his headquarters for more staff conferences and to watch the second session of the convention on television. He saw Barry Goldwater receive a hero's welcome, both nostalgic and emotional. Goldwater made a moderate—for him—speech and once again was granted an ovation by the delegates.

In Rockefeller headquarters, somebody said, "How they love a loser!" And then Rockefeller changed to a darker suit and went downstairs again to the Americana ballroom for a "Salute to Rocky" party given by the New York delegation.

He politicked nonstop, his craggy face in a fixed smile. He looked good, and he knew it. Sometime in the early hours, as the party was breaking up, he made his farewells; he and Happy, with the ever-present Secret Servicemen, took the elevator to the fourteenth floor. It was the end of the second seventeen-hour day in a row. And what has been accomplished was open to question.

In retrospect, it is intriguing to ask whether or not Rockefeller was playing a game, whether or not he was simply going through the motions of his part in the ritualistic choreography of a political ballet. But afterward Rockefeller argued that everything he had done had been essential. The battle had not been fought for appearances' sake, he said: Right to the end there was a chance of undermining Nixon's strength, and given a little extra time he might have succeeded.

Monday was also a big day for Reagan. For months he had been going through the farce of campaigning while declaring, "I am not a candidate." No one had been deceived. It was simply a matter of time before Reagan declared. Having come to the convention as a "favorite son," he finally did it. At lunchtime Reagan was in his $525 a day suite with campaign manager Clifton White for an important—perhaps a key—appointment. He was lunching with four important southern delegates, all opinion makers: Bill Murfin of Florida, Alfred Goldwaite of Alabama, Clark Reed of Mississippi, and Harry Dent of South Carolina. They began to talk about the party platform, and Reagan came on strong with his right-wing line, a line that the southerners liked. He had had time to rehearse. In the three weeks before the election, White had taken Reagan deep into the South to talk to key Republicans. There had been dozens of promises that Reagan would be a firm second choice. The southern delegates would vote for him if Nixon did not carry it off on the first ballot. Now at the convention White's strategy called for those second choices to be converted into first choices. The play began at lunch.

From that meeting came the only menace that Nixon was to face during the convention. At no time, despite all his effort, showmanship, and money, did Rockefeller ever give Nixon a moment's worry. But from Monday at midday the Reagan campaign did become a threat, a small one, but one that had to be checked before it expanded.

The Reagan scenario called for a surprise by the time the men had reached the dessert. And, with accurate timing, former California Senator William Knowland entered the room. Knowland, now a right-wing newspaper publisher, brought with him Leonard K. Firestone of the rubber-tire family and William Smith, deputy leader of the California delegation. "Governor," said Knowland, "the feeling that you should run, for the sake of the country and the sake of the party, is very strong." The California delegation, he went on, was about to caucus, and he, Knowland, was going to propose that Reagan should announce his candidacy immediately. "I want to know what you will do, Governor," he said.

"I've said all along," answered Reagan, "I'll become a candidate if and when my name is put in nomination."

Two hours later the resolution was passed unanimously, and Reagan went before the cameras to announce, "In response to a resolution I am now a candidate." As a surprise it was about as successful as a Hollywood ending, and it was swiftly overshadowed by the appearance of Nixon, who arrived in Miami like an unbeatable champion.

At the airport a well-drilled crowd was waiting to greet him. It gave a "spontaneous" demonstration for the television cameras as Nixon came down the ramp. He waved, smiled, got into his car, and began a triumphant drive to the Hilton. His motorcade, with lights flashing and outriders' sirens screaming, swung through the muggy streets and avenues of Miami, jammed with people wanting to see Nixon and to cheer him.

In front of the hotel his advance men let fly 2,000 multicolored balloons. The entrance to the hotel was flanked, as if it were the doors of a potentate's private suite, with two bands and the high-kicking Nixonettes. With rare synchronization they struck up "Nixon's the One," the campaign song, composed by Vic Caesar, a Phoenix, Arizona, nightclub owner. Its great merit was simple words.

Nixon's the one.
Nixon's the one.
Nixon's the one for me.
We believe in Nixon, N-I-X-O-N.
Nixon's the one for me.

The Nixon staff was delighted with the reception. "It was as if it was a state visit," said one. But behind the self-congratulatory smiles the alarm bells were ringing. Nixon barely had time to shower and change before his top aides started reporting on the Reagan candidacy and the Californian's determined raid into the southern delegations.

"We can hold it," he was told, "but we have to move fast."

His advisers were right. Nixon had built his strategy on national support. He had part of the North, much of the Midwest, and some of the West—but most of all he had the South, the conservative South, which was still in love with Barry Goldwater, still violently opposed to eastern liberals, and still likely to defect to a strong right winger like Reagan if there was enough encouragement.

The seriousness of the threat could be gauged from Rockefeller's reaction. The New Yorker's men were actively encouraging Reagan's raid into the South and exaggerating its success, for it was, as Nixon commented, Rockefeller's only chance. If the southern vote went to Reagan and Nixon failed to win the nomination on the first or second ballot, it was possible, even probable, that his support would fall away and that the battle would resolve itself between Reagan and Rockefeller; in that case Rockefeller would almost certainly win.

But the immaculate Nixon machine had not come all that way without a plan for just such a contingency. Indeed, it had more than a plan; it had a secret weapon in the shape of Senator Strom Thurmond, the craggy, hard-line segregationist from South Carolina who held the Senate record for filibustering against civil rights. The crucial date in Nixon's campaign may well have been June 1, 1968, when, in Atlanta, Georgia, he convinced Thurmond to help him hold the South. At that meeting Nixon ensured the nomination.

A late convert to the Republican Party (he joined after Lyndon Johnson was swept to power on promises of the "Great Society"), Thurmond was still a staunch segregationist. But he was also a pragmatic politician, and he did not see any chance at all that the

Republicans would pick a right-wing candidate again after the Goldwater disaster. He did see a chance that northern liberals might secure the nomination for Rockefeller. At that Atlanta meeting he was persuaded that Richard Nixon was the one man to prevent a Rockefeller victory, and he offered his total support.

He did not ask much in return. He knew that Nixon, if he secured the nomination, would not pick a right-wing southerner as his running mate. He said he could explain this refusal to his fellow southerners. What he would not and could not do was stop a mass southern defection should Nixon pick a northern liberal as the Vice-Presidential candidate. Nixon replied, "I understand that, Strom." The pact was sealed. Nixon would go for a middle-of-the-road running mate, definitely not a liberal, however great the pressure. The man he would choose, Nixon promised, "will not be objectionable to the people in the South."

Thurmond was an extraordinary politician. Twenty years earlier, while serving as Democratic Governor of South Carolina, he had himself run for President on the ticket of the State's Rights Party, more popularly known as the "Dixiecrats." He had carried four southern states. Two years later he was defeated in a campaign for the Senate by a mass defection of the Negro vote. "I built more schools and houses for them Nigras than anyone else before," he said ruefully, "and look what they did to me." In 1954 he became the first man ever to be elected to the Senate on a write-in vote, running against the nominee of the state Democratic Party. A total of 143,444 South Carolinians scrawled his name on the ballot paper and helped him to make a little bit of history.

Thurmond was an ascetic, given to push-ups in the office and prune juice for indulgence. He never touched alcohol or tobacco and was notably lacking in humor. Even in the closed committee hearings of the Senate he did not join in the banter that usually marked relations among members, despite their political differences. In 1957 the southern senators opposed a new civil-rights bill, but they decided not to filibuster against it because the publicity attached to a marathon debate would be counterproductive and could leave them open to charges of racism. It would be better, they concluded, to try to soften the bill's impact offstage with the help of the Senate's accommodating majority leader, Lyndon Johnson. But Thurmond the loner refused to go along. He went ahead by himself and staged the longest one-man filibuster the Senate has ever endured: 24 hours and 19 minutes with no break except when Senator Barry Goldwater took over long enough for him to nip out to the men's room.

When he left the party and ran as a Republican, his constituents did not forget that one-man filibuster. In Washington Thurmond seemed a chameleon, but in Dixie he was a champion. And so in 1966 he ran 25 percent ahead of his nearest rival, which raised him above the rank of mere eccentric convert. He became a force in the Republican Party.

Thurmond had been at the airport to greet Nixon, but the two men had not exchanged more than a few words. Now it was apparent that a great deal had to be said. Nixon picked up the phone, reached Thurmond, and asked him to make a scheduled morning meeting earlier. When would be suitable? "Now," said Nixon. Thurmond left at once for the Hilton.

When Thurmond arrived, Nixon presented him with an outline of the Reagan threat. Thurmond knew all about it. "This is the real trouble," he said, pointing to that day's New York Times. There on the front page was a story that Nixon had narrowed his Vice-Presidential choice to three men: Rockefeller, Mayor John V. Lindsay of New York City, and Senator Charles Percy of Illinois —all liberals.

Nixon told Thurmond lightly, "You know better than to believe all you read in The New York Times," then added with all the force at his command: "There isn't one word of truth in it." He then reiterated the Atlanta "arrangement." The man he would choose would "not be objectionable to the South." Then Thurmond went into action. Before that evening was over, ironically while Barry Goldwater was making his emotional address and receiving his nostalgic cheers, particularly from the southerners, at the very psychological moment when the Reagan drive should have reached its peak, Thurmond was already beginning to blunt it.

Moving across the floor from one southern delegation to another, he used the same kind of argument: "I tell you, Ronald Reagan doesn't have a chance. You vote for him now, and you're going to get yourself Rockefeller, boy. Is that what you want?" On Tuesday, starting almost at dawn, Thurmond was in there fighting, keeping up the pressure, racing up and down the beach, checking delegation after delegation. He hinted strongly that he had been given the power of approval over Nixon's running mate. Here was an argument that the South understood.

Helping Thurmond to keep the South in line was another Nixon supporter, conservative Senator John Tower of Texas. Tower was a dedicated rightist, who, surprisingly, had studied at the London School of Economics. But, unlike Thurmond, he was a "clean" politician, with none of the old Dixiecrat taint about him. Between his smooth, reasoned approach and Thurmond's ferocious brow-beating, the southern delegates showed signs of falling back into line.

Success was still not certain, but Nixon had yet another ally, of the best possible vintage. He had Barry Goldwater. The Arizonan had planned to fly west before the convention ended, but he was persuaded to remain and to join in the fight to prevent the erosion of Nixon's southern support.

When this news was reported to White, he slumped behind his desk. "This is my comeuppance," he said. His staff knew what he meant. After the 1964 election White had written a book about the nomination campaign that he had run for Goldwater. It was called *Suite 3505*, after the number of his executive suite in a skyscraper on New York's East 42nd Street. It was a candid book, particularly about the shortcomings of Barry Goldwater. "I know that Barry Goldwater did not like some of the things I said in that book," said White afterward, "and I can't be sure that he remained on to help Nixon purely as a means of paying me back, but the fact was that it was a crippling blow and did Governor Reagan no good at all, just when we had a real chance."

The Nixon camp reported that the situation was being brought under control but that the southerners still needed "soothing down." This matter was something the candidate would have to handle personally. Just how he did it was revealed in the *Miami Herald* on Wednesday; it published a transcript of a tape recording of Nixon's confidential talk with a large body of delegates from Tennessee, Virginia, the Carolinas, Arkansas, Florida, and the District of Columbia.

Nixon began to talk about the Vice-President almost from the moment he entered the room. Referring to himself in the third person, he discussed his future running mate with a mixture of judicious vagueness and heavy hints:

Now, there have been some cock-eyed stories that Nixon has made a deal with this one or that one. And I can assure you that some of those stories, which mentioned names, were,

289

shall we say, difficult as far as I am concerned. But I can say to you that, in making the decision on the Vice-President, these are the things I want:

First, would he be a good campaigner, not just in your state but in the rest of the country?

Second, will he be a man who is close enough to Nixon in his views so that Nixon could trust him, that Nixon could work with him, that Nixon, who is going to give the new Vice-President a great deal of new responsibilities, can then have that kind of pained feeling of relief?

I want to say a final thing: I am not going to take, I can assure you, anybody that is going to divide this party.

The applause was deafening after that last statement. Whatever the words, they meant only one thing to the southerners: There would be no northern liberal for Vice-President. The southerners also questioned Nixon about issues that concerned them. His answers showed how easily he could shift from a moderate center position to a conservative slant. He was opposed to the busing of Negro children from ghetto areas to the better white suburban schools, he said, which was exactly what the southerners wanted to hear: "I think that busing a child, a child that is two or three grades behind another child, into a strange community—I think that you destroy that child. The purpose of a school is to educate. That is what we have got to do."

Then he gave them what they really wanted. The busing was wrong, but what was even worse, what was terrible, was the decisions of the Supreme Court that had ruled that it was legal. "I would like to say this with regard to the courts of this land: I think it is their job to interpret the law, not to make the law."

There was tremendous applause from all over the room at Nixon's dig at the Supreme Court. He left the caucus well pleased. His meeting with the southerners was one of six such regional conferences. Delegates from the North and from the industrial Midwest, who attended other sessions, did not hear any of the arguments that he gave to those from the South.

The southern meeting paid off. Half of Mississippi's twenty delegates were for Reagan, for example, but the delegation agreed to vote as a bloc for Nixon. On Tuesday night the only remaining problem was the Florida delegation. Because of its strategic position early in the alphabetical roll call, it had to be held firm. The trouble was that it was split, 22 for Nixon, 11 for Reagan, and

Governor Kirk alone for Rockefeller. All day long the Florida people had been meeting in their splendid Doral Country Club headquarters—knowing Florida they had chosen not to stay in Miami Beach—and quarreling bitterly over whether to vote as a unit (for Nixon) or as individuals.

By Wednesday morning Nixon's strength had further eroded, as fourteen delegates declared for Reagan. But all day Thurmond kept at them, reminding them of his deal with Nixon, warning them that they would only let Rockefeller in if they defected, and telling them to "use their heads." In the end they held, and 32 votes went to Nixon.

And that is how the South was saved for Nixon and how he was saved by the South. From the 124 southern delegate votes, he received 96, which assured him of a swift, bloodless victory.

Clifton White accepted the defeat like a professional: "Florida and Mississippi were the key, and I must admit I failed there. They were voting units perhaps even as a combined bloc. That was 53 votes, and I nearly had them. I nearly had them. I came within a fraction, but the Nixon people dragged them back—and that was it."

By 7:00 P.M. on Wednesday evening, a strange lull had come over the Nixon headquarters. Suddenly the telephones were silent, their ear-shattering clamor stilled. Messengers and visitors were elsewhere. The corridor was empty except for three receptionists, the guards, and a lingering man from Southern Bell Telephone, who had installed the complex wiring for the Nixon telephone exchange and the national television networks. In several rooms down on the fifteenth floor, the staff was relaxing. Drinks were being poured in anticipation of victory.

Nixon was up in Penthouse B dictating final touches to his acceptance speech to his secretary Rose Mary Woods. Sporadically nibbling at a cheese omelet, drinking milk, eating ice cream, and sipping coffee, Nixon grew more elated as reports flowed in from his communications trailer parked at the northwest corner of the convention hall. In that trailer, sending messages to the ten Nixon "whips" on the floor, were John Mitchell, the cool, pipe-smoking campaign manager, and Richard Kleindienst, the shrewd but humorless Goldwater man who had come over to Nixon early in the spring.

The reports were more than encouraging. The South was holding, and a Nixon raid of the New Jersey delegation was going to be successful in breaking the hold of favorite-son Senator Clifford

Case. Case had lost control, and Mitchell expected at least sixteen votes from New Jersey. As it happened, the delegation had to be polled, and it gave Nixon eighteen of its forty votes.

Nixon, who watched television all through the interminable speeches, smiled when he saw his wife and their two daughters Trish and Julie with evangelist Billy Graham, an old family friend, seated like royalty at a command performance.

At the convention hall itself, every seat was filled. The climactic moment had come. But, like everything else about the convention, the moment was spun out until it became a paralyzing anticlimax. The session began at 7:00 P.M. but, in addition to the three main candidates and perennial Harold Stassen, there were eight favorite sons: Governor Walter J. Hickel of Alaska, Governor Winthrop Rockefeller of Arkansas, Governor George Romney of Michigan, Senator Frank Carlson of Kansas, Senator Hiram L. Fong of Hawaii, Senator Clifford P. Case of New Jersey, Governor James A. Rhodes of Ohio, and Senator Thurmond of South Carolina. All had to be nominated.

After each nomination there was a demonstration, about as spontaneous as the ones they have in the Soviet Union, although perhaps a little more colorful. Then came the seconding speeches. They were predictably slow, so that, although they were limited to five minutes, each seemed to last an hour. The amazing thing to foreign eyes was the seeming pointlessness of the proceedings. It was more circus than caucus.

The endless procrastination had its purpose, however. The seconding speeches (maximum of four to a candidate) were designed to give delegations time to caucus on the floor: built-in breathing spaces in which people could change their minds, settle arguments, or make final assessments.

All over the hall the managers of Nixon's two rivals were desperately enacting the classical drama of the convention's eleventh hour: pleading, cajoling, starting rumors here, damping others there. But by the time Mrs. Consuelo Bailey, the convention secretary, a lady with blue-rinsed hair that looked as if it had been set in a steel foundry, rose and called, "Alabama," in her parade-ground voice the battle was already decided. Thirty-three minutes later the ballot was complete. Nixon had 692 votes. Then Reagan swept into the hall, playing the role that he had performed in so many Hollywood movies—the good loser—to suggest that the vote be made unanimous, and it was.

Nixon experienced his greatest moment in eight years watching television in a room that reflected Miami Beach perfectly. It was circular. Over the bar a small plastic elephant stood on its hind legs, the gift of a thoughtful management. A glass chandelier lit the gilt-papered walls. A large vase of expensive plastic carnations stood in the middle of a mahogany table. On the coffee table was another elephant, a small one of jade. It was the only evidence of good taste in the whole room.

But during the week the expensive tattiness of that hotel room had been mellowed, given a special kind of homeliness in the English sense of the word, by the people who occupied it—the Nixon family. For the Nixons were a close family. They were out of *Family Circle* rather than *House and Garden,* and so they would never glitter in high society. But they had that close-knit interdependence, loyalty, and understanding that produce a special kind of warmth when they were together. And they had always been together.

In past campaigns, when Trish and Julie had appeared on the hustings, first as cute toddlers then as gangling tomboys, and finally as awkward teenagers, Nixon had been criticized for "exploiting" his family. The charges were unfair because it was impossible for Richard Nixon to exploit his family. It was unthinkable that he should embark on any course without them. His life and his career were family affairs. That night, within a few minutes of the nomination, a car with police escorts whisked the Nixon women back to the Hilton, and Richard received the embraces of his wife and daughters in the room with the plastic elephant and artificial carnations.

Pat Nixon looked more attractive at 55 than ever in the past. Her figure was still good, but time had softened the sharpness of her features. In her time, this far from insensitive woman had suffered hours of intolerable boredom and much pain as her family came under personal attack. Given her choice she would not have wanted her husband to try again, but loyalty dictated that his wishes came first. Now she shared and savored the moment of victory, holding Trish's hand, perhaps because she understood her older daughter's apprehension about the future. Trish Nixon is very like her mother. She does not like the spotlight but does not flinch from it either. But, although she wanted above everything for her father to win, she had confided to friends that she thought it would be awful to be a President's daughter.

293

Julie Nixon, one felt, was the opposite to her elder sister. She showed no doubts about the future, for herself or her father. She was a Nixon booster, an invaluable asset in the campaign, and even more valuable with fiancé David Eisenhower by her side. Young Eisenhower, an engaging young man invariably beaming the "Ike" smile, which seemed to have leapfrogged his father's generation, was clearly in love with Julie and with politics.

All present watched the nominee. He talked about his feelings:

> It is a wonderful moment, but you know I am somewhat fatalistic about it. I feel the Presidency seeks the man. I was ready. I was willing. The events all fell together. About tonight I was confident. I never doubted the team. It is a great team, which tested and perfected itself in the primaries. Yes, I expected to win tonight. I believe the nomination was won the night of the Oregon primary.

But there was an election to win too, and the first key decision had to be reached. Who would be the running mate?

Nixon said goodnight to his family and prepared to receive party leaders. The meetings went on all night. The crucial discussions took place between 3:30 and 5:00 A.M., as names of potential running mates were thrown up and shot down like ducks at a fairground rifle range. The session proved, if nothing else, that in American as in British politics big decisions were still made in smoke-filled rooms.

Strom Thurmond, who was there to collect, recalled later:

> There were objections to some of the names I mentioned, and I objected to some others mentioned. I objected to ultraliberals from the North because they were so out of thinking with the people of the South. I told them it would be impossible to carry the South with one of these ultraliberals on the ticket. Some people wanted Rockefeller or Lindsay. Others wanted Senator Percy and Senator Hatfield.

Thurmond's own first choice was Reagan, but he recognized that the combination could lose the North, so he put forward the names of Senator Tower, Senator Howard Baker of Tennessee, Senator Marvin Griffin of Georgia, and Representative Rogers Morton of Maryland, all hard-line Republicans. Nixon simply sat and listened to people from all sections of the country, a man looking for a compromise. Eventually two names were advanced and not immediately shot down: Governor Spiro Agnew of Maryland and Governor John Volpe of Massachusetts.

As Thurmond put it, "There was no particular enthusiasm for either of them but no enmity either." Agnew came from a border state and Volpe from New England. Geographic considerations entered in, and Thurmond was not surprised when Nixon went before the cameras next day to announce his choice. He was one of the few Americans who was not surprised.

The news created a sensation. If Nixon had announced that he was running with the man next door he could not have caused a greater surprise. He had repeatedly said that there were three conditions that any man running with him would have to fill: He would have to be qualified to be President, a seasoned political campaigner who could attract votes, and a man whose views were compatible with his own. Then he chose Agnew.

Who was Spiro Agnew? America just did not know. The *Miami Herald* sent a reporter onto the streets to ask people, "What or who is a Spiro Agnew?" Among the answers: "some kind of screw," "a nut with a special thread," "an insect," "something to do with cloud formations in the sky."

The Nixon machine swiftly began to pump out details of the real Spiro T. Agnew. He was Governor of Maryland, the first American of Greek descent to achieve that post. He was married to Elinor Agnew (who when interviewed said that she liked classical or semiclassical music and gave Hoagy Carmichael's "Stardust" as an example). They had three daughters, Pamela, Susan, and Kim, and one son, Randy, who was in Vietnam but expected to be home before the November election.

Within the hour, a revolt was brewing within the ranks of northern liberals. It was not only the selection of Agnew the unknown that rankled. It was the manner in which it had been done. Rockefeller and his supporters had not been consulted. To northerners the whole affair stank of a sellout to the South. It was the price that Nixon had had to pay Thurmond for that southern support. The liberals were outraged. Yet Agnew's selection was a peculiarly American event. It served as a good illustration of basic differences in British and American political parties. American parties, certainly the Republican and Democratic Parties, were really coalitions of splinter groups or factions from the different states. These splinters had different roots in ethnic groups, indus-

295

trial or agricultural areas, northern or southern states, western or central or eastern states.

When factions combined, as they did at the Miami Beach convention, they constituted a coalition of vetoes. The only acceptable compromise such a coalition could produce was an unknown leader. It would be difficult to imagine the meteoric emergence in a British party's second leadership spot of the likes of Governor Agnew. British parties are ruled by tough discipline, and the leaders are usually men who have given long service and risen to the power elite.

That night, as the convention went into its last session to approve the Vice-Presidential choice and to hear Nixon's acceptance speech, the very issues involved in Agnew's choice were being played out in a deadly way several miles across Biscayne Bay, in Miami's Negro northwest section, known as "Liberty City." In the afternoon shooting had been heard in the rather nice area along 62nd Street, with its one-story pastel-tinted houses and well-trimmed tropical gardens. It was hardly a ghetto.

But the shooting continued, and an incident grew into a riot. It was—to be fair—the first Negro riot in Miami's history, and indignant officials loudly denounced "outside agitators." "It's just too much of a coincidence that we're having this riot at the same time as we're having the Republican convention and Richard Nixon's making his nomination speech," said Florida's State Attorney.

In emulation of the happenings across the bay a group of Negro youths held a "Negro Power" rally. Their convention began on the street and ended when the police nervously moved in with clubs. Then the shooting began, after which it was the usual thing: tear gas and armored trucks on the police side and sniping and rock throwing from the Negroes. The result was also usual: three Negroes dead and seven wounded and a number of policemen injured.

While the gunshots echoed through Liberty City, a battle was developing on the floor of the convention hall. The rebels, led by Governor John Chaffee of Rhode Island, decided to try to block Agnew. The man to nominate instead, they believed, was Lindsay. In the New York Mayor they knew they would have a candidate with the appeal to pull delegates out of their seats.

Lindsay had often been called the "Republican Kennedy," and he had Presidential ambitions. It was interesting to see him in action at the convention. He had a staff almost as big as the candidates had (all kinds of New York City officials were in Miami

Beach), smiling men with charming wives who went round making friends with people and pushing very discreetly for John Lindsay.

Lindsay reminded one of a good-looking Briton who had emigrated to America immediately after leaving college. He was slim and had an easy smile. His eyes were blue with little crow's-feet around them, the kind jet pilots get from scanning the sky. His clothes were worn with a casual abandon that most Americans —who are either very starched or extremely rumpled—found very hard to achieve. His hair was a little shorter than it would have been if his grandfather had not left the Isle of Wight, but one could have taken him back to Blighty, and in three months' time he would have been playing cricket as if to the manor born.

All six foot three inches of Lindsay were pure "Wasp" [White Anglo-Saxon Protestant], but he had something beside good looks. He had political integrity, and most of all he had the power to communicate with Negroes. He was the man the rebels wanted to overthrow Agnew, and they told him so. All through that day they pursued him, urging him to join the revolt.

So strong was the pressure that some of the southern delegates were convinced that the liberal counterattack would succeed. In a last-minute panic they decided to put Ronald Reagan's name in nomination for the Vice-Presidency. Clifton White went to the Reagan command trailer and found an argument going on. At that very moment some of the Reagan men were about to telephone the California delegation on the floor to order the Governor's name put forward. White countermanded this plan and ordered the phones to be silenced.

"Some people claimed that I sabotaged this effort," he said. "I didn't. I just told them the battle was over, and no more phone calls would be sent from or accepted by the Reagan trailer. The Governor did not want his name forward, and we did not want a major split in the party when we had come so far."

But when Lindsay went to the podium to be greeted by a huge roar of applause, he went not to launch his own candidacy but to second that of Spiro T. Agnew. His speech was brief and to the point, and, when it was over, Lindsay swiftly left the hall—and the rebels without a hero. There had been one charged moment that night when Lindsay could have stampeded the convention. He could have said, "If you want me, here I am," and the time and the mood would have been right.

A German reporter said with disgust: "I hear so much about

ruthlessness in American politics. Where is the fight? Where is the killer instinct? Here is Lindsay's chance, and what does he do? Nothing." Lindsay was very determinedly doing nothing. He had told the rebels all day long that he would not join the revolt. Indeed he was extremely nervous that they might put his name in nomination without his approval, which would have been political infanticide.

Lindsay thought that the 1970s, when he would be in his fifties, would be the right decade for him, and, in backing Agnew and furthering party unity, he made a lot of friends on whom he could call in the future. By good thinking and fast footwork, Lindsay became a potential winner that night.

But George Romney was once again the loser: As the ground beneath the liberals rapidly eroded his was the only name they could put up. And the pitiless television lenses recorded the bemused Romney going down to humiliating defeat before Agnew, 1,128 to 186, with 26 delegates withholding their votes.

Then came the finale. The bands played, and Nixon arrived to make the acceptance speech on which he had worked so long. Leading him to the podium, as northerners were not slow to notice, was Strom Thurmond, wearing a smile of precast concrete. This role was an honor that he had requested and been granted. It was only a walk-on but a significant one, for it established his position in the party.

Hubert Humphrey commented on the scene a week later:

> This is the year of the New Politics, but I don't think many of us were prepared for the amazing transformation that occurred in Miami last week. We knew there was a Nixon. We knew there were some recent Republicans like Strom Thurmond, one of the first people ever to walk out on me. But who expected them to spin off, and I pray you will bear with me here, a new party, the Nixiecrats?

Nixon's acceptance speech was the product of six weeks' work. In it the trained ear could hear John Kennedy's urbanity, Martin Luther King's "I have a dream" appeal, a touch of Barry Goldwater's basic Americanism, and an echo of Billy Graham's evangelism. It was polished, comprehensive, and immaculate in its address to each of the great national issues, but it struck no sparks.

Yet Nixon received an ovation—not the polite and dutiful ovation that delegates routinely gave their chosen leaders but a genuine ovation. It expressed warmth, affection, understanding, and it explained why Richard Nixon had won the nomination. The people listening to Nixon had chosen him because they believed that this time he would be a winner. There was another reason too: Nixon was more than just "the one." He was one of *them*, of the Republican middle class. They were not millionaires, and they were not intellectuals. They were a little improved on Babbit but still out of *Main Street*. And so was Richard Nixon.

He was intelligent but not imaginative, honest but shrewd. In other words he was just like the men they did business and played golf with. That quality, helped along by endless work for the party, was why Nixon won.

And so, in a rash of tired postconvention parties and press conferences, the Miami Beach party came to a soggy close. By Friday morning, as the delegates streamed away, Nixon was feeling the strain. At the Key Biscayne Hotel on the first of the palm islands that stretch south toward Key West, he gave a buffet lunch for those closest to him. Unwinding at last, he let his mind drift back over the years. Euphoria was replacing the tension of the past months and especially the past week. "I love this stretch of beach," he said. "My girls learned to swim here. I mean fresh water is good to look at but not to swim in."

He began to talk about 1960, just after the election:

I was sitting at the Jamaica Inn just across the road when I was told that former President Herbert Hoover was trying to reach me. Mr. Hoover said: "Dick, I think the country is in enough trouble and that you and the Senator [John F. Kennedy] ought to have a meeting. He's in Palm Beach and would like to fly down to see you. Do you think that's a good idea?"

I said yes and agreed that we couldn't afford a vacuum. So I called President Eisenhower, and he too agreed we ought to get together. I got John Kennedy on the line. He said, "Dick, I think I'd like to come to Key Biscayne and have a talk." I'm sure I'm the only person who ever talked to three Presidents within five minutes!

Jack Kennedy came driving up in a convertible—he loved convertibles and was driving the car himself. His hair was windblown—it was a blowy day—so we walked to the villa, and we each had a Pepsi. We discussed campaigning. He said that somehow we had to find a way so that campaigns did not exhaust you. Although you are tired you see the crowds,

299

you wave your arm, you feel an inner strength, and you go on beyond the point of exhaustion.

Kennedy agreed that his arms got pretty tired. He said, "I'm down here in Palm Beach, and I've got to make decisions, but I'm too tired to set up the Cabinet or to work on the budget."

This preoccupation with the exhaustion inherent in the American campaign system had haunted Nixon through the 1960s:

Well, this time, at least, we are not going to wear anyone out. No man ought to come into this job physically and emotionally exhausted and be expected to make decisions. But perhaps I'm talking of the impossible dream. The three-week British system strikes me as ideal. But at least there you have a national press, and it covers the whole country. We don't have that here.

He paused reflectively, and then his mood changed. "That's enough rambling," he said. "I thought that, as you have all wondered if I really can play the piano, I would take this occasion to prove myself."

Then Richard Nixon sat down at the piano and gave a rather collegiate rendering of "Let Me Call You Sweetheart." "All together now," he cried, looking and sounding like the social director of a medium-sized resort hotel, a sort of contemporary Archie Rice. His jokes were corny, but they came fast and were well timed: "Since we are going down tomorrow for the first time for my first visit to see L.B.J. and, of course, since L.B.J.'s favorite hero was Franklin D. Roosevelt and since F.D.R.'s favorite song was "Home on The Range," where Johnson is going to be from now on unless he changes his mind, I think we ought to sing that too."

After the "singalong" he walked to the miniature golf course between the hotel and the beach. He took off his sports jacket, borrowed a golf club, and made a couple of respectable shots. "I'll never play golf again," he said. "It's like eating peanuts when you are on a diet. Once you've learned to play well, you no longer play sporadically. No, this is the game now," he went on, his mind going back to politics. "This is going to be the most exciting game in my career. The nation is ready for a great confrontation. People will be out in great numbers to hear the candidates."

Later, as if uncertain of the wisdom of choosing Spiro Agnew, he launched a major support move for him. "He's one of the most underrated men in America, a man who can show poise under pressure. You can look him in the eye, and you know he's got it. He has a good heart. He's an old-fashioned patriot, highly controlled. If a guy's got it, he'll make it. If not, Nixon's made a bad choice."

And what of the Negro vote? Had his choice of Agnew rather than a northern liberal been a calamitous blunder after months of impeccable care?

> I might get a good part of the Negro vote. When I finish this campaign, Negroes are going to know that my heart is in the right place and are going to respect me. So are whites. You bet your life I'll campaign in the ghettos. I can talk their language. These people don't go for the professional liberal, and I am not going to get the white and Negro liberal vote.

The next day Nixon and Agnew went to the L.B.J. Ranch in Texas for a briefing on world affairs, especially Vietnam. Johnson, wearing khaki, drove the two Republicans around the ranch in a beige Lincoln Continental with the top down. When he returned from the ranch, Nixon told the following story, which was destined to become a major item in his comic repertoire: "When I got back into the helicopter the President's dog Yuki ran up and jumped under my seat. The President rushed in and picked him up and said, 'Look you've got my helicopter, you want my job, and now you've taken my dog.' The President explained that Yuki always jumps under his seat. Well, the dog certainly knows where the power is now."

In San Diego the next day Ray Price, the 37-year-old Nixon speech writer credited with the brilliant "Bridges to Human Dignity" speech about Negro capitalism in the ghettos, was asked, "Is it true that Yuki is Japanese for "Checkers?" Checkers, the Nixon cocker spaniel, had been an important part of his effective but cloying television performance in 1952.

Without a moment's hesitation Price said: "No, you are quite wrong. Yuki is Japanese for chess. This time we are waging a high-class campaign."

301

.16.

CHICAGO: WILD IN THE STREETS

CHICAGO, SITED AT THE JUNCTION OF LAKE MICHIGAN, WHICH IT HAS polluted, and a river, whose course it has reversed, is the convention capital of the world. It has 5,000 restaurants, 25,000 first-class hotel rooms and the world's busiest airport. These facilities attract 13 million people every year for the great American pastime of talking shop; these people bring with them $300 million which they leave within the city limits, affording great wealth to many Chicago citizens.

Ask most any foreigner what Chicago brings to mind, and likely Al Capone will be mentioned. This automatic association is unfair. Chicago also was the home of the world's first stainless-steel building, the first zip fastener, and the first lie detector. But these attainments followed an older and more basic source of income. Chicago's wealth came originally from its role as the nation's slaughterhouse.

How fitting that the Democrats should have come to this town as if they were about to experience an apocalypse. The delegates were in a grim mood even before they descended from the planes. They were sweating because the week before the convention had been unbearably hot, and they were harassed because a strike of taximen and some bus drivers had left the city almost without public transport. They were also worried about losing touch with one another because a strike of telephone engineers had paralyzed the complex communications network so essential to a political convention.

The atmosphere was completely different from that at the Republican convention. The organizers had already decided that there would be no girls, no brass bands, no balloons, not even demonstrations. The convention was to be characterized by real politics, not phony show-business politics. The leaders had correctly sensed the mood of the party.

All summer it had been uncertain whether or not the Democrats would stick by their choice of Chicago. The strikes, with resulting lack of communications and public transport, made the city seem increasingly unattractive. Equally, all summer the student Left had been laying plans to disrupt the convention with a series of major demonstrations that, they claimed, would paralyze the city.

Faced with these hazards many Democrats—pressured by television companies and newspapers worried about communications, argued that Chicago should be abandoned for somewhere like Miami Beach. During the last days of the Republican convention the pressure had built up sufficiently so that the telegraph and television companies ceased to dismantle their equipment in Florida; they were certain that the Democrats too would come south.

But that was not to be—because of the special flavor of Chicago and the personality of Mayor Richard J. Daley. Chicago was not simply another great American city. It was the quintessential American city. New York was unique; New Orleans was a memory embalmed for tourists; San Francisco was self-consciously cosmopolitan; Houston was awkwardly Texan; and Los Angeles was nothing in particular. But Chicago, in the middle of America was rough, brutal, powerful—much tougher than New York and a long way from Europe in every sense. Thirty-one percent of its 4 million citizens were Negro. Vast numbers of the whites were of eastern European origin. The city was known for its vitality and corruption, but its citizens were proud to live there.

Chicago had rows of slums, block after foul block of torn tar paper stretched over rotting frames. Chicago had big hotels and expensive stores in "the Loop," overlooking manicured lakeside gardens. Chicago had the finest public housing in the whole United States, providing the ordinary citizen with apartments of style and comfort beyond the reach of all but the rich in many other countries. Chicago also had Richard J. Daley, the last political dinosaur in the United States. If he could only be preserved for future social historians, they would be able to learn more about mid-century American politics than all the documents together could possibly teach them.

Daley was the final survivor of a breed of Irishmen whose political talents flowered in the United States and led them to exactly the right level of power for their characteristic temperament. He was the last big-city boss. Mayor Daley ran Chicago, and he loved it. He had often said, "Chicago is the finest city in the world in which to live, work, and worship." To have that city spurned by the party to which he had devoted his life would have been an insult that Richard Daley could not and would not have tolerated. He took his argument to the President of the United States and came away satisfied. The 35th Democratic national convention took place in Chicago as planned.

That victory was a sample of how Daley operated. President Johnson had instructed his White House communications chief that, whenever Dick Daley telephoned the White House, he was to be put through to the President, no matter what time of day it was. Daley, 66 years old in 1968, had worked himself into his unique position of power by the classic route. Born just this side of poverty, he had worked as newsboy, laborer, and stockyard laborer before entering night school, then law school, then politics. In 1955 he had taken over Chicago. As mayor he controlled 40,000 jobs and through them the Cook County Democratic machine—and through it Democratic politics in the entire state of Illinois.

Devout, puritanical, and honest, Daley still lived in the same small house where he had lived all his married life, in the predominantly Irish area of Bridgeport, where he had been born. Each morning he went to mass. At noon he went home to lunch. His bank balance was open to examination, and his private morals were beyond reproach.

But behind his benign and simple exterior were an iron will and ruthless impatience at opposition. Daley *ran* Chicago, and he ran it in true dictatorial fashion: One man ruled. This man willed that the Democratic convention would not be interrupted by any of the outside events threatening it—especially the middle-class youth protest movement, which Daley despised. Together with John Crisswell, party treasurer and a Johnson man, he set about organizing the most security-conscious convention in American history, unaware that he was about to parody the whole democratic process.

Four factions confronted one another in Mayor Daley's city that August. There were the party regulars supporting Hubert Humphrey. There were the antiadministration forces of Eugene McCarthy and the leaderless Kennedy people. Outside the convention hall there were the demonstrators. Finally, there were police and the national guardsmen imported for the occasion—backed by the dour burgher opinion expressed in the words of George Wallace.

In all these groups there were many subdivisions, each of which had its skirmishes within the major battles. At the time it was impossible to determine what was the most important event of that week in Chicago. The whole circus had the impact of three Richard Lester movies exposed simultaneously nonstop.

One of the more extraordinary features, which went relatively unnoticed at the time, was a negative event, the nonappearance of Lyndon Johnson. Up to the last minute the Conrad Hilton Hotel, though inundated with requests for accommodations, saved its Imperial Suite for the President in case he should deign to descend. A Chicago branch of the Confectioners' Union baked him a birthday cake five feet high, with extra-thick icing, so that the cake would remain fresh from Tuesday until the end of the week, whenever the President might decide to come.

But Johnson decided against appearing. His decision was as much a matter of pride as of personal safety. His men in Chicago, led by poker-faced Texas Congressman Marvin Watson had warned him that he might be booed by many of the delegates if he appeared at the convention. That was one humiliation that he could avoid by settling for the lesser one of being the only incumbent in modern times (except for Franklin D. Roosevelt at the height of World War II) not to attend his party's convention.

He settled. Lonely and wounded he celebrated his sixtieth birthday in Texas with his daughter Luci and his grandson. 1968 was the worst year of his political life. Once the greatest congressional manipulator of all time he had run up a list of failures in Congress that was hard to believe. When he asked for a gun law Congress took the teeth out of it, despite the clamor for such legislation after the assassination of Robert Kennedy and Martin Luther

King. His foreign-aid bill was turned into a joke, and the International Development Authority was denied appropriations. The President's "Great Society" programs were all reduced. Furthermore the Senate refused to ratify his court appointments. The President nominated Justice Abe Fortas, a Jewish liberal and a personal friend, to be the new Chief Justice. The Senate filibustered. He wanted a Texas friend, Homer Thornberry, appointed to the Court. Again the Senate denied confirmation. It refused too to accept another old Texas friend, Barefoot Sanders, as a Federal judge. The Presidential embrace had become the clasp of death.

Abroad the President's efforts were equally frustrated. All his schemes to involve the Soviet Union in a peace drive had failed. His hopes of a grand summit in the Kremlin were smashed in the invasion of Czechoslovakia. There was no point in going to Chicago, he decided. He would content himself with giving orders through his lieutenants and watching events on television.

In Chicago the delegates spent the weekend obtaining their credentials for the most closely guarded convention in American history. First, they had to prove their identities. Then they were given sets of magnetized tickets for each day's session. These passes, which had to be worn on elastic round their necks were marked, "Insert into machine this way." Electronic eyes then scanned them. If the robots approved, a green light flashed and a delegate could enter. If they were suspicious, a red light warned the guards, and the unfortunate transgressor was ejected—and none too gently. There was no shortage of guards; more than 1,000 policemen, security officers, and private guards and ushers from the Andy Frain organization staffed the convention, in an Orwellian scene.

The Democratic delegates gathered in the second city were rather different from their Republican counterparts. There were more of them—2,989 compared to 1,333. The Democrats looked tougher. There were more union officials and more Jews than the Republicans had mustered. There were also more Negroes—337 delegates and alternates, compared to 78. Very few delegates brought their wives, for everyone knew that the Chicago convention was not going to be a very sociable affair.

The convention took place in the International Amphitheater, a huge, ugly building in the stinking stockyards. It had been provided with a perimeter defense that would have graced Khe Sanh: barbed-wire fences, armed troops, circling helicopters, and a restricted air zone in which other planes were forbidden to fly below

2,500 feet. To reach the hall the delegates had to travel four miles by special buses. Along the route newly erected strips of brown wattle fencing failed to hide the ugliness that they were supposed to disguise. The only color was in the red, white, and blue posters proclaiming "We love Mayor Daley" from almost every window.

Unlike the candidates who had arrived in Miami Beach displaying surging confidence, the Democratic contenders came to Chicago as if the fight were already over.

McCarthy arrived knowing that he had no chance of nomination. The previous Tuesday, after his last day of public campaigning (among the Pennsylvania delegates in Philadelphia), he had admitted it. "They're not going to give it to me," he had said. In vain his supporters pleaded with him to pursue the political chase to the end. The result was not sewn up, they argued. He could talk to the delegations. It was still possible to persuade them because nobody really wanted Hubert Humphrey. But that was not McCarthy's lofty style. Grudgingly he attended a mere five caucuses, at which he talked down to the delegates as if they were a particularly stupid bunch of undergraduates not truly interested in his subject.

Hubert Humphrey arrived looking but not sounding optimistic. "Chicago is not going to be easy for me or the party," he had told a friend before leaving Washington, "but if we can air our differences I know that we can unify the party once the campaign begins."

Senator George McGovern, a dove from South Dakota who had announced his candidacy only a few weeks before in an attempt to hold the Kennedy forces together, arrived wrapped in mystery. Was he a serious candidate? Was he aiming for the Vice-Presidency? Whatever his ambition, to the delegates he looked like a nonstarter.

There seemed no question that the machine would triumph and that Humphrey would be nominated. Just as the saber rattling and bombast of Miami Beach had masked the total lack of real battle, so the apparent lethargy in Chicago masked a determination for struggle that created a political sensation in that most sensational of years.

The anti-Johnson forces had one aim in common: to smash the administration's Vietnam policy plank in the official party platform. If nothing else were achieved, McCarthy said, a victory on that issue would show that democracy still worked in the party. And however the dissident Democrats divided on other issues they could unite on that one. People like Lowenstein could see farther: If the antiadministration delegates were successful in having a peace plank written into the platform, they might trigger a surge of emotion that could rob Humphrey of victory on the first ballot. And then?

And then, according to Lowenstein, the convention could be turned around. It was too late for McCarthy or McGovern, but if a new candidate could be produced and if he had a big enough name, the New Politics might triumph after all. There was still one man capable of carrying off such a staggering political coup and his name was already on everyone's mind: Senator Edward Kennedy.

This instinct to coalesce—which is the secret of the Democratic Party's long success—demonstrated how seemingly implacably opposed forces could come together in America for the sake of victory. The men who wanted Teddy Kennedy were diametrically opposed to one another on almost every score but the need to win. McCarthy would accept him in order to win the peace plank. Daley, who could not bring himself to speak to Eugene McCarthy, wanted Kennedy because he did not believe that Humphrey could carry Illinois. The Americans for Democratic Action, who loathed Daley, wanted Kennedy because they could get out the vote for him.

Daley started the Kennedy movement. A week before the election he had phoned Kennedy about his worry over the impending nomination of Humphrey. The Vice-President, he had decided, was a loser and would drag Daley's Illinois candidates down to defeat with him on November 5. "But you," Dailey said, "you are a winner. You can carry the convention, you can carry Illinois, you can carry the country."

Kennedy listened but did not commit himself. He was in an intriguing position. Richard Daley had no political ambitions beyond running Chicago except perhaps to *be* kingmaker. He was primarily interested in Democratic power in his city and state. Kennedy therefore took his words at their face value. But the family counseled caution. Could Daley be setting a trap? Was Daley luring Kennedy into the open merely to snare him into running as the Vice-Presidential candidate? The Kennedys wanted to be certain.

Only the previous week Humphrey had still been desperately shopping for a running mate. He had gone cap in hand to Eugene McCarthy and said that in his view the next President of the United States would be a Democrat from Minnesota. At that the Senator had smiled scornfully. But Hubert Humphrey had pursued his course: "If I were to beat you to the nomination."

"Which you probably will," interrupted McCarthy.

"Well, we will see," said Humphrey. "But the burden of my question is will you accept the Vice-Presidency if I offer it?"

McCarthy's reply was withering. "Don't bother to offer it." With that rejection—as cold and as cutting as the sleet storms that sweep their northern state—the two men from Minnesota parted.

Humphrey had then gone to Teddy, who said, "I am not a candidate."

"I know," answered Humphrey. "But would you consider running with me? I mean is the door ajar a little, is the key still in it perhaps, or is it locked?"

Stephen Smith, who was also a member of the New York delegation, undertook a political reconnaissance in Chicago on August 23. Kennedy had already decided to maintain a 1,200-mile distance between himself and the convention. He stayed in Hyannis Port. In Chicago Smith talked to the Mayor. The Kennedys understood Daley. If he gave his word he would not break it, and he gave his word that there was no trap. Smith came away convinced and flew to Hyannis Port for a family conference.

Edward Kennedy was 36 years old and the head of the most celebrated political family in the United States. He had only recently had to shoulder the responsibilities of his family, and they weighed heavily upon him. He had chosen a political life, and that too had brought heavy responsibilities.

He was in a most delicate position. The "draft" was a device of the American political system that enabled a party to pull in an outsider, a noncontender on a tide of emotional conviction and place him above all other candidates. But such a "spontaneous" expression of will rarely happened by accident. It had to be deftly orchestrated, building from a whisper to a thunderous crescendo, sweeping everything before it, including the qualms of its object. No man could refuse a genuine draft, not even a man who had lost two brothers in political assassinations inside five years.

Edward Kennedy was aware of this imperative. He was equally aware that all the goodwill toward him could sour in an instant should he make an active move toward the nomination. The Kennedys were a special family on the American political scene. They engendered love and hatred in equal proportions, often from the same people. Kennedy knew that many of the people who were at that moment saying that he was the only man who could save the party and the nation would become violently hostile should he openly display a wish to be President.

309

But there was no escaping the tightrope: He had to walk it. He stayed in Hyannis Port awaiting developments. The next day Daley phoned again and pressed him to attend the convention: "If you do, we can put you over the top."

When Kennedy said that he could not, Daley replied, "Well, if you must stay in Hyannis Port, you ought to at least indicate that you will consider a draft."

Kennedy said, "I can't do that either, but Steve is going back again, and he'll be in contact with you."

Before he went to Chicago Smith got in touch with members of the old Kennedy team. One of them was Pierre Salinger, who had participated in the front rank of the eighty-day campaign of Robert Kennedy in the spring. Salinger was working for Senator McGovern at the convention. He recalled afterward:

> I was working for McGovern, but I was not a Trojan horse. Rumor has it that I put into the McGovern campaign as a worker for Teddy. I was not. But I was fully informed on all the moves to draft Teddy. Smith and I met and talked before Chicago. Steve told me that he originally had not planned to go to the convention. But now he was going, and he said, "I'm going out to look around."

On Sunday Smith booked into a suite on the eighth floor of the Standard Club, in the convention-hotel area of downtown Chicago. The Illinois delegation was to caucus at 3:00 P.M.; Daley would, as he always did on the eve of the convention, announce his candidate, tantamount to instructing his 118-man delegation how to vote. Humphrey was confident that Daley would come out for him. Jeff Antevill, Humphrey's press secretary, said: "Daley may dance around and hedge a little. But he and the President are for Humphrey."

Yet two hours before the Illinois caucus Daley told Smith on the telephone: "I have not changed my mind. As far as I am concerned, Humphrey is still a loser. The only person I can see as a winner for the Democratic Party is Senator Kennedy. I am not going to announce for Humphrey tonight. I am going to give you 48 hours to see what you can put together."

Later that night Richard Goodwin called on Smith to say that he and McCarthy were actively considering throwing their support behind a Kennedy draft: "As he is not going to get the nomination, Senator McCarthy feels this is the way to make all his work on the campaign trail count for something."

On Monday, the day of the opening session, the first Teddy Kennedy buttons began to appear. They were made of cardboard like British flag-day badges, but the eager young volunteers handing them around assured everyone that real metal buttons would soon be forthcoming. All over hotel lobbies and conference rooms where delegates gathered, hastily scrawled posters began to appear: "Draft Teddy"; "Let's win with a Kennedy"; "Kennedy can beat Nixon—Humphrey can't." The excitement swept through the city, and Kennedy became the only topic of conversation. All else was forgotten: the hippies and the yippies in the park, the absence of L.B.J., McCarthy's depression, the strikes, everything. It seemed that the country might once again witness that overwhelming expression of political will, a Presidential draft. The Democrats were like a tribe lost in the desert and suddenly sighting a glittering oasis ahead.

Smith had little sleep in those first 24 hours. His suite had become the heart of a political movement that was pulsing with energy but still formless. Nor could it take shape until Kennedy spoke the word from Hyannis Port.

Directly and through Salinger and other intermediaries, Steve Smith sought out the old Kennedy loyalists up to the time that the convention opened, shortly after 5:00 P.M. He spoke to the men in each state delegation who would quietly form Kennedy cells and prepare for floor battles when they received the word. But even while he rallied the faithful, he could not say that Kennedy was, in fact, a candidate. Jesse Unruh, who was ready to commit his 174 California delegates to a Kennedy candidacy instantly, pleaded for some word from Hyannis Port. So did other leaders.

To each query Smith answered: "I can give you no answer at this time. If the Senator indicates he will accept a draft, then he is a candidate. And he is not a candidate." Still the draft-Kennedy boom gathered force. And by 5:00 P.M., before the first convention gavel had cracked, Smith was convinced that he had enough delegates to stop Humphrey on the first ballot.

It would take 1,312 to secure the nomination, and, in Smith's figuring, Humphrey could not possibly count on more than 1,100. The first ballot would thus result in no winner. On the second ballot, if Teddy's name were put in nomination and McGovern and McCarthy withdrew, Kennedy would be nominated, the youngest Presidential candidate in American history.

Early on Tuesday Jesse Unruh was in touch with McGovern headquarters in the Blackstone Hotel. He told Salinger: "Teddy is

311

my number one choice. I am going to hold off announcing for California until I know whether he is going to take a draft."

Also on Tuesday morning Goodwin made another attempt on behalf of the McCarthy camp to generate a move from Kennedy. He invited Smith to come to McCarthy headquarters. Smith went, under cover of assisting in planning New York's role in the floor fight over the Vietnam plank. Salinger insisted on this cover story. He argued: "Steve, when you show up at McCarthy's headquarters, there is going to be a lot of conjecture. The press is fanning the Teddy thing, and it might get right out of hand."

The meeting at the Hilton Hotel was only the second occasion on which Smith and McCarthy had seen each other. They got straight down to business. McCarthy said: "Look, I am beat. I can't make it. But I don't want to pull out now. I have to let my name be placed in nomination. But I am willing to pull out midway in the first ballot. I would announce my support for Ted Kennedy." Yet even in that moment of generosity, McCarthy could not contain his bitterness. Looking Smith in the eye he said, "I am doing this for Ted Kennedy, but I would never have done it for Bobby."

The cold delivery of that sentence shook Smith. He regarded it as gratuitous, but he let it pass unchallenged. He replied once more, "The Senator is not a candidate."

McCarthy considered, then said: "Well I will see my name go into nomination. Then, from the floor, I shall take myself out and urge my people to go for Teddy."

Here was the device that could be used to pull off the whole scheme. Kennedy would not declare himself a candidate, but if McCarthy, with his ability to arouse an emotional response, were himself to step down before the whole convention and mention Teddy's name, "that would be a real ball game," said Smith. "I will have to check back with the Senator."

He left convinced that the point of no return would shortly be upon them. And so it seemed. No sooner had Smith returned to the club than he heard that George McGovern had spoken to Unruh and Senator Abraham Ribicoff of Connecticut: "If this is the moment, then I am ready to pull right out and go for Teddy. There is no problem." Unruh and Ribicoff hurried over to the Standard Club, and together with Smith they reviewed the situation that they had created and had now to control.

The Kennedy movement was the nucleus of a potentially formidable alliance: Daley of Illinois, Unruh of California, McCarthy and

312

his following, McGovern, and the Kennedy cadres in many delegations. But it was still a shadowy alliance; one single overt move from Kennedy could weld it into a powerful and cohesive force in the convention hall. The nomination was within his grasp if he moved.

Salinger later recalled:

> I was on the floor of the convention. I saw more of the old Kennedy advance men there early on Tuesday evening than I had ever seen in my life. Everywhere I would turn there were guys that I knew. You could see their lips moving, and they were all saying "Kennedy." They were all there—Jerry Bruno, Don Dell, Jerry Dougherty, Ken O'Donnell—primed and willing to go.
>
> The news that McCarthy would back Kennedy was getting out, and it was getting more tense by the second in the convention. The fascinating thing to me was the number of southern delegates who came to me and identified with the Kennedy movement. They all said, "If Kennedy will go, we are for him." These were people who would never in a thousand years have supported Bobby.
>
> There was already a state senator who wanted to put Teddy's name in nomination. That was Tom Radney. In addition there was Mike di Salle, who had announced to everyone that he was going to put Ted's name in nomination. Mike was not phased in with the Kennedy movement. He was touching base occasionally with Steve Smith, saying, "Look I'm going to do it unless I get told by the man himself he does not want to run as the candidate."

But time was running out for Daley. He called Smith: "I cannot make a move for Teddy unless Teddy calls me and tells me he is a candidate." Smith relayed this information and a report on the highly volatile state of the draft movement to Hyannis Port. Kennedy said that he wanted to wait a little longer.

Shortly after 8:30 P.M. David Schuomacher of C.B.S. television reported a "leak" on the McCarthy-Smith meeting. According to Schuomacher, the meeting had lasted two hours, during which time Smith had pleaded with McCarthy to support Kennedy. Sputtering with anger, Smith called McCarthy's headquarters, reached Goodwin, and snarled, "What kind of a can of worms do you have over there?"

Goodwin said that he had not heard the Schuomacher report,

313

but he did agree to appear (and did) on television to say that, although a Kennedy candidacy had been discussed, Smith had not sought McCarthy's help. But it was too late. The original report had already fanned rumors of a Kennedy announcement to wildfire. Smith, who had been in periodic contact with Kennedy during this turbulent time, told him, "If you are not going to make an overt move for the nomination, you have to do something to head off what is happening here."

Kennedy replied, "Well, I will not make an overt move."

So the rumors flew that night. Blazing rows developed between the Smith people and the McCarthy people. Smith demanded that McCarthy himself go on television to deny the C.B.S. story. The next morning Salinger called Kennedy to urge a decision, saying, "You must either fish or cut bait."

Kennedy cut him short. His mind was made up, he said. "I am going to call the Vice-President now and tell him where I stand." To Hubert Humphrey he said, "I have been listening, but I am not a candidate."

And so the Kennedy bubble burst. Once again, to an outsider the whole thing was incomprehensible. Why had these maneuvers been conducted at all if the principal would retreat from ultimate commitment? Had Edward Kennedy been uninterested from the beginning? Did he fear that no Democrat could beat Richard Nixon? If so why had he let the movement build? Pierre Salinger was still saying after the convention that Edward Kennedy could have won the nomination: It would have been a walkover—Smith had sixteen hundred votes. And, what's more, he would have won the Presidency too."

But Edward Kennedy withdrew literally at the moment of truth. Where was the Kennedy boldness, the instinctive decisiveness that is an intrinsic part of the legend? Teddy was as indecisive and as unsure as his brother Robert had been before New Hampshire. In the end he fell back on the same familiar argument; 1972 would be the year. For personal and political reasons 1968 was too soon.

The Kennedy buildup had taken place against a backdrop of bitter fighting over the Vietnam plank. The doves were determined that the party would not endorse Johnson's war policy. Johnson was thus to be repudiated in the official Democratic platform. Several groups had begun to prepare alternative Vietnam planks in the weeks before the platform was drafted: McCarthy's men, McGovern's supporters, and the Kennedy team. Their first hope was to win the battle in the platform committee itself and to have their peace plank adopted as official policy. If that failed, they would draft a minority report and ask the convention to decide in a floor vote.

A running battle raged within the 22-man platform subcommittee. All day on the Saturday before the convention it had met without reaching agreement. On Sunday Louisiana Governor John Mc-Keithen said: "I hope that the committee does not suggest a platform for picking up and just getting out of Vietnam. That would be a disaster for the party."

Nevertheless the Committee showed every sign of taking a comparatively dovish stand on a bombing halt. A copy of the Vietnam plank draft was taken to the White House, but the wording did not please the occupant. The next the Subcommittee knew was that Chairman Hale Boggs—who had been peremptorily summoned to Washington for a "briefing on Vietnam"—appeared with White House aide Charles Murphy and some fresh wording that called for bombing to stop only when a halt would not endanger the lives of American troops in the field. The subcommittee was told that the "administration" wanted this plank. There was no more fighting. The group did its duty and passed the plank after less than an hour's deliberation.

The McCarthy, McGovern, and Kennedy forces then combined to write their minority report. It was obvious that they had to reach some agreement, for, if the floor fight was to be successful, all the doves (including those members of the subcommittee who were not necessarily allied to any one group) had to be united. But when they met—first at the Hilton, then at the Amphitheater, and finally back at the Hilton—among them the atmosphere was decidedly hawkish. No group was prepared to compromise at first. Angry words were exchanged. Goodwin accused his old colleague Theodore Sorensen, who represented the uncommitted doves, of being a Johnson-Humphrey fifth columnist, sent in to try to water down anything that the real doves might produce.

Between meetings Sorensen, who had been urging a compromise acceptable to all the party, changed his stand to go along with the stronger wording: "Although the war in Vietnam is complex, the bombing of North Vietnam serves no military purpose and must be stopped. This initiative can move the Paris negotiations forward without, in any way, increasing the risk to our troops in the south." The statement was an outright repudiation of the administration's

315

view that the bombing (which had initially been justified as a measured response to North Vietnamese infiltration) was necessary to protect American lives.

Why did Sorensen change his mind? Goodwin had no doubt: He believed that Sorensen had finally recognized that there was no chance for a compromise acceptable to the party leadership and had accepted the necessity for a floor fight.

On Monday night the minority plank was issued to the press. Then interesting things began to happen. McGovern received a telephone call from Clark Kerr, former chancellor of the University of California, who asked if he and Walter Reuther might call. They wanted to try to water down a little further the draft that had been released to make it acceptable to Humphrey. McGovern invited them to breakfast on Tuesday morning at the Blackstone Hotel. Also attending were Salinger and Ed McDermott, a director of the McGovern campaign.

Kerr and Reuther had a moderate draft of their own. It called for an all-out effort for peace, but it did not include a demand for a unilateral bombing halt. McGovern was tempted to accept it as better than all-out endorsement of the administration's policy. But Salinger argued that the doves had already compromised a good deal; why compromise further unless Humphrey would definitely accept the new draft? He said, "Go back to Humphrey, and if he will buy this draft, then we will buy it; then we shall all have the same position and there will be no further fight about it at all."

Salinger was not certain that he could persuade Goodwin and McCarthy to accept such an agreement, but he thought it was worth trying. Reuther and Kerr agreed that his proposal was fair. Said Kerr, "We'll get back to you in a couple of hours." They left at once. Later McGovern told Salinger that they had telephoned him that Humphrey after talking to the White House had, to their disgust, made up his mind to accept the majority report.

All chance for compromise was gone. The party's policy on Vietnam would have to be fought out on the floor. The McCarthy forces were pleased, for a reversal in Vietnam policy was their cause, what they had been in the campaign to achieve. The debate was set for Tuesday evening, but all through that night fractious delegates argued and fought on other issues, and it was after 1:00 A.M. Wednesday when Vietnam finally came up.

On the podium Chairman Carl Albert tried to get the debate started, but his efforts were useless. For one thing the delegates were exhausted, and for another the doves were not going to have this most crucial debate carried on while the majority of the American people were in bed with their television sets turned off.

Pandemonium broke loose. Albert was repeatedly howled down. Finally, with a gesture that in a way summed up the whole convention, Mayor Daley signaled Albert to adjourn by running his forefinger across his neck as if cutting his own throat.

The great debate finally took place on Wednesday afternoon. It was probably as thorough an argument as had ever been heard at an American convention. It reminded one observer very much of the debates at British political conferences, with one difference: It was briefer. Each side was given an hour, and no speaker was allowed more than five minutes.

The attention of the delegates on the floor did not waver during those two hours. The cases were argued well with both logic and conviction. As the afternoon came to an end the voting began. At first the tally seemed close, but the gap widened until Texas was called; in a triumphant drawl Governor John Connally did his master's work: "The State of Texas votes 104 votes no."

These exultant words scuttled the doves' plank and at the same time ensured the nomination of Hubert Humphrey. The final vote was 1,567¾ to 1,041¼, and, as it was read out the convention floor dissolved into chaos. The organizers had banned demonstrations, but the one that ensued was as spontaneous as those at Miami Beach had been contrived. The New York delegation swept the marshals and the security men aside and stormed into the aisles singing the civil-rights song "We Shall Overcome." The galleries thundered to the chant "Stop the war. Stop the war."

The doves had come prepared. Black crepe was produced to drape the standards of New York, California, Wisconsin, and Colorado. Cheerleaders coordinated the chanting. As always when rebels launched a disturbance throughout the week, Albert flashed a signal to the Lou Breese Orchestra at the back of the hall. Instantly it blared out the rousing "Off We Go into the Wild Blue Yonder," a glaringly inappropriate choice in view of the emotions being expressed on the floor; the protesters doubled their efforts to drown the best that Mr. Breese could produce.

The band seemed prone to misfortune whenever the chair activated it in an emergency. It ripped into "Happy Days Are Here Again" during protest over police brutality. The leader explained: "We're all set to go when the light flashes, but we just have to play what's on our stands. I'm not a mind reader; I can't predict the convention's mood in advance." That night no one could misjudge the prevailing mood as a cross was raised on the floor and delegates went down on their knees. The band stopped in the middle of "When Irish Eyes Are Smiling," and Rev. Richard Neuhause, a young Lutheran minister with the New York delegation, intoned a prayer in which he begged God to turn the American people from war to peace. A loud "amen" rang through the vast amphitheater. Then, supported by clapping crowds in the visitors' balconies, the delegate started to chant, "I ain't gonna study war no more."

The losers thus made defeat seem noble and victory base.

There were, of course, two battles in Chicago: the one on the convention floor and the one in the streets. Chicago being what it was and its mayor being what *he* was, everyone who came there in that hot August week knew that a confrontation would occur. When it came it was like the living theater of political struggle in America. Two extremes met and clashed, and one felt that it was only the first of similar clashes to come.

Both sides, for different reasons, sought an explosion. The organizers of the protest demonstration, who aimed to marshal 100,000 marchers into the city at the same time that the convention was already packing it, had a variety of reasons. Some extremists saw in "street power" the first stage of revolution. Another group saw an opportunity to disrupt and discredit the convention process and thus to undermine the traditional political system in America. Abbie Hoffman, the 31-year-old leader of the Youth International Party—known as "Yippies"—an eccentric prophet of revolution, turbulence, and change for the sake of change was taken to City Hall as soon as he arrived in Chicago; there he met with Deputy Mayor David Stahl.

"Now what are you boys going to be doing here?" Stahl asked.

Hoffman, a small, wiry figure with a grotesque balloon of hair replied: "I dunno, but, like, whatever it is, it'll be designed to, uh, bring down the Democratic Party." To his delight, he was taken seriously. The Yippies really were the most amusing people in a notably humorless city.

The National Mobilization Committee to End the War in Vietnam—known as "MOB"—was infiltrated by hard-core militants: Maoists, followers of Che Guevara, members of the Students for a Democratic Society. (S.D.S.). But all these elements amounted to only a handful of people. The vast majority of those who turned up to join the demonstration were simply opposed to the war. Most were students; some were young marrieds. There were very few workers and comparatively few Negroes.

There was some irony in this situation, for activists like S.D.S. leader Tom Hayden really hated the candidates who opposed the war in the way that only the extreme Left can hate liberals. Liberal leadership prevents the masses' capture by extremists. To the New Left, people like McCarthy and Lowenstein were in the way. McCarthy had advised his people not to come to Chicago, and his advice had had some effect. Instead of the army of 100,000 that Hayden and MOB leader David Dellinger had predicted, the protestors never numbered more than 15,000.

They were faced by Chicago's 11,900 policemen, 6,000 Illinois national guardsmen (called out by Governor Samuel Shapiro at Daley's bidding), and 7,500 regular army troops with riot training. The first clash came on Sunday night before the convention was even officially open. Some thousands of protesters had gathered in Lincoln Park, along the lake north of the Loop. The authorities had decided to enforce a city ordinance forbidding people to remain in the parks after 11:00 P.M. Just before midnight, the crowds were broken up by 1,600 policemen; skirmishes lasted for three hours.

It was during this melee that the first newspaper and television reporters were hurt and Tom Hayden was arrested along with about two dozen others. These two factors heavily influenced events of the succeeding week. The former started a chain reaction of public suspicion toward Daley's police among news media; the newsmen were thus singled out for further punishment, which meant even greater antipathy and led to certainty among demonstrators that they would receive maximum publicity and "a good press."

The arrest of Hayden, a hero to the protest movement, provided the immediate excuse for further protest. Late Monday afternoon several hundred demonstrators moved downtown to Grant Park, a strip of green 200 yards wide directly across Michigan Avenue from the Hilton, where both Humphrey and McCarthy had their headquarters.

In a way this hotel became the true center of the convention. Most of the lobbying took place there, for it also housed Marvin Watson and his aides and the Democratic party machinery. It claimed to be the world's "largest and friendliest hotel." It was certainly vast, an enormous pile of red brick occupying an entire city block. It had 3,000 rooms and could accommodate 4,200 people. In the milling throng that jammed the lobby a small, bespectacled man wearing a look of total bemusement was occasionally to be seen in conversation with a bellboy.

He was Bill Smith, one of the most harassed men in the whole building. After six years as manager of the New York Hilton, he had been transferred to Chicago barely a month before the opening of the convention. "It is, after all, a promotion," he said. "This is the flagship of the Hilton chain, but the timing is unfortunate. It takes a little while to adjust to a new hotel and even to get to know all the staff—we have over 2,000 people on the payroll here, and I don't know them. The trouble is," he added, "that not many of them know me yet." When one heard Mr. Smith's story, one could forgive a great deal. There was a great deal to forgive.

The elevators were totally inadequate to deal with the mass of people going up and down (McCarthy's headquarters was on the 15th floor, Watson's on the 22nd, Humphrey's on the 24th), and it was sometimes necessary to queue for twenty minutes to get one. Service in the bars and restaurants was painfully slow and the food not particularly appetizing. The booking arrangements broke down totally so that, when the huge Texas delegation arrived with reservations made three months previously, it found no rooms available. Sunday morning the McCarthy staff discovered only a few hours before the Senator's arrival that there was no bed for him. The main watering place in the hotel was the Haymarket Room, where a small ensemble sang loudly enough to discourage most conversation and where the waitresses appeared to have been selected for bosom size; their qualifications were on ample display. Chicago was, after all, the center of Hugh Hefner's *Playboy* empire. Most of the time the hotel smelled foul from gas "bombs" left there by demonstrators, who also spread blue cheese on the walls and ground it into the carpets.

Monday evening 2,000 demonstrators set out for the Hilton. They were met by police, who plunged straight in with nightsticks—the two-foot-long wooden clubs that nearly all American uniformed patrolmen carry. The previous week Chicago Chief of Police James Conlisk had told his men: "We must be constantly mindful of the welfare of others, never act officiously, and never permit personal feelings, prejudices, or animosities to influence our decisions or actions. To a substantial degree, it will be by our actions that the rest of the world will judge Chicago and to some degree our nation itself." As it happened, he was right.

At midnight a major riot broke out. An hour after the 11:00 P.M. curfew police moved in to clear the Yippies from Lincoln Park. They used tear gas and clubs, and the protestors spilled out into the streets of Chicago's Old Town. In hours of running fights, in which police cars had their windows smashed by stones, seventeen newspapermen were beaten up, and 166 people were arrested; there were scores of injured. Chicago retired to an uneasy sleep.

There was one thing to be thankful for: The weather had changed. Winds from the north lowered the temperature to the middle seventies. Had the city remained at the oven heat of the previous week, the violence would certainly have been even worse. Tuesday dawned bright and cool. Before daylight the television companies began their marathons of reportage.

The morning papers reported protests to Mayor Daley from the Chicago Daily News, Newsweek, C.B.S., N.B.C., and A.B.C. Reporters were united in their statements that charging lines of police had chanted "Kill, kill, kill." Placards and chants among the demonstrators began to compare Chicago to Prague and Daley's police to Hitler's S.S. men. Under its previous chief, criminologist Orlando Wilson, the Chicago police force had achieved quite a reputation in Britain for advanced methods of crime detection. But Wilson had gone long before the Democrats came to Chicago, and, whatever other reforms he had instituted, he had failed to reform the mentality or, obviously, the manner of the uniformed police.

It is pointless to expect all the police forces of the world to be composed of men with the patience and tolerance of the London "bobby." His personality is developed from the British character itself and reflects the city that he polices. Without arms, the British constabulary not only polices a metropolitan area bigger than New York and succeeds in maintaining one of the lowest crime rates in the world; it also successfully controls demonstrations without recourse to violence. It takes a certain kind of intelligence to be able to do so, and, having observed it more than once, the visitor feels within his rights in saying that the Chicago policemen were not only brutal but also exceedingly stupid.

Of course, Mayor Daley's city was not London. It was the last great political fiefdom in America, and to attempt to police it with bare hands would have been as futile as to try to persuade a medieval court to accept the rules of cricket. Many parts of Chicago

321

were too dangerous for policemen to walk through in pairs, let alone singly and unarmed.

But at the convention the Chicago police were not dealing with hardened criminals. The demonstrators were middle-class and idealistic. Whatever their intentions they were not capable of putting Chicago to the torch or numerous enough to disrupt the city significantly. Treated with good humor and tolerance their protest could have become a demonstration of American political maturity and democratic ideals. But the Chicago authorities did not have the wit to see this possibility, nor had the police the discipline to achieve it even had they been instructed to do so.

For the simple fact was that policemen themselves were in the vanguard of that group of frustrated Americans who did not understand the protest against the war or the rejection of basic American conventions. Even less did they understand the protestors, who, although they wore faded jeans, ripped army blouses, and torn sneakers, had arrived in gleaming cars and carried Norelco tape recorders and Bolex movie cameras. They were members of the affluent middle class and therefore their protest was even more baffling to policemen and intensified their resentment. In the confrontation the police saw an opportunity to release their frustration in the simplest and most satisfactory way: an outburst of vengeful violence.

It was more than unfortunate that the Russians had chosen the Wednesday before the convention to invade Czechoslovakia. At the convention itself the move strengthened immeasurably the hand of the "hawks" and would have weakened McCarthy even without his lukewarm statement on the subject. On the streets—which in the daytime were filled with parades of exiled, expatriate, and Americanized Czechs begging help for their homeland—the demonstrators naturally seized upon the comparison. "Welcome to Chicago" signs were altered to read "Welcome to Prague," and the police were identified with the Russian oppressors.

Later Tuesday night, as the convention adjourned its debate on Vietnam, police drove a truck through Lincoln Park, dropping off canisters of tear gas. Some of it blew back and affected the police themselves. Some of it blew on to Lake Shore Drive, where about fifty drivers were forced to stop to dry their tears. The hippies moved back into Old Town, where they contented themselves with stoning police cars.

At the Hilton the police, who had been on duty continuously for seventeen hours, were replaced by the first detachment of national guardsmen. Tension lessened immediately. Guard Commander Major General Richard Dunn said that the police had "overextended" themselves and proposed to "let the demonstrators enjoy themselves." The mixed crowd listened to folk singers Peter, Paul, and Mary as they wandered singing over the grass, and a man who claimed to have been released from the army only five weeks before bellowed into a microphone asking guests and delegates at the Hilton to blink their lights on and off if "you're with us." At first, a solitary light from the 15th floor flashed on and off, then a second, then one on the 11th; in a few minutes dozens of windows were blinking and flickering until the whole facade of the Hilton looked like a giant pinball machine. From across the road came an exultant cheer in response.

Inspired, some of the delegates came out of the hotel and crossed the road in front of the bayonets of the national guard and joined the kids. There, before the shining headlights of the jeeps, the generation gap was bridged. That was how Wednesday, August 28, began.

It was to be the worst day of all. Trouble began at 2:00 in the afternoon, with a ban on a planned MOB rally and march to the amphitheater. By 3:30 the crowd was getting out of hand. As many as 12,000 people had gathered in Grant Park; bottles and bricks were thrown at police who replied by hurling smoke bombs into the crowds.

Suddenly the police charged. There was a certain brutal beauty in that charge. The Chicago police wore shirts of robin's-egg blue, and, to meet trouble, they replaced their soft caps with helmets in the same hue. When they first began their controlled move across the greensward of the park, the harmony of color and setting were reminiscent of the charge of a nineteenth-century infantry regiment.

They thrust into the ranks of demonstrators, and the view was swiftly transformed into an all-too-familiar twentieth-century scene of policemen clubbing civilians, smashing into silence the screams of protest, uttering their own guttural shouts of encouragement. The protestors were driven from the park, but they scattered into the city itself, where they roamed the Loop seeking another place to rendezvous.

About 5:00 some of them encountered the mules and wagons of the Reverend Ralph Abernathy's Poor People's March. Abernathy had permission to proceed through the city to the convention hall. The first demonstrators fell in behind him while messengers went to inform the rest there was a chance of marching to their objective behind the mule train. By 6:00 several thousand young protestors were lined up behind Abernathy, as the mules moved into Michigan Avenue and past the Hilton. But, as the demonstrators themselves moved past the hotel, the police unexpectedly and uncontrollably attacked again.

The attack was so sudden, so indiscriminate, that the marchers were paralyzed with indecision and fear. They were assaulted by tear gas, Mace, and, most of all, swinging clubs. The tear gas wafted up to the 25th floor and reached the Vice-Presidential nostrils. The screams could be heard as well. But there was no response to either.

All the time that the clubbing continued in the streets, the trio in the Haymarket Bar continued to play louder and louder as in a scene from a bad western. Then the Haymarket itself became a scene of brutality. Outside spectators were watching the riot from behind police barriers; inexplicably a squad of policemen turned and charged them with such force that they were swept back against the thirty-foot plate-glass windows, which shattered; policemen and victims fell among the terrified patrons inside. By then completely berserk, Chicago's "finest" began to lay about them with their nightsticks spilling blood among the bloody marys while the band played on over the screams of the waitresses.

On the street itself the massacre proceeded. The police, now completely out of control, charged again and again into the stumbling, panicky ranks of protestors. They hit anything that moved; when a victim fell to the ground, he was immediately surrounded by more policemen, who continued to smash him until another collapsing protester claimed their attentions.

From the park the mass of uninjured demonstrators were chanting: "Let the whole world watch. Let the whole world watch." But the police themselves might have been chanting it, for they went about their bloody business with the pride and determination of top performers exhibiting their professionalism.

Afterward, Chicago mounted with considerable skill a propaganda drive to prove that the police had suffered intolerable provocation. It was cleverly managed and found a ready response among many Americans. The polls showed that as many as 70 percent of the people believed that the police had acted properly in their violent suppression of the demonstrators. Nevertheless, a committee appointed by President Johnson and under the chairmanship of Milton Eisenhower reported in December 1968 that the violence in Chicago had been "overwhelmingly" on the police

324

side. The demonstrators had provoked the police by words and actions, according to the report, but the police had lost control of themselves and had "rioted."

But that was not the prevailing view at the convention that night. The delegates had gone into the nominating session tired, nervous, and bad-tempered. The security precautions were oppressive, the arrogance of Mayor Daley's protection forces insufferable.

Daley and his Illinois delegation had been seated right in front of the podium, where the Mayor could be instantly recognized and given the floor; the anti-Johnson delegations had been exiled to the outer fringes of the hall. At the farthest extremes, then, were New York, California, New Hampshire, Wisconsin, Oregon, and Colorado. These delegates were constantly pestered by the troops of floor security men. Their microphones had a habit of being off when needed; when connected, they seemed curiously muted compared to the electronic power accorded to Texas and Illinois. Most of all these delegations experienced the greatest difficulty in catching the eye of Chairman Albert, another Johnson man.

Johnson and the machine controlled the convention, but his opponents were determined to show that he did not control them. As they watched the street battle on their television sets they knew they had to do something. But what? No collective action could stop the clubbing on Michigan Avenue that night. No strategy could prevent what was already arranged and about to happen on the convention floor. Only individual action was possible.

A tall, distinguished-looking rancher from Colorado, Robert Maytag, demanded that the convention be suspended until police terror on the streets of the city stopped. He was ruled out of order. Donald Peterson, the Wisconsin chairman, obtained the floor only by telling as many as twenty reporters and television commentators that the chair had refused to recognize him; the crowd of journalists around the Wisconsin delegation became so big that Albert was forced to see him. Peterson shouted into his microphone: "Thousands of young people are being beaten on the streets of Chicago. I move that this convention be adjourned for two weeks and moved to another city."

His demand was drowned in a scream of rage from the automated delegates of the party machine, and the chairman moved on to "the real business of the convention."

On the floor, former Kennedy man Larry O'Brien, who had become Humphrey's campaign manager, was cornered by Frank Mankiewicz, working for Senator George McGovern. Mankiewicz,

325

an emotional man who had not yet recovered fully from Robert Kennedy's assassination, seized O'Brien's arm and pleaded, "Larry we've got to stop what's going on downtown."

"I know it's bad, Frank," said O'Brien.

"Bad!" answered Mankiewicz. "I've just talked to George Mc-Govern; he says it's a bloodbath down there."

"Well, I know," said O'Brien, "but we don't have all the facts. We don't know."

"But I tell you the streets are running with *blood*," shouted Mankiewicz. "They're just kids being smashed down there. Mc-Govern says he's not seen anything like it since films of Nazi Germany. I tell you, Larry, we've got to do something."

"I know, Frank," O'Brien answered, "but what can we do?" Later that week O'Brien was made national chairman of the party. All he had had to do that night was to make soothing noises. He did so and passed on.

Near the New York delegation a fight between delegates and security men broke out when a West Side Manhattan delegate, Al Rosenberg, refused to show his credentials to a floor marshal for the sixteenth time that night. The forces of law and order surrounded him and ran him out of the hall. In the ensuing chaos, Paul O'Dwyer, the state's Democratic candidate for the Senate, was thrown out too, and Mike Wallace, a nationally known television commentator, ended up with a bloodied face.

The convention routine could hardly proceed for the noise, confusion, and conflict on the floor. Albert's dogged voice had shrunk to a tiny croak; still he pushed ahead with the nominations. Nothing was sacred that night.

Senator Ribicoff came to the podium to nominate George Mc-Govern. He said, "As I look at the confusion in this hall and watch on television the turmoil and the violence that is competing with this great convention for the attention of the American people, there is something else in my heart tonight and not the speech I was prepared to give. . . ." He spoke about McGovern and then, looking directly into the puce-colored face of Mayor Daley only 30 feet away, he said, "And with George McGovern as President of the United States, we wouldn't have these Gestapo police tactics on the streets of Chicago." The sentence stunned the hall into silence. For a moment time was suspended, action frozen as the handsome lawyer stared contemptuously at the men of Illinois in their places of honor.

Then it broke as separate waves of applause and fury smashed

326

together like a clap of thunder under the steel rafters of the amphitheater. Daley and his henchmen were on their feet screaming at Ribicoff. The television cameras zeroed in to show the Mayor, his face contorted with rage, shaking his fist at the Senator from Connecticut. Around him the Illinois delegation was screaming at the speaker: "Get out. Go home. Get out." Daley's mouth was working too, but, either from discretion or incoherence, no words were coming forth. The lip movements were perfectly clear, though; the muscular contortions to articulate the most famous of Anglo-Saxon expletives are quite specific.

Ribicoff stood in indestructible dignity. Then he leaned over and said quite calmly, "How hard it is to accept the truth." This comment produced a fresh outbreak of rage. He looked amused at the reaction. "How hard it is," he repeated. Then he finished very quickly, and, tearing his speech into little pieces, he left the podium.

In the uproar that followed, a rumor—one of many that swept the floor that night—worried O'Brien, Humphrey in his hotel suite, and the absent party leader, who was watching events from his daughter's Texas home. William vanden Heuvel, a Kennedy friend and supporter and a New York delegate, was, according to the rumor, going to nominate President Lyndon Johnson because he felt that "Johnson is the only man who can run on the Vietnam plank the platform has given us." By this simple device the opponents of the President could have reduced the proceedings to total anarchy instead of the mere chaos then prevailing. For, if the President were nominated, whom would the delegates vote for? They could not allow him to be defeated, but then they would have to abandon Humphrey until the President could release their votes to the Vice-President.

The more militant members of the McCarthy group were elated. "Why take the dummy when you can get the ventriloquist himself?" chortled Goodwin bitterly through cigar smoke. "It makes sense, doesn't it?"

But such a nomination could not be allowed to happen. Vanden Heuvel was reached by various members of the Democratic establishment. They all said the same thing: To put his plan into action would be to degrade the office of the Presidency and to finish the party.

That incredible evening wore on until at last the balloting began. It went exactly as predicted. At midnight Humphrey was nominated as the Democratic candidate for the Presidency of the United

States. He received 1,761¼ votes, 449¼ more than he needed. McCarthy received 601, McGovern 146½, and Channing Phillips, the first Negro ever to be nominated for the Presidency, 67½.

In the hall the convention orchestra, controlled like everything else in Chicago by Mayor Daley, was playing the Humphrey theme song, "Happy Days Are Here Again." In the Hilton Humphrey jigged to its rhythm, and, when his wife's face appeared on his television screen (from a V.I.P. spot in the convention hall), he rushed up and kissed her image. His aides reported to the waiting press that he had cried, "Muriel, I love you!"

Then the phone rang. It was the President. "You have got us here," he said, "and all you need are a few million more. We've got to get this party together and work to see this through November."

Humphrey's reply, as recorded by his aides, was touchingly reverent. "Bless your heart," he said, "and thank you."

Were the forces of liberalism completely stifled at Chicago? There were many who believed as much and thought that Daley, Humphrey, and Johnson together had set the party back fifty years. A closer examination supports the view that a true and lasting victory was won not for 1968 but for 1972 and the years beyond. The progressives believed they had scored in two very notable ways.

The first victory was on credentials, and the argument as to who should sit in the arena at all. There was an exceptionally large number of delegations whose right to sit had been challenged for having been unfairly chosen or for being unrepresentative of their states. Only 966 of the 2,622 delegates had been chosen by primary vote. The rest had been selected in state conventions, local caucuses, or simple party appointments. Four years previously a challenge to the all-white Mississippi delegation had brought uproar in Atlantic City. This time there was little dissent. Since 1964 the "regular" Democratic Party in Mississippi had made absolutely no effort to put its house in order. In 1968, by an overwhelming vote of 84 to 10, the credentials committee, chaired by Governor Richard Hughes of New Jersey, threw out the "regular" Mississippi delegation and seated the challengers.

It was a revolutionary decision and one that promised to have a profound effect in the Democratic South. An immediate reaction came from Reverend Abernathy, who sent this telegram: "Congratulations on Credentials Committee decision to recommend seating of Mississippi delegation which represents all people, including poor people in that state. This is a victory for freedom, justice and democracy."

Another success came over seating a Georgia delegation, although the committee had to make a decision something like the judgment of Solomon. The "regular" delegation was led by the extraordinary Governor of Georgia, former cafe owner Lester Maddox, a ludicrous aspirant to the Presidential nomination. The challengers were led by Negro state representative Julian Bond. The committee decided to divide the seats equally between the two factions. Maddox refused to accept that solution. The committee eventually suggested that both delegations be seated and that the Georgia votes be split equally between them. This solution was finally accepted.

The actual physical seats went to the regulars; Bond's men were given gallery passes. Bond declared, "I intend to launch a floor fight and throw that Georgia delegation out of the hall bodily." Armed with 45 floor passes lent by anonymous sympathizers, Bond and his followers entered the main hall, and a tremendous melee ensued. The Bond group was first given temporary seats with Wisconsin but tried to take its rightful place beneath Georgia's flag; all the time it was pursued by reporters and television men, who were also being harassed by security men.

While all this hullabaloo was going on, the second, even greater victory was achieved almost unnoticed. At 11:38 Tuesday evening the *minority* report of the rules committee was adopted, by a vote of 1,350 to 1,206. Earlier in the year a commission on the democratic selection of Presidential nominees had been set up in New York by the committee on rules and credentials. It had been headed by Governor Harold Hughes of Iowa, who came out for McCarthy shortly after the convention began. Also on the commission were ex-Kennedy aide Fred Dutton and Julian Bond.

In the preamble to its report the commission had said:

> This convention is on trial. The responsibilities of these committees, and all delegates to this convention, are unprecedented. To an extent not matched since the turn of the twentieth century, events in 1968 have called into question the integrity of the convention system for nominating Presidential candidates. Recent developments have put the future of the two-party system itself into serious jeopardy. The Democratic Party is in trouble.

Now, while the furore over Georgia raged, the rules committee's minority reported, against the wishes of the entrenched party bosses, what should be required in future: First the unit rule should not be used at any stage of the delegate selection process and, second, all feasible efforts should be made to ensure that delegates were selected through party primaries, conventions, or committee procedures open to public participation within the calendar year of the national convention. The convention accepted these requirements on the floor.

This endorsement meant that each delegate would in future be able to vote according to his own conscience, instead of being muted by the unit rule. These two recommendations were absolutely fundamental reforms and rang the final death knell of the old Democratic politics in the South.

Credentials and rules: technical successes for those who wanted a new kind of party. With these struggles three men emerged into new prominence, suggesting hope for the future. One was Donald Peterson, leader of the Wisconsin delegation. He was 43, married with four children, a tall man who wore glasses and a look of stubbornness. He was vice-president of a pizza-making firm in Eau Claire. Throughout the convention he seemed to stand for decency at all costs. It was he who led a torchlit march back to the Loop after Wednesday's brutality. And he led his delegation on a march to the amphitheater on Thursday in an attempt "to see if the streets of Chicago were really free." They were not, and the marchers were forced into Daley's buses. Said Peterson, after it was all over, "Basically people want to be fair, but they take a long time coming to it."

The second man was Julian Bond, leader of the Georgia Loyal Democrats' Challenge. Bond was a lithe, 28-year-old Negro, circumspect, polite, absolutely correct, but a ferocious fighter. He was very good-looking, rather light in coloring. He did not smile very much. He was from Atlanta and in 1965 had been elected a Georgia state representative, though in 1966 the legislature had refused to seat him because he had criticized the Vietnam war. He had taken his case to the Supreme Court. In 1967 it ruled in his favor, and he was seated. Of the credentials battles he said: "The mood of the convention was to seat the challenging Mississippi delegation and no one else. They could hardly refuse them since they had an overwhelming case, and it was sort of left over from 1964. What they decided in the case of Georgia was a purely political decision. It was taken in order not to anger too many southerners or too many liberals."

The decision satisfied neither side, but the moral victory was clearly with Julian Bond. Several times during the convention the liberal delegations took up the cry "Jul-i-an Bond, Jul-i-an Bond," and he became a sort of figurehead. As Ted Warshavsky of Wisconsin said in nominating Bond for the Vice-Presidency (for which he could not legally have run because of his age), "This may be a symbolic gesture tonight, but it may not be symbolic four years from tonight."

The third man was the tall Senator from Maine whom Humphrey ultimately chose as his running mate, Edmund Muskie. A youthful-looking 54, Muskie was the son of a Polish-born tailor. Attractive, craggy-faced, with a lazy, Jimmy Stewart type of charm, he had an impressive legislative record and was not hampered by ties with any particular faction. He had done great work on model-cities legislation. In 1954 he had been elected the first Democratic Governor of Maine in twenty years. He was one of a rare breed, a true rugged individualist. And he proved an excellent choice, for if anyone was to give Humphrey's campaign sparkle and a touch of originality it was Ed Muskie.

Humphrey, in his acceptance speech, tried desperately to unite the many irreconcilable factions. "We stand at the end of an era and at the beginning of a new day," he said. "Winning the Presidency is not worth the price of silence or evasion on the issue of human rights. The new day belongs to the people, every man, woman, and child." It was a speech calculated to quiet every doubt, to paper over every crack, to heal every scar, to placate every enemy.

But the divisions were too deep. Posters of Humphrey's smiling face were defaced by rebel crayons. They scrawled "the gutless wonder" underneath that picture, and they gave him a new name: "the Cowardly Lion." The Chicago convention concluded with the same implacable enmity that had characterized its entire course.

In the early hours of Thursday morning two policemen appeared with a hotel employee to investigate reports that beer cans had been thrown from the windows onto troops below. Senior McCarthy aides agreed to close and lock the windows. But just after 5:00 A.M., a dozen policemen appeared and started beating the young workers and herding them down into the lobby. A nightstick was broken over one young man's head. McCarthy was called and went downstairs. His position seemed more and more to demand the virtues of Florence Nightingale. He told his helpers to return in the lift three or four at a time.

Later that morning he called a press conference to announce that he would not be returning to Washington that morning as planned. He was, in effect, staying to make sure that his supporters left the city safely. As he said, "There seems some doubt as to whether anyone wearing a McCarthy button is entirely safe in this city."

Would the party and the country really have been better off had Chicago never happened? Could one take this convention as typical of American politics and thus demand that conventions be abolished? What was the Chicago convention? A bloodbath? A grotesque political farce? The final indisputable sign that the United States was into the final crack-up?

Judged by British standards it was perhaps all these things British reporters, among them the visitor, were appalled by what they witnessed, for in Britain it would have signified collapse. But Chicago could not—and must not—be judged by anything but American standards. It proved that Americans were a violent people, which the world already knew. Technically the battle over the platform was meaningless, for only a few weeks later Humphrey was able to take, or appear to take, a different stand on Vietnam from the one that he had taken, or appeared to take, at the convention.

But Chicago proved something else: that an expression of public will could make itself heard at an American political convention, despite all the efforts of a repressive machine to strangle it. It proved that change could come and that political machines were changing in America as elsewhere. It proved that the people's voice was heard, for the defeated majority plank on Vietnam was translated into action before the election was over.

The convention was a mirror that enabled America to look at itself. The disunity, the bitterness, and the violence in Chicago revealed the worst side of the American character, but what mattered in the long run? An open sore is usually easier than an inward cancerous growth to heal. Chicago showed all; it hid nothing of the wounds and the divisions. And after Chicago America began to heal itself. Few realized it at the time, but Chicago was the turning point. The Democrats—and the country—had gotten the poison out of the system.

332

.17.

From Traditional Beginnings

AMERICANS TAKE THEIR LAST PUBLIC HOLIDAY OF THE SUMMER ON Labor Day, the first Monday in September. Like the Late Summer Holiday in Britain, it gives everyone a chance to have a last long weekend in the sunshine. It is a day of picnics, parades, and barbecues, a bittersweet day, for it marks in effect the end of summer, when urbanites must close up their cottages and return to their city apartments. For children, it is the symbolic last day of freedom before they face new classmates and new teachers in a new grade. And every four years it is the starting day of the final stretch in that political marathon, the Presidential election.

All that had gone before in 1968—the months of slogging competition, the million-dollar advertising campaigns, the knockdown and dragout of the primaries—were just the preliminaries. Only after the conventions had picked their candidates did the official campaign begin. It would last nine weeks, and in that time the candidates and their staffs would perform prodigious feats of physical and mental effort. Their days would start before dawn and end after midnight. They would jet across time zones and come down the ramps to full days of performing in public and intensive work in private. They would rarely eat without having at the same time to speak, to confer, or to plan.

Nine weeks of such effort would punish a highly trained athlete starting fresh. But the candidates in the American election were far from fresh when called on to submit to this final test. Richard Nixon and George Wallace had been actively on the road since winter, and Hubert Humphrey had been active since April.

Traditionally, the Labor Day weekend itself was a pause for the candidates, a brief respite as they moved from the heats into the final. Richard Nixon spent it pottering about his Manhattan apartment. In the four weeks since the Republicans had nominated him he had worked at a steady yet far from frantic pace. He knew that he was the fittest of the three candidates, and he intended to stay that way.

George Wallace spent the weekend trying to shake a throat virus that kept his temperature between 100 and 101 degrees. "I must not lose my voice," he told his staff. "Whatever happens, I've got to have my voice."

Hubert Humphrey had retreated from Chicago to his home in Waverly, Minnesota, but there was no rest for him. The Chicago convention had been scheduled at such an extraordinarily late date —to coincide with the President's birthday—that there was hardly time, even with everyone working all out, for the Democratic organization to ready itself for the road. Humphrey spent Saturday and Sunday working with Larry O'Brien and his advisers in Waverly and on Monday flew to New York to lead that city's Labor Day parade.

Democratic candidates traditionally have gone to Detroit for Labor Day, but Humphrey had decided to concentrate on New York; the foundation of his strategy was to capture that state's 43 electoral votes. The first step was to demonstrate that labor's real candidate was Hubert Humphrey and not George Wallace. It was a fine sunny day in New York and not too hot; the temperature was in the middle seventies. Humphrey marched at the head of 100,000 people, not a record number, for many workers preferred to relax in the country or at the beaches rather than to march. But Humphrey was happy. He was off and running, the first of the three main finalists to take the field. [There were, of course, several fringe candidates, as there are in every Presidential election. Among them were Eldridge Cleaver, Peace and Freedom Party; Dick Gregory, Freedom and Peace Party, and Mrs. Yetta Bronstein, Best Party.]

Labor Day 1968 was not perhaps the happiest on record. Six hundred eighty-eight road deaths were reported over the weekend, an all-time high. In Boston the threat of a Negro riot was averted by a special meeting of the school board, which transferred white principals from two predominantly Negro schools and replaced them with Negroes. In Chicago Mrs. Sylvia Sewell was beaten to death with a candlestick in the basement of her antique store; she was one of more than 100 Americans murdered that holiday weekend. In New York 10,000 hotel workers went on a three-hour wild-cat strike, leaving guests to make their own beds and carry their own bags.

America was so vast that these and similar events hardly ruffled the tranquility of that summer weekend. The visitor spent the time in a small New York resort, where the police often chose not to carry their guns, so unnecessary did they seem. There in the easy warmth of an American family atmosphere, the country's problems seemed to recede.

But they were still there. That Monday evening after the last swim, while the children packed their toys and the last barbecue crackled and filled the air with that unique American smell of fine beef cooking over charcoal, people began to talk about them again. Could any of the major candidates come up with the radical programs that America needed to right itself? Was it not a condemnation of the country itself that the people were being offered a choice among a couple of political retreads and a Neanderthal populist?

A Harris poll taken in September showed that 57 percent of those questioned wished that there were other leading candidates beside Nixon, Humphrey, and Wallace; only 49 percent believed that they were being offered "a fair choice" by the available candidates, and 46 percent said that they were "disappointed" in having only those three men to choose from.

Yet it was not clear what alternative America did want. That Labor Day they behaved remarkably like the British at election time, grumbling about the choice but accepting it. They were not prepared to change the system and traditions that had produced that choice. To understand this acceptance one must look closely at Americans. Whether they were of Colonial stock or whether their parents had came off a boat from the Mediterranean only a generation before, Americans had been shaped by an Anglo-Saxon culture. The foundations of the United States were in British history and British institutions, and Americans were taught to revere those institutions.

Although the "special relationship" between Britain and America may have been fading, the "emotional" relationship was still very much alive in the mind of the average American. His history did not begin in 1776; it went back to the *Mayflower* and beyond that to Elizabethan England.

The Colonies were founded by the British, and until the first quarter of the nineteenth century the nation's white population was of primarily British descent, as New Zealand still is today. The population of the United States reached 10 million shortly after the 1820 census. It was already two-thirds that of England. Ten percent of the American population was Negro slaves; the rest was almost entirely from British stock.

Then the great waves of immigration began. The Irish came first, their arrivals reaching a peak in the years of the great potato famine in the late 1840s. The Germans were next; they kept on coming right through the century. The Scandinavians followed, then the Italians, and finally the Slavs and the Jews from eastern Europe. These continual injections of foreign culture might have smothered the Britishness of America except for two factors. First, the British had simply been there first; 8 million strong in the early nineteenth century, they controlled the country and were determined to keep it what their forefathers had fought to make it. Being wealthier, healthier, and better fed, their children prospered, enabling British-Americans to maintain their superior position.

There was, however, a second reason, less well known. Throughout the entire eighteenth century there was another great flood of immigrants, not an intermittent tidal wave but a continuous current, steady and unremarkable: more British. Speaking the same tongue and brought up in a similar tradition, they were not easily noticeable, but there was no need for them to settle in ethnic ghettos while they learned the language and customs of the new country. Swiftly they were absorbed into every area of American life. With the earlier arrivals, they maintained the traditions of an older society.

The surprising fact is that of all the great waves of immigration from across the Atlantic between 1820 and 1966, only two exceeded that of the British. Germany sent 6,862,900 people to become Americans during those 146 years; Italy sent 5,067,717; and Britain sent 4,711,711. Then came Ireland with 4,706,854, Central Europe with 4,491,312, Russia with 3,345,610, and Scandinavia with 2,498,480.

Although every European people sent settlers to the United States, no group was ever able to challenge the British-descended

336

establishment. All three 1968 Presidential candidates, incidentally, could trace their ancestry back to Colonial America and thence to Britain. Richard Nixon's maternal and paternal forebears had come from England and Wales via Ireland. George Wallace's family was from Ulster, and Hubert Humphrey's father was of Welsh descent.

Whenever important groups succeeded in entering that establishment, as the Irish did in politics, the Jews in business and academic life, and the Germans in manufacturing, it was by accepting the basic political structure of the country, and not by trying to change it. That structure was to a great extent Anglo-Saxon: the jurisprudence, the local system of government, the organization of police, education, the electoral system, all had evolved from Colonial times and thus from the small island on the other side of the water. As time passed no one fought harder to hold onto those Anglo-Saxon traditions than first-generation Americans whose parents had not been able to speak English.

It has been calculated in the extraordinary way that Americans calculate such things, that if it were possible to envision a "representative" American, descended proportionately from all the ethnic groups in his country, he would still be predominantly British: Using the size of each immigration and its length of residence in the United States (and thus the number of descendants it had produced) a computer determined that the "average" American was 35 percent British, 12.5 percent German, 9 percent Irish, 4.5 percent Scandinavian, 3 percent Polish, and, of course 11 percent Negro.

This obsession with heritage was one of America's great handicaps in 1968. For, although Americans were the most flexible people on earth in business, although their history was one of brilliant improvisation, and although they were always excited by new technology, they were far too rigid about their traditions. This stubborn adherence to the past was increasingly paralyzing Washington, and the malaise affected the great cities and was responsible for the appalling urban crisis from which so many other problems arose.

American cities were, for the most part, ruled and administered in a nineteenth-century tradition, the mayoral and aldermanic concept that to Americans was inviolate. Britain had recognized that the old forms of city government were no longer adequate to deal with modern urban problems and changed the structure of city administration.

The British did not have the same veneration for their traditions that Americans had (despite the preservation of the monarchy, it's role has also steadily changed), and they discard them when they hinder progress.

It is worth comparing post-World War II London and New York. It was recognized after the war that London's system of administration was out of date. Contemporary urban problems required less central control, and cities had to be broken down into compact subunits. In 1965 the London County Council, the biggest local administrative body in British history, was quietly eliminated. A new structure provided for 33 local boroughs within the Greater London area, each controlling welfare, social services, and to a large extent education in its own district. Each borough council, in conjunction with an overall body, the Greater London Council, shared control of roads, housing, planning, sewage, garbage collection, and parks. The G.L.C. provided and controlled fire and ambulance services, but the Metropolitan police was controlled by a separate body under the supervision of the Home Office.

New York had made changes in its city government since greater New York was created in 1898. The Board of Aldermen had been replaced by a city council, and through the years the Mayor had been given increased executive powers. But the changes were less radical than those affecting London. New York City was still centrally controlled, despite the agreement of an overwhelming number of the world's urban experts that decentralization was the only answer to the problems besetting big cities.

New York was the most progressive of all American cities, and in John V. Lindsay it had perhaps the finest Mayor it had ever produced. Yet by 1968 New York seemed to be sliding into absolute chaos. With a million people drawing welfare, the city's budget had risen 40 percent in the previous five years and stood at just under 6 billion, bigger than that of any state in the union. To subsidize this rising budget sales taxes and real-estate taxes had increased, and a city income tax had been introduced.

Yet the huge expenditures brought little improvement into the lives of most New Yorkers. The schools were appalling, and many pupils were as much as 50 percent behind the national reading norm. An intermittent teachers' strike through the autumn had turned the educational situation from bad to hopeless. The teachers' strike was only one of many citywide strikes that contributed to impending disaster. The sanitation workers, the police, the firemen seemed permanently on the verge of walkouts or slowdowns, and nothing seemed to pacify them.

On top of all this trouble, rents had been continually increasing; the cost of an average middle-class apartment had doubled in the past four years. And the residents of New York paid to live in fear. Crime in the city was appalling. In 1968 it rose 16.7 percent. In 1967 New York had had 746 murders, 1,905 rapes, 35,934 robberies, 149,765 burglaries, and 24,827 felonious assaults.

Mayor Lindsay had been able to prevent serious outbreaks in Harlem of the racial violence that had erupted in so many other American cities, but his efforts had only alienated the city's white population. New York's 2 million Jews, once his most ardent supporters, had turned against him; the Negroes had turned against them. The enmity between the Negroes and the Jews took on increasingly ugly overtones. Once Jews, propelled by their liberal traditions and their own knowledge of persecution had been in the forefront of the civil-rights movement. That role was forgotten as Negro militants became increasingly anti-semitic.

What was happening in New York at the end of the 1960s was the culmination of social upheaval that had been affecting American cities ever since World War II. More and more white people had moved to the suburbs; more and more Negroes had moved in from the rural South. Manhattan was populated most by rich white people and poor black people, middle-class family life was swiftly becoming extinct in Manhattan, and the workers were steadily evacuating the outer areas of the Bronx and Brooklyn.

Whatever reforms Mayor Lindsay tried to institute brought only more trouble. An experiment in decentralization of the school system brought on the teachers' strike. Governing the city was, as Lindsay said one autumn day, "never easy." The one hope, he said, was to "hold to reason."

> You know for every progressive soul there is there are 1,000 appointed guardians who will fight any change at all. Nobody likes change. But we must do what the British did and guide this revolution into peaceful channels. They did it for several centuries, and they did it brilliantly by and large. They used the skills of their great moderate leaders, who stayed ahead of the tides and did not allow the waves to drown them.

America had to civilize its cities. It had to reverse the great white outflow to the suburbs, as Britain had done, so that New York could become as livable as London. It had to make city life comfortable, clean, and safe. It had to eliminate ghettos, produce public housing, integrate black and white. It had to make urban education as good as suburban education. It had to find work for the unemployed; it had to produce a constructive welfare system; it had to provide free hospitals and social services to a degree rarely imagined in America; it had to tame the automobile. It had to strain all its resources and talents to reverse its decline. Then so many other problems would ease themselves: crime, racial strife, slum living, suburban despoliation of the countryside.

Lindsay called the problems of the cities the domestic task of greatest urgency facing the new President. But the new President would have to begin educating the American people to understand the problem. He would have to discuss it during the campaign.

But that never happened except obliquely. Instead the politicking centered around the issue of law and order, a phrase that meant different things to Americans. Hardly anyone could define precisely how he understood it, but it seemed to mean a return to the good old days when family life was stronger, when university students wore short hair and demonstrated at football games, when hippies were unknown and narcotics limited to the ghetto, most of all when it was safe to walk city streets and the Negro knew his place. To most Americans "law and order" meant one or more of these things. And it was George Wallace's political accomplishment that he was able to capture white Americans' longing for quieter days in that one all-purpose phrase.

To many Americans, crime was linked with Negroes. To the extent that poverty, hopelessness, and frustration led to crime, there was some truth in this association. The two main causes of the increase in American lawlessness were the magnitude of special ills and the inefficiency of American police. In the latter instance Americans once again refused to challenge the hallowed concepts of their Colonial forebears. The British had brought the sheriff and the paid-constable system with them in the seventeenth century, and, when cities began to grow in the eighteenth, the Colonists turned again to Britain for ideas on law enforcement.

Sir Robert Peel had formed the Metropolitan Police in London in 1829; nine years later Boston formed the first police force in the United States. In 1840 the New York Police Department was created. From then on cities all over the country began forming their own departments, although very small ones still maintained the old tradition of town constables. The American police were thus Anglo-Saxon in conception, a citizen force controlled locally to prevent use as a political weapon by the state or national government. The result was that America had the most decentralized police force in the world. There were more than 40,000 police departments in the United States, and standards of recruitment, discipline, and effectiveness varied wildly.

Throughout the twentieth century these local forces had only reluctantly surrendered their parochial powers. The crime wave of the 1920s and 1930s resulted in establishment of the Federal Bureau of Investigation (F.B.I.) and the various state police forces. But these forces had not been enough to contain the increase in crime.

In 1968 polls showed that 81 percent of Americans believed that law enforcement had broken down, and there was plenty of evidence to support this belief. In New York Police Commissioner Howard Leary admitted that, although he had a force larger than that of London (30,000 men, compared to 25,000) to handle a smaller population (7,781,984 compared to 8,400,000), there were nine times as many violent crimes in New York as there were in London (63,412 compared to 7,302 in 1967).

In the United States in 1967 there were 12,090 homicides (in Britain, with a quarter the population, there were 172). Urban crime, according to an F.B.I. estimate, had increased 88 percent in the first seven years of the decade. But nobody knew just how bad the story was because the compilation of crime statistics was more an art than a science in the United States. They had been kept on a national basis only since 1930 and were drawn from reports to the F.B.I. by thousands of local authorities, but there were no means of checking the accuracy of local reports, and no attempt was made to do so.

Again a parallel must be drawn with Britain. Just as handling urban problems requires decentralization, organized crime requires a centralized police force. In the last ten years, often against local opposition, the tiny city and county police forces in Britain have been eliminated to make way for more centralized police agencies. It was recognized that the nineteenth-century fear of a national police force must be forgotten when weighed against twentieth-century awareness of the dangers of high-speed crime.

Although Americans in 1968 cried for law and order and asked what had happened to their country, they did not question why some kind of modern order was not being applied to the forces of the law. Such reorganization was never mentioned by George Wallace. It would have struck no chord in his audience, to whose members "law and order" meant stopping the Negro from getting away with "murder." According to Wallace, for the criminal, Negro or white, crime did pay because the U.S. Supreme Court had made life safer and more profitable for the criminal than for the law-abiding citizen. Insofar as there was any detailed discussion of law and order during the campaign it was on this topic.

The duty of the Supreme Court, as set down by the men who framed the Constitution, was to interpret the laws of the country, but during the previous fourteen years many Americans had come to believe that the Court was *making* law, rather than interpreting it. The Court had rarely been as active. Since 1954, when Earl Warren had become Chief Justice, its decisions had affected American life far more fundamentally than anything that Congress had done.

The nine justices of the Court in 1968 included one Jew, one Roman Catholic, and one Negro. But the Court was divided along liberal-moderate conservative lines. In virtually all clashes the liberals outnumbered the conservatives two to one.

In 1954 the Court had declared school segregation in violation of the Fourteenth Amendment to the Constitution, which read: "No state shall make or enforce any law which shall abridge the privileges or immunities of citizens of the United States; nor shall any state deprive any person of life, liberty, or property, without due process of law; nor deny to any person within its jurisdiction the equal protection of the laws."

The attitude of the Warren Court was simple: Its job was to interpret the Constitution, the Bill of Rights, which included the first ten amendments, and all subsequent amendments, in the light of contemporary conditions. As Justice Fortas * said, "The problem is not to determine precisely what the framers meant but to interpret their moral thrust in the light of the problems of today."

That is what the Court had been doing for more than a decade. After declaring segregation unconstitutional, the Court, later, found "busing"—transportation of Negro children in ghettos to predominantly white schools and vice versa—to be constitutional. This issue was one of the most controversial in the United States; at a time

---

* Justice Fortas, liberal jurist, Texan, and close personal friend of President Johnson, had been appointed to set a liberal future course on civil rights. The President wished him to succeed retiring Earl Warren as Chief Justice, but congressional reaction forced withdrawal of his nomination. Congress feared that the Court would, under Fortas, encroach on legislative prerogatives, and would swing farther left. It also objected to a "lame duck" President's setting his stamp on the Court.

when it was being considered in Britain, it was interesting to watch the backlash it produced in America.

The Court had also infuriated millions of Americans by ruling against prayers in schools supported by taxes or public funds. Although many Americans agreed with the decision, it was clear that a huge segment of the population saw it as another step toward breaking down traditional values and creating an increasingly decadent society.

The Court also generally found against censorship and, in several controversial rulings on the definitions of pornography and obscenity, left the way open for publishers to print almost what they wished in this area; the publishers did just that. Worst of all, to many Americans were decisions that they thought weighted the scales of justice on the side of the criminal. In order to protect the rights of the citizen the Court made it increasingly difficult for police to arrest suspects and secure convictions. In fact the *Miranda* decision did little more than extend to suspects the same protection that their British counterparts receive. It barred the use as evidence of confessions taken from suspects in custody who had not first been warned of their rights. In other words, as in Britain, a suspect could refuse to answer questions once he had been warned that his answers might be used in evidence against him and could demand a lawyer before talking to the police. The one difference was that in the United States, if a suspect did not have or could not afford a lawyer, the state had to supply one as soon as he was taken into custody.

"What the court has done," said retired New York Police Commissioner Michael Murphy, "is to make one boxer fight to the Marquis of Queensbury rules while permitting the other to butt, gouge, and bite."

Richard Nixon, sensing public feeling on the matter said that the Supreme Court "was hamstringing the peace forces in our society." But he warned that law and order were meaningless without justice.

To George Wallace "law and order" meant "supporting the police and letting them run things their way." Wallace wanted all the Court's decisions repealed.

Hubert Humphrey addressed this issue along more orthodox liberal lines. Both he and Nixon eventually suggested more Federal aid and control of local police forces but such suggestions were lost in the heat generated by the issue.

As the campaign began, it was obvious that the issue of law and order would transcend all others, even the Vietnam war. With its simple, sinister appeal it raised the question, were Americans prepared to sacrifice their freedom for the sake of their security?

The point was made by Mayor Lindsay:

> What happens if we begin to yield to this kind of demand for "law and order"? What happens if recent Supreme Court decisions are overturned, if police are ordered to arrest without any restraints on their conduct, or if peace officers are instructed to shoot looters? What happens if, after this victory for "law and order" we find—as we will—that the crime rate is still going up, that the streets are still not safe, that more lives have been lost, and that America is being divided into armed camps?
>
> The answer, I am afraid, is that these defeated hopes will escalate into new and more dangerous demands.
>
> Perhaps some would then look at criminal law and demand to know why we need a unanimous jury vote to convict a person of a crime? Why not declare a suspect guilty if he won't talk? Why not cast aside the privilege between clients and lawyers, between confessors and priests? And why presume a man innocent until proven otherwise? If the police arrest someone, isn't he probably guilty anyway?
>
> What is next? Shall we keep order by refusing men the right to hold peaceful meetings in large cities? Shall we uphold the law by suppressing controversial newspapers? Shall we forget what history has always taught us: that those who suppress freedom always do so in the name of "law and order"?

If Americans took this path, warned Lindsay, they would eventually achieve security and order. "But what would be missing would be liberty."

Intertwined with the main issue were others: the cost of living, the war, poverty amidst plenty, the arms race, the urban crisis. They were the problems to which the candidates had to address themselves and upon which the American people would have to decide who was best fitted to handle them.

To put across their views and secure the voters' confidence and support, the candidates spent millions of dollars in those final eight weeks. In a sense there was no limit on the money spent in an American election campaign. The law said that no more than $3 million might be gathered and spent by a political committee in one year, but American politicians evaded this requirement by forming as many political committees as they found necessary.

For example, in addition to the Republican National Committee and the United Citizens for Nixon-Agnew, there blossomed a spectacular profusion of political groups: Businessmen for Nixon-Agnew, Housewives for Nixon-Agnew, Polish-Americans for Nixon-Agnew, Entertainers for Nixon-Agnew. The Democrats matched this performance, and Wallace's American Independent Party exceeded it, at least in the number of committees, including Free Americans for Wallace; Polish-, Italian-, and Irish-Americans for Wallace; and just plain Americans for Wallace.

According to Doctor Herbert E. Alexander of the Citizens Research Foundation, between $15 and $21 million had been spent on the campaigns up to the conventions. Of the Democrats, Humphrey spent $1-$2 million, McCarthy $3.5-$4 million, Johnson about $500,000, and Robert F. Kennedy more than $3 million; of the Republicans, Nixon spent $3-$5 million, Rockefeller $3-$5 million, Reagan about $500,000, and Romney about $1 million. More than twice that amount was spent in the final stretch. The Republicans exceeded $25 million, the Democrats $12 million, Wallace $10 million. Much of this money went to the television companies at $75,000 an hour (the networks sold time to candidates at half-price, as a public service).

Whatever the cost television could take the issues into every home in the United States. That autumn there were more than 200 million Americans, and their average age was 27.7 years. Eighty-five million of them were under 24, 6 million were in college, 9 million were foreign-born, 123 million went to church regularly, 91 million were married, 2 million were widowers, 9 million were widows, 33 million held white-collar jobs, 27 million were blue-collar workers, 19 million were retired, and 120 million were registered to vote.

Many of these people were uncertain, discouraged, even frightened. Many were intelligent, energetic, well-educated, tough, resourceful, and courageous. They would respond to the man who could touch the right chord in their hearts or could make the right appeal to their minds. Depending on what the candidates said or did not say, these Americans could be inspired, frightened, or merely bored. The candidates would either lead the people or be led by them. The country and the world waited to see which way they would go.

345

.18.

WALLACE: WHERE DOES THE SOUTH END?

GEORGE CORLEY WALLACE CAME OUT OF THE SOUTH WITH A PLAN. IT was to begin the campaign as a spoiler and to end it as kingmaker. He had as much chance of entering the White House as a Negro field hand had of becoming Mayor of Montgomery, Alabama. He knew that. But he could still effectively help to deadlock the election and then exact his price—or so he believed. He believed that little was required to make his plan work: a little money, which he could raise; a major issue, which he had; and just one speech, which he had written. Applied correctly these weapons could pry loose enough states to ensure that neither of the two major candidates would achieve a majority of the electoral votes. Then, George Wallace could exercise the balance of power.

Americans voted for a President indirectly. In every state each candidate had a slate of electors pledged to vote for him in the Electoral College. Each state had an elector for each seat that it held in both Houses of Congress. New York had 43, New Hampshire 4. The candidate who received 270 of the total 538 votes in

346

the Electoral College would win. If no one received a majority, Wallace intended to trade his votes to the candidate who would agree to include the maximum amount of Wallace thinking in his policy.

To this end, he had already secured notarized affidavits from his electors in *every* state that they would vote either for him or for the candidate to whom he saw fit to transfer their votes. Although he knew that this procedure would be bitterly contested in court and in public if he ever put it into effect, the constitutional position was unclear on the point, which made his menace all the greater.

Wallace was a politician of instinct. To be effective he knew that he had to show that his plan would work. From the beginning, then, he made himself absolutely clear: "When this happens, this deadlock, I would not be the next President of the United States. But I would have the power to say just who *would* be the next President. And I make no secret that I would want something in return before I make my choice."

What he wanted in return was also spelled out very clearly. The new President would have to promise to restore to individual states full control over their own affairs and to summon Federal bureaucrats back to Washington. In particular, the states would have to be given free rein in deciding how they were to run their schools. Hospitals would decide who would use which bathrooms. Houseowners could refuse to sell their homes to whomever they liked. Labor unions would decide for themselves just how they would operate their seniority and job-option systems. All these demands were clearly aimed at depriving the American Negro of all the hard-won advances of the previous two decades.

Wallace believed that his policy would be as popular outside the Deep South as in it. He recognized the frustration of blue-collar Americans, he knew how right-wing Republicans felt, and he believed that he could form a coalition of the discontented that would give him as many as ten states.

So began an extraordinary campaign. The American Independent Party was not a party at all in the accepted American sense. Wallace had no "machine" working for him, no speech writers, no high-level advisers or "brain trust." He did most of the work himself. True he was surrounded by men like "National Campaign Chairman" Seymore Trammell, "National Campaign Coordinator" Bill Jones, "National Campaign Director" Cecil C. Jackson, Jr., and "National Campaign Organizer" Ed Wing. But one had the impression that these

347

mostly unremarkable men—dressed in slightly shabby suits and always bustling about anxiously—were like the water boys and trainers who accompany professional prize fighters. The Wallace campaign was a one-man performance, but from the moment that it took to the road it drew crowds.

In the unlovely midwestern industrial towns, which all looked alike, Wallace would descend from his battered DC-6 and give effusive greeting to the local police, who were always out in force to meet him. "It's good to see you boys," he would say. "Ah want you to know that millions of decent Americans do appreciate their law-enforcement departments, and many will be saying so tonight." The subsequent rally was virtually identical in every town. An early-October evening in Canton, Ohio, was typical.

The civic auditorium was filled with a raucous crowd, many wearing the plastic "straw" hats that proliferated during American campaigns. The hats had Wallace ribbons on them. On the floor there were scores of homemade placards proclaiming: "Keep America Free"; "Support Your Police"; "Stand Up For America." In the balcony was the opposition, perhaps 100 young Negroes carrying their own placards: "One Hitler Was Enough" and "Wallace Is a Racist." They were led by a white clergyman, who carried a cardboard cross.

On stage the warm-up was proceeding full blast. The crowd had already heard the national anthem and the Lord's Prayer, and it was being treated to the music of Sam Smith and his Travelers, an Alabama rock combination with a tearaway beat. Before a backdrop of Confederate flags the Travelers played "Dixie" and "When the Saints Go Marching In"; had it not been for the jeering Negroes in the balcony, the whole affair might have seemed a massive Saturday-night social.

Next on the bill were an Alabama harmony duo, Mona and Lisa Taylor. As the entertainment was free and the audiences cheerful, Mona and Lisa usually received a good hand; they always came offstage saying, "That was the greatest audience, you know." Some of Wallace's supporters thought that, if he was going to present himself as a national rather than a sectional figure, he should dispense with the Travelers and Mona and Lisa before moving north. The entertainment smacked too much of "Alabammy," they said, at which Wallace would bristle and demand, "What the hell's wrong with Dixie?"

And what was wrong with it? Mona and Lisa might not ever

348

make the Palladium, but they were exactly right for the frenzied revivalist atmosphere so necessary to raise political money. As they sang, Wallace girls started the collection in the audience, not with trays but with plastic buckets. The whole atmosphere was out of *Elmer Gantry*. Between songs, Dick Smith, the cochairman of the Wallace Finance Fund, made the appeal. Smith had the rolling tones of a Bible Belt preacher:

> Good folks, they said it couldn't be done—but it *is* being done. Wallace is setting this country on fire, and those liberals —those liberals [spoken the way a preacher would say "the devil"]—they're really scared to death. We've got to keep them running, folks, because they've done enough harm to this great country of ours. But, oh Lord, it costs money. It costs $200 a minute—*a minute*—so help us, good folks, when those girls pass among you; help us all you can.

And they did help, with dimes, quarters, dollar bills, fives, even tens. It was hard-earned working-class money, "respectable" money, money that could have been used for down payments on cars and television sets or perhaps even for the kids' college education. But the cause was worth making sacrifices for, and Wallace was *the* cause. Smith watched the buckets carefully as they filled, and, when every last section of the crowd had been covered, he signaled to Mona and Lisa and to the blasting guitars. They then sang, to the tune of "Are You from Dixie?" the campaign song, "Are You for Wallace? 'Cos we're for Wallace too-ooh."

Then the candidate appeared. Small, dapper, almost dainty in his movements, he walked into the spotlight with perfect timing. His eyes were his best feature, and he used them to great effect, widening them, narrowing them, rolling them almost coquettishly from side to side. But his most riveting feature was his mouth.

When he campaigned in the South and the border states, Wallace was never subjected to heckling. But as he moved north he had to face opposition. There was no heckling in the British sense of the word, for Americans did not appreciate the art. Instead the opposition would attempt to drown his speech with counterchants and slogans. It happened in Canton. No sooner had the roar of welcome died away than the Negro group in the balcony came to life. It was clearly well drilled and rehearsed, for its epithets were bellowed in precise chorus. "Go home pig; go home pig; go home pig."

Wallace remained unperturbed. He was one American politician who would make a superb opponent for British hecklers, for his wit was quick, and he never lost his temper. Although he was frequently compared to Adolf Hitler during the campaign, his oratory was not that of the Führer. He did not rant or rave and rarely even raised his voice. Only in his constant repetition of a clearly inflammatory theme did Wallace resemble Hitler.

He let the Negro opposition group shout for perhaps two minutes and then minced to the edge of the stage nearest the balcony, peered at them quizzically for a moment, and blew them a kiss. The effect was comic and drove the chanters into paroxysms of rage, thus disrupting their synchronization. They left the gallery and descended to the floor, to march shouting toward the platform. Wallace, increasing the pitch of the microphone, could be heard saying sarcastically, "Ah thank you, Ah thank you; you've just got me another 200,000 votes."

Then he tired of them, and the police, ever willing to respond to their candidate, moved in. After some confused shoving and yelling, the Negroes were ejected, none too gently, into the street. As he always did when the going got rough, Wallace played the great soother. "That's all right folks; everything's quite all right," he drawled. "Jes' leave it all to the police, good folks." And, as the last of the hecklers disappeared, he threw out his arms and said: "See what Ah mean about the an-*ar*-chists, folks? See why Ah'll deal with them real hard when Ah get to be President?" The crowd roared its delighted approval.

Then came "the speech." The visitor heard Wallace deliver it on scores of occasions, and it never varied from the basic pattern. It contained key phrases and quaint turns of speech that acquired a sort of life of their own. The audiences knew them well, and, as Wallace, straight-faced, would begin to cross the well-trodden ground, a groundswell of appreciative laughter and applause would ripple through the audience.

He began indignantly, assuring his audience that, although he did not see eye to eye politically with Lyndon Johnson, he yielded to no man in his respect for the office of President of the United States. He therefore found it reprehensible that when the President —at this point there might be a slight variation, depending on whether or not Wallace was fatigued or momentarily forgetful— "went to the funeral of the Cardinal last year," or "went to the funeral of Cardinal Spellman, up there in New York," he was forced, by threats of anti-Vietnam demonstrators to lie down in front of the Presidential motorcade, to approach "that Cathedral," or "the Cathedral," from a back street and enter by a side door instead of by the main entrance. "Ah tell y'awl this," continued Wallace, "if, when Ah'm President, any an-ar-chists lie down in front of *mah* automobile, it'll be the very last time they lie down in front of *any*thing." Delighted roars of applause followed.

Another great crowd pleaser was the "law and order" quip: "You leave this gathering, and when you get on the street outside you get hit on the head by some criminal, and y'awl know as well as I do that that criminal will be out of jail before y'awl can get into hospital." Then there was a pause whose timing only Bob Hope could match, and then:

Next Monday the police officer who made the arrest will be in court for trial himself. Now, when Ah'm President, we're going to change all that. Ah shall appoint an Attorney General who will indict these criminals and will seek to ensure convictions of these criminals and an-ar-chists and long-haired people. And these people will be dragged by the hair of the head and thrown under [sic] a good jail.

Wallace began to zero in on the issues close to home, issues like school integration:

Now you get this business of busin' yore children to school. Well, if you good folks of Canton really want to bus yore children way over to school out of your district, well that's yore affair, and the people of Alabama won't interfere with you. But Ah tell you this: When Ah become President there won't be one thin dime available from Federal funds to pay for all this school busin'—you can rely on that.

By now the applause was so enthusiastic that Wallace had to hold up his hand for silence. The movement was hypnotic; silence was instant.

It will be a sorry day when you can no longer have a free choice about who you sell your home to. With the new law that this absurd and ridiculous Supreme Court has approved, if you refuse to sell yore house to somebody you don't want

to sell it to, you can be tried before a jury and sent to jail. Well, Ah think that a man must be left free to sell his house

351

to just whom he chooses. We got too many of these bureau-crats comin' down from Washington into the various states and tryin' to tell us what to do. When Ah'm President Ah'm goin' go gather together all of these pointyhead bureau-crats and send 'em back to Washington where they belong and sling all of their briefcases into the middle of the Potomac.

Cheers, screams, whistles followed. Wallace moved on to Vietnam: "If the peace talks in Paris with the representatives of Hanoi finally break down, then Ah shall lean on the military—lean on the Joint Chiefs of Staff, to see what they have to say about ending this war by military means. But Ah shall end it with the use of conventional weapons." He never said what he would do if the Joint Chiefs were to tell him that the war could not be ended by conventional weapons, but the audience did not care. It was on its feet cheering.

It was a very clever speech. When the visitor went among the crowd immediately afterward to ask people why they liked it, he heard answers like "He is saying what we all feel"; "Wallace is one of us; he knows what we think"; "Wallace is his own man; that's why he can tell us the truth."

It had taken Wallace a long time to reach such perfection. "I composed that speech myself," the candidate proudly told the visitor. And indeed he had, out on the campaign trail, testing every line for audience reaction, discarding any that brought weak applause, expanding those that drew roaring responses, until in the end the speech perfectly reflected what a Wallace audience thought. He truly told his people what they wanted to hear.

In city after city in the Midwest and other parts of the North Wallace would shout, "People always say that George Wallace just appeals to the crackers, the peckerwoods, and the rednecks." He would pause. Then leaning forward, pointing his finger directly at the spellbound audience, he would continue, "Well, George Wallace says there's an awful lot of us rednecks in this country—*and they're not all in the South.*" That would bring the audience to its feet, standing on chairs and shouting approval to the rafters.

George Wallace put electricity into the campaign. If one wanted to see Americans turned on, one went to a Wallace rally. He was the only candidate who could do it. Richard Nixon's crowds were polite, mechanical, civilized. Hubert Humphrey's audiences were sedate, worthy, and bored. Yet there was nothing special in the look of the Wallace crowds—at least in the North—to identify them

352

as different from everyone else. Whatever one may have expected, they did not look like fat-bellied thugs or neurotic women. They were neat, respectable, decent-looking people, yet when Wallace called them to his redneck's standard they responded with alacrity.

In New York the visitor spent some hours talking to Thomas Sutton, a middle-aged construction worker and Wallace supporter who had collected several hundred dollars from his fellow workers to support the cause.

> I'm voting for Wallace. Let me tell you why. I have two boys; one is working his way through college now. I'm a building laborer; he'll be an architect, I hope. I help him all I can, but he mostly pays his tuition by working through his vacation. He works for the City of New York. The second boy's in high school and won't be able to go to college. You want to know why? Because the city's decided that all these summer jobs, they have to go to the underprivileged, to the Negroes who sit around in Harlem all day. Which means a white boy who's trying to improve himself doesn't stand a chance any more. And don't tell me my boy can get another job because the whole scheme these days is to give the temporary work to Negroes. That's what these liberals have done; they've persuaded the big stores and the supermarkets and all the concerns who usually employ college kids through the vacations to change their policy. "Why give work to those privileged college kids?" they said. "Your duty is to give it to the poor underprivileged Negroes." Of course, these liberals—they're mostly Jewish, you know—are really loaded. They think everyone is like them, that every kid going to college is driving his own Corvette Stingray, just like their kids. It never occurs to them that maybe a lot of kids in college came from poor families and have to work hard and spend every penny they make to pay for their education.

Sutton and the visitor were talking in a bar.

> I was in England during the war, and I really miss your beer. Do they still serve it warm? The other day my car was stolen. When the cops got it back, the fender was crumpled, the windshield smashed, the paintwork scratched to hell—$700 worth of damage. The cops got the kids who did it, and they asked me did I want to prosecute. "You're damn right I do," I said, and the cop told me, "Mr. Sutton, you're simply going to waste everyone's time." And you know something? He was right. I

353

went down to the court; I lost a day's pay; and the judge just reads these kids a lecture and gives them a suspended sentence. Two brothers. It was their fourth conviction, and they walked out of court laughing. One of the cops ran out in front of them shouting: "Lock your cars up, everyone; the Murphy's are comin'," and the kids just laughed more than ever. And, before you ask me, let me tell you that they aren't Negroes. The Negroes shouldn't get blamed for everything, but they should get blamed for what they do.

Now let me tell you about my mother. She lives in the city. She's 72 and has lived on the same street down there all her life. She's a widow now, and she goes out to do her bit of shopping. So one day these two Negro punks, just kids, come up and one of them grabs her bag. Well she's a tough old lady, see, so she hangs on and hollers like hell, and the other kid he's got a stick, so he starts hitting her first across the arms and then the head, and she's still hollering, and this is broad daylight—*broad daylight*—and no one comes to help her, and finally she goes down, and they get her bag and run away.

Sutton took a long draught of beer.

She's still in the hospital. We try to get to see her every day. She had a cracked skull and a fractured arm, and she's very slow at getting well. You want to know why? It's not the physical injury; it's the shock. To think that that kind of thing could happen on her street and no one came to help her; she can't get over it. When I said to her, "Mom, it happens all the time in the city; that's why none of us kids live there anymore," she just looks at me.

The visitor asked how Sutton thought Wallace could change any of these undoubtedly bad situations.

Well, Wallace knows how we feel. Don't get me wrong. I'm not against the Negro; he's got to have a fair crack the same as anyone else. And some of the best fellows I work with—best at hard work, I mean—are Negroes. Can't say I'm particularly friendly with them. But they're all right; they give a fair day's labor and all. But in my opinion there's a hell of a lot more who don't want to work, who are happy to live off welfare, and it's my money going to support them.

The real thing is that I'm against discrimination. And you know what the discrimination is today; it's against the working

354

man. All these liberal intellectuals, they don't understand us. What contact do they have with us? We service their cars or paint their houses or sweep their drives, but they never see us.

They've got this great guilt thing about the Negro and integration and all, so *we* have to be forced to do things; *our* children have to be bused to different schools; *we* have to sell our houses to Negroes. They don't because there isn't a Negro in a thousand with the money to buy their kind of houses, and anyway they send their kids to private schools.

Well I'd just like to redress the balance. One law for the Negro *and* the working man *and* the rich liberals. I think Wallace will do that. I think he'll be fair to all. And I think he'll be tough with young hoodlums. The country's gone too far in one direction. It's too liberal, and it's coming apart; we need someone pretty strong to slow it down and hold it together.

Sutton's attitude was no different from that of a dozen other working-class voters who discussed the Wallace appeal. Confused though they seemed about what Wallace could do to ease their frustration, they were desperately seeking someone to express their point of view. Although not all were racist, in the sense of being pathologically anti-Negro, the apparent emphasis on Negro social problems at their expense was steadily increasing their hostility toward Negroes.

So the Wallace drive built up. By the third week in September the polls were giving him between 21 and 22 percent of the vote.

Without organization or any of the complicated machinery of the two traditional parties, the Wallace campaign had simply grown naturally. It was the phenomenon of the election. Hundreds of volunteer workers had collected 2.5 million signatures to put his name on the ballot of every state in the union.* Mail contributions to Wallace headquarters in Montgomery were running at tens of thousands of dollars a week. Wallace posters and buttons were appearing everywhere, and more significant, according to political ob-

---

* A legal battle developed in Ohio. The state constitution was invoked to prevent Wallace's name from being put on the ballot. The matter went to the U.S. Supreme Court, a body that Wallace had repeatedly described as "absurd and ludicrous." The Court decided six to three in favor of Wallace. Justice William O. Douglas pointed out in his opinion that the fifty states tended to think in terms of only two parties, the Republicans and the Democrats. The Constitution, he said, was thus being flouted; a third party, of whatever complexion, had a right to due process under the electoral regulations.

servers, Wallace bumper stickers were no longer appearing only on old cars but on new Fords and Chevrolets as well, which meant that his appeal was spreading steadily upward through the economic strata.

By the end of September his campaign had reached its peak. His plane was hedgehopping from city to city—nerve-racking for him because he did not like to fly and takeoffs and landings made him particularly uneasy. He never hid his fear. On one flight he was talking to the visitor when the plane began to bucket and bump as it hit a pocket of turbulence.

Wallace, who had until then been lively and informative, fell silent and began staring intently out the window. Further questions brought no reply. Eventually he remarked: "Ah'm trying to figgah out the weathah. Ah'll answer yore questions when Ah got the weathah figgered out." The turbulence continued, and the "Please Fasten Seat Belts" sign lit up. Wallace was sunk in thought. Then he went up to the flight deck and talked earnestly with the pilot. It turned out that he had advised him—the pilot was from Alabama —to avoid the dark clouds immediately ahead and to veer right. A few minutes later we found ourselves back in the sunshine. Wallace slapped the visitor triumphantly on the knee. "See?" he cried. "Got y'awl through the weathah."

There was a valid reason for this particular fear. During World War II he had served as a flight engineer on a B-29, "The Sentimental Journey," and had flown combat missions against the Japanese over the Pacific. Of those days he said with his customary candor: "Man, it like to scared me to death. Mah hands would be all sweaty, mah heart thumpin' an' all."

There is nothing wrong with that kind of honesty. In 1963 Senator Wayne Morse of Oregon disclosed on the floor of the Senate that Wallace was receiving a 10 percent disability pension for a psychoneurotic condition resulting from his World War II service. Morse saw fit to quote from a private file that he had obtained from the Veterans Administration, which said:

He was last examined by the V.A. in November 1956 when he gave his age as 37, married, three children and was occupied as a circuit judge. He was tense, restless and ill-at-ease; frequently drummed on the desk with his fingers, changed position frequently; sighed occasionally; showed a tendency to stammer, resulting in a diagnosis of anxiety reaction. The 10 percent rating was continued.

356

To this attack Wallace responded: "I received a 10 percent disability pension for a nervous condition, caused by being shot at by Japanese airplanes and antiaircraft guns in combat missions during World War II. To what does Senator Morse attribute *his* condition?"

The beautifully timed counterthrust was George Wallace's great talent, which is why he was so good at dealing with hecklers. To one bearded hippie dissenter who shouted, "We know you," Wallace replied, "Fine; if you come down here then, I'll autograph your sandal." He used his best lines over and over again—why waste them?—and his audiences loved them. "Now, take it easy *honey*," he would shout to his hippie hecklers. "Oops, it's a he; sorry I thought it was a she."

Wallace scored so well in his verbal battles—it was always the interrupters who lost their tempers—that he welcomed, even encouraged the heckling. His campaign men always carried enough spare tickets to provide anti-Wallace pickets outside meeting halls with passes to get in. Those who entered did so at their own risk. For, despite the hillbilly picnic atmosphere, despite the well-scrubbed faces and the clean collars of the audience, there was always an underlying menace at Wallace meetings. His appeal was to the dark side of American character, and his talent—which was chilling to watch in operation—was in the way he revealed it without unleashing it. Wallace showed in those months that he had at his disposal a social nuclear weapon and that he was the man with the fuse.

In that feverish atmosphere, his critics, white and black, had to run the gauntlet of the crowd, which became increasingly dangerous. At almost every meeting scuffles and fist fights broke out in the audience. Any poster that read, "Let's Not Turn America into a Police State" or "I Laid Down in Front of Wallace's Car and Lived" would barely last a minute before they were seized and ripped to pieces and their carriers set upon. In the end things became so rough that Wallace's opponents were forced to change their tactics, and from this change developed the one original bit of political heckling in the campaign.

The dissenters vanished. In their place appeared groups of clean-cut American kids, all wearing Wallace hats and buttons and carrying placards proclaiming, "This Is Wallace Country; We Love George." As soon as the candidate appeared this "support group" would begin to cheer and stomp and whistle. Then the shouting would begin: "We want Wallace"; "Give us law and order"; and all

357

the other slogans of the American Independent Party. The crowd would pick it up. The candidate would bask in this adulation for a few moments and then raise his arms for silence, but it would not come. The hecklers would continue their shouts of encouragement, determined to drown George Wallace in his own applause.

This technique was the only one that really got to him. He would stand there behind his portable bullet-proof podium, his eyes glittering in supressed fury. "You'd better have your fun *now*," he would shout, "because after November the fifth *you're through*."

His faithful allies, the police, would be ordered to "throw those troublemakers out." But the psychology of the protest was designed to confuse the officers of the law, and it frequently did. It went against their instincts to push around people wearing Wallace campaign badges. And occasionally they made mistakes, as in Youngstown, Ohio, where an American Independent Party steward, equally bedecked with Wallace buttons, was the first man they set upon.

The disruptive effect of this new-style heckling was considerable, and sometimes Wallace would have to wait fifteen minutes or more before he could begin the speech. But still his popularity rose; the polls showed his support remaining steadily above a fifth of the vote. Although he never strayed from his declared strategy of wielding the balance of power, he occasionally allowed himself a pleasurable lapse into fantasy. Things were going so well, he said, that he "figured" that he might capture as many as seventeen states: the whole South, some of the border states, and maybe a couple of the big industrials.

But then the slippage began. After October the polls revealed a steady erosion of Wallace support, as it dropped below 20 percent to 19, 18, 17 percent. What went wrong? Three main factors were operating against Wallace as the campaign entered its last two or three weeks. First, he became the victim of his own inspired choice of law and order as a major theme of his campaign oratory. It was so obviously successful, hitting hard and deep and arousing enormous enthusiasm among his audiences, that both Nixon and Humphrey were forced to adopt it. Wallace thus lost his copyright on the burning issue. There was also the almost inevitable swing away from a third-party candidate as Election Day approached. Supporters began to worry about wasting their votes.

After the election the observer asked Sutton whether or not he had voted for Wallace. He revealed that he had gone for Nixon

358

instead. "I had two reasons," he said. "I began to have doubts about Wallace in late October; he was still saying the same thing, which wasn't very impressive, and then I thought, 'hell, a vote for him is wasted. I've got to stop Humphrey and the liberals.' So I voted Republican for the first time in my life."

The most crucial factor of all was the Vice-Presidential candidate. If Wallace could have succeeded *early on* in attracting to his cause a respected figure for his running mate, it might have made a big difference. To satisfy the law in various states, he had named Marvin Griffin, an elderly segregationist, who had once been Governor of Georgia, as his Vice-Presidential candidate. But this pairing was merely a ruse to get on the ballot. He had decided to announce his real running mate later in the campaign. But how much later? It was not until October 3 that Wallace unveiled the American Independent Party's number-two candidate, former Air Force General Curtis LeMay.

At a Pittsburgh press conference Wallace introduced the General as a "man of peace but a man of courage." LeMay's reputation was hardly a peaceful one. He was a hawk's hawk, a man of clear-cut views who believed that North Vietnam should be bombed "back into the Stone Age," who was known to favor the use of nuclear weapons against America's enemies. His obsession with "nukes" was of Strangelove proportions. No sooner had Wallace introduced him than he began talking compulsively about the bomb: "We seem to have a phobia about nuclear weapons," he declared. "I think most military men feel that a nuclear weapon is just another weapon in our armory. And I think there are many occasions where it would be most efficient to use nuclear weapons."

This message was the last thing Wallace wanted the world to hear, and, as LeMay plunged on, saying that he would "much prefer to be killed by a nuclear bomb than a rusty knife," Wallace tried to bring the proceedings to a swift conclusion. But LeMay was unstoppable. He had seen a film of Bikini Atoll, where nuclear tests had taken place twenty years before, he continued, and everything was fine there now. Even the rats were bigger and fatter. So, although you couldn't *win* a nuclear war, you could certainly survive it.

By then Wallace had grasped that LeMay was potentially as dangerous as one of his much-admired nuclear bombs, and the General was swiftly silenced and led away to the airport. Shortly afterward, he was dispatched on a "fact finding" tour to Vietnam.

Wallace had made a bad choice. General LeMay was a man with a distinguished past, a World War II hero, a controller of the Berlin Airlift, former Commander in Chief of the Strategic Air Command, and former Air Force Chief of Staff. He was thus a figure of truly national proportions, exactly the kind of personality George Wallace needed to give his campaign respectability.

But all these advantages were outweighed by LeMay's frightening reputation as an exponent of nuclear war. In his last year as Air Force chief his reputation as a brilliant general had disintegrated. "He became emotional and fretful," one of his senior colleagues said of him. "He really disqualified himself because of the 'ultimates' he kept on proposing and pressing for."

Opponents of the American Independent Party swiftly recognized the destructive potential in Wallace's Vice-Presidential candidate. New placards appeared, to disturb the faithful: "Vote for Wallace —and the End of the World"; "Wallace *Will* Eliminate Your Problems—And You"; "Bombs Away with Curt LeMay."

In the last weeks before the election General LeMay—a dismal speaker—added nothing to Wallace's campaign and actively lost him votes. Immediately after his candidacy was announced a Gallup poll showed a marked decline in Wallace's popularity among women fearful of the bombing General's influence, and by the end of the month the polls gave him only 15 percent of all votes.

The final thrust of the Wallace campaign came on television; his funds were sufficient for him to invest more than $2 million in air time. He was as good on television as in personal appearances, moderating his performance to that of a friendly community leader at ease in any household. He spoke as he always spoke, clearly. He always expressed himself more lucidly than either Humphrey or Nixon, ignoring the polysyllabic jargon that asphyxiates so many American political speeches.

The rise and fall of third parties was a constantly recurring cycle on the American scene. The Electoral College was in some ways similar to the British parliamentary system, in that third parties had little hope unless they could benefit from a deadlock between the two giants. The chances of such a deadlock were small, and so splinter parties usually rose only to fall.

But George Wallace seemed to have had more impact during his campaign than had any other third party in recent history. It had been an extraordinary campaign—all 70,000 miles of it—conducted on a shoestring, and a frayed shoestring at that. Wallace made no secret that he traveled on the cheap because he liked it that way. He was happier in second-rate hotel rooms, eating the $1.90 chef's special (always drowned in catsup), because he was at home in such surroundings.

The other candidates provided their staffs, their press corps, and themselves with streamlined jets on which the bloody marys never ran out and the sirloin steaks were always hot. Press releases came hourly from the duplicating machines in the staff section, and hand-picked stewardesses were always there to smile and serve.

On Wallace's DC-6 there were no stewardesses and no hot food. Nor was there any drink (Wallace was a teetotaler) or any duplicating machinery. If one was lucky, one might find a doughnut and a bottle of that ubiquitous southern soft drink, Doctor Pepper; but the candidate himself had no more. Flying back to Montgomery in these austere surroundings toward the end of the campaign, Wallace expounded his philosophy. "Money doesn't worry me," he said, and it must not have, for like royalty he never seemed to carry any.

> Not for myself. It's only when it's other people's money and the government is wasting it that I get concerned. Now the people understand that, and they understand me. The polls and the big-time politicians, they don't understand me, and they don't understand the people. That's why we're going to give them a shock come Election Day.

George Wallace had come out of the South—that strange, tragic country that is so different yet so much part of the United States—but he had never left it behind. He had taken it with him everywhere he went because at heart he was a chauvinist. The South was the true America, he told the visitor; southerners were still pure-blooded pioneer stock, still English, Scots, Welsh, and Scots-Irish. The South was not like the North, where the races had mixed to produce a mongrel breed.

Nevertheless in the North he had found a response to his southernism. He told with satisfaction the story of a Polish-American who had come up to him in Wisconsin and had said, "Governor, I've never been farther south than south Milwaukee, but I am a southerner." What Wallace had discovered, he said, was that the whole of America was full of southerners. Nervously the country waited to see whether or not he was right.

.19.

Nixon: Letting the Clock Run Out

THE NIGHT BEFORE THE REPUBLICAN CANDIDATE OFFICIALLY BEGAN HIS
campaign, he did something highly characteristic of the "new
Nixon." He invited the correspondents who would be traveling
with him for the next nine weeks to join him and his staff for
cocktails at the Regency Hotel in New York. It was a good party.
Friendships formed in the dim, distant days of the primaries were
renewed, and anticipation gripped everyone in the room. Much of
this atmosphere was owing to the candidate. He moved from group
to group with gay confidence. He was like a boxer about to enter
the ring in perfect shape. He was the odds-on favorite, and he
intended to act as such.

Among the guests were the flight crews from the two chartered
United Airlines Boeing 727 jets. Nixon's staff had picked the
stewardesses for intelligence as well as looks. The planes were first
class throughout. It was clear that the Nixon press corps would
travel in style. "I am naming these planes *Tricia* and *Julie* in honor
of my daughters," said the candidate, outlining his plans. The

scheme was to cover most of the country, but he would use television much more than before; also, he would be available to talk to the press much more than before. The long feud between Richard Nixon and the fourth estate seemed to be over. "We will have two periods of time off," he continued, showing again how much he had learned since 1960. "We will all need it."

That was true. The campaign that was about to begin would carry the candidate and his entourage more than 50,000 miles into 30 states and 121 cities. The Nixon staff, many times larger than its preconvention size, would have to organize about 10,000 hotel rooms; budget millions of dollars; negotiate with city authorities, police departments, television and radio executives; and at every stop set up a complex communications network for the press, the network men, and the candidate himself.

No European political party had ever been called upon to handle such a complex operation. In Britain party leaders hit the road hard during the general election, but distances are short, and the campaign is over in three weeks. The difference in logistics between these two kinds of campaign is the difference between sending one man on a leisurely poetry-reading tour round the British provinces and flying the British Royal Ballet, complete with orchestra and sets, around the world for a series of one-night stands. Everything depends on timing and keeping to schedules, but the schedules must be realistic. The Nixon team set itself the task of organizing the most efficient political campaign of modern times. When it was over the veterans who had traveled with Nixon admitted that the staff had met and exceeded its objective.

The first stop was Chicago, which showed how luck and instinct combined in Nixon's political planning in 1968. When he had scheduled that city to open the campaign, he had had no idea that he would be arriving a few days after the shambles of the Democratic convention. When he landed at Chicago's Midway Airport, Senator Charles Percy of Illinois waited on the tarmac. "On behalf of Mayor Richard J. Daley, I wish to welcome you to Chicago," Percy said with a smile. The quip was well spoken; the fortunate timing of Nixon's first day's campaigning in the heart of Daley's demoralized fiefdom was too delicious to ignore.

Nixon's reception was fantastic; a half-million people lined the streets to cheer him. There was not a police club in sight. Mayor Daley was involved at that moment in a propaganda campaign to clear the name of the Chicago police and prove that they had merely been defending themselves and the city from virtual revolution the previous week.

That night on the first Nixon television question-and-answer show, the basic format of his campaign in that medium, the topic of Daley, the police, and the Democratic convention naturally came up. Nixon's reply was calm and unsensational. America was a free country, he said, and he welcomed "dissent within limits." He deplored "overreaction from police" anywhere in the world, but he did not "rule out the need for control" on some occasions. He thus neatly said something for everyone.

Or almost everyone. Senators Thruston Morton of Kentucky and Edward Brooke of Massachusetts had been Rockefeller men but had loyally lined up behind Nixon when the convention had selected him. Both were disappointed at his refusal to come down hard on Daley and the Chicago police. Both believed that it was imperative that Republicans not be pushed to the right on the explosive "law and order" issue. Immediately after the telecast, Booke and Morton sat down and drafted a statement expressing a more liberal line on the student demonstrations and a harder line on police brutality. They submitted the draft to the Nixon staff— some members of whom agreed with it—and suggested that the candidate endorse and release it within 48 hours. They would be available for any discussions on the matter, they said.

To their astonishment nothing happened. They were ignored. Morton, talking to the visitor the following day, openly expressed what was later termed the "mini revolt."

"We cannot allow Nixon to be like Dewey, who was afraid to say that the sun was shining in case that might be termed too controversial," he said. "Dewey was sure he had it made and did not want to rock the boat. We fear Nixon too thinks he's got it made, and we're afraid that he won't speak out. That could be disastrous."

Later that week in Houston, Texas, the two senators called a sudden press conference to talk about their "differences" with Nixon. They still supported him but commented, "We are sure the candidate is not going to let the heady wine of being the leader prevent him from being definitive on issues." The conference took a nasty turn as Senator Brooke stood up to face the press. Late the night before a *Vogue* reporter, referring to the fact that he was the only colored member of the Nixon team, had asked him, "What is it like to be the house Negro?" He had dodged the abusive question then. Now it was asked again, in more acceptable terms, as the candidate continually described him as a man who had clawed his way out of the ghetto into the U.S. Senate.

"When I first heard this, I blushed. I do occasionally," said Brooke. "But when I heard him say it again, it did not offend me, and I am a very sensitive man." He had never lived in the ghetto, and his family was comfortably off. Richard Nixon was "only using me as an example of what could be done. However, I don't like being singled out as *the* Negro Senator, any more than Senator Javits would enjoy being singled out as *the* Jewish Senator."

Was he still mad at the candidate's evasiveness? Brooke paused. "I don't think that the candidate should necessarily spell out all the issues in the first week. There are eight weeks to go." He had thus given his warning. He was leaving the way open for Nixon to come to terms with the liberal wing of the party.

American Presidential candidates tended to speak in generalities. They did not say, "If elected we shall nationalize the steel industry," as British politicians do. They were helped in this vagueness by the fact that their platforms were more general than the British equivalent. There were fewer promises to be broken and more room for maneuver if they were elected.

In fact, Nixon was little more evasive than Humphrey or Wallace. He was trying, he told reporters, to chart a sane and reasonable course between the orthodox and impotent liberalism of the former and the radical extremism of the latter. Such a course, though practical and moderate, was hardly spectacular. But the American public, he believed, would not doubt where he stood.

While Richard Nixon remained firmly on middle ground, however, it became clear that Spiro Agnew was capable of plunging in any direction. First, the Vice-Presidential candidate accused the Chicago police of overreacting at the Democratic convention; then a few days later he charged that the riots had been inspired by Communists. Worse was to follow. Within ten days Agnew had managed to send a shudder through older voters by conjuring up some ghosts of American politics. "Hubert Humphrey," said Agnew, "is squishy-soft on Communism." So reminiscent was this phrase of the Joseph McCarthy witch-hunt era that the response was loud and immediate. The joyful Democrats howled that the Republicans were bringing back the smear, proof positive that Richard Nixon had not changed at all.

It was the first Republican mistake of the campaign. But Nixon did not lose his cool. Agnew, he told his staff, had to be straightened out; he would mention it to him, and the Nixon men attached to the Vice-Presidential candidate would *have* to educate him on the niceties of American politics. The first lesson, he added, was how to apologize gracefully. Agnew's teacher was 27-year-old lawyer John Sears. Within 48 hours Agnew had learned. "Had I ever realized what an effect this phrase would have, I would have avoided it like the plague. If I had known that I would be cast as the 'Joe McCarthy of 1968' I would have turned five somersaults. I said 'squishy-soft,' and I am not proud of it."

After the Republican convention, at which he had selected the Maryland Governor to be his running mate, Richard Nixon had put Agnew through a crash course in campaigning at Mission Bay, near San Diego, California. There the campaign strategy had been developed. Nixon, the "elder statesman" would take the "high road," behaving as if he were already President, not deigning to reply to personal attacks and dealing only with the important affairs of state. Agnew would take the smaller towns on his campaign route and would handle the "gut fighting," just as Nixon had done for Dwight Eisenhower in 1952. Agnew had been told that he could be abrasive, but it became obvious that his technique—or lack of it— would have to be kept under control.

"We are in the first stage of our campaign strategy," said William Safire, the New York public-relations man who served as an unpaid adviser on the Nixon staff. "In a nutshell it is the Woodrow Wilson approach, which was 'never murder a man who is about to commit suicide.'"

Two weeks after the campaign began, Nixon found that Humphrey was so far behind in organization, money, and popularity that frontal attack was the wrong strategy. He began publicly to sympathize with Humphrey, saying that it was disgraceful that unruly dissenters had embarked on a campaign to stop him from being heard at public meetings.

Agnew, or "Joe America," as the Republican candidate had taken to calling his running mate, still had his uses. The real threat, Nixon had decided, came not from the demoralized Democrats but from the rampages of George Wallace. Agnew was the perfect weapon to use against the Alabama spoiler. On this point Nixon was correct. Agnew's campaign through many southern and border states blunted Wallace's impact and helped to hold them for the Republicans.

No American campaign seemed complete without an exposé of

one or another of the candidates; in the last week before Election Day the spotlight fell on Agnew. *The New York Times,* which had already endorsed Humphrey for President, questioned Agnew's fitness for the Vice-Presidency. According to the *Times,* Agnew had become a director of the Chesapeake National Bank, thus developing a conflict of interest with his position as Governor and the man in charge of enforcing Maryland's banking laws. Worse, he had joined with a group of wealthy speculators to buy land on the probable approach route to a new bridge, said the *Times,* and then as Governor he had approved the route. Later, because of criticism, he had sold the land.

The exposé did not cause much of a sensation. Agnew angrily accused the *Times* of trying to "smear" him. Nixon came to his defense, declaring that the *Times* story was the lowest form "of gutter politics a great paper can possibly indulge in." The Washington papers and the Baltimore *Sun* also came to Agnew's defense: "In Maryland none of this is a new story or even a big one," said the *Sun.*

The Nixon staff calculated that the *Times* story had won votes for the Republicans. Vast areas of the United States, it said, regarded *The New York Times,* not as the most distinguished newspaper in the country, which it was, but as a foreign and anti-American influence. On moral grounds, Americans seemed quite indifferent to the charges. Whatever Agnew had done or not done, they were hardly surprised. Politicians often had activities on the side; "So what?" was the common attitude. Had any newspaper been able to expose a breath of scandal in a candidate's matrimonial or sexual life, the visitor was assured, the reaction would have been entirely different. It could have cost a man the election. On this point it seemed that the British and American people had virtually opposite points of view. Charges of financial irregularities would have shocked the British, but they would have been more tolerant of disclosures of sexual indiscretions. It must be remembered that in the Profumo case the British cabinet was shocked not that War Minister John Profumo had been sleeping with Christine Keeler but that he had lied about the association to the House of Commons.

Richard Nixon moved easily from city to city, as his superb organization smoothed the way for his ever-growing entourage. A third plane had been added; it had been christened *David* after Julie's fiancé, but it was known to everyone as the *Zoo* because it carried only television technicians and engineers, whom some lordly newspapermen called "the animals."

At each town Nixon was received by neat, decent crowds; he would then make a speech as bland as the food served on his planes. He faced no opposition; the crowds were as polite and respectful during the campaign as they had been during the primaries. The barracking, the crude attempts at heckling that were a feature of this campaign and against the tradition of modern American elections, affected only Wallace and Humphrey. The radical Left seemed disinterested in Richard Nixon.

The campaign was thus so placid as to be almost boring. In Pittsburgh Nixon was asked: "Why are you running such a super-safe campaign? Some of your staff have criticized you for not dealing with issues. How do you answer that?"

For a moment, Nixon bristled. A nerve had been touched. Then he answered in a machine-gun rattle:

> If you gentlemen have read the various statements I have made, I have now to date taken positions, and completely forthright positions, on 167 major issues in this campaign, more than any other candidates in the primaries to the final campaign. I do not play games in a supersafe way. I take risks, just as I took risks in the primaries. I went into every one of them when any one of them might have knocked me out of the box.

It was an extraordinarily precise figure that he had given and seemed to have been chosen at random, or such was the press reaction. But 39 days later, as the campaign entered its last fortnight, every newsman was presented with a well-produced paperback book entitled *Nixon on the Issues*. His staff had done a good job. There in direct quotes were Richard Nixon's views on, not 167, but 227, issues.

In Pittsburgh at the same time as Nixon was his old friend Billy Graham, a nice coincidence. The Nixons were invited to attend Graham's rally that afternoon. They received maximum exposure, for Graham attracted 35,000 people. The Graham organization used the same financial technique that Wallace used, but it made Wallace seem an amateur, which, by Graham's standards, he was. Ushers passed the "plate"—the same white plastic buckets—*before* the service. Beside the collection, each member of the congregation found on his seat a yellow postpaid envelope with an easily detachable stub; it said: "This is a check for spreading the gospel.

Pay to the order of the Billy Graham Evangelistic Association $——."
On the back there was a space for a weekly or monthly pledge of
a sum, to be circled by the donor, of up to $100. The donor was
reminded that "all contributions to the Billy Graham Evangelistic
Association are income tax deductible."

The Nixons entered to respectful, almost worshipful, applause.
The candidate took a bow. He would receive many votes from that
Graham congregation.

The following day he appeared before a very different religious
group, a less friendly one. The Jewish charitable organization B'nai
B'rith was holding its 125th-anniversary convention at the Shoreham
Hotel in Washington. In general the American Jewish vote went
to Democrats, and it was clear when Nixon rose to speak that he
was in hostile territory. He told a suspicious audience, "Order without progress is tyranny; progress without order is anarchy." Then
he made a statement that took some courage before *that* audience:
"For Israel to take final possession of the occupied Arab territories
would be a mistake," he said. Applause was lukewarm.

Outside the Shoreham, Solomon Goldstein was selling sheet
music of a song that he had written, "Richard Nixon; He Is the
Great." The visitor asked Goldstein to sing it and the lyrics, sung
horribly off key and without tempo, rang through the Washington
dusk. On the back page of the sheet music was stamped: "Expert
Piano Tuning and Repairs. Licensed. Fourty [sic] years experience.
Solomon Goldstein." There was at least one American Jew for
Nixon.

At the end of the first week of campaigning, Nixon went back to
New York for a break. A Gallup poll greeted him with the news
that the public had more confidence in the Republicans' ability to
cope with major problems facing America than in the Democrats'—
56 percent to 44 percent. Four years earlier, when Lyndon Johnson
had faced Barry Goldwater, the reverse had been true—62 percent
to 38 percent. Nixon could be happy as he surveyed the situation
from his study on Fifth Avenue. His wife too was happy just to be
back home.

Pat Nixon's back-seat attitude toward politics is more like that of
a British or Continental politician's wife than that of the usual
American polititian's wife. Unlike Jacqueline Kennedy, who sparked
intense social activity; or Lady Bird Johnson, who spoke on issues;
or Muriel Humphrey who traveled in relative discomfort by herself
about 26,000 miles for her husband, Pat Nixon was a silent orna-

ment, ever by her husband's side. She much preferred to be at home.

The fact was that she did not want to move from 810 Fifth Avenue, New York, with its atmosphere of home, to 1600 Pennsylvania Avenue, with the glare of the lights, the probing of reporters. Her husband's shift from $30,000 a year as Vice-President to $250,000 as top man in a New York law firm had meant something to Pat Nixon. She had found in New York since 1962 a social and family stability that had been missing in the earlier turbulent years of her married life. As an American political wife, she had attended rally after rally, day after day, week after week, month after month, year after year. She had sat on platforms of all descriptions in cities and towns of all sizes, with her ankles primly crossed, her hands demurely clasped, and her eyes riveted on her husband as he spoke.

Americans expected their political candidates to take their wives with them wherever they went, in the tradition of togetherness. American political wives were expected to have exactly the same philosophies and views that their husbands had and to expound them on the campaign route like dutiful echoes.

Whatever specific views Pat Nixon had she kept to herself. Early in the campaign she was asked what kind of first lady she thought she would make. She answered: "It would be too presumptuous of me to say. I live from day to day." When asked about her passive campaign role, she said: "I have always campaigned this way. You see I'll always be the same person. I would never change and try to pattern myself after someone else." Her self-control was remarkable, and she rarely allowed an interview to uncover her true feelings. Her defense was to respond to all questions with unrevealing clichés. Occasionally there was an exception.

In midcampaign writer Gloria Steinem sat next to Pat Nixon during a flight from Denver, Colorado, to St. Louis, Missouri, and reported in *New York* Mrs. Nixon's reaction to some probing questions:

> Then the dam broke. Not out of control but low-voiced and resentful, like a long accusation, the words flowed out.
>
> "I never had time to think about things like that—who I wanted to be, or who I admired or to have ideas. I never had time to dream about being anyone else. I had to work. My parents died when I was a teenager and I had to work my way through college. I drove people all the way cross-country so I could get to New York and take training as an X-ray technician so I could work my way through college. I worked

in a bank while Dick was in the service and talked with people and learned about all their funny little customs.

"Now I have friends in all countries of the world. I haven't just sat back and thought of myself or my ideas or what I wanted to do. Oh no, I've stayed interested in people. I've kept working. Right here in the plane I keep this case with me, and the minute I sit down I write my thank you notes. Nobody gets by without a personal note, I don't have time to worry about who I admire or who I identify with, I never had it easy. I'm not like all you . . . all those people who had it easy."

Pat Nixon had learned to live with criticism. A great deal of her share was overspill from the bitterness that her husband had engendered in his early days. Some had been directed at her personally for her public stiffness, her lack of spontaneity, her correct manner, which seemed without warmth or femininity.

The visitor was left with two memories of Pat Nixon gleaned from watching her unobserved. The first was the sight of her fussing with her daughter's clothes in a corridor behind a suburban high-school gymnasium before a rally. Shaking her head, she muttered under her breath, "These girls simply have no clothes because there's so little time to buy them any." The second took place in San Antonio, Texas. The Nixon plane had landed, and its passengers had disembarked; among them was Julie Nixon, who had a temperature of 102 degrees from a throat infection. Her mother, oblivious to everything else, took her into the V.I.P. lounge, where she put her arm around her and sat comforting her daughter. She sat very still and said nothing. She looked rather sad.

Richard Nixon's strength was in organization. Organization required plenty of volunteers and money. The Republicans had both. The grass-roots foundation of the Nixon campaign was the United Citizens for Nixon-Agnew, a political association outside the regular party conceived, established, and disbanded inside 100 days.

One wondered whether or not a politician of any other nation would be capable of creating a perfectly coordinated 5 million-member machine in such a short time. Almost certainly not. U.C.N.A. was a uniquely American concept, which could have been realized only by American drive and efficiency. From a tiny nucleus of organizers in each state, U.C.N.A. reached a membership of more than 2 million by the end of August and its target of 5 million by the end of September.

It thrived on a curious mixture of brilliant improvisation and precise computer planning. By the end of September headquarters had been established in the empty shell of the nostalgic Willard Hotel in Washington. The hotel, which had fallen on bad times and had lost $1.25 million since 1965, had closed down on virtually an hour's notice. It was a sad ending to a great history. Carl Sandburg once wrote, "Willard's Hotel more justly could be called the center of Washington than either the Capitol or the White House or the State Department." Lincoln lived there before his inauguration in 1861 and General Ulysses S. Grant often occupied a strategic position in the dimly lit lobby while he was President. Julia Ward Howe wrote "The Battle Hymn of the Republic" in her room there, and it was at the hotel tobacconist that Woodrow Wilson's Vice-President, Thomas R. Marshall, angrily uttered the immortal "What this country needs is a good 5-cent cigar."

The twelve-story Willard was perfect in location and size for the headquarters of the U.C.N.A.; the group arranged to use it for the price of heating, electricity, and water taxes. By October 700 full-time workers, assisted by twice as many volunteers, had lent the Willard an air of activity such as it had not seen in decades.

The people running U.C.N.A. were like Nixon workers everywhere: cool and businesslike. Pipe smokers appeared to outnumber cigarette users. These people always paused thoughtfully before answering questions, and they did not always agree with positions taken by the candidate. The hallmark of the 1968 Republican worker was that he had a mind of his own.

Charles Sylvanus Rhyne, a former classmate of Nixon's from Duke University, was chairman of U.C.N.A.; his national director was John Warner, a handsome 41-year-old Washington lawyer. The air of purpose that pervaded the whole organization was exemplified in these two executives. "There's not a man in this building who is a full-time politician," said Warner. "No Salingers, no Sorensens. No, they are just ordinary and in most cases successful Americans who don't make news. They just get on with the job."

A volunteer came in to show Warner a newly designed poster with the Republican slogan "Nixon's the One" on it. "Print 5 million," ordered Warner, "and get them moving. Time's running out."

He showed the visitor a colored postcard of Nixon playing the piano as his wife, his daughters, and David Eisenhower looked on:

> Seven million of these are going out this week to people who have shown a personal interest in the candidate. What does that picture say? It says that the Nixons are a tightly

knit family group with youth on their side, capable of re-laxed self-confidence. That picture is the complete message. We have exceeded 5 million volunteers. Their names and addresses are all on tape. We have tied up computers all over this country processing our mailing lists. In addition, we have several million people, who, while not active members, are in-terested in the candidate. There has never been anything like this before.

U.C.N.A.'s biggest contribution to the Republican campaign and, incidentally, to the computerization of politics was the "listening post" project. Seven hundred portable recording booths, which were set up in fresh positions daily throughout America, made it possible for citizens to speak to Richard Nixon "personally." In fact they tape-recorded their messages to him, giving their names and ad-dresses at the end. The tapes—45 miles of them—were flown to Washington daily. As each message was transcribed, the gist of it was encoded on a punch card. This card then went to a letter-writing computer, programmed with 67 Nixon paragraphs on the major issues. Many of these paragraphs overlapped, expressing subtle shades of difference. There were twelve on Vietnam, for example. The computer would analyze the coding and then compose the best six-paragraph letter within its range.

The operation was totally American: slick, custom-tailored, im-pressive. It gave excellent value at a production cost of 20 cents a letter. Taking a copy from one computer, Warner handed it to the visitor, and suggested that he wet his finger and rub it across the signature "Richard M. Nixon." The visitor did so, and the signature smudged.

"Neat, isn't it?" said Warner. "A lot of people do that to see if the signature is printed or written by hand. Our computer has developed a technique which is exactly the same as if each letter *were* signed in ink by the candidate. It's impossible to tell the difference."

Rhyne was the man behind the computers. Before he joined U.C.N.A. he had worked feeding legal information into memory banks for swift reference; he published a monthly magazine, *Law and Computer Technology.* In his view, it was no longer possible to run a competent political campaign without computers. "It is the only efficient way of knowing the swing of the issues," he said. To demonstrate, he invited the visitor to "the war room." It was a windowless area in which nine U.C.N.A. workers kept up to date the trends of public interest. An analysis of the tapes from the "listening posts" would produce a daily digest of major topics both nationally and area by area for "the war room."

This digest would be compared with latest statistics from opinion polls and with what the opposition candidates were saying. A Republican official could thus tell at a glance that the Democrats were gaining in opinion pools in, say, Iowa because they were campaigning for a new highway that was of major concern to the Iowans.

The four walls were covered with charts. The charts were covered with lines and flags. A set of interlocking glass panels could be superimposed to provide more complex information. One chart showed the "key issues" and how they shifted. By the end of October law and order had slipped below Vietnam, as the chances for peace talks rose. Word went out immediately to Nixon strategists and to U.C.N.A. state chairmen that Vietnam was a more suitable topic for emphasis.

"The war room is invaluable as a statistical backstop, where errors in editorials or in the official polls can be detected and corrected before damage is done," said Gay Fletcher, who was in charge of it.

Away from this electronic brain center, in the towns and suburbs and villages of America, the citizens worked in a more traditional manner, putting posters in their windows and stickers on their car bumpers, calling on their neighbors with literature, and always raising money.

Locally, U.C.N.A. was organized into clubs to cover specific areas and specific professions.

"A club is nothing more than a vehicle for people who don't wish to be formally affiliated to a party. There are even a lot of Republicans who don't want to be known as politically active," said Biehl Clarke, the club organizer. It was a natural American instinct to form clubs and join them, he explained:

> De Tocqueville pointed out that the essence of America was the people's voluntary nature. But it's dying, you know; fewer and fewer people are joining organizations today.
>
> Despite the fact that we've got the biggest voluntary political organization ever going here, it took a lot of setting up.
>
> We are running across many people who, rather than set up a club on their own, think they have to have permission first. We tell them: "You are free Americans. Set up your own club. You don't need permission." Then we help them all we can.

374

Fortified by this superb organization, unlimited funds, and determination never to go down into the arena to debate with Humphrey, Nixon conducted a campaign whose pace and flavor hardly varied. The visitor found the stops blending in a repetitive blur. In each town—and American towns could look so much alike—the routine was the same. There were the same speech, the same kind of young girls organized by U.C.N.A., the same kind of policemen with telescopic rifles on the same kind of rooftops.

Humphrey was moving up fast in the polls, but the Nixon strategy did not change. Nixon concentrated on winning all the states that he had won in 1960 plus at least two more big ones like Texas and Illinois. Nixon was still untroubled by hecklers and was supplementing his television appearances with coast-to-coast radio broadcasts costing $4,000 for fifteen minutes. A final television blitz was planned for the last week, and $2 million were put aside to finance it.

Everything went as planned. But, as that last week arrived, Republican nerves began to fray. The workers braced themselves for a last-minute shock, which came in the announcement by the President of a complete bombing halt in North Vietnam—what American doves had been crying for all year.

The announcement sent a chill through Nixon's camp. In the days preceding it there had been much discussion of how much harm it could do to the Republican candidate. Pessimists feared that it would cost him the election. Afterward some Nixon people suggested that, had the bombing halt come 48 hours later, on November 2, it would have won the election for the Democrats. Either Johnson mistimed it, or it was just coincidence, they said.

Was the announcement a political move? In the Nixon camp everyone thought so. "*Anything* that Johnson does is political," said one Nixon man, "and he has timed this to give Humphrey that last-minute surge."

Robert Finch of California formally charged that the bombing halt was politically inspired and made headlines across the nation. But before the press runs had finished, the candidate, aloof and dignified, denied having entertained such thoughts about the President's action. The Republicans thus had the best of both worlds. A seed of doubt had been sown in the public's mind, yet Richard Nixon's patriotism and dignity remained publicly unsullied. He had kept his cool to the end.

.20.

HUMPHREY: SOME TALK CHANGE

HUBERT HUMPHREY STARTED HIS CAMPAIGN WITH HANDICAPS. CHICAGO had left scars in the defection of the young liberals. In the field he was hamstrung by the broken-down and demoralized Democratic machine. And psychologically he was crippled by his loyalty to and dependence on the President, who still maintained his self-imposed exile in Texas. In addition, the Democratic candidate had literally no time to organize himself before he went on the road. One can see why Richard Nixon was so confident.

Yet, from this abyss of disorganization and despair, Hubert Humphrey pulled himself and his party back into the race and came close to winning the biggest political upset America had seen in decades. To see this remarkable comeback in perspective one must examine in detail the problems facing the Democrats at the beginning of the campaign. First, there was the possibility that a fourth party would be formed by McCarthy dissenters enraged at the events in Chicago. It's establishment would finish Humphrey before he began. Second, the labor vote, traditionally Democratic, was, according to the polls, going to Wallace. It had to be brought back but without resort to the appeal that many experts believed counted most among blue-collar Americans: the veiled racism of George Wallace. American Negroes were watching Humphrey closely; any suggestion that he might be moving to the right in his efforts to regain the labor vote would have resulted in immediate withdrawal of Negro support.

Third, the party had no money. On the night that Richard Nixon was nominated, Republican National Committee Chairman Ray Bliss presented him with $1 million for his campaign. On the day after Hubert Humphrey was nominated, he was told that the Democratic Party not only had no campaign funds but was also more than $100,000 in debt. Finally, Humphrey, as Vice-President, was identified with an administration and a war that were not only extremely unpopular among the American people but also violently opposed within his own party. Somehow the candidate had to break with the President's policies without seeming to betray him.

The man who assisted Humphrey in overcoming these almost insurmountable obstacles one by one was Larry O'Brien, the former Kennedy aide who had remained in the Johnson Cabinet as Postmaster General until resigning to run Robert Kennedy's campaign. After the assassination O'Brien had eventually agreed to assist Humphrey. In Chicago he had consented to run the campaign and to take the job as Democratic National Committee Chairman until the election was over.

The first postconvention strategy session between O'Brien and Humphrey was devoted to the risk of massive defections from the party. O'Brien did not think that McCarthy would attempt to run as a fourth-party candidate; he was right, for at that moment the Minnesota Senator was taking legal action to prevent overenthusiastic supporters from putting his name on the Presidential ballot. But O'Brien *was* afraid that McCarthy would sit the whole election out.

McCarthy's organization had many useful elements that were lacking in the regular Democratic machine, which was run-down and incompetent. His supporters had experience at improvising, enthusiasm, and drive. It was essential to harness these qualities to the main Democratic campaign, said O'Brien. The one way to do so was to obtain McCarthy's endorsement.

Serious attempts had been made to persuade McCarthy to close the ranks in the traditional way at Chicago, but he had contemptuously rejected them. And, when his antiwar rival George McGovern had told him that he was "going to fall in behind Hubert," Mc-Carthy's reply was withering. He did not believe in "betrayal," he said. McCarthy had then been approached by such diverse figures as cartoonist Jules Feiffer, former Robert Kennedy speech writer Adam Walinsky, actor Paul Newman, and writer Gore Vidal all with one idea: to form a fourth party. But he had rejected their suggestions too.

McCarthy left Chicago as if his whole Presidential effort had been an academic exercise, but his unemotional veneer hid bitter and petulant disappointment. O'Brien had sensed his mood well. The risk to Humphrey was that McCarthy would sit out the campaign and that his supporters would follow suit.

The Minnesota Senator left the United States in mid-September. He needed a vacation, he said, and he also wanted to think. He chose France out of season as a civilized site for both pursuits. Through his campaign manager, Blair Clark, he found lodgings at the Auberge Le Mas des Serres, below the old mountain village of St.-Pol-de-Vence. There, dining on the vine-shaded terrace or lounging in the Riviera sunshine, McCarthy relaxed and reviewed for the visitor his own part in the astonishing turmoil of the Democratic Party that year.

He told a story, which he had previously kept to himself, that he believed might explain his attitude. There was a time, he said, just before Primary Day in New Hampshire when he had glimpsed the possibility of success. It was slim, but he had realized for the first time the real depth of feeling against the war and the administration and, among the young, the dissatisfaction with old, tired party politics. He believed that it was vital that this new coalition not be fragmented before it could be truly established. Accordingly, he had telephoned Robert Kennedy and had asked to see him. The meeting had taken place in Edward Kennedy's Washington office just a few days before the New Hampshire vote.

There McCarthy explained his feelings. He recalled: "I said to Kennedy: 'I think I have a chance. But I must have a clear run. You can have it all in 1972. I pledge my support for that, but in return I want you to leave it to me in 1968. Will you give me that clear run?' "

And, according to McCarthy, Kennedy had replied that he would: "I tell you what I am telling everyone. I shall not run. You can count on it." McCarthy had thanked him and repeated that, whatever happened, he would support a Kennedy effort in 1972. Ken-

378

nedy had asked some desultory questions about New Hampshire, and the brief meeting had ended. McCarthy had flown back to New Hampshire elated. His mood had been further enhanced by his astonishing performance there—only to be shattered by Kennedy's reversal and announcement of his own candidacy.

From that moment, whatever chance I had was written off. I knew it the day he announced. The game was over, for me and for him. It could not be either of us.

I do not think that he would ever have voted for me had I defeated him, nor do I think that I and my supporters could have voted for him. So, had he lived, the antiadministration movement would have remained divided to the end. Thus his entrance into the campaign meant that the Democratic candidate had to be Johnson or Humphrey.

When he died, I knew it would turn out exactly as it did. You see, the Kennedy camp was very different from ours. About one-third of Bobby's people were with him because they really cared about the issues. The others were there because they were seeking power in the style of old-fashioned politics. When Bobby was killed, they refused to throw in their lot with us. They preferred to return to the old party loyalties, the old party groupings. That changed everything for me.

If he had not been killed, we could, between us, have controlled the party platform. On the Vietnam issue our joint delegate strengths, I know, would have carried the minority plank. The nominee would have almost certainly been Humphrey, since neither Bobby nor I would have agreed to support the other. But it would have been a Humphrey nominated on a very different platform.

That was the reason why, in Chicago, I tried to bring Teddy in. It was the last chance of rallying the Kennedy strength and winning the platform fight over Vietnam.

McCarthy, his face immobile, let his mind wander back over the year. "It is enigmatic to reflect," he said at last, "how one decision can alter so many things. Had Bobby Kennedy stuck to his word, not only would he almost certainly be alive today but most probably he would have emerged as President of the United States in 1972."

But all that was in the past. What would McCarthy do now? Was he content to remain on the sidelines and watch the victory go to Nixon? Back in the United States Humphrey desperately needed

379

his endorsement. Surely he had to give that endorsement or withhold it and start a fourth party. Merely to opt out would be unworthy. McCarthy reluctantly conceded the point. There would be no new party, as far as he was concerned. Not during this election anyway. He would go back to America before Election Day, and he would endorse Humphrey. "After all, he *is* a liberal you know," he said bitterly.

The visitor said that the prospective endorsement sounded rather grudging. McCarthy answered that it need not be. If Humphrey would dissociate himself from the President's Vietnam policy everything would alter; he would receive McCarthy's endorsement at once. If Humphrey was worried about gaining support from the young, McCarthy went on, the solution was the same. He leaned forward: "Let him break away from the White House war policy. Let him renounce the bombing."

McCarthy's pride and integrity thus mingled in steely unforgiveness. He was not, as the kids thought, merely cool; he was cold, implacable. His terms were conveyed to Humphrey, who seriously considered them. The pressure on the Democratic candidate to break with the President began to mount, but Humphrey was the opposite of McCarthy in almost every way. He was a warm man, emotional, excitable, and loyal. He refused to renounce the President publicly. Lyndon Johnson had suffered greatly during his term of office, and Humphrey would not betray him.

The pressure increased. O'Brien thought that it was "essential" for Humphrey to show his independence from the White House. Joe Napolitan, Humphrey's director of advertising, insisted not only that the candidate break with Johnson but also that he do it in a very dramatic way. "By that I mean that you must resign as Vice-President," said Napolitan.

Humphrey's reply was in character, sincere yet pompous: "That I will not do. I have a contract with the American people, and I will not break it."

Although Humphrey's loyalty helped to hold him back, there were two other reasons for his refusal to break with the President. To understand them, we must examine the activities of President Johnson since April.

The President did not abandon his people, even though he may justifiably have felt that they had abandoned him. All through the summer he worked for an accommodation on Vietnam. Humphrey was aware of this Presidential effort, although he had not been given the full details. He was aware, too, that, if the President succeeded, he himself would be the major political beneficiary.

The President's first move was to try to secure a meeting with the Kremlin. He almost succeeded. Five days before the opening of the Democratic convention the White House alerted senior correspondents to the possibility of a special briefing. That briefing was to have included an announcement of a "summit meeting" between Johnson and Alexei Kosygin. But plans for the summit—and the briefing—were canceled abruptly at the news of the Soviet takeover of Czechoslovakia. A minor casualty of the Czech tragedy was President Johnson's personal plans, for the summit meeting was to have led to a triumphant birthday appearance at the Democratic convention.

In September the President turned his attention once again to the lagging peace talks in Paris. If Hanoi's representatives would give certain guarantees—to cease military activities in the demilitarized zone, to halt attacks on the southern cities, and to participate in "meaningful" discussions—then the bombing would stop, he said. A tiny gleam of cooperation shone through the implacable Oriental front, and at the beginning of October chief American negotiator Averell Harriman reported to the White House that for the first time the talks looked as if they might move forward.

To break with the President in light of this possibility would be not only disloyal but also disastrous, Humphrey argued. He might say something about the bombing, in view of what was going on, but he would not resign as Vice-President.

There was a second reason. Lyndon Johnson might have sunk to an all-time low in the popularity polls, but he still carried weight with party professionals, conditioned as they were to obeying their leader. Humphrey badly needed their support, and Johnson was the man who could deliver it. Johnson's influence was essential if Humphrey's strategy was to succeed.

That strategy called for capturing the eastern industrial states—New York, Massachussetts, Pennsylvania, and New Jersey—for a total of 103 electoral votes. He would also have to take the three big midwestern industrial states, Michigan, Ohio, and Illinois, for another 73. He could count on his own state, Minnesota, to bring the total to 186; Muskie would deliver Maine for 190. Democratic West Virginia would raise the total to 197. The final necessity was to take California with 40 votes and Texas with 25, bringing the Democrats to within 8 votes of the necessary 270. The extra votes could come from the border or even the South, where it was hoped that Nixon and Wallace would cancel each other out.

Such was the strategy, but its application was another matter. Texas and California were also key states in the Republican plan, and obviously both were going to be bloody battlegrounds. To win, the Democrats needed at least a unified party machine, yet the organizations in both those states were bitterly divided. Only one man could start the wheels moving: Lyndon Baines Johnson.

Texas was the first problem. Proud, suspicious, susceptible, it was ripe for George Wallace. Democratic Governor John Connally, an arrogantly handsome conservative, had been feuding for years with liberal Democratic Senator Ralph Yarborough. There were no feuds quite like Texas political feuds. In 1963 President John F. Kennedy had journeyed to Dallas to attempt to heal the party breach, and there he had died. Even that tragedy had failed to mend things. Now Connally, still angry at the convention's decision to abolish unit rule, was sulking in the Governor's mansion. Yarborough and his friends, all McCarthy supporters, refused to assist Humphrey in any way.

While United Citizens for Nixon-Agnew moved through the state picking up membership and drowning the area in Republican posters, speakers, and literature, Humphrey's Texas propaganda at the beginning of the campaign was entirely in the hands of one sixteen-year-old boy. All the Humphrey literature was mailed to Tom Prentice, a Dallas high-school boy, who, with the help of friends, redirected it around the state. "I think the McCarthy kids showed what amateurs could do," said young Prentice. "And I feel we're not doing too badly here. It's really up to us kids because the adults are afraid to stick their noses out for fear of getting smudge on them, which could affect their political record." Eventually O'Brien set the professionals to work, but he could not bring the party leaders around. When Humphrey arrived in Texas, he was contemptuously ignored by Connally.

The first phase of the Democratic campaign showed no sign of any resurgence. Preoccupied with the problems of dissociating from the President's Vietnam policy without betraying the President himself, Humphrey could not hit his stride. All the impressive "American" traits that the visitor had observed in the Republican campaign—streamlined organization, split-second schedules, superb backup by computers—were absent from the confused Democratic effort. The candidate was always late. His staff was never quite sure what was happening. Information was never ready when it was needed. Minor things went wrong. The whole campaign was rather British in character. Humphrey muddled through.

One positive feature of the first month of Democratic campaigning was the impact of Edmund Muskie. The Maine Senator had been selected as Democratic running mate because of his sectional appeal as, in part, Spiro Agnew had been selected by the Republicans. But though Agnew revealed himself as a liability, Muskie swiftly proved a considerable asset. His dry, relaxed, natural style appealed to the American people.

Muskie had a very simple approach to campaigning. He told his own story, which was extremely effective because it revealed more about the strength and greatness of America and its people than did all the words of the highly skilled speech writers attached to both camps. Muskie, in his New England voice, told how a young tailor's apprentice named Stephen Marciszweski had fled from Poland to escape Czarist tyranny and had made his way to America. He told how American officials, as they had done countless times, had anglicized the immigrant's Slavic name at the port of entry and how Steve Muskie had learned English and finally settled in the northernmost part of New England, where he had been accepted and where his son had grown up, attended college, and become first a lawyer, then Governor, and finally Senator. That was the personal history lesson that Senator Muskie delivered to his audiences.

All his techniques were very simple. He evaded the shadow of Lyndon Johnson by making no mention of the President in his speeches. On the bombing issue he ignored specifics and said only that the Democrats would end the war more quickly than the Republicans. He could handle with simple dignity topics that were embarrassing to the Vice-President. Muskie concentrated on the theme of trust:

> Lack of trust in each other is the greatest single threat to America. We bet on horses, yet we will not take chances on people. Certainly at this time there is no way of reconciling the people by government action or executive order. The American people, with all the distances separating them, with all their different sorts of faces and different colors, their different educational and social backgrounds, must learn to trust each other. For without this trust our society won't work.

383

Muskie was most effective in dealing with hecklers. "You want the microphone? You can have it," he would say. He would let the hecklers speak, and they would grant him the same favor. As time passed, Muskie came to be interrupted hardly at all.

The same could not be said of Humphrey. In the primaries, the visitor had noticed how quiet and well-behaved American political audiences were. The traditional British art of heckling—in which the audience attempts with superior wit and knowledge to embarrass the speaker—was unknown in the United States. But in 1968 the country produced its own form of heckling, which involved none of the tolerant give-and-take of British political repartee.

The object was not to score points but to shout the speaker down, and the major victim was Hubert Humphrey. Everywhere he went he was met by groups of unruly young opponents, whose sole aim was to drown whatever he had to say in a torrent of abuse. At meeting after meeting the Democratic candidate would rise to be greeted by chants of "Dump the Hump, Dump the Hump."

Humphrey would look round the auditorium, attempt a trembling smile, and raise his hands. This gesture would provoke screams of fury punctuated by shouts of "Fascist pig," "murderer," and "child killer." Humphrey was as indecisive in dealing with his tormentors as he was in other aspects of his campaign. He tried appeals: "Now, my friends, you've had your say; let me speak now." He tried countershouts: "Your actions are going to disgust the American people." He tried ridicule: "Did you ever see such nonsense in all your life? Now let's just laugh them out of our hair. Haha, hahaha."

None of these devices was effective and, as the weeks passed, the interrupters became bolder and Humphrey more easily rattled. In the end it was the hecklers' excesses that brought about the turning point in his campaign. Humphrey arrived in Seattle on September 31. He was extremely tense. His staff was worried because early reports suggested that the barracking at the rally to be held in Seattle's Center Arena would be worse than usual. It was. The object of the radical-Left campaign against Humphrey was to stop the meetings before they began and to vilify the candidate in every way. The dissenters saw Humphrey as an extension of the President and sought to identify him with the President's policies and errors.

As soon as Humphrey walked into the hall the chanting began, amplified through electric bullhorns: "Murderer! Fascist! War Lover!" As he took the rostrum, the noise increased.

384

Humphrey waited. The uproar continued. He tried an appeal: Now, let's all settle down." The noise drowned him out. Only then did he finally become angry: "Knock it off!" he shouted. "Shut up!"

The howling increased. Some minutes went by without Humphrey's being able to speak, and the atmosphere in the hall was so charged that the Secret Service official in charge of the detail attached to the Vice-President approached him saying: "We've got to get these people out. We need an order from you, sir."

Humphrey gave the order. "Tell the police to evict them," he said. As fighting and scuffling broke out, Humphrey waited angrily. Finally, he raised his hands and said, "Let us get on with it." He spoke then about the need for increased social-security benefits, about the economy, about racial harmony. It was a good speech, but it was hardly mentioned in the news reports. The dissidents had achieved their objective of obscuring Humphrey's words and gaining publicity for themselves.

But that was the end. That night Humphrey discussed the matter with his staff. Perhaps he should not have become so angry, he said; the publicity had not been good. But he had had enough. The dissidents who hounded him from meeting to meeting were not young idealist. Their ideas were totalitarian. They had contempt for the democratic process. They used the same street-power tactics that had brought Adolf Hitler to power, and Humphrey was not going to take any more.

The next day, in a national telecast from Salt Lake City, Utah, Humphrey gently cut the umbilical chord to the White House.

As President, I would stop the bombing of the North as an acceptable risk for peace because I believe it could lead to success in the negotiations and thereby stop the war. This would be the best protection for our troops. In weighing that risk—and before taking action—I would place key importance on evidence, direct or indirect, by deed or word, of Communist willingness to restore the demilitarized zone between North and South Vietnam.

The surgery was skillfully done. Humphrey had not moved far from the President's line. He had, like Johnson, made a bombing halt conditional upon Hanoi's showing some sign of cooperation. But the way that he spoke had impact. Humphrey had recovered his political skill; he had said something that had different shades of meaning to different groups and had satisfied them all.

From that moment, the Humphrey campaign hit its stride. Confidence was regained; the pace increased; the machinery meshed; and the Democrats began to close the gap. McCarthy supporters began to drift back into the fight singly and in groups—and finally in organized bodies. All over the country the remnants of the McCarthy crusade began to reform under the title "McCarthy Supporters for Humphrey-Muskie." Two distinguished doves, George Ball and Arthur Goldberg, both former U.S. Ambassadors to the United Nations, began actively to campaign for the Vice-President and, in doing so, brought in more doves who had previously been holding back.

With them came money. The problem for the Democrats had been not only how to raise funds but also how to raise them *in time*. The money was needed in early October, but O'Brien and Humphrey knew from experience that it probably would flood in only in the last week when it would be virtually useless, for then it would be too late to spend it on productive television and radio spots. Democratic Party Treasurer Robert Short solved this problem by raising a number of short-term loans from party angels.

"Let us have the money now, when we need it," said Short "and we will be in a position to repay it after the election is over." In this way, he raised more than $10 million, mostly in loans of six figures.*

The money came exactly when it was needed, for the tactics of the campaign had at last been established. The candidate would cease trying to debate issues and would go over to all-out attack on Nixon personally, on his fitness to lead the American people. The constant reiteration of this question, it was hoped, would produce a double dividend. First, it might rattle Nixon sufficiently to dissolve the blandness and bring out the "gut" fighter. Second, the chilling thought of their old enemy within a footstep of the White House would certainly bring back all those doubtful Democrats who were still sitting out the campaign.

The man who planned these tactics was Joe Napolitan former public-relations partner of O'Brien turned professional campaign manager. This profession has not yet been developed in Britain.†

---

* The Democrats ended the campaign $6 million in debt. The money was owed to fewer than thirty wealthy supporters, according to Short. It was estimated that it might take two years to raise sufficient funds to repay them.

† After the election Napolitan was instrumental in forming the first professional association of political-campaign organizers—The International Association of Political Campaign Consultants.

Napolitan offered a complete service to men of political ambition as long as he approved of them. "I only work for Democrats," he said.

His method was to move in with a staff, organize polls, analyze them, direct the candidate to the main issues, organize meetings, write speeches, produce campaign literature, book television and radio time, and make political commercials. For these services he charged a five-figure fee.

O'Brien had brought Napolitan into the Democratic organization to take charge of television advertising. There was no limit on the amount of time or space that a political party could buy on American television during an election campaign, provided that it had the money. Political advertising was not banned, as it is in Britain, nor did any government body apply the equal-time rule to paid party advertising, as it does in Britain.

Napolitan budgeted some $4 million for television, which he decided to concentrate in the last month of the campaign. The commercials would concentrate on the question of Nixon's ability to be President and secondarily would project Humphrey as a dynamic yet humane man who was fit for the job. The first tactic was successful, but the second failed.

Ridicule was used to attack the Republicans' weakest spot, Spiro Agnew. One of the first and most effective Democratic commercials showed the words "Spiro Agnew for Vice-President?" for twenty seconds against a sound track of hysterical laughter. Then the message changed to "This would be serious if it weren't so funny."

Napolitan also controlled the Democrats' newspaper advertising, which was much superior to that of the Republicans. "Where Does Nixon Stand on Education?" was the headline of one layout; the answer was "In the back of the bus with Thurmond." Another devastating Democratic headline appeared in newspaper advertising across the country. It said simply, "Nixon's the One—To Beat."

Napolitan called in Tony Schwartz, brilliant commercial-television director and consultant in auditory perception at Fordham University, to make the commercials and biographical producer Shelby Storck to project Humphrey's image. Storck was a believer in the ability of film to capture the essence of personality. He would shoot hundreds of thousands of feet of film to make a one-minute commercial, but that commercial would reveal the truth of its subject, he believed.

He assigned two camera crews to Humphrey with orders to keep their lenses trained on him at all times. Later, ankle-deep in film, Storck would splice together shots of what he considered the essential Humphrey. The resulting film biography *What Manner of Man?* came to the television screen in time to aid the Democratic upswing, and it was believed to have helped Humphrey considerably.

Some of the film showed Humphrey talking about his retarded and obviously much-loved granddaughter Vicky Solomonson. The subject was delicate and perhaps illustrated an essential difference between British and American politicians. In Britain a politician's personal life is kept out of the campaign. To the visitor, the sight of Humphrey talking about his grandchild's misfortune was distasteful and embarrassing.

Americans were more natural when they talked to children in general than the British are. Some argued that they liked children more than the British do. Perhaps. But it often seemed that, when Americans talked *about* children, they found it difficult not to be sentimental or even mawkish.

Hubert Humphrey frequently drew attention to his granddaughter, who had been born with a disease called Down's Syndrome. He spoke with sincerity, and tears usually came to his eyes. "Why, I have learned more about the goodness of other people through her eyes than I could have learned in a century otherwise. To me Vicky is the greatest spiritual experience I have had in my life." Had Humphrey been campaigning in Britain, the use of Vicky might well have lost him many votes. Presumably Americans reacted differently, for he spoke of her often.

One of the best campaigners in the Democratic Party was the candidate's wife. Unlike Pat Nixon, Muriel Humphrey did not remain at her husband's side. She went off on a 26,000-mile solo swing, speaking in thirty cities. Republicans uncharitably claimed that she did so to escape the nightly agony of listening to her husband's nonstop monologues. But Muriel Humphrey was a good political operator in her own right.

One day she attended a rally of the Amalgamated Clothing Workers in Baltimore. Mrs. Humphrey was late for her next meeting but showed no sign of impatience as the ritual of a typical American union political rally began. First came a ten-minute harangue against the Republicans. Then everyone stood for the union anthem, sung to the tune of "The Battle Hymn of the Republic."

> Our Amalgamated Union is fulfilling destiny
> We're glad of it, we're proud of it,

She's making history
Her star of hope shines brightly in
The economic sky
Amalgamated ever more we cry.

Mrs. Humphrey never blinked, but some of her staff wore glazed expressions as 350 souls swept into the chorus:

Glory! Glory! Amalgamated!
Glory! Glory! Amalgamated!
Glory! Glory! Amalgamated!
We'll stick until we win.

Mrs. Humphrey's speeches, most of which she wrote herself, were never slipshod. Deep in potential Wallace territory, she put over a message of tolerance and understanding with understated skill:

Just a week ago, in Detroit, I had the opportunity to tour Wayne County Juvenile Home. The building itself is modern and clean. It is also overcrowded. And the dominant impression is of sad, confused, homesick youngsters adrift in a society they neither like nor understand.

I talked with some girls, aged eleven to seventeen. I didn't know, of course, what unhappy home situations they had left behind or what law they had broken. I do know they were pale, forlorn, dejected. One girl about fourteen years old sobbed when I came near her, and I held her in my arms and tried to comfort her.

I went into a classroom of young boys. I asked them some questions, and they had some for me. And one boy with a sad smile asked, "If Mr. Humphrey is elected President, will he help me get out of here?" And I told him that the Vice-President would help him but that first he would have to help himself by studying hard.

I am telling you about these youngsters because they are very much an issue in this campaign. They come under that broad topic law and order we hear so much about.

You want law and order. So do I. So does Hubert Humphrey.

But, beyond that slogan, just what are we talking about? Better-trained and better-equipped police, certainly. More court officials and speedier trials, certainly.

That is part of the answer but only part of it. We shall not have a law-abiding society until we get at the causes of delinquency in Detroit, in Baltimore and every city and town in this nation.

389

That is why we Democrats do not view law and order as a simple matter of massive repression. That is why we Democrats do believe in strong Federal support for education at all grade levels from Head Start for preschool toddlers to loans for college students.

The speech went over well. Muriel Humphrey made government aid sound respectable.

Gradually the unions were growing more favorable. Local revolts against the national leadership's endorsement of Humphrey were fizzling out. Wallace's appeal was fading. Racial backlash was not as strong as had been feared. The main issue for the workers was prosperity. To this issue Humphrey addressed himself with vigor. The Democrats had given America 93 months of uninterrupted economic prosperity, he said in his closing speeches. If the people wanted that prosperity to continue, let them vote for him. If they wanted a recession, let them vote for the Republicans. Inspired by the polls, which daily charted Humphrey's progress, the Democratic campaign reached its peak in the last week.

The week began with an infusion of money and spirit at a $1,000-a-plate dinner at the Waldorf-Astoria Hotel in New York. Humphrey was confident enough to acknowledge openly the fear that he had been suppressing for weeks—that he might be defeated. He told the audience at the Waldorf-Astoria that he had suffered from a bad attack of intestinal flu the previous week. "So a week ago I wasn't feeling too good. Two weeks ago I wasn't feeling too good politically. Today I'm feeling good physically and politically. I can say to you tonight that nobody ever felt more despair and heartache than I did at the beginning of the campaign."

The tone was jocular, but Humphrey's emotion showed as he went on: "If the British after Dunkirk hadn't improvised, Hitler would have had England. I knew that if the Democrats after Chicago didn't improvise, Nixon would have had America."

The week ended at Carswell Air Force Base in Fort Worth, Texas, with a reconciliation that few Democrats had anticipated even in their most optimistic moments. Waiting on the tarmac, side by side, were Governor Connally and Senator Yarborough, their enmity at least temporarily buried in their mutual willingness to help Hubert Humphrey. Only one man could have brought about this reconciliation. Lyndon Baines Johnson had come through in a typically Texan way. The previous week he had phoned both men and given them the same message: "We're not going to see the state of Texas going to the Republicans. Hubert Humphrey needs help. Now get the lead out of your pants, and give him the help he needs."

Both men obeyed their leader's wish and stuck with Humphrey for his tour of Texas. In Dallas Connally, not known for his sweetness, caught the mood of optimism. He told an open-air rally: "People say that Vice-President Hubert Humphrey lacks the capacity to bring unity and reconciliation to the Democratic Party and to the nation." He turned and grinned broadly at Yarborough, who smiled back, and added, "I say to you that, if you look at the people on this platform here today, Mr. Humphrey is a miracle worker when it comes to unity." Texans—including Mexican-Americans and Negroes—appreciated the joke and roared approval.

On October 31 President Johnson went on television to announce that he had ordered a bombing halt in North Vietnam, and Hubert Humphrey flew to California to wind up his campaign. There were no hecklers to greet him, only enthusiastic crowds, including many former McCarthy supporters. Humphrey had achieved what virtually every political commentator two months before had predicted was impossible. He had reunited the Democratic Party in only nine weeks after the Chicago convention. It was as impressive a feat as the 1968 Presidential campaign would produce.

.21.

The Man and the Moment

TUESDAY, NOVEMBER 5, 1968, WAS THE KIND OF ELECTION DAY THAT
politicians pray for. The weather came up as forecasted, mostly
clear with seasonable temperatures and little rain—just a few
showers on the West Coast and in the Northwest. It was the kind
of weather that gave the voters no excuse to stay indoors. Throughout the United States that day the bars remained shuttered; they
could not be opened until the polls had closed, an American custom
that, if nothing else, encourages sobriety in the voting booth.

Americans were fond of talking about the democratic process
and the right to vote as the most precious possession of a free
people, but their actions belied their words. In fact millions of
Americans were not registered to vote, and millions more did not
bother to vote. The Johnson-Goldwater election of 1964 had produced the biggest vote in U.S. history yet drew only 62.1 percent
of the electorate to the polls. The average percentage of Americans
voting in Presidential elections since 1920 was 55.3. The postwar
average was 60.2. But it must be compared to an average of 77
percent in Britain, 85 percent in Sweden, and 86 percent in West
Germany.

In 1968 the experts predicted a lower-than-average turnout because, they said, the campaign had been listless and the candidates lacked personality. The pundits were wrong. The voting percentage was no lower than average; it was 60.2, exactly the norm. The campaign had come to life in the final weeks. The opinion polls reflected the story: In September Humphrey had rated only 28 percent of the vote according to Gallup and only 31 percent according to Harris. Nixon had received 43 percent in both. Wallace had reached his peak of 22 percent toward the end of September.

But in October Humphrey's popularity in the polls began to rise. By the end of the month he was only two points behind Nixon. The penultimate Harris poll showed him with 43 percent to Nixon's 40 percent (which led Nixon to complain that the Harris Poll had always shown a Democratic bias). But the final polls agreed: Nixon 42 percent, Humphrey 40 percent, Wallace 17 percent.

Symbolically the two major contenders ended their campaigns in California. They had started in New York nine weeks before. In those nine weeks, Humphrey had traveled 98,000 miles and Nixon 50,083, carrying their respective messages "from sea to shining sea."

But after all the jet whistle-stops, the last effort was electronic. Each candidate made his final pitch on national television. George Wallace had bought time on C.B.S. to present for the umpteenth time "the speech," direct from Montgomery. The Democrats and Republicans both presented four-hour "telethons" in color from California. Humphrey's, on the A.B.C. network, cost $300,000; Nixon's, on N.B.C., went to more stations and cost $400,000. Each program reflected the personality of the contender and the character of his campaign.

Nixon's telethon was thoughtful, controlled, and produced with cool professionalism. It did not expose him directly to the public. Swiveling gently in a pedestal chair on a blue-carpeted dais, he fielded questions lobbed to him by an ardent supporter, popular sports broadcaster Bud Wilkinson. The questions, which aides selected from those phoned in by viewers, were the same ones that Nixon had answered a thousand times before, for example, "Mr. Nixon, just what credentials would you bring to the White House that would make it possible for you to solve the war in Vietnam?"

"Well, if I may say so, I have quite a lot of experience in foreign affairs. I am a good negotiator if I say so myself."

In contrast, Humphrey required no intermediary. With obvious relish he answered the telephone calls himself and took the questions as they came. They were broadcast live through the microphone for everyone to hear, and some of them were very tough indeed. Helping Humphrey answer the phones and answer questions were Muskie and "Hollywood Stars for Humphrey," among them Nancy Sinatra, Burt Lancaster, Paul Newman, and Edward G. Robinson. Elation and optimism, based on the polls, shone through the performance. Afterward, instead of immediately flying back to Minnesota as he had planned, Humphrey went to a Hollywood party, given by former U.S. Chief of Protocol Lloyd Hand, where he danced cheek to cheek with his wife.

Nixon's exit from his telethon was totally in character. He raised his arms in a victory salute to the studio audience, then hurried into his car with his face set. He went straight back to his hotel, Los Angeles' Century Plaza, ate a sandwich, drank a glass of milk, and went to bed. He slept well and regained his confidence, waking early and bursting into young assistant Dwight Chapin's room to wake him. Then his mood evaporated. He breakfasted alone on his usual oatmeal; made some telephone calls, including one to his brother Ed and another to Mrs. Mamie Eisenhower; and drove to the airport for his last flight on *Tricia*.

Election Day was the longest day of all for the candidates. No matter how well they had done their work, no matter what their experts or their computers told them, there were still uncertainties. It was a day when the mind roamed back over the campaign, worrying about events that had been mishandled, fretting over errors in judgment. It was a day on which emotions swung between wild confidence and lonely defeatism. Richard Nixon, a mercurial, solitary man, knew the torment—and it *was* torment—of such a day only too well.

It seemed fitting that Nixon spent the daylight hours in a kind of limbo seven miles above the American continent, crossing the U.S. time zones from coast to coast, from California, where he had been born, to New York, where he had finally found a home. He went forward to the plane's private compartment, changed into a sports jacket, and sat alone for a while. As the jet crossed the first mountain range on the flight eastward—the Sierra Nevada—he called Chapin: "Ask Mrs. Nixon and the girls to come in."

They came, and Richard Nixon gently handed his wife a jewel box. She opened it and said the only thing a woman says at such a moment: "They're beautiful." Inside was a pearl-and-diamond pin with matching earrings. They were very beautiful and very expensive. The girls asked to look at them and Julie handed them to David Eisenhower, who repeated, "They're beautiful."

Nixon had bought the jewels during the campaign and had saved them for this moment. The gift was his expression of thanks to his wife, but it was also something more. He knew what his defeats had cost her in suffering; now he was warning that he might be defeated again but reassuring her too that defeat was never the end.

The girls had never allowed themselves to contemplate anything but victory. A defeat would come as a traumatic experience, but they had to prepare themselves to face it. Nixon began to talk. It had been a good campaign, he said, one that the country need not be ashamed of. This time he thought that he would win, but victory was by no means certain. Despite what he had said in public— that he would win by a popular majority of 3 to 5 million votes— the election might not turn out that way. No one knew. So, he went on, looking at his daughters, they must be ready in case he was defeated. After all, someone had to lose. Julie interrupted to say that he could not lose, and Richard Nixon smiled and said that he could, that he had proved it in the past. He did not think that he would lose this time, but he wanted to talk to them just in case, just in case.

Having psychologically prepared his family for a tight race rather than a runaway victory, the candidate began calling in his advisers. They came in small groups and sat with him, sipping coffee and reviewing the situation. First came the speech writers, James Keogh, on leave from *Time*, where he was assistant managing editor; Pat Buchanan and Ray Price, young newspapermen; and Bill Safire, New York public-relations man.

Then came the communications men, Len Garment, Nixon's law partner; Frank Shakespeare, on leave from C.B.S.; and Wilkinson. This group was more relaxed. The sound of laughter floated back to the main cabin. It was caused by discussion of Nixon's final campaign gaffe, which had occurred during the telethon. In answering a question, he had begun, "Well, that's getting down to nut cuttings, as they say." The expression, which had slipped so readily from his tongue, did not belong to the polite, middle-class society at which the program was aimed. It was a colloquial expression for the castration of young bulls, a task that goes to the toughest ranch hands, men who are not afraid of any part of their job. In the plane Nixon began to speculate humorously on how his lapse had been received in the nation's drawing rooms.

Then the drinks came round; the candidate sipped white Dubonnet on the rocks and talked to the third group, the press-political section of his entourage: Herb Klein, Bob Finch, and Charles McWhorter. Lunch was served—chopped steak, milk, a bowl of peaches, and coffee for Nixon—and afterward the rest of the staff men came forward to pay their respects.

As the plane crossed the Midwest, he set his watch forward to Eastern Standard Time. It was 4:12 P.M., and the voting was reaching its peak. Nixon suddenly flagged. He went to the couch, removed his jacket, lay down, and pulled it over him. But he did not sleep; he reflected.

He was still confident, but, as a professional with firm theories about the pitch and rhythm of campaigns, he knew that Humphrey had performed brilliantly. Nixon had always believed that a classic Presidential campaign should be run like a long-distance track event; that the competitors should try to force each other's pace, always keeping some of their own strength in reserve so that they could increase the pressure toward the end; that in the final lap they should spend those reserves to peak in impressive bursts of speed. He had to admit that Hubert Humphrey had done just that. But discussion was all academic now. His own campaign had been controlled and cool, and his head start, he believed, had been enough to outweigh Humphrey's unexpected dramatic and final effort.

Just before 5:00 he rose and gave himself his second shave of the day. As *Tricia* began its slow descent to New York, Nixon invited the wives of his staff to join him for coffee and thanked them too.

The first part of that long day was over. It was dark and the landing lights were already on as *Tricia* touched down at Newark Airport at 6:30 P.M. His Cadillac limousine was waiting with a police escort, and 35 minutes later it drew into the garage under the Waldorf-Astoria Hotel; the Nixons went swiftly to their adjoining suites on the 35th floor. Thirty-two floors below the Nixon campaign workers were gathered, awaiting the results and the victory celebrations that they were sure would follow.

Humphrey had landed in Minneapolis, while Nixon was still asleep in Los Angeles. He had then driven for an hour to his local polling place in Marysville. Nixon had voted in advance by absentee ballot. But Humphrey wanted to be seen voting, and he and his wife lined up with men in plaid jackets and peaked caps to be photographed taking their turn at the Marysville town hall.

All the candidates voted. In Alabama Wallace cast his vote in Clayton Courthouse in Barbour County, where he had grown up; afterward he stood on the steps talking to hundreds of white Alabamans, saying, "Our movement, yours and mine, has changed the course of this country."

In Johnson City, Texas, there was a double break with tradition. For the first time that many people could remember the name Johnson was not on the ballot, and Lyndon Johnson was not the first man to vote. He had always insisted on having ballot number one at the Pedernales Electric Cooperative Inc., which, a large tablet proclaimed, was "a product of the faith, ability and foresight of Lyndon Baines Johnson, President of the United States, while a Congressman from the tenth district, 1938." This time the President appeared shortly before 9:00 A.M., driving his own car; he and his wife voted quietly and returned to the ranch.

Muskie voted in Waterville, Maine, where he had practiced law, joshing with old friends outside the South Grammar School. In Annapolis, Maryland, Agnew voted and then played golf. In Belair, California, LeMay, all military precision, voted without a smile.

The day passed. For the first time in months there was nothing for the candidates to do, except to vote, like millions of other Americans who were lining up outside the schools, libraries, and town halls of the country to record their choices. Getting out that vote was the party machine's job. And political machines all over the world are made up of ordinary people. Election Day was their day; they checked lists, sent cars for the aged and infirm, telephoned, telegraphed, knocked on doors.

Despite all the trouble that had plagued America in 1968, the election itself was quiet and orderly. There were no riots. The national guard was not called out. November 5 was a day on which democracy worked. As the day slid into night, Americans gathered round their television sets to watch the results, which normally came in swiftly. Voting machines in the big cities tabulated ballots as they were cast and could produce their totals within a few minutes after the polls had closed. But smaller towns and rural areas where officials still counted ballots by hand, as they do in Britain, reported more slowly.

It was the statewide results that mattered. The first results from the eastern cities were usually heavily Democratic, but they were later whittled by suburban and rural results. In the old days,

Americans had had to wait, as Britons still do, until every vote was counted before a final result could be declared. But with computers programmed with "voter profiles" from every district, it was possible in 1968 to know in some instances who would win a state well before all the votes were tabulated.

To monitor the vast American electorate and to feed the necessary data to the computers were titanic tasks, beyond the capability of party organizations. The Federal government provided no organization to handle them. It was left to private enterprise, to the national television networks and the two major wire services to project the results for the nation and the world.

In the past the media had fought for this honor. But the cost had become prohibitive, and a truce had been called in 1964. The three television networks had agreed to cooperate in establishing News Election Service, which was later joined by the two wire services. The center of N.E.S. operations on Election Day was in Rockefeller Plaza, where the Associated Press had its headquarters. Two IBM-360 model 40 computers were moved in, together with 26 data receivers; they were backed up by seven regional computers. The N.E.S. covered all 167,000 precincts in the United States, using a combination of staff men, local journalists, and volunteer students and housewives to collect data. Data were flashed to the center and fed into the computers, which tabulated results at lightning speed.

All the media depended on this operation, which had cost $2 million to set up for one day's work. The President, the personnel of the U.S. government, the candidates, and the heads of foreign governments, not to mention the American people, all received their information by courtesy of the computers.*

* In the event, the computers almost failed, although the experts blamed the humans who fed them. The "soft ware" for the machine was based on the 1964 race, in which there had been only two main contenders. The result was uncertainty in handling voting patterns for three leading candidates. Then too the operators handling the inputs were not sufficiently trained and sometimes the same results were fed into the machines two or three times. At 10:00 Tuesday night comedian Dick Gregory, the Freedom and Peace candidate, was reported by one computer to have almost 10 million votes in Pennsylvania. At 10:11 N.E.S. reported 18 percent of the vote tabulated, with Nixon's total at 6,198,354. Nine minutes later it said that 34 percent was in and that Nixon's total was 6,662,824. At that point, A.P.'s general news editor Sam Blackman realized that the computers were unreliable and switched to the backup system of seven regional computers, which were slower but more accurate.

The computers were waiting. Ten thousand man-hours had gone into programming them, and their circuits held the secrets of thousands of precincts: ethnic patterns, key issues, voter incomes, percentages of home ownership, voting performance in previous years. The high priests of American communications, the David Brinkleys, Chet Huntleys, and Walter Cronkites, surrounded by acolytes and flanked by their counterparts from 26 other countries (watching live results by satellite) were in position to convey and interpret the predictions of the computers. Everything was done with "newspeed," thanks to the most elaborate electronic setup yet conceived to handle a national election anywhere. Not only would N.E.S. receive, digest, analyze, and regurgitate the results in milliseconds, but also secondary computers, hired and programmed by rival networks, would refine and reanalyze those results in the light of special information.

So precise was the operation of these secondary computers, their programmers claimed, that they could project the final statewide results when only 20 percent of the ballots were counted. At certain points during the evening their lights would flash, and their tapes would issue incontrovertible statements that this or that state was going Republican or Democratic. Then the networks would decide to "give" that state to one or another of the candidates. The actual tabulation of the vote would take several more hours, but all urgency went out of the officials' handling of it, for they had been cheated of their moment of drama; their only task was to confirm what the computers had predicted.

There is a classic ritual to the pattern of election results in all countries. Some areas, because of their composition and size are able to record their results more rapidly than others, which brings them a certain reputation. They are like well-loved performers who traditionally open the bill at command performances. In Britain there is usually a contest between the Parliamentary district of Cheltenham and the surburban Essex constituency of Billericay to be the first to declare in a General Election. Both are proud of achieving this distinction, and their officials train their counting staffs like Olympic athletes, constantly striving to shave seconds from the tabulating time in order to beat their records in each election and to stay ahead of the rest of the country.

In the United States the first results came in from the hamlets of upper New England. Then there was a small flurry from the villages of Kansas, for in both those places the polls closed in the afternoon, and ballots were counted while the rest of the nation continued to vote.

At 6:00 P.M. Kentucky closed its polls and strove to be the first state to declare. Then came a wave of results from the southern states, closely followed by the New England cities. Then the eastern industrial states began to report. By then the polls had closed in the mountain and western states, and shortly after midnight their results began to flow in.

The first predictions were made by the computers before 8:00 P.M., E.S.T., but the first results with any real meaning did not begin to register until 10:00 P.M. From then until midnight the patern began to emerge; usually, unless the vote were perilously close, one would expect the final results to be known by the early hours.

For the candidates in 1968 the first part of the evening was agonizing, a twilight period between the rising tension of the day and the predawn release. In Minnesota the Humphreys joined some old friends, Mr. and Mrs. Dwayne Andreas, for dinner. They ate slowly and well—boned pheasant in cream sauce, French beans with water chestnuts, caramel rolls, and apple pie topped with cheddar cheese and ice cream. After coffee, they drove to the Leamington Hotel, where Humphrey had his headquarters. It was a pleasant hotel, whose charm derived from a certain old-fashioned quality. It was a fitting place for Hubert Humphrey.

In the Leamington's Hall of States ballroom on the first floor, a devoted crowd of 5,000 supporters had been waiting for Humphrey since early evening. But he had decided firmly against presenting himself until there was reason. He slipped in the back way and took a freight elevator to a suite on the fourteenth floor. On the way, he called in at Larry O'Brien's communications center and picked up Senator Fred Harris of Oklahoma and his wife. The two couples entered the suite, where Humphrey took off his coat and turned on the three television sets in the living room. He settled down for a long night.

In the Waldorf Towers 1,100 miles away Nixon's first order on entering his suite was "Turn off the television." His aides flicked the switches of the three sets in the sitting room, and the screens blanked out. They would not come to life again until Nixon knew that he had won. He disliked watching himself on television intensely, although he had spent many hours doing so to improve

400

his technique. He also disliked hearing himself discussed by television commentators.

Nixon strolled into the bedroom. His movements were controlled and unhurried. He had programmed his day carefully to fill the void, and there were still contingencies to be planned for. Opening his travel bag, he selected a dark suit and asked Chapin to have it pressed, joking "We'll need it for either a victory appearance or a concession." As Chapin left, Nixon said: "I'm going to get some sleep, Dwight. Call me at 8:30." He started to undress, then changed his mind about sleeping. Instead, he filled the bath with steaming water and stepped in. He lay there for forty minutes, turning on the hot tap again and again to keep the heat up, letting the water soothe his tired body. He could not remember the last time that he had taken a bath; he was a man conditioned to brisk, efficient showers, but the bathtubs in the Waldorf Towers were more than six feet long, relics of a more leisurely age, and that evening the long soaking was perfect for Richard Nixon.

When he stepped out, it was already 8:00, and the N.B.C. computers had made their first projections: Wallace would win Alabama; Nixon would win Kentucky. C.B.S. meanwhile projected a Nixon win in Tennessee.

The candidate knew nothing of these predictions as he toweled himself and picked up his freshly pressed suit, which had been left outside the door. He was about to step into the trousers when he changed his mind and put them back on the hanger. He put on the suit in which he had traveled. He would save the fresh one until he appeared before the cameras; his experience and instinct told him that that moment was still a long way off.

The Waldorf Towers suite consisted of a bedroom, a large sitting room with an orange Oriental carpet and French Provincial furniture, a dining room with a bar, and a room that had been converted into the command post. It bristled with telephones and television sets. From there, Haldeman and Chapin monitored the results, supplementing the television reports with information from telephone calls to Republicans all over America. Down the corridor, Nixon's other aides, under Mitchell and Finch, monitored key areas all night.

At 8:20 Richard Nixon came into the sitting room dressed in his wrinkled suit and asked Chapin to buy him some cigars. Haldeman gave him a written report on the first projection, which was how Richard Nixon liked to receive facts. He liked to read words, ab-

401

sorb them, then throw the paper away. He noted with satisfaction that he was well ahead in the first 2 percent of the votes counted. That was the last written report he would receive that night. As the speed of tabulation increased, Nixon, like everyone else, had to settle for verbal reports.

Chapin returned with a box of medium-priced Floridan cigars, as Haldeman appeared with the first of the verbal reports. Nixon lit a cigar, the first of five that he would smoke that evening, and listened. The news was not bad, Kentucky was officially his, with the nine electoral votes; in the other border states he was beating Wallace and Humphrey. The Deep South results were not so good; Wallace was way ahead. In New England the Democrats were doing better than expected; they would hold Connecticut with its eight votes, but staunch Vermont was coming through for the Republicans.

Just after 9:30 Haldeman told the candidate that Indiana was safe but that Massachusetts seemed to be lost. At 9:42, with 16 percent of the votes counted, the gap between the two main contenders was only 1 percent; Nixon had 41 percent of the votes, Humphrey 40 percent, and Wallace 19 percent. "It's going to be close," said Nixon, pacing up and down the room. His nerves were showing. The whole evening was shaping into an agonizing replay of 1960, when the fight had gone through the night and the decision had remained in doubt until dawn.

At 10:00 C.B.S. predicted that Humphrey would win New York State with its 43 votes. That was the worst moment, but it was also the turning point for Nixon. He went into action. Figuring on one of his yellow pads, he issued a stream of names for his staff to telephone. He did not trust the computers, this man who had himself been accused of being as heartless as an IBM machine; he depended on people. And the people he ordered his men to telephone were the local chairmen and ward captains of Republican precincts across the country, people he knew personally and trusted.

For the next hour the reports flowed in, and the candidate noted them on his pad. He was disappointed. Even worse than losing New York was the heavy Negro vote in Philadelphia, which would probably cost the Republicans Pennsylvania. To offset those defeats, it seemed that he would hold Ohio; but things were touch and go in Illinois. Nixon knew that state and what Daley could do there. "Keep a very close eye on Illinois," he ordered.

At 11:00 he called in his top men for a review of the situation.

Humphrey had taken Rhode Island, the District of Columbia, and West Virginia. Wallace had Mississippi and Alabama; it was by then obvious that the majority of Americans had rejected his demagoguery and that he would carry no state outside the Deep South. The border states were going to Nixon but with 17 million votes counted the percentages were still 41 for him and 41 for Humphrey.

Finch, Chortiner, and John Mitchell were all in the room. "How do we stand?" asked the candidate. "How do we look?" Mitchell thought that the outcome remained promising. The rural vote was still not counted. Most of the Middlewest would go for the Republicans. The Democrats needed a big lead at that time of night if they were going to amount to anything, he said.

"But what about Illinois?" asked Nixon. "If we can carry Washington we can write off Illinois, but we'll have to carry something else to really clinch it." At 11:30 the Democratic vote rolled ahead of the Republican total for the first time. At that point, Nixon insisted that it was necessary to make an announcement to the press. It should express confidence, and it was Klein's job. "Tell them I will be down when we've won," said Nixon. At 11:35 Klein walked through the jammed press room, a bedlam of typewriters, phones, teleprinters, and dozens of television sets, and into the briefing room.

Raising his voice a couple of octaves, he announced: "Mr. Nixon's plans are to come down at victory, but it may be a long night. We still think we can win by 3 to 5 million, but it looks closer to 3 million at this point." His words were whistling in the dark. There could be no such majority of the popular vote, and everyone knew it. But the Republicans still had the edge in the Electroal College, where it counted.

Shortly before midnight Maine went to the Democrats, and just after midnight Florida went to the Republicans. "Well, at least we've got Florida," said Nixon. "We need not alter our plans."

Those plans—win, lose, or draw—called for the Nixon family to fly to Key Biscayne for a vacation after the election. Only one thing could have altered them, and that was a Democratic victory in Florida. Then, Nixon had decided, he and his family would have to go elsewhere—San Diego's Mission Bay or even their New York home.

At 12:40 A.M., still figuring his returns, the candidate was informed that Governor Rockefeller had arrived in the hotel and

403

wanted to see him. He permitted himself a smile. Beside being an old rival, Rockefeller was a man with whom the candidate had little in common beyond an interest in politics. After the convention, Rockefeller had swallowed his bitterness and had campaigned for Richard Nixon, but the two men were never easy on the same platform.

Presumably he was coming now to apologize for having failed to deliver New York, which was indisputably going Democratic. The candidate considered for a moment, then told his aides to apologize to the Governor and to say that he could not see him. Rockefeller replied, "I well understand that Mr. Nixon is busy," and left the hotel. Nixon's behavior was petty perhaps, but he was irritated by Rockefeller's call at such an awkward point. He thought it presumptuous. He wanted to finish the vigil alone with his team, and there was no room for outsiders until it was finished one way or the other.

The results were coming fast. At 12:26 the television screens revealed that Humphrey had carried Minnesota. Then one after the other the mountain and western states went to Nixon, as Mitchell had predicted. At 12:39 he received Iowa and Montana, for thirteen votes; at 12:44 Oregon, for six votes; at 1:26 Wyoming, for another three votes. Humphrey took New York officially at 1:41, but that shock had already been absorbed and forgotten when nine minutes later North and South Carolina were delivered to Nixon with 21 votes between them, later, Idaho with four, and finally Kansas with seven would be his also.

Nixon walked down the corridor to talk with his wife and children. They were watching television in the living room of a nearly identical suite. Their faces revealed their anxiety, and he reassured them with a smile. "It all depends on California," he said, "but California is all right." It did indeed depend on California. At that point it was clear that neither man could win without the Golden State and its forty votes. The race was desperately close in California, but Nixon had done his work well, and the verbal reports from Haldeman and Finch had satisfied him that he had the edge.

His judgment was based on what his people told him, beyond the computers. The voting was so close that the machines could not predict the outcome. And this uncertainty raised the specter that haunted American elections every time a third party made any real impact. What if no candidate succeeded in securing a majority of the electoral votes?

404

Reuters, the British news agency, underlined the threat in its lead for the first editions of Europe's afternoon papers:

The U.S. Presidential elections edged towards deadlock today with the outcome hinging on close-run races in the key big states. With seventy percent of the votes counted in a near record turn-out, both Democrat Hubert Humphrey and Republican Richard Nixon had 42 percent of the popular vote. But in most of the big states carrying the heaviest prizes in Electoral College votes, the situation was so tight that few cared to predict the outcome at this stage.

The threat of deadlock and constitutional crisis became the main subject of television comment as the computers steadfastly remained silent on further predictions. To see how serious the threat was—and many commentators were thoroughly alarmed by it—it is necessary to reexamine what Americans had been doing that day.

They had been voting for President but only indirectly. For legally the only people whom the American public had elected that day were the members of the Electoral College. Hardly any American could say who his state's electors were. This ignorance was understandable, for they were usually drawn from that breed of anonymous citizen who does good works all his life and, in Britain, ends up with the O.B.E. To serve as an elector was a similar honor in America, a reward for unglamorous civic service or party loyalty.

The electors would assemble on the first Monday after the second Wednesday in December to cast their ballots for President. The ceremony would be a mere formality, however; they would perform a ritual, the result of which was already known, each elector giving his vote to the candidate with the majority of popular votes in his state. A candidate had to have a clear majority of 270 of the 538 electoral votes; a strong third-party showing could prevent any candidate from receiving enough electoral votes.

During that early-morning pause, some television commentators imagined the dread possibility to be a probability. Psychologically they were predisposed to look for it. The whole election year had brought unprecedented drama and disaster. Everything appeared to be going wrong for the United States; a paralysis would be a fitting finale. Or so they were saying, and they made a frighteningly persuasive case, for Humphrey had won Pennsylvania, and Nixon

405

had taken New Jersey. The tally was Nixon 195, Humphrey 159, Wallace 45.

Clearly, even if Humphrey took California (40 votes) Illinois (26 votes), and Ohio (26 votes), his total would not be high enough. But, equally, if he took even two of those states, Nixon could not win a majority either. There would thus be no winner.

If no candidate had a majority, the responsibility for selecting a President would go to the House of Representatives. But there was another possibility. What if Wallace made a deal for his 45 electors, trading their votes to one of the candidates in return for a promised hard line on civil rights? Would such a deal be constitutional? No one knew.

Even if that problem were avoided, it would still be January, when Congress was scheduled to reassemble, before the House of Representatives could ballot; even then disaster was possible. The Constitution provided that each state delegation in the House be given one vote in balloting for President. A simple majority would be required for nomination. Twenty-six states would thus have to vote for the winner, but there was no guarantee, in view of the regional loyalties of the congressmen dominating some southern delegations, that either Nixon or Humphrey would receive a majority.

So the conjectures ran, and they ballooned. Inauguration Day could come still with nothing decided. Then the scene would shift to the Senate, for selection of a Vice-President. A Democratic majority there would undoubtedly give the job to Senator Muskie, who would assume the role of Acting President until the House could finally discharge its duty.

The thought of such protracted and perilous decision making chilled every listener. Understandably, when the election was over and such a crisis averted, determination to eliminate such a risk swept America. This determination was to alter a sacred precept of the Founding Fathers and abolish the Electoral College. A Gallup poll showed that 79 percent of the public was opposed to the system, and congressional reformers, striking while the issue was hot, announced that they would begin hearings on appropriate constitutional amendments as soon as the House resumed sitting.

Nixon's confidence was not impaired by the television drama. He was more concerned with a piece of symbolic theater of his own. He was not a superstitious man, but his mood often bordered on the mystical. The evening had evoked memories of eight years before most disturbingly, but his intelligence told him that 1968 was different and that he *would* win by a narrow margin. During the evening he had dwelt on the events of 1960 more than somewhat, and slowly an idea had come to him. He would exorcise the ghostly memory of that year.

He took Chapin into a corner of the living room and said: "Dwight, at 3:00 I'm going to be in the bedroom. I want you to find Mitchell, Chotiner, Finch, and Haldeman; bring them in, and—and get them to sit in these chairs. Then come and get me. Make it exactly 3:00." Chapin did as he was told. As he entered Nixon's bedroom, the telephone rang. It was Governor Agnew calling from Annapolis. "Tell him I will call back," said Nixon, looking at his watch. "It is almost 3:00."

At 3:00 A.M. precisely, on November 6, Richard Nixon entered the living room and confronted his four closest assistants. "Don't get up," he said. Eight years ago in another hotel, he reminded them, he had confronted three of them—Mitchell was the exception —at exactly the same hour and had asked them the question he was asking now: "How do we stand?" Then they had been forced to review a situation that was hopeless. And Nixon had known then that he had lost to John F. Kennedy.

Once again they reviewed the situation, but this time it was different. California was safe; Ohio was safe; the lead in Illinois was safe, even from Mayor Daley. There could be only one conclusion: Nixon and the Republicans had won. The candidate puffed on his cigar. "That is how I see it," he said. "Perhaps it is time to go downstairs."

Everyone in the room was exultant, but they all voiced a warning note. They knew that Nixon had won—barring an incredible unforeseen event—but the public did not. It would be better and more dignified to accept victory than to claim it, better to wait until Humphrey conceded before making a public appearance. Nixon agreed.

But there was someone whom he could tell—Spiro Agnew. He put through a call to Maryland and spoke to his controversial running mate for the first time in several days. "Well, Ted," he said, "we have won."

The time was 3:15 A.M.

In Minnesota Humphrey had been elated earlier that night. "By golly," he cried when C.B.S. gave him New York, "we might do it!"

The Democrats were nowhere nearly as well organized as the Republicans and depended more on television and less on their own men for the count. They were therefore behind on results and still had hopes for a stalemate, even while Nixon was already certain of victory.

Hubert Humphrey had decided to go to bed at 2 A.M., but first he had appeared before the crowd in the Leamington's ballroom. He was exuberant, and, amid shouts of "Sock it to 'em Hubie!" and "We want Humphrey!" he assured his supporters that he would be down in the morning for a victory celebration.

Then he went upstairs to sleep. While he slept Nixon's victory was confirmed by the computers. At 5:18 A.M. the Los Angeles *Times* computer gave California to Nixon. At 8:12 the victory became official. At 8:25 he took Ohio. Only Illinois remained uncertain. Despite the fact that there appeared to be "something wrong with the balloting" in Cook County, A.B.C. predicted a Nixon victory at 8:55. At 10:40 N.B.C. chalked up Illinois for Nixon and from that point began calling him "President Elect."

The Democratic candidate awakened after five hours' sleep to find himself defeated. At that moment dignity took hold of Hubert Humphrey. With a smile for his wife and his staff he said, "Now I don't want any sympathy from any of you," and steeled himself to perform the loser's ritual.

First, through an aide, he alerted the press that he would be making an announcement at 11 A.M. Then he drafted his concession telegram to Nixon:

> According to unofficial returns, you are the winner of this election. My congratulations.
> Please know that you will have my support in unifying and leading the nation. This has been a difficult year for the American people. I am confident that, if constructive leaders of both our parties join together now, we shall be able to go on with the business of building the better America we all seek—in a spirit of peace and harmony.

The losing candidate in an American Presidential election was totally defeated. Unlike Britain, where more often than not the defeated party leader retains his seat in Parliament, an official title, and a salary as Leader of the Opposition, the United States provided no institutional niche for the loser. He was out, and Humphrey accepted this bleak prospect without a whimper, even though he knew that for him there probably would never be another chance.

He came down to the Hall of States, with its torn bunting, dirty glasses, and smell of stale food and tired people; it took him seven minutes to concede. He had spoken hundreds of thousands, if not millions, of words during the campaign, words that bored reporters, after the first few hearings, had noted as if in a trance; now they applauded him. His supporters came crowding back into the hall to shout the old, now pointless slogan, "We want Humphrey."

On the election trail his response had always been, "Well let me tell you that Humphrey wants you too." Now his reply was a little wan, and his voice quavered: "Well, thank you very much. It is nice to know." His chin was up and his eyes filled with unshed tears. He had telegraphed his congratulations to the winner, he said. Then he thanked his supporters and his family.

I shall renew my personal commitment to the cause of human rights, to peace, and to the betterment of man. If I have helped in this campaign to move these causes forward, I feel rewarded. I have done my best. I lost. Mr. Nixon has won. The democratic process has worked its will. Now let's get on with the urgent task of uniting our people. Thank you.

He made a faint little joke about mowing the neglected lawn of his lakeside home at Waverly; then he left.

In New York the Republicans had been celebrating ever since 4:00 A.M. The candidate had invited all the key staff men in for drinks and sandwiches. At one point he had joked, "This is taking so long to settle I may not accept." He was nursing a beer so that the others would not feel constrained. He was in a jovial mood and, noticing Chapin, whose willingness and total loyalty throughout the campaign had deeply impressed everyone, he declared loudly, "Chapin, I want you to know that you've been totally worthless through this whole thing." In the resulting laughter, Chapin took a bow, and somebody said, "Now we're back to the 'nut cutting' again," and everyone laughed at that. Just after 7:00 A.M. Nixon quietly went into the bedroom.

The crowd downstairs, where Lionel Hampton's band—the only black faces in the room, someone noted, but that was not quite true —had been playing for dancing, had already dispersed until the morning. John Nidecker, a Nixon advance man, had announced: "You might as well go home now. Because of the indecisive situation, Mr. Nixon will greet you tomorrow. He is not coming down tonight." A groan went up. "Go home," said Nidecker. "Get down on your knees and pray." The band struck up "Good Night, Ladies," and the guests began to drift away.

Just before 9:00 A.M. the candidate awoke and summoned Haldeman and Finch to his bedroom. His first question was about Illinois. Finch told him, "Illinois is okay." He digested this news, then arose, put on a robe, and padded down the corridor to see his wife and daughters. They were watching television. He bade them a cheerful "good morning" and kissed them one by one. Everything was all right.

A little later he went back to bed but could not sleep. At 10:40 when N.B.C. announced that he had Illinois, Chapin rushed in. "We've made it," he shouted. The candidate followed him into the command room as the N.B.C. announcer was saying, "at 55 Richard Nixon will be the 37th President of the United States." The candidate listened, then flopped into a chair and watched television for the first time since his arrival in New York.

He let the full impact of the Illinois victory seep in. Ironically, it was Illinois, where Mayor Daley's notorious grip on Cook County had allegedly cost Nixon the 1960 election, that had put him over the top. One aide said that Nixon had "a faraway look" in his eyes but wore no outward expression of jubilation. But a low key had been the trademark of the whole campaign. Nixon turned to Chapin and said, "Dwight, will you show me where the family is?" Though he failed to show his feelings, these words proved that he was deeply moved. He could not even remember the way down the corridor to his family's suite.

There were embraces all round, and Julie took advantage of the family meeting to give her father her personal present, upon which she had been working throughout the campaign: a crewel work Great Seal of the United States. To Nixon, a man who believed in symbols and in loyalty, his daughter's trust, illustrated by the present, was deeply moving. He turned at once and hurried to show it to his staff. He did not realize that everyone had seen it in the making over the weeks.

At 11:45 A.M. the telephone rang. It was Vice-President Humphrey. He told Nixon that he would be conceding at 11:00 A.M.–noon in New York. Fully aware of Humphrey's feelings, Nixon did most of the talking, reminding Humphrey of his own emotions in 1960 and how he had eventually overcome them. "You put up a great fight," he said, "a great fight."

Then he started to jot down ideas for his acceptance speech, which he would deliver at 12:32. He stopped and went to tell his family about Humphrey's call. Again his behavior was out of character. In the past, when he had had anything to tell the family, he had called it to him. Now he went to the family.

Just before noon a call came from the White House. A message of congratulations in the form of a telegram was dictated. President Johnson wanted Nixon to have the text before he went down to the ballroom.

Billy Graham, evangelist and long-time Nixon supporter, was the first outsider to enter the suite. Then Mrs. Nixon, the girls, and David Eisenhower came in. Pat Nixon wore a bright-blue dress. Tricia's blonde hair sparkled over a bright-red dress, and Julie wore pink. Eisenhower still looked as if his suit had never been pressed. Nixon, in his own freshly pressed suit, grinned.

The group chatted until 12:25. Then came the walk down the carpeted corridor to the Tower lift. Lining the corridor like a guard of honor were the people who had worked so hard for this moment, as well as some old friends. Someone started applauding. It was very formal applause, for friendship and affection were now overlaid with respect for the office of the Presidency. "Everyone knew," said Chapin, "that it was no longer just Richard Nixon walking down the corridor, but the next President."

In the ballroom the television cameras zeroed in, sending the President Elect's acceptance via the satellites to the world. He hoped that he would be worthy of the votes he had received. Vice-President Humphrey had sent him a gracious message. Nixon had thanked him and had told him that he had always admired a fighter. Winning was a lot more fun than losing, as he knew. Then he added, "A great philosophy is never one without defeat but always without fear." Nixon had given substance to the American dream that a man can always make a comeback if he tries.

The party pushed back into the lift. Nixon slumped into a small seat in the corner, sighed, and said to Pat: "You know, as President, I have certain prerogatives. And I am going to exercise them today. I'm going to take you and the girls to lunch at Twenty One." They were thrilled, but the staff and the Secret Servicemen panicked. Within five minutes, Nixon learned that his prerogatives were not quite as great as he had thought. The Secret Service simply did not have enough time to "secure" the restaurant. The idea was abandoned. Nixon was now the property of the American people and in many ways a slave to his office.

In order not to disappoint his womenfolk, Nixon said, "Well, never mind, we'll eat in Peacock Alley," the restaurant in the Waldorf-Astoria. "You can get that secured, can't you?" he asked the security men.

The suite was packed with accredited well-wishers. The phones rang constantly; they were answered with the words "President Elect Nixon's suite." The President Elect was shaking hands; he ordered his staff to provide champagne, and within minutes four cases had arrived.

It was a good party, but the Nixons did not stay long. As always in moments of private joy or distress, Nixon wanted only to be with his family and the faithful Bebe Rebozo. They said their goodbyes and went into the elevator, where they were told that Peacock Alley had still not been "secured." "In that case," said the President Elect, "we will go home."

So they drove to the Fifth Avenue apartment, which was empty when they arrived. Their housekeepers Manola and Fina Sanchez had taken the day off. The Nixons looked at one another and laughed. Fatigue and, of course, victory had replaced any possible hunger for the small family. That plus the absence of their domestic help caused them to end up having a Spartan snack of cold tinned salmon and a small salad. "It makes little difference" Rebozo told the visitor, "the Nixons always prefer light lunches."

The election had been very close. Nixon had staged his comeback with a minority vote, although the experts said that he would have won a majority in a two-party fight. But that was conjecture. The fact was that he had received 43.48 percent of the popular vote, to Humphrey's 42.97. His plurality was 324,000 votes, more than Kennedy's margin in 1960. He had carried 32 states and won 302 electoral votes to Humphrey's 191 votes from 13 states and the District of Columbia and Wallace's 45 votes from 5 states.

The nation had also elected 21 governors, 34 senators, and all 435 members of the House of Representatives. In those elections the Republicans had not fared as well as they had expected. American voters had rejected straight party tickets and had split their ballots as never before. Nixon would therefore have to work with a Congress in which the Democrats had majorities in both Houses.

The American people made other dispositions on November 5 as well. The voters of Massachusetts abolished the death penalty in their state; the voters of Utah rejected a proposition legalizing the sale of liquor by the glass. In Alabama George Wallace finally won his point: The voters decided that future governors would be allowed to succeed themselves. New Hampshire voters decided that it was time that their Governor lost his right to declare war and took it away from him. Despite the fact that there are few places named after African cities in the United States, the people of East Palo Alto, California, who were predominantly Negro, overwhelmingly turned down a motion to rename their city Nairobi. Providence, Rhode Island, citizens decided against a new sports arena; St. Louis, Missiouri, voted for a new airport.

The election results confirmed rather than disproved that the United States was divided. The negroes voted overwhelmingly—91 percent—for Humphrey. The Deep South went for Wallace. The blue-collar vote split among all three candidates. The Midwest went mainly to the Republicans, the cities mainly to the Democrats. The ethnic groups split: Italian-Americans, traditionally Democratic, gave 22 percent of their vote to George Wallace; the Jews, perhaps because of increasing Negro anti-Semitism, gave him 13 percent of their vote. The great suburban vote went to Nixon and ensured his victory.

Great though the divisions were, however, they did not break up the system. There was no deadlock, no constitutional crisis. That in itself was the first step toward unity and restoration of national confidence. It was from the events that had not occurred that the strength of America could be gauged at the end of that eventful year.

First there had been no massive swing to the extreme right. Despite Wallace's demagogic appeal, the American people had quarantined him in the backwoods of the Deep South, where he belonged.

Second, for the first time in four years there had been no major outbreak of Negro violence during the summer. Some experts believed that, in the riots following the assassination of Martin Luther King, America had seen the last of that particular form of Negro protest. Negroes had participated fully in the campaigns: more than 85 percent of registered Negro voters had exercised their right to ballot; all six Negro congressmen were reelected, together with three new ones.

Third, the American people had not turned their backs on the democratic process. There was no massive abstention; 72 million people voted. And they did not vote mechanically, responding only to party reflexes, but selectively.

Finally, the youth of America did not "drop out." Despite the

413

Chicago disaster, in the end the young Democrats stayed within the political framework and campaigned for Humphrey. Nixon too had his share of the young.

The Democratic process had not been found lacking. Eugene McCarthy had not been elected president but the aims which he and his supporters had set out to achieve had been accomplished. Everything they had sought was now a fact—the bombing had been stopped and peace talks were taking place in Paris.

The New Politics had not triumphed; no inspirational figure had emerged to lead Americans out of a wilderness of their own creation. But perhaps the country was not looking for a messiah. The problems of the United States in 1968 could not be solved by personality and style alone. Too much inspiration can lead to too many expectations, and in retrospect one sees that many of the country's troubles arose from the unfulfilled expectations aroused by John F. Kennedy's magic words. He had encouraged the world to expect too much of America and the American people to expect too much of themselves. As a result, the United States had aimed beyond its potential both at home and abroad.

Anglo-Saxons have a frequent habit (which is a form of self-congratulation) of worshiping their newly elected leaders and ascribing to them almost superhuman talents. When the fantasy fails, they turn on them for not living up to these false expectations. The British did so with David Lloyd George, Ramsay McDonald, and Anthony Eden. The Americans would almost certainly have done so with John Kennedy if he had lived; they certainly did with Lyndon Johnson.

The United States avoided this mistake in 1968. No American saw Richard Nixon as a political superman; he had no magic. The vision of Camelot was not his because he knew—and always knew—that Camelot was unreal. He would not set America's sights too high, and in that he might well achieve more for his country than all the visionaries. Americans and the rest of us had been looking for radical answers to the problems of the United States. But now it became clear that radical answers had been tried and had been found wanting. What was needed was a solid, undramatic approach to these problems without fanfare and without rhetoric. America turned to a man who could provide this.

Richard Nixon embodied the not-to-be-undervalued virtues of ordinary Americans: patience, persistence, hard work, and realistic

414

ambition. He would take office in a nation that was badly over-extended, a nation that needed to consolidate its gains and concentrate on its major problems before it could move ahead.

Earlier in the year, he had spoken of his conviction that "the man and the moment came together." At the beginning of 1969 there was growing confidence in America that he could be right.

417

418

426

Tet offensive, 34-5, 38, 93, 101, 102, 103, 124
Texas, University of, 258
Theiss, Rev. Norman, 134
Thompson, William, 153
Thornberry, Homer, 306
Thurmond, Senator Strom, 190, 286-8, 291, 292, 294, 298, 387
Tonkin Resolution, 16-17
Torres, José, 227
Tower, Senator John, 289, 294
Trammell, Seymore, 347
Tree Grows in Brooklyn, A., 146
Truman, Harry S, 123, 125
Tydings, Senator Joseph D., 257

Uecker, Karl, 244, 245
underground press, 126-7
unions, labor, 169, 217, 338-9, 388-9, 390
United Auto Workers' Union, 217
United Citizens for Nixon-Agnew, 371-5, 382
United Democrats for Humphrey, 206
United Nations Organization, 47
University administration, student control in, 44
Unruh, Jesse, 60, 241, 245, 311-12
urban renewal, 142
U.S. News and World Report, 165

Vance, Cyrus, 123
vanden Heuvel, William, 104, 327
VanDrusen, Richard, 81
Vassar College, 273
Vaughn, Robert, 59-60
Vidal, Gore, 378
Vietcong, 23, 34-5, 254
Vietnam war, 3-4, 9, 16, 22-4, 34-5, 38, 39-41, 48, 50-3, 56, 58, 62, 63, 66, 68, 74, 93, 99, 101, 102, 115, 142, 203, 208, 226, 231, 282, 375; peace talks on, 118, 119, 121, 122, 123-5, 236-7, 352, 377, 381, 385
    See also bombing halt
Vietnam plank at Democratic convention, 312, 315-18
Village Voice, 109
Volpe, John, (Gov. of Mass.), 203, 295

Volstead Act, 257
Vulcania, 144

Wackenhut Agency, 272, 278
Walinsky, Adam, 101, 112, 378
Wallace, George Corley, 111, 134, 169-74, 258, 305, 334, 335, 340, 342, 343, 345, 346-61, 365, 366, 368, 377, 382, 390, 393, 397, 401, 402, 406, 413
Wallace, Lurleen, 173
Wallace, Mike, 326
Walter, Paul, Jr., 266-7
"War Room, the," 373-4
Warden, Charles, 13-14
Warner, John, 372-3
Warren, Chief Justice Earl, 342n.
Warshavsky, Ted, 331
Warsoff, Louis, 46
Washburn, C. Langhorne, 280
Washington Post, 190
Waterman, Homer, 138, 305, 319
Watson, Marvin, 100, 305, 319
Watts, 139, 224, 228-9
Wayne, John, 282
"We Shall Overcome," 317
Weaver, Robert, 21, 135
Welch, Raquel, 226
welfare, Negroes and, 157, 165-6, 167
Wellesley College, 273
Westmoreland, General William, 3, 38, 61, 93, 119, 122
What Makes Sammy Run, 195
What Manner of Man, 388
Wheeler, General Earle, 123, 125
White, Clifton, 204, 284, 289, 291
White, Mary, 159
White House, value and maintenance costs of, 18-19
White House press corps, 20
White House situation room, 38
Whitman, Charles, 258
Wilkins, Roy, 135
Wilkinson, Bud, 393, 395
Williams, Jack, 185
Willnauer, James, 26, 29
Wilson, Harold, 11, 12, 15, 16, 122, 216, 239
Wilson, Malcolm, 273
Wilson, Orlando, 321
Wilson, Woodrow, 191, 366
Wing, Ed, 347

427